Lecture Notes in Computer Science 14717

Founding Editors

Gerhard Goos
Juris Hartmanis

The series Lecture Notes in Computer Science (LNCS), including its subseries Lecture Notes in Artificial Intelligence (LNAI) and Lecture Notes in Bioinformatics (LNBI), has established itself as a medium for the publication of new developments in computer science and information technology research, teaching, and education.

LNCS enjoys close cooperation with the computer science R & D community, the series counts many renowned academics among its volume editors and paper authors, and collaborates with prestigious societies. Its mission is to serve this international community by providing an invaluable service, mainly focused on the publication of conference and workshop proceedings and postproceedings. LNCS commenced publication in 1973.

Matthias Rauterberg
Editor

Culture and Computing

12th International Conference, C&C 2024
Held as Part of the 26th HCI International Conference, HCII 2024
Washington, DC, USA, June 29 – July 4, 2024
Proceedings

 Springer

Editor
Matthias Rauterberg
Eindhoven University of Technology
Eindhoven, The Netherlands

ISSN 0302-9743   ISSN 1611-3349 (electronic)
Lecture Notes in Computer Science
ISBN 978-3-031-61146-9   ISBN 978-3-031-61147-6 (eBook)
https://doi.org/10.1007/978-3-031-61147-6

This Springer imprint is published by the registered company Springer Nature Switzerland AG
The registered company address is: Gewerbestrasse 11, 6330 Cham, Switzerland

If disposing of this product, please recycle the paper.

Foreword

This year we celebrate 40 years since the establishment of the HCI International (HCII) Conference, which has been a hub for presenting groundbreaking research and novel ideas and collaboration for people from all over the world.

The HCII conference was founded in 1984 by Prof. Gavriel Salvendy (Purdue University, USA, Tsinghua University, P.R. China, and University of Central Florida, USA) and the first event of the series, "1st USA-Japan Conference on Human-Computer Interaction", was held in Honolulu, Hawaii, USA, 18–20 August. Since then, HCI International is held jointly with several Thematic Areas and Affiliated Conferences, with each one under the auspices of a distinguished international Program Board and under one management and one registration. Twenty-six HCI International Conferences have been organized so far (every two years until 2013, and annually thereafter).

Over the years, this conference has served as a platform for scholars, researchers, industry experts and students to exchange ideas, connect, and address challenges in the ever-evolving HCI field. Throughout these 40 years, the conference has evolved itself, adapting to new technologies and emerging trends, while staying committed to its core mission of advancing knowledge and driving change.

As we celebrate this milestone anniversary, we reflect on the contributions of its founding members and appreciate the commitment of its current and past Affiliated Conference Program Board Chairs and members. We are also thankful to all past conference attendees who have shaped this community into what it is today.

The 26th International Conference on Human-Computer Interaction, HCI International 2024 (HCII 2024), was held as a 'hybrid' event at the Washington Hilton Hotel, Washington, DC, USA, during 29 June – 4 July 2024. It incorporated the 21 thematic areas and affiliated conferences listed below.

A total of 5108 individuals from academia, research institutes, industry, and government agencies from 85 countries submitted contributions, and 1271 papers and 309 posters were included in the volumes of the proceedings that were published just before the start of the conference, these are listed below. The contributions thoroughly cover the entire field of human-computer interaction, addressing major advances in knowledge and effective use of computers in a variety of application areas. These papers provide academics, researchers, engineers, scientists, practitioners and students with state-of-the-art information on the most recent advances in HCI.

The HCI International (HCII) conference also offers the option of presenting 'Late Breaking Work', and this applies both for papers and posters, with corresponding volumes of proceedings that will be published after the conference. Full papers will be included in the 'HCII 2024 - Late Breaking Papers' volumes of the proceedings to be published in the Springer LNCS series, while 'Poster Extended Abstracts' will be included as short research papers in the 'HCII 2024 - Late Breaking Posters' volumes to be published in the Springer CCIS series.

I would like to thank the Program Board Chairs and the members of the Program Boards of all thematic areas and affiliated conferences for their contribution towards the high scientific quality and overall success of the HCI International 2024 conference. Their manifold support in terms of paper reviewing (single-blind review process, with a minimum of two reviews per submission), session organization and their willingness to act as goodwill ambassadors for the conference is most highly appreciated.

This conference would not have been possible without the continuous and unwavering support and advice of Gavriel Salvendy, founder, General Chair Emeritus, and Scientific Advisor. For his outstanding efforts, I would like to express my sincere appreciation to Abbas Moallem, Communications Chair and Editor of HCI International News.

July 2024   Constantine Stephanidis

HCI International 2024 Thematic Areas and Affiliated Conferences

- HCI: Human-Computer Interaction Thematic Area
- HIMI: Human Interface and the Management of Information Thematic Area
- EPCE: 21st International Conference on Engineering Psychology and Cognitive Ergonomics
- AC: 18th International Conference on Augmented Cognition
- UAHCI: 18th International Conference on Universal Access in Human-Computer Interaction
- CCD: 16th International Conference on Cross-Cultural Design
- SCSM: 16th International Conference on Social Computing and Social Media
- VAMR: 16th International Conference on Virtual, Augmented and Mixed Reality
- DHM: 15th International Conference on Digital Human Modeling & Applications in Health, Safety, Ergonomics & Risk Management
- DUXU: 13th International Conference on Design, User Experience and Usability
- C&C: 12th International Conference on Culture and Computing
- DAPI: 12th International Conference on Distributed, Ambient and Pervasive Interactions
- HCIBGO: 11th International Conference on HCI in Business, Government and Organizations
- LCT: 11th International Conference on Learning and Collaboration Technologies
- ITAP: 10th International Conference on Human Aspects of IT for the Aged Population
- AIS: 6th International Conference on Adaptive Instructional Systems
- HCI-CPT: 6th International Conference on HCI for Cybersecurity, Privacy and Trust
- HCI-Games: 6th International Conference on HCI in Games
- MobiTAS: 6th International Conference on HCI in Mobility, Transport and Automotive Systems
- AI-HCI: 5th International Conference on Artificial Intelligence in HCI
- MOBILE: 5th International Conference on Human-Centered Design, Operation and Evaluation of Mobile Communications

List of Conference Proceedings Volumes Appearing Before the Conference

1. LNCS 14684, Human-Computer Interaction: Part I, edited by Masaaki Kurosu and Ayako Hashizume
2. LNCS 14685, Human-Computer Interaction: Part II, edited by Masaaki Kurosu and Ayako Hashizume
3. LNCS 14686, Human-Computer Interaction: Part III, edited by Masaaki Kurosu and Ayako Hashizume
4. LNCS 14687, Human-Computer Interaction: Part IV, edited by Masaaki Kurosu and Ayako Hashizume
5. LNCS 14688, Human-Computer Interaction: Part V, edited by Masaaki Kurosu and Ayako Hashizume
6. LNCS 14689, Human Interface and the Management of Information: Part I, edited by Hirohiko Mori and Yumi Asahi
7. LNCS 14690, Human Interface and the Management of Information: Part II, edited by Hirohiko Mori and Yumi Asahi
8. LNCS 14691, Human Interface and the Management of Information: Part III, edited by Hirohiko Mori and Yumi Asahi
9. LNAI 14692, Engineering Psychology and Cognitive Ergonomics: Part I, edited by Don Harris and Wen-Chin Li
10. LNAI 14693, Engineering Psychology and Cognitive Ergonomics: Part II, edited by Don Harris and Wen-Chin Li
11. LNAI 14694, Augmented Cognition, Part I, edited by Dylan D. Schmorrow and Cali M. Fidopiastis
12. LNAI 14695, Augmented Cognition, Part II, edited by Dylan D. Schmorrow and Cali M. Fidopiastis
13. LNCS 14696, Universal Access in Human-Computer Interaction: Part I, edited by Margherita Antona and Constantine Stephanidis
14. LNCS 14697, Universal Access in Human-Computer Interaction: Part II, edited by Margherita Antona and Constantine Stephanidis
15. LNCS 14698, Universal Access in Human-Computer Interaction: Part III, edited by Margherita Antona and Constantine Stephanidis
16. LNCS 14699, Cross-Cultural Design: Part I, edited by Pei-Luen Patrick Rau
17. LNCS 14700, Cross-Cultural Design: Part II, edited by Pei-Luen Patrick Rau
18. LNCS 14701, Cross-Cultural Design: Part III, edited by Pei-Luen Patrick Rau
19. LNCS 14702, Cross-Cultural Design: Part IV, edited by Pei-Luen Patrick Rau
20. LNCS 14703, Social Computing and Social Media: Part I, edited by Adela Coman and Simona Vasilache
21. LNCS 14704, Social Computing and Social Media: Part II, edited by Adela Coman and Simona Vasilache
22. LNCS 14705, Social Computing and Social Media: Part III, edited by Adela Coman and Simona Vasilache

23. LNCS 14706, Virtual, Augmented and Mixed Reality: Part I, edited by Jessie Y. C. Chen and Gino Fragomeni
24. LNCS 14707, Virtual, Augmented and Mixed Reality: Part II, edited by Jessie Y. C. Chen and Gino Fragomeni
25. LNCS 14708, Virtual, Augmented and Mixed Reality: Part III, edited by Jessie Y. C. Chen and Gino Fragomeni
26. LNCS 14709, Digital Human Modeling and Applications in Health, Safety, Ergonomics and Risk Management: Part I, edited by Vincent G. Duffy
27. LNCS 14710, Digital Human Modeling and Applications in Health, Safety, Ergonomics and Risk Management: Part II, edited by Vincent G. Duffy
28. LNCS 14711, Digital Human Modeling and Applications in Health, Safety, Ergonomics and Risk Management: Part III, edited by Vincent G. Duffy
29. LNCS 14712, Design, User Experience, and Usability: Part I, edited by Aaron Marcus, Elizabeth Rosenzweig and Marcelo M. Soares
30. LNCS 14713, Design, User Experience, and Usability: Part II, edited by Aaron Marcus, Elizabeth Rosenzweig and Marcelo M. Soares
31. LNCS 14714, Design, User Experience, and Usability: Part III, edited by Aaron Marcus, Elizabeth Rosenzweig and Marcelo M. Soares
32. LNCS 14715, Design, User Experience, and Usability: Part IV, edited by Aaron Marcus, Elizabeth Rosenzweig and Marcelo M. Soares
33. LNCS 14716, Design, User Experience, and Usability: Part V, edited by Aaron Marcus, Elizabeth Rosenzweig and Marcelo M. Soares
34. LNCS 14717, Culture and Computing, edited by Matthias Rauterberg
35. LNCS 14718, Distributed, Ambient and Pervasive Interactions: Part I, edited by Norbert A. Streitz and Shin'ichi Konomi
36. LNCS 14719, Distributed, Ambient and Pervasive Interactions: Part II, edited by Norbert A. Streitz and Shin'ichi Konomi
37. LNCS 14720, HCI in Business, Government and Organizations: Part I, edited by Fiona Fui-Hoon Nah and Keng Leng Siau
38. LNCS 14721, HCI in Business, Government and Organizations: Part II, edited by Fiona Fui-Hoon Nah and Keng Leng Siau
39. LNCS 14722, Learning and Collaboration Technologies: Part I, edited by Panayiotis Zaphiris and Andri Ioannou
40. LNCS 14723, Learning and Collaboration Technologies: Part II, edited by Panayiotis Zaphiris and Andri Ioannou
41. LNCS 14724, Learning and Collaboration Technologies: Part III, edited by Panayiotis Zaphiris and Andri Ioannou
42. LNCS 14725, Human Aspects of IT for the Aged Population: Part I, edited by Qin Gao and Jia Zhou
43. LNCS 14726, Human Aspects of IT for the Aged Population: Part II, edited by Qin Gao and Jia Zhou
44. LNCS 14727, Adaptive Instructional System, edited by Robert A. Sottilare and Jessica Schwarz
45. LNCS 14728, HCI for Cybersecurity, Privacy and Trust: Part I, edited by Abbas Moallem
46. LNCS 14729, HCI for Cybersecurity, Privacy and Trust: Part II, edited by Abbas Moallem

47. LNCS 14730, HCI in Games: Part I, edited by Xiaowen Fang
48. LNCS 14731, HCI in Games: Part II, edited by Xiaowen Fang
49. LNCS 14732, HCI in Mobility, Transport and Automotive Systems: Part I, edited by Heidi Krömker
50. LNCS 14733, HCI in Mobility, Transport and Automotive Systems: Part II, edited by Heidi Krömker
51. LNAI 14734, Artificial Intelligence in HCI: Part I, edited by Helmut Degen and Stavroula Ntoa
52. LNAI 14735, Artificial Intelligence in HCI: Part II, edited by Helmut Degen and Stavroula Ntoa
53. LNAI 14736, Artificial Intelligence in HCI: Part III, edited by Helmut Degen and Stavroula Ntoa
54. LNCS 14737, Design, Operation and Evaluation of Mobile Communications: Part I, edited by June Wei and George Margetis
55. LNCS 14738, Design, Operation and Evaluation of Mobile Communications: Part II, edited by June Wei and George Margetis
56. CCIS 2114, HCI International 2024 Posters - Part I, edited by Constantine Stephanidis, Margherita Antona, Stavroula Ntoa and Gavriel Salvendy
57. CCIS 2115, HCI International 2024 Posters - Part II, edited by Constantine Stephanidis, Margherita Antona, Stavroula Ntoa and Gavriel Salvendy
58. CCIS 2116, HCI International 2024 Posters - Part III, edited by Constantine Stephanidis, Margherita Antona, Stavroula Ntoa and Gavriel Salvendy
59. CCIS 2117, HCI International 2024 Posters - Part IV, edited by Constantine Stephanidis, Margherita Antona, Stavroula Ntoa and Gavriel Salvendy
60. CCIS 2118, HCI International 2024 Posters - Part V, edited by Constantine Stephanidis, Margherita Antona, Stavroula Ntoa and Gavriel Salvendy
61. CCIS 2119, HCI International 2024 Posters - Part VI, edited by Constantine Stephanidis, Margherita Antona, Stavroula Ntoa and Gavriel Salvendy
62. CCIS 2120, HCI International 2024 Posters - Part VII, edited by Constantine Stephanidis, Margherita Antona, Stavroula Ntoa and Gavriel Salvendy

https://2024.hci.international/proceedings

Preface

Culture and computing is an important research area which aims to address the human-centered design of interactive technologies for the production, curation, preservation, and fruition of cultural heritage, as well as developing and shaping future cultures. There are various research directions in the relations between culture and computing: to preserve, disseminate, and create cultural heritages via ICT (e.g., digital archives), to empower humanities research via ICT (i.e., digital humanities), to create art and expressions via ICT (i.e., media art), to support interactive cultural heritage experiences (e.g., rituals), and to understand new cultures born on the Internet (e.g., net culture, social media, games).

The International Conference on Culture and Computing (C&C), an affiliated conference of the HCI International (HCII) conference, arrived at its 12th edition and provided an opportunity to share research issues and discuss the future of culture and computing.

Submissions this year explored the multifaceted landscape of user experience, art and culture, offering an inspiring compilation of groundbreaking research and visionary ideas. A key theme across many of the submissions was the exploration of user experience facets for cultural experiences. Whether it's enhancing museum and tour guide apps, reshaping language learning experiences through play, or exploring the Metaverse, these studies underscore the importance of cultural sensitivity and user-centric design principles in fostering meaningful interactions and seamless cultural experiences. In the realm of art, topics explored include the fusion of data with interactive installations and music experiences, the impact of synesthesia theory on art design, the design of immersive art spaces, and the transformative power of technology in shaping artistic expression. The role of technology in preserving and celebrating heritage has also been emphasized through the fusion of tradition with innovation for the creation of captivating new narratives expanding from traditional herbal medicine culture to teaching folk dance and preserving traditional weaving skills or to the integration of AI tools in enhancing cultural identity. Finally, articles have also taken a philosophical perspective expanding on the contemporary theory of Biemodernism and its implications for cultural computing. Overall, each paper delves into diverse themes and offers a unique perspective, with the collective volume encompassing a broad range of topics allowing the reader to get familiar with the current state of the art. I encourage every reader to enjoy the academic topics they are passionate about.

This volume of the HCII 2024 proceedings is dedicated to this year's edition of the C&C conference and focuses on topics related to User Experience Design for Seamless Cultural Experiences, Technology, Art, and Culture, Innovations in Digital Cultural Representation, and Biemodernism and Cultural Computing

Papers of this volume were accepted for publication after a minimum of two single-blind reviews from the members of the C&C Program Board or, in some cases, from members of the Program Boards of other affiliated conferences. I would like to thank all of them for their invaluable contribution, support, and efforts.

July 2024   Matthias Rauterberg

12th International Conference on Culture and Computing (C&C 2024)

The full list with the Program Board Chairs and the members of the Program Boards of all thematic areas and affiliated conferences of HCII 2024 is available online at:

http://www.hci.international/board-members-2024.php

HCI International 2025 Conference

The 27th International Conference on Human-Computer Interaction, HCI International 2025, will be held jointly with the affiliated conferences at the Swedish Exhibition & Congress Centre and Gothia Towers Hotel, Gothenburg, Sweden, June 22–27, 2025. It will cover a broad spectrum of themes related to Human-Computer Interaction, including theoretical issues, methods, tools, processes, and case studies in HCI design, as well as novel interaction techniques, interfaces, and applications. The proceedings will be published by Springer. More information will become available on the conference website: https://2025.hci.international/.

General Chair
Prof. Constantine Stephanidis
University of Crete and ICS-FORTH
Heraklion, Crete, Greece
Email: general_chair@2025.hci.international

https://2025.hci.international/

Contents

User Experience Design for Seamless Cultural Experiences

Research on Museum App Service Design from the Perspective of User
Experience 3
   Qihan Guo, Xing Fang, and Mingxi Shi

Preliminary Exploration of User Experience in the Learning-Through-Play
Language Learning App Duolingo 21
   Hsiu-Ching Laura Hsieh and Yi Zhen Liao

Taking Culture as the Axis to Discuss User Experience in Tour Guide
Mobile Application of Taichung City 31
   Hsiu-Ching Laura Hsieh and Wan-Ting Lin

Market-Driven HCI Design Education Analysis and Cultivation Strategy 42
   Yiyuan Huang, Yichun Huang, Xueqing Sun, and Linyou Sui

ContentRank: Towards a Scoring and Ranking System for Screen Media
Products Using Critical Reception Data 55
   *Chris Kim, Cris Paano, Anantha Chickanayakanahalli, Yulei Xiao,
   and Sara Diamond*

Discussion of User Experience for Streaming Platform by Using Mouse
Trajectory 74
   Shih-Yun Lu, Wei-Her Hsieh, and Chang Yuan Ku

Feasibility Study on Touch Screen Interaction Technology Based on "The
Sword of King Goujian" Exhibit 90
   Yuanyuan Song

Exploring User Behavior Based on Metaverse: A Modeling Study of User
Experience Factors 99
   Siqin Wang and Sunghee Ahn

Research on AR Cultural Heritage Museum Application Design Driven
by User Demands 119
   Kexin Yi and Yongkang Chen

Technology, Art, and Culture

Studying the Usability of the Yunlin Puppet Theater Website 137
  Hsiu-Ching Laura Hsieh and Tsu-Chi Shen

Construction of Immersive Art Space Using Mirror Display and Its
Evaluation Through Heart Rate Measurements 150
  Go Kazawa, Naoko Tosa, and Ryohei Nakatsu

Color Constancy Assuming Viewing Works Using a Display 167
  Meeko Kuwahara, Hiroki Takagi, and Masaki Hayashi

Application of Interactive Installation Art Design Based on Generalization
Theory 180
  Lin Liu, Yue Mi, Xinyi Cheng, and Yu Shi

Effect of Art's Increasing Human Creativity and Motivation When Viewed
in an Immersive Environment 196
  Ryohei Nakatsu, Naoko Tosa, Yunian Pang, Satoshi Niiyama,
  Yasuyuki Uraoka, Akane Kitagawa, Koichi Murata, Tatsuya Munaka,
  Yoshiyuki Ueda, Masafumi Furuta, and Michio Nomura

Data Shed: Interactive Art in the Service of Data Fluency 214
  Adit Verma, Sara Diamond, and Alexis Morris

The (Un)Answered Question: A Data Science Powered Music Experiment 233
  Lynn von Kurnatowski, Benjamin Wolff, Sophie Kernchen,
  Adriana Klapproth-Rieger, David Heidrich, Carina Haupt,
  Andreas Schreiber, Thoralf Niendorf, Andreas Kosmider,
  Marcus Lobbes, and Martin Hennecke

Innovations in Digital Cultural Representation

Spatial Interaction Elements in AR-Glasses-Based Touristic Service
Scenario Design 249
  Sunghee Ahn, Juhee Lee, Hyungmin Kim, Seong Lee, and Jong-Il Park

The Inheritance of Traditional Weaving Skills of Indigenous Settlement
and the Practice of Micro-industry and the Dream of Weaving Craft Village 259
  Shyh-Huei Hwang and Hsiu-Mei Huang

Design of Interactive Digital Virtual Display Application for Chinese
Heritage Traditional Herbal Medicine Culture 274
  Haoru Li, Binlin Feng, Mingyang Su, and Zhuohua Liu

AI Tools to Enhance Cultural Identity in Traditional Visual
Communication: A Case Study of Milan Chinatown 293
    Xinxi Liu and Yuan Liu

A Preliminary Study on the New Southbound International Co-creation
and Design Empowerment of Ethnic Studies - A.R. Application
of the Taivoan Tribe 309
    Li-Hsun Peng, Chi-Yu Pan, Indarti, and Mohammad Adam Jerusalem

Digital Storytelling of Intangible Cultural Heritage: A Multimodal
Interactive Serious Game for Teaching Folk Dance 325
    Yun Xie, Mingyang Su, Xiaomei Nie, and Xiu Li

Biemodernism and Cultural Computing

Bie-Modernism Cultural Computing of Literary Works of "Three
Musketeers of Tie Xi" Based on the Pre-trained Dialogue Models
ChatGLM3 339
    Jiafeng Lin and Zhaoyang Sui

Bie-modernism: From Cultural Computing to Social Computing 361
    Jiafeng Lin

Calculation of the Proportion of Modernity in Dao Lang's Lyrics
from a Bie-Modernist Cultural Computing Perspective 377
    Jianjiang Wang, Haiguang Chen, Hui Wang, Muyun Wang,
    Hong Ni, and Juan Wang

Writing Education Research in the Context of Cultural Computing
in Bie-modernism 391
    Yingying Xu and Jianjiang Wang

Research on Social Welfare Under the Perspective of Bie-modernism Life
Equity Theory - Prediction Based on Machine Learning Algorithm 408
    Peng Zhe

Author Index 431

User Experience Design for Seamless Cultural Experiences

Research on Museum App Service Design from the Perspective of User Experience

Qihan Guo[1] , Xing Fang[1]([✉]) , and Mingxi Shi[2]

[1] Wuhan University of Technology, Wuhan 430070, Hubei, China
1156165712@qq.com
[2] Kyungpook National University, Daegu 41566, South Korea

Abstract. With the arrival of the era of digital intelligence, the way information is disseminated has changed, and the form in which users receive information has also undergone significant changes. As a public welfare institution focused on cultural education and dissemination, museums not only collect, store, and research natural and human cultural things, but also provide services such as knowledge popularization and education for the public. The main function has shifted from displaying "objects" as the main focus to serving "people" as the center, providing various experiences for education, appreciation, contemplation, and knowledge sharing. People's visits to museums have entered a stage of cultural enjoyment that focuses on experience, from shallow cultural relics viewing. This has put forward higher requirements for the level of experiential service in museums. On the one hand, expanding people's participation and achieving the popularization of cultural relics education; on the other hand, the surge in the number of visitors has put enormous pressure on museum operations and service facility configuration. In this context, how museums optimize their service system is a topic worthy of social attention and research to solve. This paper takes museums as the research object, based on service design theory, analyzes the internal connection and value between stakeholders, user profiles, user experience maps, touchpoints, and other aspects of the museum system, explores the service design methods and strategies of the museum app, and achieves the goal of improving the quality of museum services and optimizing user emotional experiences.

Keywords: User Experience · Service Design · Museum App

1 Introduction

In the era of digital advancements, museums, as custodians of cultural heritage and educational repositories, are increasingly leveraging mobile application technologies to enhance their service offerings. At present, there are more than 5,000 different types of museums in China. However, with the growing demand for mass spiritual culture, Chinese museums currently have problems such as monotonous exhibit content, weak curatorial ability, patterned exhibition decoration, and users' lack of deep memory of exhibit information. In the era of big data and artificial intelligence, users are also paying more attention to humanization and emotional satisfaction [1], and more and more museums have begun to pay attention to the provision of "online + offline "service content, so as to improve the visiting experience of the audience. At present, there are still many museums that only provide offline visit services for the public, which not only limits the communication capacity but also makes the museum's service system unable to form a complete closed loop, reducing the audience's visiting experience. Therefore, starting from the people-centered concept of service design, this paper takes the Shanhaiguan Great Wall Museum as an example to put forward a service design strategy to improve the current situation of insufficient museum service capacity, maximize the display value of the museum while meeting the personalized needs of users [2], realize the unity of knowledge experience and interesting experience, and improve the service efficiency of the museum.

2 Related Theories

2.1 Service Design

Service design is a multidisciplinary field that has its origins in the intersection of design, business, and user experience. The evolution of service design as a distinct discipline can be traced back to the latter half of the 20th century, gaining prominence as organizations recognized the need to improve the quality and delivery of services in an increasingly service-oriented economy.

As a new interdisciplinary approach and a new mode of thinking, service design is influencing the way people live and work, and more and more organizations and enterprises realize that services can be designed and need to be designed [3]. Service design was first introduced to solve the problem of total quality management, so service design is regarded as a value-added service that drives economic growth in the business field. The roots of service design can be found in the principles of design thinking, which emerged in the 1960s and 1970s. Design thinking emphasized a human-centered approach to problem-solving, focusing on empathy, iteration, and collaboration. This methodology became foundational for service designers as they sought to address the complexities inherent in service systems. In 1991, Bill Hollins formally proposed the concept of "service design" in the field of design in the book "Total Design", explaining how "service" as a product should be designed to enhance the user's experience [4]. The goal of service design is to focus on the user's overall experience from the perspective of "people", including all aspects of service before, during, and after contact [5]. Pay attention to the user's expectations and expectations from the moment the service is contacted, and ensure that the user can easily find and understand the service by providing clear information and guidance. In Service Contact, we are committed to providing a user-friendly interface and process that enables users to easily use the service to solve problems and have a satisfactory experience. After the service contact, we value the feedback and evaluation of users, and continuously improve the service to provide a better user experience. In addition, service design not only focuses on the user's feelings but also considers the perspectives of other stakeholders, so as to enhance the attractiveness of the service by assisting the enterprise or organization to design an effective service.

In the 21st century, service designers face challenges related to the integration of emerging technologies, the globalization of markets, and the increasing demand for sustainability. Service design continues to evolve as a dynamic and responsive discipline, adapting to the changing landscape of user expectations and technological possibilities. In conclusion, service design has its roots in design thinking, responding to the demand for improved service experiences in an evolving economic landscape. Its development has been shaped by pioneers, the rise of the service economy, and the integration of business strategy, making it a crucial discipline for creating meaningful and effective services in the modern world.

2.2 User Experience

User Experience, commonly abbreviated as UX, is a pivotal aspect of design and technology that focuses on enhancing user satisfaction and interaction with a product, system, or service. It encompasses a broad range of factors, including usability, accessibility, aesthetics, performance, and overall user satisfaction.

The concept of "User Experience" discussed in the design community today was first proposed by the American cognitive psychologist Donald Norman in the mid-90s of the 20th century [6]; According to Donald Norman, user experience encompasses all aspects of the human-to-system experience, including industrial design, graphics, interfaces, physical interactions, and more. In 1998, the Harvard Business Review magazine published by B. Joseph Pine and James H. Gilmore, who first proposed the concept of the "experience economy", further confirmed the great influence of "user experience", and was quickly accepted and adopted by the industry. Many UX researchers have made their own arguments about user experience, and Jean-Marc defines user experience as a multidimensional structure that defines the overall role of the user in interacting with the system in a given environment [7]. According to Hassenzahl, user experience is a description of the user's changing inner emotional state during and after the interaction with the product, so the user experience should not be limited to a certain stage, but throughout the entire use process [8]. According to Pettersson et al., the user experience has shifted from simply determining usability and product performance to interactive emotion and pleasure, and after usability is reached, the user experience will expand to advanced features such as aesthetics, stimulation, and identity self-fulfillment [9]. In general, user experience is a macro concept with a very broad dimension, and many definitions are both common but different. UX design is gradually being widely used, and its connotation is constantly expanding, involving more and more fields, such as psychology, human-computer interaction, and usability testing are all incorporated into the relevant fields of user experience [10].

3 Analysis of Museum Service Design

3.1 Introduction to Shanhaiguan Great Wall Museum

The Shanhaiguan Great Wall Museum is situated at the foot of the 'First Pass Under Heaven' in Shanhaiguan District, Qinhuangdao City, Hebei Province, China. Established in 1991, it stands as a large thematic museum dedicated to the Great Wall. Spanning a total area of 1.21 hectares, the museum boasts a comprehensive collection of cultural artifacts, including stone tools, pottery, porcelain, bronze artifacts, jade items, currency, and inscriptions. Notably, it features a distinctive focus on Great Wall construction materials and weaponry, showcasing over 1,100 pieces and sets of various relics.

Accolades include designations as a National Patriotic Education Demonstration Base, National Popular Science Education Base, one of the first batch of National Defense Education Demonstration Bases, and recognition as a National Secondary Museum. Renowned for its exquisite design, well-planned layout, grandeur, and rich cultural content, the Great Wall Museum serves as a showcase for historical culture, a patriotic education base, and a platform for popularizing scientific knowledge among youth. It plays an immeasurable role in the inheritance of Great Wall culture and the promotion of the spirit of the Great Wall.

However, the current challenge lies in the extensive but somewhat monotonous collection within the Shanhaiguan Great Wall Museum. The majority of exhibits consist of textual and pictorial descriptions, making it difficult for visitors to grasp the historical knowledge behind the artifacts. This results in a less impactful and memorable experience for users. Online offerings are limited to a WeChat mini-program, allowing users to explore a VR digital museum and access audio explanations for exhibition halls. Nevertheless, the overall online service system is not fully developed, restricting the museum's outreach and impact.

In light of this, the Shanhaiguan Great Wall Museum urgently requires an App to facilitate a diversified and enhanced service experience through a combination of online and offline channels. This app aims to unlock the museum's service potential, improve efficiency, and provide visitors with a more engaging and immersive experience, both physically and virtually.

3.2 Stakeholders of Shanhaiguan Great Wall Museum

Stakeholders are individuals and groups that can affect or are affected by the achievement of an organization's objectives [11]. For the Shanhaiguan Great Wall Museum, there are many stakeholders, such as tourists, the government, media, universities, designers, related businesses, museum staff, and so on. In the service process, stakeholders engage with each other through the exchange of goods, information, and funds, which leads to the establishment of certain relationships. This interaction encompasses the various needs of different stakeholders (see Fig. 1).

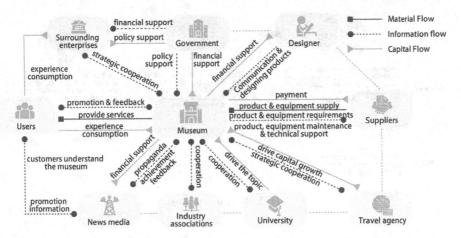

Fig. 1. Stakeholder Service System Diagram of Shanhaiguan Great Wall Museum

3.3 Service Design Value of Shanhaiguan Great Wall Museum

Firstly, the research subject is characterized by its holistic nature. In the realm of service design thinking, it is imperative to consider all stakeholders of the Shanhaiguan Great Wall Museum comprehensively. This extends beyond visitors to include the perspectives and service needs of the government, media, other enterprises, and related staff, treating all interconnected stakeholders as a unified entity. Through detailed research and surveys of different entities, a more complete understanding of their diverse service requirements can be achieved. Subsequently, compatible design strategies are proposed, laying a foundation to support the practical development of the museum's app.

Secondly, the design process is systemic. Guided by service design thinking, designers must grasp every aspect of the service system, which involves understanding various touchpoints during service stages—static, interactive, interpersonal, and even environmental touchpoints—as well as their interrelationships. It also includes the interaction between various software and hardware components [12], enabling the Shanhaiguan Great Wall Museum app to function optimally within the service system.

Lastly, the design outcome exhibits interdisciplinary characteristics. Service design is inherently systemic and multidisciplinary, and the process is interdisciplinary [13]. Therefore, the Shanhaiguan Great Wall Museum app will be related to fields such as design theory, communication studies, marketing, sociology, psychology, and more. This interdisciplinary research will ultimately enhance the design product, elevating the museum's service efficacy.

4 Investigation and Analysis on Service Demand of Shanhaiguan Great Wall Museum

4.1 Research Process

The research process is mainly divided into the following three stages: problem exploration, problem analysis and demand summary stage (see Fig. 2).

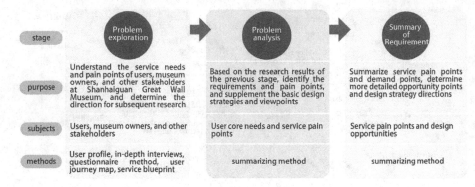

Fig. 2. Research process

4.2 Stakeholder Research and Analysis

The Main Service Object of Shanhaiguan Great Wall Museum. The primary service audience for Shanhaiguan Great Wall Museum comprises visitors who come to explore its offerings. To gain insight into visitor behaviors, attitudes, and service needs, the museum conducted an onsite survey by distributing 200 questionnaires. The specific content of these questionnaires (see Table 1). Out of the distributed questionnaires, 187 were returned with valid responses, resulting in an effective response rate of 93.50%.

Table 1. User survey content

Problem Dimension	The content of the problem
User Visiting Behavior	How many museums do you visit a year on average?
	What is the purpose of your visit to the museum?
	How long do you usually spend in a museum?
	Which route will you choose to visit the museum?
	What is your visiting preference?
	What kind of narration do you prefer?
User Perspectives and Attitudes	What do you focus on when you visit the museum?
	Why did you choose to visit the museum?
	What are some of the problems you usually have when visiting a museum?
User Expectations	What do you expect from the Shanhaiguan Great Wall Museum?

To facilitate an in-depth analysis of the 'human' element in service interactions, the author has primarily categorized visitors into four types: child visitors, elderly visitors, expert visitors, and general visitors. For each category, a user persona model has been employed to examine the service needs of groups with common interests or similar behavioral patterns (see Fig. 3).

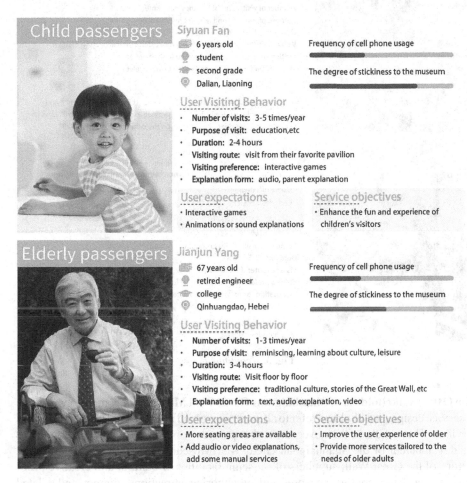

Fig. 3. User portrait building

Fig. 3. (*continued*)

The Other Stakeholders of Shanhaiguan Great Wall Museum. From the perspective of service design, stakeholders refer to all groups involved in or affected by the museum's services. These include the government that provides policy and financial support for the development of the Shanhaiguan Great Wall Museum; universities promoting the culture of the Great Wall; suppliers of museum facilities or cultural and creative products; media that increase exposure; and neighboring attractions, dining, and related businesses. Through in-depth interviews and field research, stakeholders' pain points and service needs for the Shanhaiguan Great Wall Museum have been identified (see Fig. 4). Therefore, a singular service or design fundamentally cannot satisfy the diverse needs of different stakeholders. In proposing subsequent service design strategies for the Shanhaiguan Great Wall Museum, a deeper consideration of the relationships between stakeholders is necessary. By employing specific methods, it is important to ensure the personalized needs of various stakeholders are met, thereby clarifying the unique importance of different groups and encouraging them to proactively perform their distinct functions.

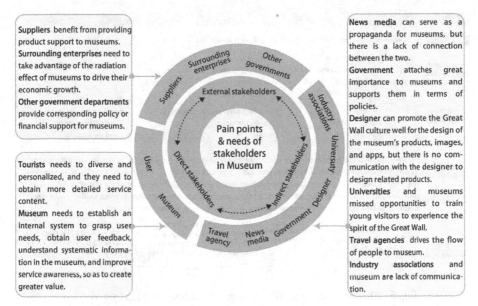

Fig. 4. Stakeholder pain points and needs analysis of Shanhaiguan Great Wall Museum

4.3   Service Flow Investigation and Analysis

By employing the user journey mapping method, an analysis of the service processes at the Shanhaiguan Great Wall Museum is conducted. The user journey map vividly visualizes the customer's experience, behaviors, touchpoints, and satisfaction throughout the service via a visual format, thereby offering further insight into user needs and potential opportunities for design innovation. Based on the user personas and insights gleaned from in-depth interviews regarding user evaluations and behaviors, the entire service process is divided into three stages: pre-visit, during the visit, and post-visit (see Fig. 5, Fig. 6, Fig. 7).

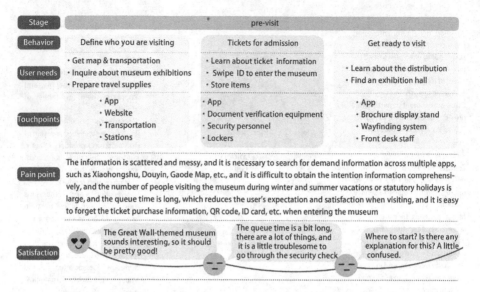

Fig. 5. Shanhaiguan Great Wall Museum User Journey Map (pre-visit)

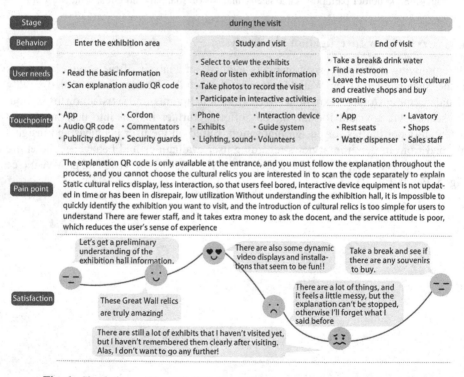

Fig. 6. Shanhaiguan Great Wall Museum User Journey Map (during the visit)

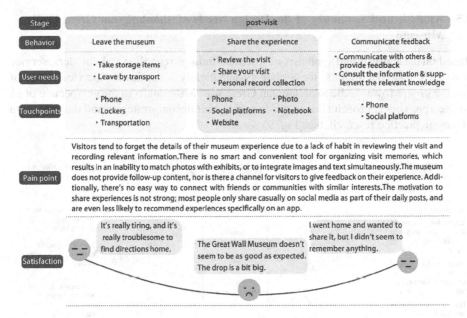

Fig. 7. Shanhaiguan Great Wall Museum User Journey Map (post-visit)

4.4 Touchpoint Research and Analysis

Touchpoints are one of the central domains within service design research and play a crucial role in advancing subsequent theoretical studies and practical design implementations. The service touchpoints at the Shanhaiguan Great Wall Museum encompass all external interactions that occur during service delivery. Based on the dimensions of the museum's communications, the touchpoints have been categorized into static, interactive, and interpersonal touchpoints. Furthermore, an analysis and organization of the museum's service touchpoints have been conducted according to the different stages of the visitor experience, (see Fig. 8).

Service Contact Point	pre-visit			during the visit			post-visit		
	Define who you are visiting	Tickets for admission	Get ready to visit	Enter the exhibition area	Study and visit	End of visit	Leave the museum	Share the experience	Feedback
Static touchpoints	Station, vehicle	Document verification equipment, lockers	Brochures, Showcase, Wayfinding system	Displays, Information wall, Cordon	Lighting, sound, LED Showcases, exhibits	Navigation system, Seats, escalators Toilets, shops	Lockers, Vehicle		
Interactive touchpoints	App, Official account, Other websites	App, Official account	App, Other websites	App	App, Camera, Website		App	App, Camera, Website	App, Website
interpersonal touchpoints	Driver	Security personnel	Front Desk Staff, Security personnel, Volunteer	Security personnel, Volunteer	Explanators Security personnel volunteer	Salesperson Security personnel Cleaning	Security personnel	Family Friend Netizens	Museum staff

Fig. 8. Analysis of service touchpoints at Shanhaiguan Great Wall Museum

4.5   Analysis and Summary of the Design Needs of Shanhaiguan Great Wall Museum

Based on the analysis and synthesis of research findings regarding stakeholders, service processes, and touchpoints, the author systematically identifies the service needs of diverse groups towards the Shanhaiguan Great Wall Museum from the perspective of an online app. This approach aims to guide subsequent design strategies and the unfolding of design practice research, (see Fig. 9).

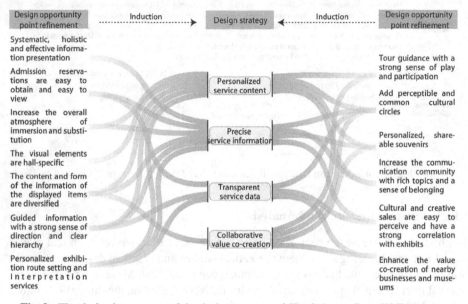

Fig. 9. The derivation process of the design strategy of Shanhaiguan Great Wall Museum

5   Shanhaiguan Great Wall Museum App Service Design Strategy

After analyzing the specific design requirements of the Shanhaiguan Great Wall Museum through three dimensions: stakeholders, service processes, and touchpoints, the final proposal presents a service design-based strategy for the Shanhaiguan Great Wall Museum App. This strategy emphasizes four key aspects: personalization, precision, transparency, and collaboration. By focusing on these areas, the design of the Shanhaiguan Great Wall Museum App aims to enhance both the experiential and the value aspects of the user experience.

5.1   Create Personalized Service Content Provision

Personalized Interaction Framework Design. In the era of digital intelligence, humanizing the interactive framework of the Shanhaiguan Great Wall Museum App makes it easier for users to access information and provides content services that are more intuitive and user-friendly, thereby enhancing the convenience of interaction. Thus, the many elements of the Shanhaiguan Great Wall Museum are flattened, by spreading the scattered hierarchical parent-child elements across the same interface structure to reduce the number of layers in the information architecture. By laying out these elements on the same interface, the complexity of the information structure is minimized while maintaining a linkage between them. Parent elements are placed at the top of the interface, and child elements at the bottom. Interaction with parent elements leads to corresponding changes in the child elements. Design techniques such as contrast, neutralization, and segmentation clearly delineate the primary and secondary relationships between elements within the interface. Building on this, the Shanhaiguan Great Wall Museum App separates permanent exhibition information from thematic exhibition information. Thematic exhibitions can be updated with relevant exhibit content and information according to different themes, meeting the dynamic needs of exhibition content. This not only ensures consistency in the structure of the museum's permanent exhibition information but also facilitates the operational management of thematic exhibitions by museum staff, enhancing the flexibility of the App.

Personalized Guided Interactions. The Shanhaiguan Great Wall Museum often caters to a diverse range of visitors and must provide different participatory guidance and interaction methods tailored to the individualized needs of its users. For instance, child visitors may be intrigued by dynamic and entertaining interactions. For these young users, the integration of gamified elements with museum information can guide them, shifting from a passive didactic approach to a proactive and self-directed learning mode, thereby enhancing their cognitive engagement with the museum. This change in approach can elevate their understanding of the Shanhaiguan Great Wall. For the general public, immersive guiding techniques can be employed to delve into the personalized desires of the user groups for socialization, learning, and entertainment. The addition of semi-intelligent guide assistants within the App system, combined with narrative and logical cultural exhibits and offline materials, can lead users into a state of immersion in exploring the cultural content of the Great Wall Museum, deepening their comprehension and awareness of the Great Wall culture. Elderly visitors, on the other hand, may benefit more from clear and concise interface indexing, reduced operational steps, and the use of audio or video explanations to guide them through the museum, facilitating active participation in the visit through conversational interactive components.

Personalized Community Facilitation. By establishing a personalized community guidance mechanism that offers topics, items, and interaction models capable of triggering social behaviors, user social needs can be met. The mode of knowledge acquisition has shifted from the traditional search and reading to a group-based model of cultural knowledge sharing and co-creation. Tailoring to the visitors' hobbies, interests, and focal points, online communities are formed within the Shanhaiguan Great Wall Museum App platform, where groups share similar motivations for visiting and consumption perspectives. Under this community guidance mechanism, visitors' sense of participation in the museum can be enhanced, and it also serves as a powerful tool for brand promotion for the museum.

The Great Wall cultural theme serves as a focal point to maintain the interactive relationships among users within the community. For example, in addition to displaying and introducing photos of the Great Wall's historical artifacts in the museum, the App allows users to engage with the Great Wall's cultural relics through commonly seen social networking actions such as liking, expressing curiosity, following, showing disinterest, commenting, and leaving messages. Within the community, users can post content related to exhibition information, educational activities, stories of the Great Wall, and interpretations of the collections. Users may share their own insights based on their visit experiences, cultural knowledge, and any questions or confusions regarding the topics posted in the community. Through mutual Q&A and sharing of insights, they can find museum friends with similar interests and form personalized communities.

5.2 Focus on Accurate Service Information Support

Enhance Visual Information to Attract Users' Attention. Experimental psychologist Treichler has proven through numerous studies that up to 83% of human information is acquired visually. Therefore, in the product shaping process, the efficient conveyance of information can be significantly improved by the sensible arrangement of colors, graphics, and typography. In designing the Shanhaiguan Great Wall Museum App, consideration should be given to visual imagery that aligns with the cultural and artistic characteristics of the Shanhaiguan Great Wall, to accurately highlight the themes that need to be displayed and better capture the attention of visitors and users. Moreover, the judicious use of contrast principles and designing the App's interactive interface according to the priority of related information can help users promptly focus on important information. For instance, by employing strong contrasts in color, font, and layout, the main body of information to be conveyed can be emphasized, catching the user's eye and thus stimulating their desire to explore.

Optimize Navigation and Reduce the User's Visual Load. It is crucial to prevent visual overload, which can increase cognitive costs for users and affect the accurate provision of service information. To make navigation more explicit, the Shanhaiguan Great Wall Museum App could be conceptualized as a virtual exhibition hall model of the Shanhaiguan Great Wall Museum.

The design process of the Shanhaiguan Great Wall Museum App can be likened to setting up an exhibition, where using the App to learn about the museum is akin to entering a virtual exhibit hall. A clear navigation system can help users efficiently find the various types of information they need. Thus, optimizing navigation to reduce cognitive load can be implemented in the following ways:

Firstly, present navigation information precisely using visual forms. For example, consolidate similar information on the same page or within the same section, hide less important information and functions, and place the most frequently used and most cared-about information and functions in the most intuitive area to reduce confusion while using the App.

Secondly, clearly indicate the user's current position within the interface hierarchy. This means that different hierarchical levels within the App should have visual guidance, providing a clear current location index, enhancing the visual findability of the Shanhaiguan Great Wall Museum App, and offering precise information service functions to users.

Lastly, provide timely and accurate operation prompts. In the process of providing services, timely operation prompts act like a manual throughout the use of the Shanhaiguan Great Wall Museum App. They are also one of the most effective ways to accurately convey functional methods to users. The Shanhaiguan Great Wall Museum App contains a variety of functions, some of which require timely operational prompts to help users better grasp the information they need.

Refine User Data and Provide Information Services. Gathering user data is one of the most critical pathways for delivering precise push services. By conducting preliminary research on users, collecting user data according to different needs and preferences, and selecting specific tags or characteristics to build user profiles, these profiles shed light on the user's personal basic information, behavioral traits, habitual preferences, and interests. The design of the Shanhaiguan Great Wall Museum App should start from these profiles to push relevant information to users, presenting it in the form or content they most look forward to, thus facilitating the easy realization of precision in information provision. For instance, by utilizing Bluetooth technology and embedding data points within the interface, one can gather behavioral data such as the number of searches for exhibits, dwell time, likes on artifacts, and saved content. This data helps to predict the information users may find interesting and allows for the precise pushing of related review information or products in subsequent pushes. It is necessary to match user data with user preferences to enhance the efficiency of information conveyance and the precision of promotional efforts for the Shanhaiguan Great Wall Museum.

5.3 Standardized and Transparent Service Data Display

Real-Time Feedback on Service Needs. During their visit to the Shanhaiguan Great Wall Museum, users expect to see real-time and detailed service processes, and the museum's backend needs to timely capture the visitors' immediate needs and thoughts to better provide service. For instance, after users have scheduled a guided tour, the application of big data calculations and test optimization allows them to monitor the guide's progress in real-time, estimate the time until the end of the current session, and, at the end of the service, to display detailed service information (service process, chargeable items, billing details), etc. This transparency lets users clearly understand the breakdown of their expenses, instilling confidence and reflecting the museum's service attitude. Additionally, the museum should offer functionalities for rating and providing feedback on the guide at different stages, which facilitates subsequent service feedback and ensures the timely supervision and regulation of the guides' service quality.

Real-Time Updates on Service Status. Utilizing big data and internet technologies to update service statuses is particularly critical for the reservation and cultural product purchase stages. For booking tickets, local attractions, and dining options, displaying dynamic progress indicators for statuses like 'in reservation', 'reservation successful', or 'reservation failed' can mitigate users' impatience and reduce waiting time. In the cultural product purchase phase, especially when users opt for personalized customization of museum cultural products, it's essential to present transparent consumption details and service statuses (such as 'customizing', 'in transit', 'being delivered'). If users have questions, they should be able to inquire with service personnel at any time. The detailed service status provided by the museum can also serve as evidence for service review, facilitating subsequent service and communication processes.

5.4 Promote Collaborative Service Value Co-creation

Motivate User Engagement and Feedback. Collecting and mining user feedback through the Shanhaiguan Great Wall Museum App during the service provision process is key to optimizing service quality. This feedback mechanism is multidimensional, encompassing not only reactions to the museum's service effectiveness but also responses to exhibits, promotional news, and cultural creative products within the Great Wall Museum. The goal is to co-create value from user data and information in interactions and to transition it towards association.

For example, different forms of feedback channels can be established to motivate user participation through incentives such as red envelopes, tickets, discount coupons, and souvenirs. After receiving user feedback, the content should be systematically organized and categorized. Users should be actively informed about the improvements made in response to their feedback and the valuable help provided to other users. Additionally, by setting up a tipping interface, users are encouraged to reward museum staff such as guides and security personnel with certain amounts. This rewarding action allows employees to feel the value and return of their labor, spurring them to strive for higher levels of service in the future.

For users, the act of tipping is a sign of respect for the staff's work and achievements. In the process of this action, they can experience the value of service and respect for labor, which reflects a significant aspect of the service culture.

Present Stakeholder Needs. Appropriately presenting stakeholders' needs not only facilitates positive interaction and communication with users but also maximizes the co-creative value between museums and stakeholders, thus transforming value. For example, after visitors finish touring the Shanhaiguan Great Wall Museum, the "Surroundings" interface on the App could suggest local delicacies, tourist attractions, and unique cultural customs nearby. Additionally, for visitors ready to leave, the App could collaborate effectively with other ride-sharing or navigation platforms to recommend routes home, addressing visitors' needs for clothing, food, accommodation, and transportation, and thus driving the economic development around the museum.

Collaborating with higher education institutions, the App could allow for the advance booking of large-scale student tours, enabling the museum to arrange guides and plan schedules timely, spreading knowledge of the Great Wall culture among students. Moreover, students passionate about the Great Wall culture could sign up for volunteer activities through the App, using their vacation periods to serve as volunteer guides at the museum, enhancing their personal expression skills and enriching their extracurricular activities, fostering a beneficial cycle between the Shanhaiguan Great Wall Museum and various universities.

Construct an Emotional Value Identity. Value co-creation, centered around a diversity of agents, involves their participation in an open public service system where the construction of emotional value identification is crucial. Emotional value is built among subjects, objects, media, and environments, and collaborative services are provided under the integrated resource value, combining emotional motivation to serve users. This approach enhances users' cultural value identification with the Shanhaiguan Great Wall Museum, stimulates emotional resonance, and thus constructs a positive emotional interactive relationship.

For instance, in the App design, mobile smart positioning and internet technology can be used to accurately gather information on visitors' footprints, the content of their visit, and the duration. After visitors conclude their tour, a personalized, exclusive, and narrative tour report can be pushed to different users. This report, even long after the visit, can help visitors easily recall the entire process of their museum tour, evoking emotional memories and transforming and expanding the co-created value through emotional means. The service system of the Shanhaiguan Great Wall Museum, guided by the service design philosophy, is the means to achieve the goal of App value co-creation. The continuity of value is the extension of service, which can strengthen user consciousness and attract new social forces to continue to participate.

6 Conclusion

From the perspective of user experience, research on the service design strategy of museum Apps not only reveals the importance of integrating technology with cultural services but also emphasizes the central role of a user-centered design philosophy. By delving into users' needs, preferences, and behavioral patterns, we can design museum Apps that offer more interactive, emotional, and personalized services. This research also demonstrates the effectiveness of data-driven design and the power of open participation and co-creation of value.

As technology advances and user requirements become increasingly complex, museum App service design will continue to evolve, seeking to enhance the depth and breadth of the user experience while fulfilling functional needs. We hope this research can provide innovative ideas for the field of museum service design, encourage the exploration of more design practices, and advocate for continuous optimization and iteration. Ultimately, we aim to achieve the best alignment between museum services and user needs, making the dissemination of cultural heritage more vivid and enduring.

References

1. Desmet, P., Fokkinga, S.: Beyond Maslow's pyramid: introducing a typology of thirteen fundamental needs for human-centered design. Multimodal Technol. Interact. **4**(3), 38 (2020)
2. Liu, W., Lee, K.P., Gray, C.M., Toombs, A.L., Chen, K.H., Leifer, L.: Transdisciplinary teaching and learning in UX design: a program review and AR case studies. Appl. Sci. **11**(22), 10648 (2021)
3. Miaskiewicz, T., Kozar, K.A.: Personas and user-centered design: how can personas benefit product design processes? Des. Stud. **32**, 417–430 (2011)

4. Zhang, L.H., Zhang, S.F., Zhu, Q.Y.: Smart appliance interaction: a new paradigm for systematic experience design thinking. Decoration **08**, 17–23 (2021)
5. Zhang, C., Yin, X.H.: Research on service design methodology to reconstruct the regional brand of Shenyang. Old Brand Mark. **10**, 9–11 (2022)
6. Donald, A.N.: The Design of Everythings, p. 11. CITIC Publishing Group, Beijing (2016)
7. Prahalad, C.K., Ramaswamy, V.: Co-creation experiences: the next practice in value creation. J. Interact. Mark. **3**(1), 5–14 (2004)
8. Hassenzahl, M.: User Experience(UX): towards an experiential perspective on product quality. In: Proceedings of the 20th Conference on l'Interaction Homme-Machine, pp. 11–15. Association for Computing Machinery, New York (2008)
9. Pettersson, R.: BasicID-concepts, Concepts & Terms, 4th edn. International Institute for Information Design (IIID), Austria (2012).https://www.iiid.net/PublicLibrary/Pettersson-Rune-ID-It-Depends.pdf. Accessed 6 Jan 2024
10. Nielsen, J.: A 100-Year View of User Experience (2017). https://www.nngroup.com/articles/100-years-ux/
11. Goldman, S., et al.: Assessing d.learning: capturing the journey of becoming a design thinker. In: Plattner, H., Meinel, C., Leifer, L. (eds.) Design Thinking Research. UNDINNO, pp. 13–33. Springer, Heidelberg (2012). https://doi.org/10.1007/978-3-642-31991-4_2
12. Bødker, S.: Through the Interface: A Human Activity Approach to User Interface Design. CRC Press (2021)
13. Norman, D.A. (ed.): User Centered System Design: New Perspectives on Human-Computer Interaction, 1st edn. CRC Press, Boca Raton (1986)

Preliminary Exploration of User Experience in the Learning-Through-Play Language Learning App Duolingo

Hsiu-Ching Laura Hsieh and Yi Zhen Liao[✉]

National Yunlin University of Science and Technology, Douliou, Yunlin 64002, Taiwan, R.O.C.
jenny199798@gmail.com

Abstract. In modern society, online learning has become another major knowledge acquisition route beyond traditional classrooms. Through network platforms, students could conveniently acquire multiple courses to expand the knowledge with self-directed learning. Language learning applications, with the convenience, therefore become the popular learning style with modern people.

Duolingo, a world-famous language learning application, provides rich and multiple language learning courses, including more than 40 languages. Designed with gamification, users learn through task and challenge completion; and, it is famous for the simple and easy-to-use interface, real-time feedback, and social media interaction. Gamification learning model does not simply provide challenging learning environment, but could also satisfy students' personalized needs for effectively promoting learners' comprehensive development.

Excellent user experience results in millions of Duolingo users in the world. This study focuses on user experience in learning-through-play, containing challenge, preference, interactivity, learning effectiveness, and satisfaction. The research method covers the following steps. First, relevant data are collected through literature review. Second, the interview outline with 5 dimensions is designed and the semi-structured interview is preceded for collecting user feedback and experience. Finally, the qualitative research results are induced and explained for the preliminary comprehension of Duolingo user experience.

By deeply understanding user experience in learning-through-play, the advantages and potential improvement of Duolingo are exposed. Furthermore, this study could enhance cross-cultural understanding so that Duolingo could better match Taiwanese users' expectations to build a friendlier, pleasant, and inclusive learning platform. By deeply understanding Taiwanese users' cultural characteristics and learning needs, Duolingo could be more flexibly adjusted the learning styles and resources to provide better learning experience for users all over the world.

Keywords: User experience · Gamification · Duolingo

1 Introduction

In the time with rapid development of technology, the broad application of mobile applications has deeply changed people's lifestyles so that mobile phones become the major information search and collection tool. Such a trend further promotes the formation

M. Rauterberg (Ed.): HCII 2024, LNCS 14717, pp. 21–30, 2024.
https://doi.org/10.1007/978-3-031-61147-6_2

of new-style learning habits with mobile devices as the core [1]. Along with the multiple development of mobile applications, including various learning APP, a lot of learners start to explore learning opportunities on mobile phones and tablets. They eager to grasp the learning initiative that results in larger motive and participation [2].

Duolingo, promoted in 2011, is a free online language learning platform. The statistics by 2023 shows that it provides courses more than 40 languages and over 5 hundred million downloads to become one of the education applications with the most downloads. Duolingo is popular due to the unique gamification elements and social media interaction. In comparison with other language learning software, Duolingo, through the ingenious gamification elements, provides learners with rich interactive experience. For this reason, it is necessary to discuss the user experience.

Based on the essential emphasis on user experience [3–6], it becomes the consensus of designers to place users in the core of the design to ensure the good and pleasant interactive experience. Such an idea is especially important for discussing Duolingo application. By deeply understanding factors of culture, language, and user habit in such countries and areas, the application better adapting to their needs and closer to local users' expectation with rich interactive experience could be provided. This study first focuses on applicable people in Taiwan, and will be expanded to more countries for user needs in different countries and areas.

2 Literature Review

2.1 Duolingo

Duolingo, a language learning application with the slogan of "The world's best way to learn a language", was created by Luis Von Ahn and Severin Hacker, allowing users creating a free account and choosing the learned language. It presents several advanced language learning methods, ensures students to learn well through courses, activities, tests, and games, including tracking progress, motivation, feedback, and vocabulary, and assists students in comprehending the learned content, inducing the interests, and enjoying learning fun. The application also tells learners about the information of points acquired, models watched, and time spent. The asynchronous forums link learners to enhance a lot of learning communities, allowing users reflecting and responding time in the forums [7–9].

Duolingo, the language learning App, uses gamification as the core, creates game roles to become the reading partners in the learning, and converts language learning contents through challenging and interesting game challenges. The App supports social media interaction, allowing users seeing the learning progress of each other to commonly promote the motivation to learn (see Fig. 1). Along with upgrading challenges, the App offers rewards, e.g. badges and encouraging dialogues, to induce users' learning interests (see Fig. 2). Duolingo provides more than 40 languages for learning choices; meanwhile, it provides individualized learning plans to ensure each user being able to appropriately learn in different courses. Moreover, the App would organize wrong answers for users' review to reinforce the memory (see Fig. 3).

Fig. 1. Challenges in the learning-through-play Duolingo

Fig. 2. Duolingo learning incentive interface

Fig. 3. Duolingo creating individualized learning courses

2.2 User Experience

The idea of user experience (UX) was first proposed by Norman, a psychologist and designer, in 1988. Norman, for the first time, introduced the term "User Experience" in the writing The Design of Everyday Things, to describe the overall perception and emotional experience in the interaction between people and products or systems. Nielsen emphasized that user experience was a comprehensive idea, which did not simply contain the actual interaction with products, but also the expectation before use and memory after use. Such comprehension had the evaluation of user experience become more comprehensive and consider users' feelings and emotion in the entire use process. Aiming at the term "user experience", ISO 9241-210 defined it as users' feelings and responding feedback after using and participating in products, systems, and service.

2.3 Gamification

"Gamification" was first proposed by Pelling, a British computer program designer and inventor, in 2002. Pelling contributed to introduce the interactivity and fun in games into other fields, such as business and education. Deterding [10] defined gamification as using game design elements in non-gaming environment. It revealed that gamification applied the design idea of games in situations not in traditional gaming scenes. Non-gaming environment referred to fields or scenes not in traditional games. In such situations, people participated in activities mainly for learning, enhancing skills, or fulfilling goals. According to the comments in studies on gamification, it was one of the most common applications in education or learning [11, 12]. Hamari pointed out positive learning outcome of gamification in education or learning practice and stressed on the potential advantage of gamification in enhancing education effect. Tsai [13] revealed that learners regarded gamification as a reward, being able to eliminate learning dullness for enjoying the learning process and strengthening the motivation to learn. The research result indicated that Duolingo combining Arabic grammar audio and video with games allowed learners learning with easy and interesting ways [14].

3 Methodology

This study aims to understand Taiwanese user experience in using Duolingo for learning-through-play and discuss challenge, preference, interactivity, learning effectiveness, and satisfaction in order to comprehensively understand users' feelings and points of view in the learning process. User feedback is collected through semi-structured interviews, and the study focuses on deep discussion of such topics, but remains the flexibility for the respondents providing personal opinions and experiences for richer data.

3.1 Research Subject

6 heavies Taiwanese Duolingo users are selected as the respondents for this study to show the preliminary exploration of Taiwanese user experience in learning-through-play with the language learning App (Table 1).

Table 1. Basic information of respondents

User	Occupation	Native language	Language learned in App	Time for using Duolingo App
u1	Student	Chinese	Japanese	About a year
u2	Student	Chinese	English	3 years
u3	Student	Chinese	Korean	2 years
u4	Accountant	Chinese	Korean	1 year
u5	Teacher	Chinese	Cantonese	3 years
u6	Teacher	Chinese	English	2 years

3.2 Interview Design

To understand Taiwanese user experience in learning-through-play with the language learning App, the interview is set the experience in learning-through-play and focuses on the dimensions of challenge, preference, interactivity, learning effectiveness, and satisfaction. Three questions are designed for each dimension for the respondents' feedback with the past use experiences.

Challenge. Hammer [15] mentioned that introducing gamification elements, e.g. tasks or challenges, into education could help provide learners with more challenging experiences. Zichermann [16] proposed a similar viewpoint that introducing challenging goals could induce the participants' positivity. Such goals might cover completing tasks with higher difficulties, solving complicated problems, or achieving certain achievement. Those studies emphasized that the introduction of challenging elements in the gamification learning experience could induce learners' positive participation and further enhance the learning experience.

Preference. Helander [17] indicated that a designer could better adapt to the user interface, promote user satisfaction, and enhance good interactive experience by understanding user preference. Considering and comprehending user preference in the product or service design could have the product better approach users' expectation to enhance the acceptance and satisfaction.

Interactivity. Interactivity, referring to a two-way or multiple-way communication and operation process, generally occurs between users and systems or users and contents. In human-computer interaction and digital environment, interactivity is one of important elements in user experience, covering several layers of interaction. Interactivity might positively affect users' satisfaction, effectiveness, efficiency, and overall attitudes [18].

Learning Effectiveness. Clark [19] considered that learning effectiveness was mainly relied on teaching objectives and students' learning activities. Learning effectiveness was the effect of learning activity or education interference, aiming to ensure whether students successfully achieve expected learning goals. This study intends to discuss users' learning effectiveness in using Duolingo, with gamification, interfering the learning process.

Satisfaction. Satisfaction, as users' subjective evaluation of products or service, reflects the feelings and attitudes after the use. Such evaluation covers several dimensions and is affected by the interaction between users' previous expectation and actual perceived performance [20]. Hassenzahl and Tractinsky [21] regarded satisfaction as an important indicator of user experience that understanding satisfaction could help more comprehensively discuss user experience.

4 Results and Discussion

This study aims to understand user experience in learning-through-play with Duolingo. According to the semi-structured interview results, dimensions of satisfaction, challenge, preference, interactivity, and learning effectiveness are organized to respond to the research objective of the preliminary study on Taiwanese user experience in learning-through-play with the language learning App, Duolingo.

4.1 Challenge

From the interview, it is discovered that the learning-through-play Duolingo App successfully corresponds to learning diverse challenges, which do not simply provide opportunities for skill growth, but also increase rich and fun learning experience. Users, during the use of the App, encounter two major challenges, including learning diverse challenges and challenge to complete learning objectives.

Learning Diverse Challenges
The newly contacted courses causing increasing errors result in frustration. (U2-Q3 21012024) Particularly difficult and challenging tasks have not yet perceived. (U3-Q3 22012024)
    Users encounter several learning challenges in the learning-through-play Duolingo App. The course design shows moderate difficulty for beginners, but might be inadequate for learners with basis, revealing the subjectivity on challenge.

Challenge to Complete Learning Objectives
The major challenge now should be turning on the App for learning at fixed time every day. (U2-Q2 21012024)
    Logging in every day to update learning records is an effective way to cultivate learning habit; however, the respondents generally regard it as a challenging task. It reflects people's needs for continuous learning and the difficulty to cultivate good learning habits.

4.2 Preference

In the process of the respondents using the learning-through-play Duolingo App, the users reflect the preferred functions or characteristics on individualized learning path, social elements, pronunciation assistance, language preference, and the comfort of visual style. Such elements successfully attract users to have learning become more interesting and attractive. User preference is classified into individualized learning experience and fascinating gamification mechanism.

Individualized Learning Experience
Individual *error exercise allows me knowing the shortage.* (U1-Q4 21012024)

In the process of using the learning-through-play Duolingo App, individualized learning experience is one of the favorite elements of users. It reflects on several parts where error exercise wins users' favor, as it offers targeted learning directions to have users clearly understand the weakness and frequent mistakes and further reinforce the learning effect.

Gamification System
Gamification elements are friendly to people lack of concentration. (U3-Q6 22012024).

Duolingo successfully introduces a fascinating gamification mechanism to outstand the language learning field. The design of counting the number of continuous using days induces users' continuity to be full of learning motivation every day.

4.3   Interactivity

The learning-through-play Duolingo App presents excellent achievement on interactivity. The ingenious design of feedback mechanism successfully induces users' positive participation in learning and motivation of continuous participation. Through the interview, users' interactive experience is classified into feedback mechanism of interactivity and incentive effect of social media interaction.

Feedback Mechanism of Interactivity
The "jingle" sound for right answers is nice to feel being awarded. (U4-Q7 22012024)

The feedback mechanism design in the learning-through-play Duolingo App successfully integrates multiple elements to induce users' positive participation in learning and motivation of continuous participation, containing promotion of challenge, real benefit incentive, praise of game role, sound encouragement for correct answers, guide with the number of loves, and shaking encouragement.

Incentive Effect of Social Media Interaction
Benign *competition is the motive of progress and is more effective than struggling alone.* (U2-Q8 21012024)

The social media interaction function of the learning-through-play Duolingo App, such as linking good friends and checking learning progress, shows positive effects on users. The respondents stress on the positive effects of social media interaction, including incentive of benign competition, promotion of motivation to learn, and satisfaction with observing good friends' learning progress. Such a social media interaction mechanism successfully induces users' learning interests and enhances the entire learning experience.

4.4   Learning Effectiveness

6 heavy Duolingo users are interviewed for this study. The learning gain from Duolingo contains improvement of learning attitude and actual application.

Improving Learning Attitude
The climate is comparatively less serious that the use is persisted to cultivate the habit of continuous learning. (U2-Q12 21012024).

Improving learning attitude: The users, after using Duolingo, feel the improving attitude towards language learning, no longer feel pressure, increase vocabulary through daily practice, and perceive the motivation to learn common words, revealing that the design of Duolingo induces users' initiative in learning.

Actual Application
I *use it for review before the TOEIC exam and receive favorable score. (U1-Q11 21012024)*

The language learning application of Duolingo presents significant effects on the promotion of language ability and actual application. First, Duolingo shows extraordinary performance on promoting test results. Some users perceive the promotion of learning effect in specific language tests, e.g. TOEIC exam. It highlights the practicability of Duolingo on the preparation for tests. Users could more confidently cope with language tests and enhance exam performance.

4.5   Satisfaction

Users show positive satisfaction on the learning-through-play Duolingo. Satisfaction in this study covers two dimensions of user interface and special impressive function or design.

Evaluation of User Interface
Simple and easy operation interface allows finding out the required buttons. (U6-Q13 22012024)

Most the respondents show positive evaluation on the user interface, interactivity, and learning effect on the App, and the design of switching language is reputable. Nonetheless, there are some suggestions for improvement, including fluency of sentence translation, unity of pronunciation for word questions, and reduction of advertising frequency.

Impressive Function or Design
The challenge mechanism is similar to playing games that I unconsciously learn a lot. (U3-Q14 22012024)

The error review function is regarded as a considerable function to help users clearly understand the part for reinforcement. Furthermore, the application of challenge mechanism is praised to have learning be similar to playing games and interesting. It offers help for people who are tired of traditional learning from textbooks. The lively animation and picture design has language learning become interesting and the emphasis on shaking effect promotes the operation motivation.

5 Conclusion and Suggestions

This study delves into user experience within the gamified learning app Duolingo. It concludes that users are generally satisfied with the app, attributing this satisfaction to its excellent user interface, interactivity, and gamified learning effects. Duolingo effectively addresses diverse learning challenges and, through personalized learning goal setting, enhances users' motivation and sense of challenge. The gamification mechanisms and interactive community successfully engage users in positive learning participation, showcasing tangible learning benefits through gamification.

Future research could delve further into the varied feedback from users in Taiwan and other cultural contexts, examining differences in user preferences, needs, and challenges. Through future cross-cultural studies on Duolingo user experiences, insights into cross-cultural preferences, needs, and challenges can be uncovered, offering more refined and specific cross-cultural design recommendations to enhance user experiences. This will facilitate better understanding and optimization of cross-cultural user experiences, promoting enhanced cross-cultural interaction and comprehension in language learning.

Acknowledgments. The authors gratefully acknowledge the support for this research provided by Taiwan Council of Science and Technology [grant number NSTC 112-2420-H-224-022-].

References

1. Pachler, N., Cook, J., Bachmair, B.: Appropriation of mobile cultural resources for learning. J. Int. J. Mob. Blended Learn. **2**(1), 21 (2010)
2. Niño, A.: Language learners perceptions and experiences on the use of mobile applications for independent language learning in higher education. IAFOR J. Educ. **3**(SE), 73–84 (2015). IAFOR, Online
3. Norman, D.: The Design of Everyday Things: Revised and Expanded Edition, 2nd edn. Basic Books, New York (2013)
4. Nielsen, J.: Usability Engineering, 1st edn. Morgan Kaufmann Publishers, Boston (1994)
5. Krug, S.: Don't Make Me Think, Revisited: A Common Sense Approach to Web Usability, 3rd edn. New Riders, Berkeley (2013)
6. Garrett, J.J.: The Elements of User Experience: User-Centered Design for the Web and Beyond, 2nd edn. New Riders, Berkeley (2010)
7. Purwanto, A.A., Syafryadin, S.: Students' perception on using Duolingo for learning English vocabulary. J. Engl. Teach. **9**(1), 70–82 (2023)
8. Neuschafer, T.: Understanding Duolingo discussion boards as social-emotional support during the Covid-19 pandemic. J. Educ. Online **21**(2), 16 (2024)
9. Teba, S.C.: Using Duolingo to improve Beninese secretarial advanced learners' oral communication skills. J. Educ. Sci. **9**(1), 25–38 (2022)
10. Deterding, S., Dixon, D., Khaled, R., Nacke, L.: From game design elements to gamefulness: defining gamification. In: Proceedings of the 15th International Academic MindTrek Conference: Envisioning Future Media Environments, pp. 9–15. ACM, Tampere (2011)
11. Koivisto, J., Hamari, J.: The rise of the motivational information systems: a review of gamification research. Int. J. Inf. Manag. **45**, 191–210 (2019)
12. Majuri, J., Koivisto, J., Hamari, J.: Gamification of education and learning: a review of empirical literature. In: Jonna, K., Juho, H. (eds.) Proceedings of the 2nd International GamiFIN Conference, CEUR, vol. 2186, pp.11–19. Pori, Finland (2018)

13. Tsai, N.: Learning Polish with Duolingo: a case study in Taiwanese academic setting. Acta Universitatis Lodziensis Kształcenie Polonistyczne Cudzoziemców **29**(29), 31–52 (2022). University of Lodz, Lodz

14. Ritonga, M., Febriani, S.R., Kustati, M., Khaef, E., Ritonga, A.W., Yasmar, R.: Duolingo: an arabic speaking skills' learning platform for andragogy education. J. Educ. Res. Int. **20**(1), 1–9 (2022)

15. Lee, J., Hammer, J.: Gamification in education: what, how, why bother? J. Acad. Exchange Q. **15**(2), 1–5 (2011)

16. Zichermann, G., Cunningham, C.: Gamification by Design, 1st edn. O'Reilly Media, California (2011)

17. Helander, M.G., Landauer, T.K., Prabhu, P.V.: Handbook of Human-Computer Interaction, 2nd edn. North-Holland, Amsterdam (1998)

18. Venkatesh, V., Morris, M.G., Davis, G.B., Davis, F.D.: User acceptance of information technology: toward a unified view. J. Manag. Inf. Syst. Q. **27**(3), 425–478 (2003)

19. Clark, R.E.: Media will never influence learning. J. Educ. Technol. Res. Dev. **42**, 21–29 (1994)

20. Oliver, R.: A cognitive model of the antecedents and consequences of satisfaction decisions. J. Mark. Res. **17**(4), 460–469 (1980)

21. Hassenzahl, M., Tractinsky, N.: User experience - a research agenda. J. Behav. Inf. Technol. **25**(2), 91–97 (2006)

Taking Culture as the Axis to Discuss User Experience in Tour Guide Mobile Application of Taichung City

Hsiu-Ching Laura Hsieh and Wan-Ting Lin[✉]

National Yunlin University of Science and Technology, Yunlin 64002, Taiwan, R.O.C.
kylielin0114@gmail.com

Abstract. Many existing tour guide Mobile Applications provide the information of attractions, but lack deep presentation and introduction to culture, places, scenery, and humanities. This study therefore intends to explore the deep cultural heritage in old Taichung City, expecting that visitors could experience the history and culture through the design of the tour guide Mobile Application. Taichung City presents rich cultural heritage. A lot of historical local ancient buildings evidence the boom and change of Taichung, present unique cultural appearance, and become the cultural symbols of Taichung. It is a pity that such features are seldom mentioned in existing Taichung City tour guide web pages and applications. To have visitors to Taichung receive more humanistic experiences, the Taichung City tour application is developed and designed with the cultural content as the axis to enhance visitors' desire for exploring Taichung local history and culture as well as the deep understanding so as to further realize the cultural content and value of Taichung.

This study aims to collect and analyze the attractions in Taichung area, integrate and induce the cultural characteristics based on such information, and design the culture-centered Taichung tour guide Mobile Application as well as evaluate user experience in the Taichung tour guide Mobile Application

The research methods contain 1. applying the analyses of anthropology and culture theory [1] and city image theory [2] and integrating the interview of culture and history workers and the actual reconnaissance contents, 2. integrating above contents as well as inducing and extracting historical stories and highlights with Taichung cultural characteristics for integrating into the Taichung tour guide Mobile Application, 3. thinking about visitors' (people) instinctive behaviors and senses about exploring above-mentioned special historical stories and highlights of Taichung to develop the Application RP, 4. outputting the Application RP, and 5. recruiting users to participate in the test to evaluate the Application RP and collect user feedback.

This study is expected to improve the cultural shortage of existing tour guide Mobile Applications. The development and design of the Taichung tour guide Mobile Application would provide tourist experience with humanistic value for visitors. According to the feedback, it would be continuously optimized for users' better experiences. The successive studies, according to the research results, could propose cultural tour programs for different places.

M. Rauterberg (Ed.): HCII 2024, LNCS 14717, pp. 31–41, 2024.
https://doi.org/10.1007/978-3-031-61147-6_3

Keywords: Mobile applications · Travel experience · Travel app · App satisfaction · Cultural dimensions

1 Introduction

1.1 Research Background and Motivation

Taichung City, being a cultural town in Taiwan, presents rich history and unique cultural features. Tour guide mobile applications in the market provide basic functions, but do not fully consider user needs for cultural depth and historical story presentation. Cultural characteristics of Taichung City are therefore seldom mentioned in existing Taichung City tour guide mobile applications that visitors could not deeply experience the rich history and cultural connotation of Taichung. This study intends to introduce the design idea with culture as the core to discuss user experience in Taichung City tour guide mobile applications, expecting to promote visitors' desire for discovering and understanding local history and culture of Taichung.

The usability of mobile applications is a key element to evaluate and improve mobile applications [3]. Particularly, the importance of user experience is getting highlighted in the new travel era, especially the structure and attribute [4]. Unfortunately, such studies do not fully get into the culture, while cultural user experience indeed is the core factor in promoting tour guide mobile applications [5].

The provision of richer and deeper cultural experience by current tour guide mobile applications requires deeper study [6]. To solve existing problems, Lowdermilk [7] stressed on the importance of user-centered design. Such a method could provide actual suggestions to improve user experience in mobile applications. Accordingly, this study aims to integrate design theory and deeply discuss user experience in Taichung City tour guide mobile application with culture as the core. With deep research, this study expects to develop a more user-friendly tour guide mobile application with rich culture to provide users with deeper and satisfactory cultural travel experience as well as to better present the unique history and cultural connotation of Taichung City.

1.2 Research Objectives

According to the research background and motivation, the following research objectives are discussed.

To collect and analyze attractions in Taichung area and, based on such information, to integrate the cultural features in order to design a Taichung tour guide mobile application with culture as the core.

To evaluate user experience in Taichung tour guide mobile application.

2   Literature Review

2.1   Cultural Travel Mobile Application Related Design Theory

Along with the rapid development of technology, tour guide mobile applications become an inevitable part in modern travel. Nevertheless, current tour guide applications in the market provide rich information of attractions but lack deep and rich cultural presentation. By analyzing three relevant literatures, the existence of culture is short in current tour guide mobile applications, and cultural connotation should be promoted through design theory.

Buhalis and Law [8] stressed on the development and situation of e-tourism in the research. They reviewed the effects of information technology on tourism management in past 3 decades and emphasized the importance of research on e-tourism. However, cultural elements are generally ignored or superficially introduced in existing tour mobile applications, without fully digging out the deep cultural heritage of destinations.

Hashim and Isse [9] mentioned several usability indicators, including effectiveness, effect, and satisfaction, to evaluate the overall performance of tour App. The research emphasized the direct and indirect effects from interface design to system response time on user experience, in the evaluation process. Such evaluation should be based on users' needs and expectation to ensure the design and function of tour App being able to satisfy broad user groups. Nonetheless, such an evaluation method has not yet fully applied to current tour mobile applications for presenting cultural elements.

To more deeply discuss the effect of technology on visitor experience, Neuhofer et al. [10] provided a comprehensive study and stressed on the driving and obstacle of technology to visitor experience. The design of cultural tour guide mobile applications should emphasize the inspiration of such technology so that applications do not simply provide information of attractions, but could deeply present local culture and history.

To make up the shortage of cultural content in existing tour guide mobile applications, the design should concern more about a tour guide mobile application with culture as the core. UX design and HCI design should pay more attention to include rich cultural elements in the application design for providing richer and deeper user experience.

In sum, the future research should further discuss the application of such theories to integrate into advanced mobile application design theory so as to enhance cultural connotation and provide rich and deep user experience in cultural travel.

2.2   Application of Cultural Anthropology and City Image Theory

Cultural anthropology and city image theory play important roles in the design of cultural tour guide mobile applications. Referring to Hofstede's theory of culture study [1] and Lynch's city image theory [2], better expression of the cultural features in Taichung could be more deeply understood to promote user experience in local culture.

Hofstede's theory of cultural anthropology [1] focused on four core points of value, rituals and norm, heroes, symbols, and the deep influence of culture on value, belief, and behavior. Such a theory could be applied in the design of cultural tour guide Mobile applications to deeply understand users' cultural difference and expectation. For instance, different cultures might appear distinct opinions about the interpretation and importance of specific locations. With Hofstede's cultural theory, a developer could better adapt to the content of mobile applications to cater users with different cultural background and promote the cultural experience.

Lynch's city image theory [2] stressed on the importance of city image to the perception and experience of residents and visitors. In Taichung City tour guide mobile application, the application of such a theory could create the application with more stories and visual attraction by integrating the history, building styles, and public art of the city. Through the guide of the application, users could more vividly feel the unique appearance of Taichung City and strengthen the deep knowledge of the city.

Using the theories of Hofstede and Lynch for the actual application, the cultural characteristics of Taichung City and the residents' city perception are collected and analyzed through in-depth site study and user interview for better defining the content structure and interaction design of the mobile application to better match user expectation.

2.3 Research on Cultural Tour Guide Mobile Application

Users' expectation and experience of cultural tour guide mobile applications is the key in enhancing the attraction of applications and satisfaction. By analyzing the following literatures, users' expectation and feedback about existing tour guide applications could be deeply understood, especially the needs for cultural depth and historical story presentation.

Ye et al. [11] focused on the effects of online user comment on hotel room selling, which could be applied to cultural tour guide mobile applications. User comment reflected their direct perception of experience in mobile applications, particularly the satisfaction with cultural depth and historical story presentation. Understanding user comment could help a developer better satisfy user expectation.

Hashim and Isse [9] concentrated on the indicators for the usability of tour mobile applications, which directly involved in users' actual experiences. The design of a cultural tour guide mobile application should ensure that users could easily browse cultural information and be interested in historical stories. With the usability evaluation, possible problems encountered by users in the using process could be discovered and improved to enhance the ease of use and satisfaction with applications.

To sum up, users expect that cultural tour guide mobile applications could provide basic information of attractions as well as in-depth and fascinating cultural content and historical stories. It reflects users' strong needs for cultural depth and expectation of deep understanding of unique culture and history of the destinations through applications. The researcher emphasizes such elements in the design to satisfy user desire for rich and in-depth cultural travel experience.

2.4 Test of SUS

Sauro [12] introduced the use of System Usability Scale (SUS) for user experience. SUS is a broadly applied standard evaluation tool and presents actual value on evaluating the usability of tour guide Mobile applications with culture as the core. The tool provides a single-number evaluation to quantify user satisfaction with the entire experience in applications.

In the development of cultural tour guide mobile application, test of application and analysis of user feedback are essential. SUS could rapidly and simply acquire the overall satisfaction index and provide valuable data for evaluating the usability of applications.

3 Methodology

Based on above literature review and research objectives, multiple research methods are adopted in this study to comprehensively and deeply discuss user experience in Taichung City tour guide mobile application with culture as the core. Particularly, SUS is used for quantifying and evaluating user satisfaction with the overall usability of the application.

3.1 Research Process

First, applying the analysis of cultural travel mobile application related design theory and integrating the content of literary and historical workers' interview and actual field survey.

Subsequently, integrating above-mentioned contents and abstracting historical stories and highlights with cultural features about Taichung for integrating into Taichung tour guide Mobile application.

Furthermore, thinking of how visitors (people) explore above-mentioned specific historical stories and highlights with the instinct behaviors and senses to develop Application RP.

Next, outputting application RP.

Lastly, recruiting users to participate in the usability test for actually evaluating application RP and collecting user feedback.

3.2 Research Tool

SUS (System Usability Scale). SUS (System Usability Scale), a standard tool to evaluate system usability, was proposed by John Brooke in 1986. SUS is a simple and effective questionnaire for measuring users' subjective perception and satisfaction about specific systems. The questionnaire contains 10 sentences; users have to score 1–5 for each sentence to show the agreement with the statement. The score of parts of the sentences requires reversion to ensure the consistency. The scores, through calculation, are converted into final SUS scores with 0 to 100. The researcher uses the questionnaire for the actual survey and collects the subjects' feedback to calculate the SUS score. 12 subjects, aged 20–30 with the education above colleges, are invited for the SUS test in this study. The test is preceded in Lab DA203 in Department of Creative Design, National Yunlin University of Science & Technology. Each test lasts for 30 min, when the subjects personally experience and use the Taichung City tour guide application with culture as the core constructed in this study, fill in SUS questionnaire (Appendix 7.1), and receive individual interview after the SUS questionnaire survey.

3.3 Application Interface

The application RP constructed in this study applies culture as the core, particularly stressing on the rich cultural heritage of Taichung City and, through well-designed application interface, inspiring users' understanding of profound history and cultural connotation of Taichung City.

The application does not simply provide basic guiding functions, but stresses more on the integration of cultural elements. Mixing unique illustration style and rich visual design, an attractive and narrative interface is created for users deeply experiencing the uniqueness of Taichung City in the travel (Figs. 2, 3 and 4).

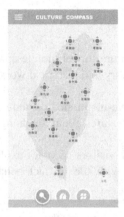

Fig. 1. Interface: Selecting site

Fig. 2. Interface: Selecting attraction

Fig. 3. Interface: Attraction picture

Fig. 4. Interface: Attraction introduction

4 Results

4.1 SUS Questionnaire Analysis

The SUS questionnaire used for this study contain 10 items. After integrating the original scores of all subjects' SUS questionnaire, odd number questions (positive questions) and even number questions (negative questions) are preceded score conversion, according to the calculation process of SUS. The conversion is to deduct 1 from the score of odd number questions, and to deduct the original score from 5 for the score of even number questions. The original score of each item is summed and converted into percentage (multiplying total score by 2.5) to acquire the final SUS score.

After completing the calculation of SUS scores, it is expected to deeply understand such numbers. In order to enhance the comprehension of SUS scores, Bangor et al. (2009) preceded an important research on user perception of SUS scores. They divided SUS scores into 6 grades and compared such grades with common evaluation in schools

(A, B, C,...F), as shown in Fig. 1: SUS score 90–100 (A), 80–89 (B), 70–79 (C), 60–69 (D), 0–59 (F).

The final score of each subject's SUS questionnaire as well as the corresponding adjective rating and the acceptable range of system usability are integrated (see Table 1 in Appendix) and analyzed. Each grade is further explained.

Interpretation. User satisfaction changes among participants; the scores cover from 65 to 95. Most users (U1, U2, U3, U5, U8, U9, U10, U11) evaluate "Excellent" of the mobile application constructed in this study, revealing high user satisfaction. The scores appear in the "Acceptable" range of SUS scale. User U4 and U12 show "Marginal" acceptance, but the scores of U4, U7, and U12 reveal "Good" satisfaction. It is worth noting that not a participant evaluates the system below "Marginal", showing users' positive acceptance on the mobile application with culture as the core constructed in this study.

Adjective Ratings and Acceptability Ranges. According to Appendix, the correlation of SUS scores with adjective rating provides qualitative description of user satisfaction for this study. Adjective rating includes "Best Imaginable", "Excellent", and "Good", and the corresponding acceptable range contains "Acceptable" and "Marginal".

Overall System Usability. As reflected in the sum of SUS scores, the overall system usability is regarded as "Acceptable" and most users present high satisfaction.

4.2 Interview Analysis of Users' Feedback

SUS questionnaire survey is an important step for evaluating system ease-of-use. Nevertheless, quantitative data might not fully catch users' true experience and feeling about the mobile application constructed in this study. To deeply understand the subjects' user experience, individual interview is preceded after the SUS questionnaire survey, aiming to understand their specific points of view and confusion in the use process as well as the expectation of the system.

The deep interview analysis helps explain the factors in SUS scores and provides actual users' points of view. The interview content of each subject is integrated to supplement and enrich the comprehension of system ease-of-use of the mobile application constructed in this study.

Interview analysis of user feedback. Summing up the subjects' feedback, it is discovered that the evaluation of the cultural tour application focuses on visual design, operation experience, and information presentation. Such evaluation provides valuable insight for the researcher better understanding user needs and the improvement.

Positive Evaluation. The color match, illustration uniformity, and quality illustration style of attraction design receive good comment.

Improvement Focus. Indefinite return button, dull introduction, and map button design are important directions for improvement.

Development Insights. Increase in gaming elements, provision of more practical information, and enhancement of introduction clarity are suggestions for further development.

Strategic Collaboration. It can be considered to cooperate with governments and locals to promote gamification activity to increase users' participation.

Overall speaking, users give positive evaluation about illustration style and convenience of overall operation. However, some indefinite operation process and interface design require further improvement. Regarding introduction to attractions, more practical information, gamification elements, as well as deep historical and cultural contents would enhance user experience.

5 Discussion and Suggestions

5.1 Discussion of Results

This study provides comprehensive understanding of the usability test of Taichung City tour guide mobile application with culture as the core as well as user feedback and interview. Most users reveal high satisfaction and classify the application into "Excellent" in the "Acceptable" range of System Usability Scale (SUS). Positive evaluation concentrates on visual attraction, uniform illustration style, and simple operation.

The improvement directions are also discovered, mainly involving in the clarity of some buttons, dullness of introduction to attractions, clearer return button, and needs for interactive map function. Users appreciate the visual function, but also emphasize some indefinite operation process and interface design, which require further improvement. In terms of introduction to attractions, more practical information, gamification elements, and deeper historical and cultural contents would promote user experience.

5.2 Conclusion and Suggestions

The research results could reinforce cultural elements in tour applications and make up the gap in the unique cultural features of Taichung City. By stressing on the cultural richness, the developed mobile application successfully provides users with deeper and satisfactory cultural travel experience.

The positive correlations between SUS score and adjective rating reveal the effectiveness of integrating cultural elements to the mobile application. The users do not simply consider the mobile application being acceptable, but evaluate it being excellent, showing the positive effects on the overall satisfaction and experience.

Based on user feedback and usability analysis, some suggestions for future design directions and reinforcement are further proposed.

Improving guiding clarity: Enhancing the clarity of return button and optimizing the entire guiding process to reduce users' confusion.

Diverse Contents. Introducing more diverse and fascinating contents, including gaming elements and interactive function, to enrich user experience.

Cooperating with Local Units. Cooperating with local governments and cultural organizations, providing real-time update, and holding activities to create more dynamic and participatory cultural exploration.

Expanding the Integration with Augmented Reality (AR). Exploring to integrate AR technology and providing users with more immersive and interactive cultural exploration experience allowing them participating in historical sites with novel ways.

Continuing User Participation. Building the feedback loop with users and constantly improving the mobile application according to needs and preference.

Acknowledgments. The authors gratefully acknowledge the support for this research provided by Taiwan National Council of Science and Technology [grant number NSTC 112-2420-H-224-022-].

Appendix

Table 1. The final score of the SUS questionnaire and the corresponding adjective ratings are indicative of the acceptable range for system usability

User	SUS score	Adjective ratings	Acceptability ranges
U1	80	Excellent	Acceptable
U2	95	Best Imaginable	Acceptable
U3	80	Excellent	Acceptable
U4	70	Good	Marginal
U5	87.5	Excellent	Acceptable
U6	75	Excellent	Acceptable
U7	72.5	Good	Acceptable
U8	85	Excellent	Acceptable
U9	80	Excellent	Acceptable
U10	75	Excellent	Acceptable
U11	85	Excellent	Acceptable
U12	65	Good	Marginal

References

1. Hofstede, G.: Cultures and Organizations: Software of the Mind. McGraw-Hill, New York (2010)
2. Lynch, K.: The Image of the City. MIT Press, Cambridge (1960)
3. Zhang, P., Adipat, B.: Mobile application usability: conceptualization and instrument development. Int. J. Hum.-Comput. Interact. **18**(3), 293–308 (2005)
4. Gretzel, U., Yoo, K.H.: User experience in the era of new tourism: the importance of mobile apps for structural and attributive aspects. J. Tour. Hosp. **2**(5), 99–110 (2008)

5. Vermeeren, A.P., Law, E.L.C., Roto, V., Obrist, M., Hoonhout, J., Väänänen-Vainio-Mattila, K.: User experience evaluation methods: current state and development needs. In: Proceedings of the 6th Nordic Conference on Human-Computer Interaction: Extending Boundaries, pp. 521–530 (2010)
6. Kennedy-Eden, H., Gretzel, U.: A Taxonomy of Mobile Applications in Tourism (2012)
7. Lowdermilk, T.: User-Centered Design: A Developer's Guide to Building User-Friendly Applications. O'Reilly Media, Inc. (2013)
8. Buhalis, D., Law, R.: Progress in information technology and tourism management: 20 years on and 10 years after the Internet—The state of eTourism research. Tour. Manag. **29**(4), 609–623 (2008)
9. Hashim, N.L., Isse, A.J.: Usability evaluation metrics of tourism mobile applications. J. Softw. Eng. Appl. **12**(7), 267–277 (2019)
10. Neuhofer, B., Buhalis, D., Ladkin, A.: Technology as a catalyst of change: Enablers and barriers of the tourist experience and their consequences. In: Tussyadiah, I., Inversini, A. (eds.) Information and Communication Technologies in Tourism 2015, pp. 789–802. Springer, Cham (2015). https://doi.org/10.1007/978-3-319-14343-9_57
11. Ye, Q., Law, R., Gu, B.: The impact of online user reviews on hotel room sales. Int. J. Hosp. Manag. **28**(1), 180–182 (2009)
12. Sauro, J.: A Practical Guide to the System Usability Scale: Background, Benchmarks & Best Practices. Measuring Usability LLC (2011)

Market-Driven HCI Design Education Analysis and Cultivation Strategy

Yiyuan Huang[1]([✉]), Yichun Huang[1], Xueqing Sun[1], and Linyou Sui[2]([✉])

[1] Beijing Institute of Graphic Communication, Beijing, China
yiyuan.huang@bigc.edu.cn
[2] Shandong Vocational University of Foreign Affairs, Weihai, China
695188592@qq.com

Abstract. In the digital age, the significance of HCI design education is escalating, playing a pivotal role in nurturing creative talent and revolutionizing the dissemination of design concepts. This paper delves into the market-driven HCI design education through case studies. We scrutinize the strengths and weaknesses encountered in HCI design education and underscore the varied global demands, accounting for social cultures and technological progressions. Our research advocates for a holistic approach amalgamating studio-based education, artistic and technological fusion, and socio-cultural values to meet the digital market's multifaceted requirements effectively. Research avenues entail addressing cultural diversity, enhancing multidisciplinary collaboration, and staying abreast of technological advancements and societal shifts.

Keywords: Market-driven HCI design education · studio-based strategy · talent cultivation · art and technology · transdisciplinary integration · social and cultural values

1 Introduction

In today's digital landscape, the importance of HCI design education is increasingly evident, shaping a new wave of creative talents and revolutionizing the transmission of design expression.

As digitalization advances rapidly, HCI design education must cater to students' emotional and creative needs and equip them with proficiency in relevant tools and media, aligning with evolving trends in the digital market and societal segments.

Internationally, the landscape of market-driven HCI design education is diverse, reflecting varying demands and considerations influenced by cultural traditions and developmental stages across different countries and regions. While HCI design education faces challenges posed by swift technological updates, it also presents significant opportunities. Collaboration on a global scale and cross-cultural exchange drive innovation in digital technology, opening unprecedented avenues for market-driven HCI design education.

M. Rauterberg (Ed.): HCII 2024, LNCS 14717, pp. 42–54, 2024.
https://doi.org/10.1007/978-3-031-61147-6_4

In disciplines like human-computer interaction design, educational methodologies emphasize practical experience accumulation, enabling students to apply theoretical knowledge to real-world scenarios and enhance their design capabilities.

While practice undoubtedly holds significance, it's crucial to recognize the equal importance of theory in market-driven HCI design education. Emphasizing theoretical knowledge can significantly aid students in achieving a profound comprehension and mastery of HCI design philosophy, thereby enriching their creative thought processes and practical abilities.

This perspective finds validation in the research study titled Design in the HCI Classroom: Setting a Research Agenda [1], which directs attention to formulating theory and establishing disciplinary frameworks. This study underscores the importance of crafting theoretical systems, methodologies, and conceptual models within HCI design, highlighting their pivotal role in advancing the field.

Educational methodologies operate in interconnected spheres, mutually influencing one another. For instance, integrating market-driven education methods can enrich students' understanding, thus bolstering their design proficiency. Likewise, incorporating theoretical education approaches can elevate students' overall competence by leveraging multidisciplinary education methods, fostering enhanced theoretical reasoning capabilities.

While combining practice with theory, market demand has fostered close collaboration across multiple domains. A multidisciplinary approach to education fosters holistic development, aiding students in enhancing their overall capabilities and creativity. This philosophy is evident in the research study titled A Framework for Digital Media Literacies for Teaching and Learning in Higher Education [2]. The study underscores the necessity of comprehensive digital literacy for effective digital artifact creation, which encompasses technical, audio-visual, behavioral, critical, and social skills.

The authors propose a framework to cultivate digital media literacies and train students in digital creation. This framework comprises three interconnected domains: conception, function, and audio-visual creation. The "conception" focuses on fundamental concepts crucial, while the "function" emphasizes students' proficiency in storyboard and content writing. Lastly, the "audio-visual creation" enhances students' skills in basic video shooting techniques and editing.

Educators can identify gaps in student's knowledge and skills through this framework, facilitating targeted training interventions to bridge these gaps effectively.

Meanwhile, in their exploration, Sara Cruz, Célia Vieira, and José Bidarra advocate for leveraging design thinking to promote environmental sustainability awareness within higher education, demonstrated through practical case studies. They stress the importance of infusing sustainability thinking into multidisciplinary digital design education within the arts, spanning theoretical and generalist knowledge [3].

Hence, an integrated approach in market-driven HCI design education, encompassing practical, theoretical, and multidisciplinary components, is essential for a comprehensive educational strategy. Practical approaches facilitate students' application of learned principles in experimental settings, enhancing their design skills, deepening their theoretical understanding, and fostering the holistic development of innovative thinking capabilities.

2   Cultivation and Construction of Market-Driven HCI Design Education

The HCI design market is intricate and interconnected. It's essential to recognize that in terms of creativity and market sensitivity, educators may only sometimes possess superior understanding compared to students, especially if they need to be more closely aligned with the digital industry. This discrepancy arises from differences in environment, awareness, and focus, creating what is known as the "knowledge gap effect."

Therefore, market-driven HCI design education should prioritize fostering an environment of equal idea exchange with students. Educators must be receptive to inspiration and insights from students while also imparting knowledge and skills. Cultivating creativity, curiosity, innovative thinking, and hands-on research is paramount in professional HCI design training. Programs should encourage students to approach challenges from diverse perspectives, empowering them to devise unique solutions that theoretically and practically address market demands. Educators should not only serve as instructors but also as collaborators in practical creation.

Simultaneously, students should be encouraged to develop independent study and research skills as needed. Knowledge development should be facilitated through interactive teaching and learning methodologies, including academic platforms, hands-on workshops, peer-to-peer seminars, and individual/group tutorials, creating a diverse and integrated learning ecosystem.

A project conducted by Dr. Austin, in relationship with market-driven HCI design education, particularly within the domain of HCI, categorizes practitioners and educators into four types: all-practitioners (no involvement in education), all-educators (no involvement in practice), both-practitioners (involved in education), and both-educators (involved in practice) [4]. This categorization offers insights into market-driven HCI design teaching and training requirements.

The essence of market-driven HCI design education lies in combining theoretical knowledge with practical experience, fostering students' digital creation skills through hands-on learning. Given its market-oriented nature, educators must collaborate closely with industry professionals. As designers and experts, these practitioners offer invaluable insights and opportunities for students to engage in practical and theoretical learning in real-world industry settings.

Hence, we advocate establishing a symbiotic relationship between both-practitioners (involved in education) and both-educators (involved in practice) within the education system. This approach ensures alignment with the integrative nature of HCI design. Additionally, all-practitioners can serve as consultants, providing crucial feedback to validate market-driven needs, thus bridging the gap between academia and industry (see Fig. 1).

In their paper titled Enhancing Human-Computer Interaction and User Experience Education through a Hybrid Approach to Experiential Learning [5], the authors present a hybrid methodology for human-computer interaction (HCI) and user experience (UX) education.

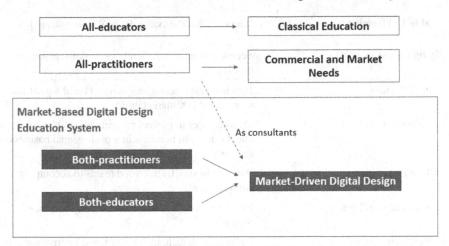

Fig. 1. Deployment of teaching staff for market-driven HCI design education (inspired from Dr. Austin's classification)

Their initiative, the UX Lab, serves as a crucial complement to students' HCI coursework by providing real-world application opportunities beyond the classroom. This experiential learning environment significantly contributes to and enriches IT pedagogy (See Table 1) relevant to HCI education. Recognizing the importance of hands-on experience in a professional setting, students benefit from exposure to a business environment, enabling them to grasp the practical skills required for their future careers and enhancing their problem-solving abilities. Moreover, market-driven HCI design education prioritizes practicality and real-world application in curriculum development. Consequently, curricula often encompass the study of prototyping theories, techniques, and tools.

The Table 1 shows the construction of IT pedagogy, which delineates seven critical categories: applying course concepts, student motivation, professionalism, team communication, mentoring and feedback, interdisciplinary focus, and understanding industry expectations. Each category provides specific descriptions elucidating their application and significance within real-world work settings.

Table 1. IT pedagogy established by Talone, A. B., Basavaraj, P., & Wisniewski, P. J.

Applying Course Concepts	Seeing how coursework relates to skillsets needed on the job
Student Motivation	Hands-on experience necessary to build a portfolio of work for UX marketability
Professionalism	Opportunities to present project deliverables to clients and communicate in a professional business setting
Team Communication	Working in small, structured teams to accomplish a common goal
Mentoring and Feedback	Having a direct line of support when assistance is required
Interdisciplinary Focus	Refining both technical, design, and interpersonal skills
Understanding Industry Expectations	Students realize that the real-world is often very different than what they learn in the classroom, requiring refinement of problem-solving skills

It's paramount to acknowledge that the realms of "teaching" and "learning" are inherently embedded within the market. Given the specialized nature of HCI design, characterized by its distinct knowledge structure and depth, adopting the traditional model of large class sizes, coordinated skill development, and classroom-centric knowledge dissemination is impractical in teaching and training. Hence, it becomes imperative to integrate teaching and learning into the industry, society, and everyday life to broaden the scope of education's role.

This evolution expands the role of education from narrowly defined scenarios to encompass broader, non-specific contexts, extending beyond the traditional educator-student dynamic to encompass the entirety of society and oriented training. In transitioning to a societal level, the teaching unit becomes merely one component of the entire education system, serving a guiding, regulatory, and corrective function. In this paradigm, students predominantly engage in self-awareness-driven, independent exploratory knowledge absorption and feedback within an educational ecosystem centered around the teaching unit.

3 Studio-Based Educational Models and Benefits

In the realm of internationalization, HCI design is primarily market-driven, emphasizing a holistic educational model that integrates hands-on learning, teamwork development, user engagement, innovation, creativity, and respect for cultural heritage and national identity. This comprehensive approach caters to market demands and addresses societal needs and talent structures. Notably, teamwork skills development is prioritized to align with the prevalent interdisciplinary collaboration in real-world scenarios.

Educators commonly adopt a studio-based training model to replicate practical experiences in the production process. This model underscores the fusion of creativity, strategic analysis, technical skills, and teamwork.

In the study Pedagogical Strategies for Reflection in Project-based HCI Education with End Users [6], the authors underscore the importance of participation. They structure course design, lectures, and studio time to guide students through the human-centered design process of prototyping, incorporating hardware prototyping, digital fabrication, and low-fidelity forms of creation. This approach emphasizes design practice and encourages students to reflect and remain attentive during the design process.

Regarding cultivation models, Professor Alma L. Culén has successfully trained computer science students specializing in design, usage, and interaction. She demonstrates the effectiveness of HCI education by assessing results in creativity, novelty of ideas, and body language. Her approach leverages the Studio Thinking Framework (STF) to cultivate students' observation and imagination in traditional and digital environments. The STF process includes encoding teaching moments, analyzing learning and teaching, detecting learning modes, maintaining teaching reflection, and providing a structure for learning and researching design [7].

Furthermore, Koutsabasis and Vosinakis proposed a Project-Based Learning (PBL) teaching method (See Fig. 2) [8] to enhance students' general skills in the design process through problem-based learning. They integrate the PBL and studio-based learning pedagogies to help students reflect on HCI methodology and develop self-directed learning, intrinsic motivation, and critical thinking competencies. The PBL method incorporates seven essential project design elements to build seven teaching practice processes, combining student practice with teacher guidance and cultivating students' digital design abilities from conceptualization to implementation.

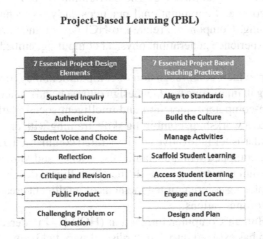

Fig. 2. Project-Based Learning (PBL) proposed by Koutsabasis and Vosinakis

4   Comprehensive Training for Art and Technology Integration

The market-driven HCI design education aims to cultivate interdisciplinary talents who are both skilled and innovative. This domain requires faculty proficient in both art and technology, a convergence that demands significant time and effort in terms of knowledge and ideology. Effective disciplinary integration must be accompanied by practical experience to develop a mature ideology of innovation. However, the challenge of cultivating talents who seamlessly integrate technology and art has resulted in a need for more relevant professionals in the market.

In the paper Practice-led Strategies for Interactive Art Research [9], the authors emphasize collaboration and interaction among artists, technicians, and audiences, conceptualizing, realizing, and evaluating artworks in studio settings and presenting them in public spaces to gather feedback, effectively creating a "living laboratory." The research underscores dynamic performance and experiential aspects across various environments, employing diverse data collection and analysis methods to study the processes and effects of interactive art from multiple perspectives and levels.

Through the Inter Art program [10], Duarte, E. F., and Baranauskas, M. C. C. exemplify the fusion of artistic creativity and technology, infusing new energy into HCI education. The program adopts a hands-on teaching approach, encouraging students to utilize tools like Arduino for creating interactive artwork. The curriculum features open-ended scenarios that challenge students to question assumptions and leverage symbolic frameworks.

Market-driven HCI design programs may choose to admit students from diverse academic backgrounds to reflect the multifaceted nature of the digital market. Students entering with a foundation in digital commercial creation will expand their computing skills and programming knowledge. The curriculum should integrate these skills into creative production and computational practices early, as technical skills require early hands-on training. Components related to HCI design encompass digital sound, image processing, experience generation, physical computing, embedded development, sensors, etc.

As students deepen their comprehension of computation, they transition into digital production, engaging in innovative work in design outreach and content services, such as experimental human-computer interaction and intelligent social platforms. This phase could be structured as a workshop, combining skills training with creative production to meet real-world standards for innovative and integrated commercial development. In the final stage, students, equipped with substantial experience and knowledge, explore the future of the HCI design universe, such as artificial intelligent development. Instructors guide students in exploring computational methods of intelligent creation and the digital ethical implications of innovations.

Carroll's book Human Computer Interaction (HCI) [11] underscores how human-computer interaction has evolved into an interdisciplinary field, attracting professionals from various disciplines. It highlights HCI as a multidisciplinary body of knowledge, merging different epistemologies and paradigms beyond computer science and drawing expertise from multiple disciplines.

5 Society, Culture, and Ethics in Market-Driven HCI Design Education

Market-driven HCI design plays a vital role in serving the market and society. Therefore, in addition to market and transdisciplinary integration, education should also focus on cultivating students' abilities in digital humanities and social-cultural creation, seamlessly integrating all educational elements.

Margolin, V. and Margolin, S. review the social model of design, exploring its application to address social needs. They advocate for further research and theorization of design for social needs to complement the existing emphasis on market-driven design [12]. In the paper Integrating Socially Relevant Projects into HCI Teaching [13], the authors highlight the significance of incorporating socially relevant projects into human-computer interaction (HCI) instruction. By engaging with real-world users and situations, students develop a deeper, more empathetic understanding of user needs, potentially inspiring them to pursue careers in HCI.

Social factors encompass the dynamic interplay between designers, individuals, and diverse groups. The significance of user participation is underscored in the study Pedagogical Strategies for Reflection in Project-based HCI Education with End Users [14]. The course design, lectures, and studio sessions are intentionally structured to scaffold students through the human-centered prototyping design process. This approach prioritizes design practice and fosters a culture of reflection among students.

Concerning the implementation, the interactive art practice InstInt [15] strives to foster collaborative co-design of small-scale interactive installations by engaging participants in a holistic design process that integrates technical and creative skills. The study underscores the significance of participants expressing and actualizing their goals and values throughout the design journey, culminating in creating artwork that is a tangible embodiment of their diverse ideas and intentions. By introducing the concept of a social design process, the study emphasizes the importance of perceptual and cognitive activities during physical construction and the necessity of collaboration and communication among participants.

In the study Using Community-Based Service Projects to Enhance Undergraduate HCI Education: 10 Years of Experience [16], the authors examine the benefits of incorporating community-based service projects into undergraduate HCI education. Such projects provide students with invaluable real-world experience, allowing them to work with users and organizations and navigate real-world challenges. However, educators must ensure proper infrastructure, structured processes, and contingency plans to manage unforeseen circumstances effectively.

Lazar, J., Feng, J., and Hochheiser, H. emphasize the importance of implementing community-based projects in real-world settings to understand better the complexities and tradeoffs involved in design [17]. Traditional passive educational models may not adequately cover design's multifaceted aspects and challenges; hence, engaging in community-based projects allows students to delve into real-world scenarios and comprehend the nuanced tradeoffs inherent in design processes.

Similarly, Mankoff, J., researched integrating Human-Computer Interaction concepts with practical service-learning projects to engage the non-technical community [18]. This approach aims to enhance the visibility and awareness of HCI within the broader community. Students bridge academic concepts with real-world issues by interacting with community members, fostering a more comprehensive learning experience.

The cases above underscore the significance of social engagement and participation, situating works within a social and experimental context. Furthermore, an educational strategy amalgamating societal and market dynamics, theoretical knowledge, and practical application can enhance large-scale evaluation methods. This approach aids in understanding the impact of HCI design on public behaviors and attitudes, as well as gathering feedback and evaluations from various stakeholders. Social and cultural research can foster interdisciplinary collaboration and exchange among artists, technicians, curators, researchers, and the public.

In the research on A Taxonomy for Learning, Teaching, and Assessing: A Revision of Bloom's Taxonomy of Educational Objectives [13], the authors introduce a framework named Applab, integrated into courses focusing on HCI, interactive media design, and creative technologies. This framework facilitates multidisciplinary team learning throughout the curriculum and collaborates closely with urban stakeholders in projects such as "Meaningful Design in the Connected City."

After integrating social, cultural, and ethical values into market-driven HCI design education, the educational system has evolved into a complex organism, challenging educators to construct a unified system in a nuanced and intricate way.

In the paper Rethinking design education-a study for the importance of general education in design [19], Lin, C.H. underscores the significance and direction of integrated design education in universities. The article emphasizes the role of integrated design education in developing students' problem-solving abilities, understanding of human behavior, strategic planning skills, values, social ethics, service design, and aesthetics. The goal is to mold students into forward-thinking, problem-solving, creative designers, strategists, and leaders equipped with strong communication and negotiation skills. The curriculum development direction is illustrated through a diagram (See Fig. 3) emphasizing the comprehensive impact of design education on students' career development.

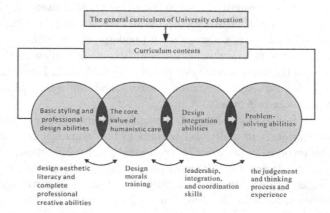

Fig. 3. Original diagram captured from *Rethinking design education-a study for the importance of general education in de-sign* of Lin, C.H., describing an integrated design education system.

Moreover, in the paper Teaching for Values in Human-Computer Interaction [20], the authors propose a pedagogical strategy to assist educators in prioritizing general values in HCI design. This strategy positions Ethics & Values and Designers & Stakeholders as core elements of education, establishing a holistic educational approach that reflects the organic integration of ethics, values, design, technology, and market relationships.

The strategy comprises four dimensions (See Fig. 4):

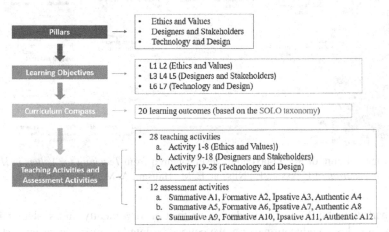

Fig. 4. HCI design pedagogical strategy in *Teaching for Values in Human-Computer Interaction* of Eriksson, E., Nilsson, E. M., Hansen, A. M., & Bekker, T.

- Pillars: Three core competency pillars for educating responsible designers—Ethics and Values, Designers and Stakeholders, and Technology and Design.
- Learning Objectives: Seven overarching learning objectives that guide teachers when teaching for values in design.
- Curriculum Compass: A curriculum compass containing 20 learning outcomes based on the SOLO taxonomy (See Fig. 5), outlining progression in learning design for values.
- Teaching Activities and Assessment Activities: 28 teaching activities and 12 assessment activities respectively, which expand, concretize, and integrate learning outcomes in step-by-step activities, ensuring that teaching objectives are achieved.

This educational strategy serves as both a guide for educators to design teaching methods and a reference for students' learning paths. It is based on integrating social humanities and design technology, bridging concepts, programs, courses, practices, and evaluations. It significantly contributes to market-driven HCI design education. This strategy can seamlessly combine with studio-based teaching methods, promoting collaboration between educators and practitioners.

The abovementioned cases emphasize that a comprehensive approach to market-driven HCI design education should extend beyond merely pursuing market dominance. Instead, it should encompass the implicit needs of social humanities, moral values, and sustainability. Therefore, a synthetic educational ecosystem must be integrated into

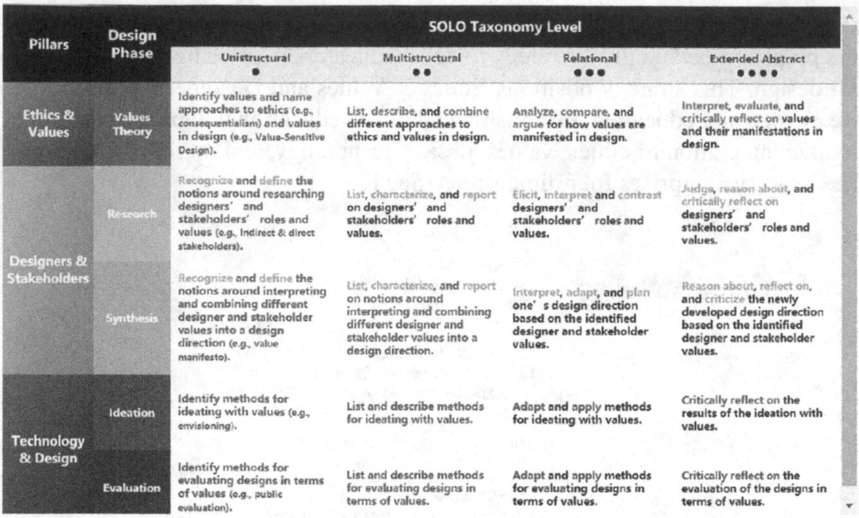

Pillars	Design Phase	SOLO Taxonomy Level			
		Unistructural ●	Multistructural ●●	Relational ●●●	Extended Abstract ●●●●
Ethics & Values	Values Theory	Identify values and name approaches to ethics (e.g., consequentialism) and values in design (e.g., Value-Sensitive Design).	List, describe, and combine different approaches to ethics and values in design.	Analyze, compare, and argue for how values are manifested in design.	Interpret, evaluate, and critically reflect on values and their manifestations in design.
Designers & Stakeholders	Research	Recognize and define the notions around researching designers' and stakeholders' roles and values (e.g., Indirect & direct stakeholders).	List, characterize, and report on designers' and stakeholders' roles and values.	Elicit, interpret and contrast designers' and stakeholders' roles and values.	Judge, reason about, and critically reflect on designers' and stakeholders' roles and values.
	Synthesis	Recognize and define the notions around interpreting and combining different designer and stakeholder values into a design direction (e.g., value manifesto).	List, characterize, and report on notions around interpreting and combining different designer and stakeholder values into a design direction.	Interpret, adapt, and plan one' s design direction based on the identified designer and stakeholder values.	Reason about, reflect on, and criticize the newly developed design direction based on the identified designer and stakeholder values.
Technology & Design	Ideation	Identify methods for ideating with values (e.g., envisioning).	List and describe methods for ideating with values.	Adapt and apply methods for ideating with values.	Critically reflect on the results of the ideation with values.
	Evaluation	Identify methods for evaluating designs in terms of values (e.g., public evaluation).	List and describe methods for evaluating designs in terms of values.	Adapt and apply methods for evaluating designs in terms of values.	Critically reflect on the evaluation of the designs in terms of values.

Fig. 5. Original figure of SOLO taxonomy level captured from *Teaching for Values in Human-Computer Interaction* of Eriksson, E., Nilsson, E. M., Hansen, A. M., & Bekker, T.

social, market, technological, and design cultivation organically and systemically. In doing so, HCI design education can move beyond isolated points of focus and establish a holistic approach that addresses various facets of the discipline.

In conclusion, market-driven HCI design education will undergo self-iteration when coupled with considerations for social value and sustainability. This iterative process will enhance market relevance and contribute to societal well-being and long-term sustainability.

6 Discussion and Conclusion

Globally, market-driven education has emerged as a prominent trend, propelled by advancements in science, technology, and digitalization. The rising demand for talents in digital media, interactive design, and human-computer interaction underscores the need for practical experience and professional knowledge.

Key findings from the study of market-driven HCI design education reveal an international trend towards workshop-based strategies, integration of art & technology, and social-cultural emphasis. Education prioritizes practical training, teamwork, and market collaboration to nurture professionals with hands-on skills. Moreover, it emphasizes disciplinary frameworks and theory construction, fostering students' deep understanding of theoretical principles within the digital market. This comprehensive approach also emphasizes global academic exchange, multidisciplinary integration, critical thinking, and global awareness.

Most students in the HCI design field are undergraduates in both domestic and international contexts. Hence, the primary focus is employment and skill cultivation as fundamental training goals. Market-driven HCI design education emphasizes practical, vocational, and innovative skills, distinguishing it from other skill-based majors.

It underscores the importance of marketable skills and creative and innovative thinking applied to design practice.

This emphasis on practical skills remains consistent across undergraduate and graduate levels, albeit with varying degrees of focus and depth. In the foundational training stage, education fosters interdisciplinary thinking, including developing technical, operational skills (such as media software programming and hardware operation), artistic design skills (drawing from both traditional and electronic art), and humanistic theory skills (grounded in history, communication, and psychology).

The study Design in the HCI classroom: Setting a research agenda [1] sheds light on the current state of design education in HCI, emphasizing the growing significance of interaction design. It identifies a need for more awareness and integration of different design approaches in HCI classrooms. It underscores the need for pedagogical research to help educators recognize the value and applicability of various design approaches. This research advocates for the integration of studio-based pedagogies into HCI courses to foster a balance between creativity and evidence-based choices.

Promoting interdisciplinary education models is recommended to address the diverse needs of the market-driven HCI design field. Academic institutions are encouraged to establish international HCI design education programs to facilitate global educational exchanges and cooperation. Additionally, closer collaboration with market stakeholders is essential. Schools should invite designers and experts to provide practical learning opportunities for students on and off-campus, ensuring alignment with market needs and enhancing students' career readiness. Furthermore, to bolster technical skills, programs should offer opportunities for students to strengthen their engineering skills, thereby ensuring comprehensive development in design creation and technical proficiency.

Future research directions will explore the challenges of cultural diversity in market-driven HCI design education within the context of globalization. Efforts will also focus on researching disciplinary integration to foster interdisciplinary thinking approaches and prepare for the evolving landscape of the HCI design field. Concurrently, attention will be directed towards technological advancements, integrating concepts with society, optimizing human-machine collaboration, and enhancing educational outcomes.

Acknowledgments. This research is supported by Beijing Institute of Graphic Communication: the Beijing Association of Higher Education Project, the program of The Characteristic Talent Training and Innovation Practice Of "ZhiXing", and BIGC Project (Ea202421).

References

1. Wilcox, L., DiSalvo, B., Henneman, D., Wang, Q.: Design in the HCI classroom: setting a research agenda. In: Proceedings of the 2019 on Designing Interactive Systems Conference, pp. 871–883 (2019)
2. Reyna, J., Hanham, J., Meier, P.C.: A framework for digital media literacies for teaching and learning in higher education. E-Learn. Digit. Media 15(4), 176–190 (2018)
3. Cruz, S., Vieira, C., Bidarra, J.: Digital art, sustainability and design thinking: study of a case in higher education. In: E3S Web of Conferences, vol. 436, p. 06004. EDP Sciences (2023)

4. Austin, A.: The differing profiles of the human-computer interaction professional: perceptions of practice, cognitive preferences and the impact on HCI education. Doctoral dissertation, University of West London (2018)
5. Talone, A.B., Basavaraj, P., Wisniewski, P.J.: Enhancing human-computer interaction and user experience education through a hybrid approach to experiential learning. In: Proceedings of the 18th Annual Conference on Information Technology Education, pp. 83–88 (2017)
6. Schultz, N., Christensen, H.P.: Seven-step problem-based learning in an interaction design course. Eur. J. Eng. Educ. **29**(4), 533–541 (2004)
7. Culén, A.L., Mainsah, H., Finken, S.: Design practice in human computer interaction design education (2014)
8. Koutsabasis, P., Vosinakis, S.: Rethinking HCI education for design. Problem-based learning and virtual worlds at an HCI design studio. Int. J. Hum.-Comput. Interact. **28**(8), 485–499 (2012)
9. Candy, L., Amitani, S., Bilda, Z.: Practice-led strategies for interactive art research. CoDesign **2**(4), 209–223 (2006)
10. Duarte, E.F., Baranauskas, M.C.C.: Interart: Learning human-computer interaction through the making of interactive art. In: Kurosu, M. (ed.) HCI 2018. LNCS, vol. 10901, pp. 35–54. Springer, Cham (2018). https://doi.org/10.1007/978-3-319-91238-7_4
11. Carroll, J.M.: Human computer interaction (HCI). In: Interaction Design Encyclopedia (2009)
12. Margolin, V., Margolin, S.: A "social model" of design: issues of practice and research. Des. Issues **18**(4), 24–30 (2002)
13. Shneiderman, B., Bishop, A., Friedman, B., Lazar, J., Marsden, G., Nass, C.: Making a difference: integrating socially relevant projects into HCI teaching. In: CHI 2006 Extended Abstracts on Human Factors in Computing Systems, pp. 41–44 (2006)
14. Roldan, W., et al.: Pedagogical strategies for reflection in project-based HCI education with end users. In: Designing Interactive Systems Conference 2021, pp. 1846–1860 (2021)
15. Duarte, E.F., Gonçalves, F.M., Baranauskas, M.C.C.: InstInt: enacting a small-scale interactive installation through co-design. In: Proceedings of the 30th Australian Conference on Computer-Human Interaction, pp. 338–348 (2018)
16. Lazar, J.: Using community-based service projects to enhance undergraduate HCI education: 10 years of experience. In: CHI 2011 Extended Abstracts on Human Factors in Computing Systems, pp. 581–588 (2011)
17. Lazar, J., Feng, J.H., Hochheiser, H.: Research Methods in Human-Computer Interaction, 2nd edn. Elsevier Science, Amsterdam (2017)
18. Mankoff, J.: Practical service learning issues in HCI. In: CHI 2006 Extended Abstracts on Human Factors in Computing Systems, pp. 201–206 (2006)
19. Lin, C.H.: Rethinking design education-a study for the importance of general education in design. Int. J. Lib. Arts Soc. Sci. **2**(9), 88–97 (2014)
20. Eriksson, E., Nilsson, E.M., Hansen, A.M., Bekker, T.: Teaching for values in human–computer interaction. Front. Comput. Sci. **4**, 830736 (2022)

ContentRank: Towards a Scoring and Ranking System for Screen Media Products Using Critical Reception Data

Chris Kim[✉], Cris Paano, Anantha Chickanayakanahalli, Yulei Xiao, and Sara Diamond

OCAD University, Toronto, ON M5T 1W1, Canada
chriskim@ocadu.ca

Abstract. ContentRank applies cultural analytics to screen media reception. Its goals are to 1) create recognition benchmarks from festival screenings and awards appropriate to genre and assess and integrate earned media scores; 2) analyze audience perceptions of the media that they watch and its impact on their lives. 3) support producers with the means to amplify audience engagement and impact over the course of the production; and 4) provide funders with an understanding of the impacts of their investment. It supplies and visualizes two scores, one that measures recognition and the second, immediate and longitudinal audience impact. It maintains and updates a comprehensive reference database allowing industry-wide comparison. Our partner is Magnify Digital, an agency that delivers audience development strategy, training, and technology for the creative industries. They will integrate ContentRank into ScreenMiner, their cloud-based software solution that supports content discoverability and strategy.

Industry interest in the success of media products has historically focused on quantitative metrics, such as audience numbers, retention, and earnings. However, producers, public funding agencies and investors are increasingly concerned with the qualitative impacts of the media products that they create and fund. Qualitative data collection and analysis tools extend beyond conventional domains such as marketing to fields such as ethnography and health studies. In addition, narrative, documentary, and interactive media are applied to encourage healthy behaviors. Despite opportunities to draw from these insights, media industries lack reception analysis tools and a consolidated database to allow comparative analysis. ContentRank addresses this opportunity.

Keywords: Screen Media · Cultural Data Analytics · Survey Data · Interactive Visualization · User Centered Design · Screen Media · Qualitative Analysis

1 Introduction

ContentRank applies cultural analytics to screen media reception. Its goals are to 1) create recognition benchmarks from festival screenings and awards appropriate to genre and assess and integrate earned media scores from mainstream, specialized and emerging online sources; 2) analyze audience perceptions of the media that they watch and its

M. Rauterberg (Ed.): HCII 2024, LNCS 14717, pp. 55–73, 2024.
https://doi.org/10.1007/978-3-031-61147-6_5

impact on their lives; 3) support producers with the means to amplify audience engagement and impact over the production; and 4) give funders an understanding of their investment's impact. It supplies and visualizes two scores, one that measures recognition and the second, immediate and longitudinal audience impact. It creates, maintains and updates a comprehensive reference database allowing industry-wide comparison. Results are aggregated, visualized, and assigned an impact score. ContentRank captures a snapshot of the Canadian screen media landscape [BUR20]. Our partner is Magnify Digital, an agency that delivers audience development strategy, training, and technology for the creative industries. They will integrate ContentRank into ScreenMiner, their cloud-based software solution that supports content discoverability and strategy.

Industry interest in the success of media products has historically focused on quantitative metrics, including audience numbers, retention, and earnings. However, producers, public funding agencies and investors are increasingly concerned with the qualitative impacts of the media products that they create and fund, that is, that they engage, and impact intended audiences and do so in ways they are intended. Funders such as the Canada Council for the Arts, which supports the not-for-profit arts sector, express value not only in the quantity of audience members but in the positive benefits of arts projects in the short, medium, and long-term [BRO19]. Audience demand for diverse, personalized content is both a challenge and opportunity that warrants analysis [DUP13, LAR14]. Impact analysis is particularly telling when addressing a defined demographic or those grappling with an illness or personal challenge. Audience and critical engagement with a screen media product offer valuable insights into its ability to retain viewers and influence attitudes and behaviors. This recognition helps stakeholders assess a project's cultural, social, and economic potential, discoverability, audience reach, and offers comparisons for future projects. Producers can establish strong feedback loops with viewers through providing personalized or complementary content [DES15, WAL16]. ContentRank allows producers to respond to audiences through the cycle of the product, whether pre-production, where they can adapt their product (for example a soundtrack), production, or release and longtail distribution.

A consolidated database of critical reception of screen media products was needed to illustrate the relationships between data points and enable extension to online publications, blogs, and social media data. Qualitative data collection and analysis tools extend beyond conventional domains such as marketing to fields such as ethnography and health studies and one-off survey tools exist. However, seamless, multidimensional tools for continuous screen media audience response analysis are currently unavailable. ContentRank addresses this challenge by consolidating survey and analytics tools, integrating reception rankings, and building a database.

2   Related Work

Research drew from three sources: 1) an extensive literature review of academic and grey literature that considered the changing landscape of critical reception of screen media; 2) an overview of interdisciplinary qualitative analytics methods including ethnography, health analytics, media; 3) a review of current tools and algorithmic approaches that could be adapted to build ContentRank.

2.1   Audience and Critical Reception of Screen Media Content: Symbolic, Social, and Economic Relevance

Distribution allows many different audiences the ability to access screen media. Distribution is impacted by festival buzz, awards and earned media. Distribution is one of the key themes for earned media where it is valued towards screen media's success. Distribution helps with the purchase and consumption process of movies and TV [BAE22, NGU14]. Distribution becomes a crucial factor for the success of screen media because it relies on media releases [HEN15]. The engagement from earned media is affected by its intent and volume which in turn impacts brand/screen media awareness, customer satisfaction, emotion-based engagement, and audience loyalty. Earned media engagement volume affects brand awareness and purchase intent but not customer satisfaction, while earned media positive and negative valence have the largest effects on customer satisfaction [COL18]. Word of mouth via social media plays an escalated role in contemporary recognition as it amplifies earned media and festival presence.

Dupont et al. (2013), Larrazet and Rigoni (2014) and Verboord (2014) observed that festivals and earned media retain their economic, cultural, and symbolic relevance despite the influence of social media, word of mouth, online reviews, audience commentary, and peer reviews which complement but at times overshadow the conventional authorities like judges and critics [DUP13, LAR14, VER14]. Iordanova (2015) underscores that festivals, while being cultural and economic events in their essence, are also markets, and battle to adapt in the ever-evolving marketplace whilst reflecting the dynamics of the market [IOR15]. Despite such fluctuations, awards continue to offer dual benefits of financial and symbolic capital for screen media products [BUR20].

Program selection and award distribution can be perceived as indicators of prevailing cultural trends [ARC11]. Festival "buzz" considers festivals as cultural events while recognizing that their impact spills into the discoverability and popularity of screen media content beyond the event. Qualitative tools are deployed to gauge the experience of festival audiences [PAR10]. Drawing parallels with festivals, researchers assert that earned media critical reviews and star power still wield considerable influence on early box office earnings [KIM14]. These studies validate that screen media recognition by festivals, events, media critics and their audiences continue to hold valence.

Social media and word of mouth through social media increasingly act as potent financial indicators in the contemporary digital landscape. Social media also serves as a source of audience assessment of screen media. Audience interaction occurs in relation to events, nominations, and awards, in response to earned media and on social platforms where audiences engage with producers, celebrities and influencers. Walmsley's (2016) studies prove that well-structured social media platforms and other digital strategies offer a deeper, and democratic form of engagement with viewers than traditional media have [WAL16]. Other studies highlight that through content personalization, robust feedback loops between viewers and creators can be established fostering genuine engagement and sharing [DES15].

2.2 Qualitative Research

Audience Segmentation. Rivard-Boudreau (2019) observes that a trend in media content is an increase in personalization, driven by the successful audience segmentation within advertising and social media. Audiences seek content that mirrors their experiences in a saturated content and delivery platform market [RIV19, PLO20]. Studies point toward approaches that are respectful of users' cultural backgrounds and identities, whether mainstream or specialized products as potentially yielding superior engagement and impact [STO13, FIE17]. Using segmentation to understand varied audience demographics, as well as specialized recognition opportunities is a goal of ContentRank.

Health and Wellness. Fancourt and Finn's (2019) comprehensive literature review documents the ways that myriad arts and culture, including media productions have facilitated health education, promoted health regimen adherence, and bolstered overall wellbeing [FAN19]. Narrative, documentary, and interactive media forms are proven to enhance healthy actions particularly when they are integrated with continuous engagement strategies such as complementary content, support groups and online dialogues [UNG17, PER18, QUI11]. A substantial amount of evidence such as Hill Strategies' The Arts and Individual Wellbeing in Canada denotes that cultural engagements induce positive health behaviors and foster mental wellbeing; however, the focus of cultural impact analysis has largely been on immediate benefits [FAN19, CHU09, HIL10]. Studies indicate that the type of media consumed (the frequency and the content), has a considerable influence on individual wellbeing [NEI21].

Health and wellness tools offer capabilities to assess long-term levels of retention, behavioral compliance with health regimes and change over time. For example, Most Significant Change (MSC) "involves generating and analyzing personal accounts of change and deciding which … is the most significant – and why" [BET21] at regular intervals. It derives from healthcare research but is universally applicable, and often used to develop and sustain communities around a process of change. Kirkpatrick (2016) offers a four-level model of Reaction, Learning, Behavior, and Results [KIR16]. Applying best practices from qualitative audience impact analysis in concert with those from health and wellness studies can potentially yield more effective tools and methodologies for immediate and longitudinal qualitative data collection and analysis.

Audience Impact Media Analysis. Qualitative analysis is not new to the screen media sector. Several initiatives have sought to understand the impact of documentary production in changing audience behaviors. The Participant Index (2020) was housed at University of Southern California in partnership with Philanthropy.com and aimed to understand the conditions that led an entertainment product to inspire activism, defining types of escalating impacts [PHI14]. It evaluates knowledge gleaned from a screen media product, changes in individual attitudes and behavior changes, and whether and how those changes result in outcomes that could be quantified through other means (health, institutional change, sustainable practices, reduction of conflict). The Media Impact Project considers the "offline" impact of documentary film, including whether a film has had an impact on individual viewers, groups or organizations or made advances towards structural change [MIP14]. It uses a four-part scale of micro, macro, meso and media impacts and offers a set of action subtypes that range from information sharing to lifestyle change [MIN22]. Rigby et al. (2019) have assessed levels of engagement with interactive media and linear media in a rigorous study that used survey techniques relevant to ContentRank [RIG19]. These sources supported the division of ContentRank analysis into 1) categories that address audience attention and engagement, as well as 2) those that reflect impact and sustain interest and action motivated by the screen media products as well as motivators for audiences.

An observational study of platforms (TikTok, Instagram, Facebook, YouTube) by the research team considered social media audience behaviors to understand levels of commitment that audiences expressed in relation to content. Actions range from a thumbs up, to tagging content, to recommendations, to commentary, to remakes [STO14, JAA17]. The study reviewed the ways that such analytics tools collected data and analyzed and rewarded behaviors These analyses were particularly relevant in relation to social media focused generations and consistent users [CAN15], and these escalating forms of engagement contributed to the ContentRank scoring system.

Qualitative Tools. Recent advancements in computational power, artificial intelligence, and machine learning have propelled the research community to use quantitative methods, such as Natural Language Processing, to devise and analyze qualitative tools [DAV11]. When data is available text mining and sentiment analysis, that aid in extracting social media trends on different scales, can eliminate the need for audience surveys [LUO19, BAT15]. However, privacy laws restrict access to databases outside of public forums. The agency of humans as co-designers remains vital, in establishing and reviewing analysis categories, identifying biases and in the practical application of these tools [BOW18, KIM14, DIA21, BUR12].

Whether scraped from social media or derived from surveys, analytics platforms require input across a broad range of audience engagement and impact facets. These include variations in audience behavior, thoughts, and emotions, and subjective well-being—capturing emotional states like happiness, grief, anger, or suffering [STO13]. A platform must incorporate means to identify audience demographics [DES15], associating these with collective wisdom gleaned from personal narratives beyond the traditional monolithic audience ratings [ROC21]. Another essential factor is temporality: concurrent impact during the experience, experienced impact appearing hours or days post the event, and extended impact symbolizing the cumulative effects of individual events over time [BRW19].

A component of research methodology was to identify which existing tools were appropriate, identify gaps and then plan the inclusion or creation of tools. Computer-aided qualitative analysis software, also known as qualitative data analysis software (QDAS), was first introduced in the early 1980s, and there are now many different programs (e.g., ATLAS.ti, Dedoose, MAXQDA, NVivo, Transana) [HUM19]. Research included a similar mapping of visualization tools [WES18] and visualization typologies [BOW18]. Online questionnaires or surveys are widespread across myriad domains, due to the ease of deployment and scalability, for example Survey Monkey, Typeform, and Google Forms. However, none of these provide standard screen media impact questions or are embedded in a platform that serves producers. Producers could employ these to accumulate user reactions to a production pilot [DUA20], gather preliminary audience profile data prior to a main feature screening [BUR18], or to involve a large participant pool regarding broader policy alterations post-screening a documentary or narratives with focal issues [LEH21]. Time-sensitive questionnaires could enable the evaluation of enduring impact from a screen media experience.

3 Methodology

3.1 Industry Collaboration

Magnify Digital has been a research and development partner throughout the creation of ContentRank providing industry advice and the opportunity to integrate ContentRank into the ScreenMiner platform. Magnify Digital delivers audience development strategy, training, and technology for the creative industries, and has designed ScreenMiner, a pioneering, cloud-based software solution. The TELUS Fund provided resources and feedback in partnership with Magnify Digital. Funding agencies, firms that undertake impact analysis of screen media and academics participated in an industry advisory committee, acting as a focus group for each stage of prototype. Producers were engaged in evaluating the usefulness and usability of ContentRank through deploying the survey tools in a series of screenings and follow-up semi-structured interviews.

3.2 Implementation Strategies

ContentRank sets out to supplement Magnify Digital's system with a mix of manual and automatic inputs enabling recognition scoring and audience impact surveys.

Visualization. ContentRank uses easily legible visualization to aggregate and compare individual productions against industry aggregates of festival/event representation, awards and earned media, including geographic representation of recognition [WAR21].

Data Processing. ContentRank analyzes unstructured content with the help of multimodal data parsers and machine learning (ML) capabilities [MEO19]. Sentiment analysis tools are built upon the interdisciplinary domain of emotion detection algorithms and datasets to inform business decisions, ranging from product improvements to predicting user behavior [MED14]. Largely categorized into dictionary- and ML-based approaches, such as NLP (Natural Language Processing) and emotion detection algorithms, they dissect user-provided texts and classify their lexical and semantic characteristics to identify everyone's emotional state and conclude the sentiment of a larger cohort. Such tools and techniques are used to gauge emotionality from a large volume and variety of people's opinion pertaining to different media products, [ROC21] and have been employed to further segment and analyze the collected audience data.

3.3 Building the ContentRank Survey Tool

Questionnaires and Surveys. Surveys typically comprise a mix of close-ended and open-ended questions, facilitating respondents' expanded thoughts on a matter [REA14] and allowing contextual analysis. In ContentRank these tools act as a bridge between qualitative and quantitative research. The research team designed a two-stage survey instrument that intertwined a Likert scale, multiple questions, or binaries, flanked by open-ended queries. Follow-up with a second survey within a month, provides a means to assess retention of interest, affective impacts, action taken in response to the media production. The number of respondents to a follow-up survey also conveys retention of engagement. Natural Language Processing tools are used to analyze text responses. Online surveys in relation to media production can be effectively used by researchers to solicit audience response to a pilot production [DUA20], undertake focus groups, gather basic audience demographic data prior to the screening of the main feature [BUR18], and engage a vast group of viewers regarding broader policy alterations after viewing a documentary or narrative-centric production that focuses on particular issues [LEH21]. It is crucial to ensure a minimum sample size and response rate to the questionnaires, along with verifying that responses originate from humans and not automated bots.

Scoring and Ranking Survey Data. Survey questions were designed to be used with documentary and narrative productions. Questions were informed by established models, the Participant Index from within the screen industries [CIE14], the offline impact study, and from outside the screen industries and the Kirkpatrick model [KIR16] to cover Reaction, Learning, Behavior, and Results; or similarly, Knowledge, Attitudes, Behaviors, Actions). Further, survey design adapted Rigby et al.'s video product immersion questionnaire [RIG19]. Survey questions applied to individual and group reactions to media products. Each question in ContentRank links to one of the six categories - Attention, Emotion, Reaction, Understanding, Watch, and Intent to Act. For instance, a question like "To what extent did the film hold your attention?" aligns with the 'Attention' category. A first survey considers levels of intention, immersion, engagement with story and characters, emotions elicited, the impact of production elements, intention to recommend and share and types of sharing on social media or face to face, changes in attitudes and feelings on topics in the film. A second survey considers whether the media production retained their attention, emotional engagement and whether they followed up on intended actions and behavioral change. All questions are consistent across the deployed surveys to allow for between-subject design experiments and feature a variety of input types (Likert scale, free text, and drop down) to allow for quantitative and qualitative analysis.

3.4 Building the ContentRank Recognition Reporting Tool

Largely characterized by live event participations (festivals and awards) and earned media citations (critical reviews and media coverage), recognition helps producers, distributors, and funders to gauge the project's potential cultural impact, and can influence financial success and as well as uncover opportunities to for discoverability, to reach new audiences against other comparable products. Events and earned media categories have expanded over the last decades with the growth of online forums, social media, and specialized publications. However, academic research indicates that these still matter in the promotion and reception of screen media products. ContentRank provides a comparative cohort of comparable products generated by attributes such as the type of screen media, genre, scripted/unscripted, language, featured events.

Learning from Past Recognition Scores. Per the request by the Canadian Radio and Television Commission (CRTC) to establish an evaluation framework that reports on audience data and reception, Telefilm Canada (2021) [TEL21] has reframed its method of analyzing success to consider Cultural Resonance (national and international) and Audience Engagement (broad outreach, community reflection, targeted audiences), and the Canada Council for the Arts new strategic plan (2021) establishes impact criteria and will soon release an evaluation framework [CAN21]. Building on these earlier initiatives, ContentRank brings together rankings gleaned from traditional earned media revues with leading online platforms, such Rotten Tomatoes, Metacritic, and IMDB, and is capable of tracking and integrating blog data and specialized media. ContentRank can serve producers who seek to meet Telefilm's evaluation goals.

Reference Database. The reference database is a consolidation of varied publicly available data sources that span from institutional and government datasets to crowdsourced wiki pages. It is designed to counteract the algorithmic marginalization and discrimination of screen media products, facilitating contributions and extensions by other collaborators.

Combating Data and Algorithmic Bias. To ensure credibility, the database features a clearly defined primary source for each data point, for example, academic sources and web page URLs, that the user can directly access. The data points can be further supplemented using a web scraper script or through manual submission by the producer, which are all subject to stringent human or AI-assisted validation. The ranking algorithm also considers the production's niche-market status, with a positive modifier for smaller venues with a cult following. To ensure producers can review and understand the resultant rankings, utmost transparency is maintained within the ranking algorithm and in presenting the available data.

Calculating Ranking. A percentile rank is calculated based on a series of comparable variables across available festival/events, awards, and earned media citations within the cohort. Wins and nominations, diversity of featured locations, recognition across a range of categories, consistency of earned media coverage, conveyed sentiment in text are analytics factors, drawing from literature assessments of factors driving festival and event acceptance, nominations, and wins, and earned media.

3.5 Usefulness and Usability Strategies

The ContentRank tools were tested for usefulness and usability through a user trial as well as industry advisory evaluation. Recognition tools were evaluated solely by an industry committee and funders and have not been tested by a wider usefulness and usability trial. Usability strategies drew from wellness application evaluations as well as standard HCI (Human Computer Interaction) practice and included video focus groups, the think-aloud protocol in our interviews with producers, user journey evaluation, Likert scales, and System Usability Scales (SUS) to deliver user-centric designs for the survey interface and the producer interface [DIA21]. These methods further draw from Nielsen Usability Heuristics [NIE05] and ISO 9241 [ISO10]. These frameworks provide guidelines that are reliable for usability testing and assessment of the user interface and the user's interaction journey. This method (and ContentRank) can scale up with growth in participation numbers including on-demand screenings.

4 Prototype Overview

ContentRank facilitates the reporting, generation of text reports, result summarization, and comparison of individual screen media products with industry counterparts. The compared elements encompass similar aspects such as genre, form, region of origin, and budget.

4.1 Qualitative Survey Tool (Audience Survey Tool)

Qualitative survey tool facilitates the collection and measurement of audience engagement and impact through individual and combined screenings.

- **Survey** is a flexible form builder tool specially designed for producers. It allows them to create, edit, and deploy various survey projects to a diverse and sizeable group of participants.
- **Introspection** enables producers to curate and launch asynchronous longitudinal studies, encouraging participants to self-report longer-term responses to screen media.
- **A submission database** is a robust database that has been designed to receive and efficiently organize data collected from respondents.
- **E-mail follow-up** is available for longitudinal studies.
- **Visualization tools** offer visual representations of both individual and aggregated (anonymized) data for each survey question (Fig. 1).

Scoring Algorithm. Data collected from 7-point Likert (summative) scale questions, treated as interval-level data, is associated with one of six categories. An unweighted average of each dimension forms the foundation for the cumulative impact score. Provided the sample sizes are substantial enough, these total impact scores can facilitate comparison between diverse surveys and productions.

Visualizations. The tool displays the score for each category for Surveys 1 and 2. This information is available individually, but it can also be viewed in comparison or

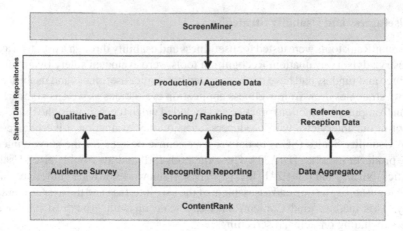

Fig. 1. Diagram illustrating the relationship between the platforms and their components.

aggregated to provide an overall picture of the feedback. In addition to the dimensions that contribute to the overall score, the system also offers insights from other analyzed data. Additional aspects include demographic data and production elements collected but not factored into the score calculation. Upon testing and engagement with stakeholders, charts include bar and pie charts for data representation. These tools were favored due to stakeholder's preference to small multiples and visualization techniques that require minimal interaction (Figs. 2, 3, 4 and Table 1).

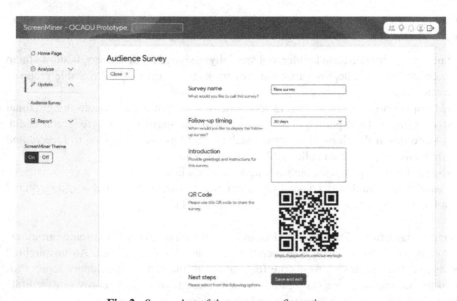

Fig. 2. Screenshot of the survey configuration page.

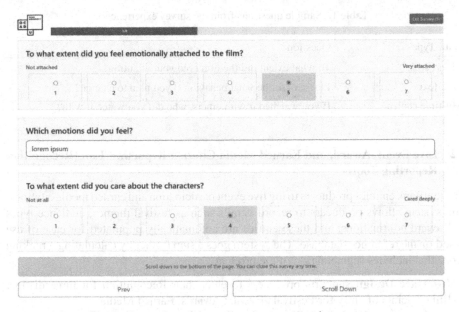

Fig. 3. Screenshot of the end-user survey experience page.

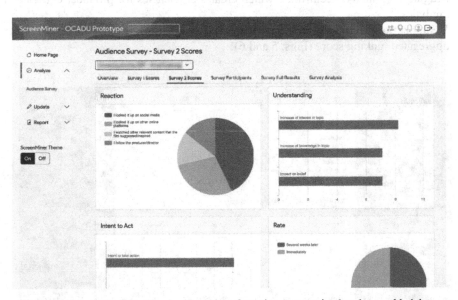

Fig. 4. Screenshot of the "Analyze" section, featuring anonymized and scrambled data.

Table 1. Sample questions from the survey experience.

Data Type	Question
Likert scale	To what extent did the film hold your attention?
Free text	Please describe what behavior(s) you plan to change?
Multiple choice	If you watched it with others, who did you watch it with?

4.2 Live Event, Award, and Earned Media Citation Reporting Tool (Recognition Reporting Tool)

ContentRank enables producers to log live event participation and earned media citations. The system allows producers to record details such as festival themes, audience types and award nominations, and these entries are automatically populated for ease of use based on the reference database. The system goes a step further by calculating a ranking score that includes segmentation of the product.

- **Interface Design** supports producers to enter their Recognition for three distinct linked points of entry for Festivals/Events; Awards; Earned Media.
- **Optimization for Integration** as the system is designed to be engineered into Magnify Digital's ScreenMiner, which creates efficiencies for producer entries and analytics.
- **Visualizations** tools present individual and aggregated results, along with the aggregated ranking score (Figs. 5 and 6).

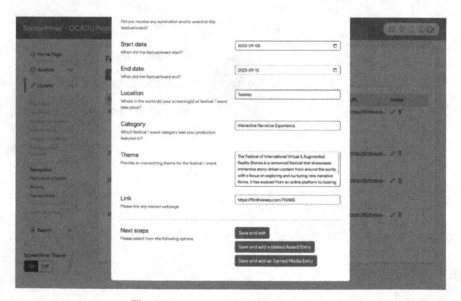

Fig. 5. Screenshot of the data entry page.

Fig. 6. Screenshot of the "Comparison" section, featuring anonymized and scrambled data.

Clustering and Ranking Algorithm. ContentRank generates a cohort of comparable products based on multiple attributes such as type of screen media, genre, whether it is scripted or unscripted, language, and featured events, among other aspects. The system then dynamically calculates a percentile rank based on a series of comparable variables across available festivals or events, awards, and earned media citations within this cohort. These variables can range from wins and nominations, the diversity of featured locations, and recognition across multiple categories to the consistency of earned media coverage and the sentiment conveyed in the text. Producers are incentivized to provide more recognition entries, enhancing both the accuracy of the results, and potentially elevating their ranking.

5   User Testing Trial for Survey Tool

5.1   Goal

The trial's main objectives were to collect audience responses using the survey tools, then analyze the depth and retention of user responses. An integral part of this process was to conduct a usability test for these tools. The trial provided participating producers with a configuration interface, which would enable them to launch surveys and receive data. This step also involved a thorough usability and usefulness (did they find the tool worthwhile and would they use it) test to optimize the system further. We assessed use of the toolset in two different contexts - festival screenings and scheduled virtual screenings, akin to an online focus group. Based on the response data and feedback, the interface is being improved in small ways to align it more closely with user needs and preferences.

5.2 Study Design

Films. Survey tool usefulness (to producers and funders) and usability testing took place over eight events that presented four films—'A Better Man', 'Milk', 'Connecting the Dots', and 'Magnitude of All Things'. These films were screened in two settings, including the Regina International Film Festival (RIFF) and scheduled focus group screenings featuring the films and a Q and A with producers. To foster awareness and encourage participant engagement for these screenings, Magnify Digital created promotional assets, such as digital ads, organic social media posts, and email marketing campaigns, which were disseminated by various partners, including TELUS Fund, OCAD U, the producers, and RIFF.

Survey Participation. Attendees were given the opportunity to participate in a survey either by scanning a QR code or visiting a specific URL. Tat the end of each screening. This process attracted over 100 participants, yielding a high response rate. The data collected from these surveys were securely stored in cloud storage. To gauge long-term reception, a second survey named "Introspection" was sent to participant emails.

Analysis. The collected data were then anonymized, analyzed, and disseminated as a roll-up of the results and visualizations to producers, researchers, and a summarized report for the funders.

5.3 Results

Technical Stability. The robustness of the system was demonstrated through its successful handling of thousands of entries in the testing phase.

Engagement and Retention. There were high completion rates of both the immediate and follow-up surveys, and significant supplementary text provided by participants although there was a small sample size (less than 100). It elicited an 80% and above response rate from screening participants, with high survey completion rates also noted. The second "Introspection" survey observed an average completion rate of over 40%.

Demographics. The demographic profile of the respondents was diverse, with age, gender, race, ethnic and Indigenous participation range. And they provided insightful commentary in response to the films. This allowed demographic differences to be associated with responses such as identification with characters.

Commentary. The surveys proved effective in eliciting responses on subjects spanning from engagement to the impact of the films. We were able to gain insights into changes in actions, beliefs, and understanding instigated by viewing these films and the influential role of specific production elements. Audience commentary was aggregated and analyzed using LLM (Large Language Model) solutions to indicate themes in their response to the film (Table 2).

User Feedback. Audience usability questions embedded in the survey indicated that respondents found the questionnaire's length to be acceptable, and there were high scores for ease of use. Usability and usefulness interviews with producers gathered encouraging feedback on the system. The producers commended the system's simplicity and ease of use, while also offering valuable suggestions for improving certain visualizations.

Table 2. Responses that attest to the intended impact of the film as indicated in Surveys 1 and 2.

Category	Text
Action audience will take after screening	*"The responses provided indicate a variety of ways in which individuals plan to address and support mental health. Some responses focus on personal actions, such as listening more, talking about feelings, and checking on loved ones. Others express a desire to take more active steps, such as hosting screenings, pushing for support in their community, and engaging with students"*
Action audience took after screening	*"The respondent shares that they have spoken to their little cousin who is struggling in high school, suggesting that they are reaching out to offer support and guidance"*

- **Value:** Producers praised the system for its ability to provide a thorough analysis of audience response, a feature they attested was currently lacking in available tools. They recognized the extensive demographic data that could be associated with engagement and impact as a strength of the system. The system's ability to assess the influence of production elements on engagement and impact was also seen as a distinct advantage.
- **Use cases:** The value of longitudinal analysis and the capacity to identify factors for audience retention were underscored. Producers appreciated the potential of the survey tool as a resource during the production and editing stages, seeing it as a tool for gauging audience strategies before finalizing the production. Moreover, the producers indicated they would apply the analysis to make marketing adjustments during the production screening. As well as aiding in distribution, the analysis could support building complementary content and related social media content and outreach strategies. They highlighted the significant value that the system offers for impact analysis (Table 3).

Response to User Feedback

- **Custom questions:** Responding to requests for customization, ContentRank will provide the capability for producers to add their own questions to the survey form. Data aggregation and visualization capacity for these producer-generated questions will support this new feature.
- **Custom timing:** The next version of ContentRank will diversify the time intervals in which surveys can be sent. This adjustment will even enable distribution prior to release and facilitate the analysis of series.

Table 3. Highlights from comments collected during interviews with producers.

User	Testimonial
Producer 1	*"I would have loved this...A lot of documentarians stepping out and not having data makes it hard to gain trust, to be able to gather and prove response. With this you would not gather things out of thin air in terms of what you think you know. It would help with corporate funding and less traditional funding sources. Numbers do matter, especially to do this work.... Really great project"*
Producer 2	*"The responses to the film are emerging in the ways that I hoped. It is a complex film...I would use this not only in an impact campaign but in post-production or even to test elements in production"*
Producer 3	*"We are collecting responses now via (named brand) – we design surveys, our team writes them. If we were able to use your surveys through Magnify, we would get out of (named brand) which is very expensive and bring our use of surveys to ScreenMiner™ and add our questions to its survey"*

- **Visualizations:** In response to producer feedback visualizations were simplified and color schemes attached to factors (such as soundtracks) and carried through the dashboard.
- **Tooltips:** Future tooltips will provide additional data on how scores are calculated.

6   Conclusion

ContentRank is an integrated system that scores and ranks screen media products based on critical and audience reception data, featuring cultural analytics to qualitatively analyze screen media reception and influences on stakeholders such as producers and funders. To overcome the lack of a consolidated database and responsive analysis tools, ContentRank provides a range of tools, including a user-friendly interface, to record events, score and rank content, measure audience engagement, and maintain a reference database, further validated by methods such as partnerships, surveys, usability assessments, interviews, and advisory board feedback.

6.1   Future Work

Usefulness and Usability of Recognition. The usefulness and usability of the recognition features will be user tested in future trials with Magnify Digital producers.

Additional Research. A future prospect involves further integration to yield an augmented score for a screen media product, amalgamating aspects of qualitative and quantitative analysis with social media rankings.

Acknowledgments. This research study was supported by Mitacs Accelerate Fund, Magnify Digital and the TELUS Fund. We thank Joanne Johns for her time on the project. A special thank you to Moyra Rodger, CEO Magnify Digital.

Disclosure of Interests. Authors Have Received Research Grants from Magnify Digital and OCAD University.

References

[ARC11] Archibald, D., Miller, M.: The film festivals dossier: introduction. Screen **52**(2), 249–252 (2011)

[BAE22] Bae, G., Kim, H.J.: Interdependent relation between earned media and TV ratings. Asia Pac. J. Mark. Logist. **34**(1), 132–158 (2022)

[BAT15] Batrinca, B., Treleaven, P.: Social media analytics: a survey of techniques, tools and platforms. AI Soc. **30**, 89–116 (2015)

[BET21] Better Evaluation. Most significant change (2021)

[BOW18] Bowes, J., et al.: User-centered taxonomy for urban transportation applications. In: Nah, F.H., Xiao, B. (eds.) HCIBGO 2018. LNCS, vol. 10923, pp. pp. 577–593. Springer, Cham (2018). https://doi.org/10.1007/978-3-319-91716-0_46

[BRO19] Broersma, M.: Audience engagement. Int. Encycl. Journal. Stud. 1–6 (2019)

[BRW19] Brown, A., Carnwath, J., Doeser, J.: Canada council for the arts qualitative impact framework (2019)

[BUR12] Burkett, I.: An Introduction to Co-design, p. 12. Knode, Sydney (2012)

[BUR18] Burns, N., et al.: The impact of creative arts in Alzheimer's disease and dementia public health education. J. Alzheimer's Dis. **63**(2), 457–463 (2018)

[BUR20] Burgess, D.: Capturing film festival buzz: the methodological dilemma of measuring symbolic value. NECSUS Eur. J. Media Stud. **9**(2), 225–247 (2020)

[CAN15] Canada Media Fund. The Digital-Only Media Consumer (2015)

[CAN21] Canada Council for the Arts. Art, Now More than Ever - 2021–26 Strategic Plan (2021)

[CHU09] Chung, B., et al.: Using community arts events to enhance collective efficacy and community engagement to address depression in an African American community. Am. J. Public Health **99**(2), 237–244 (2009)

[CIE14] Cieply, M.: Participant index seeks to determine why one film spurs activism, while others falter. New York Times **7** (2014)

[COL18] Colicev, A., Malshe, A., Pauwels, K., O'Connor, P.: Improving consumer mindset metrics and shareholder value through social media: the different roles of owned and earned media. J. Mark. **82**(1), 37–56 (2018Jan)

[DAV11] Davis, C., Michelle, C.: Q methodology in audience research: bridging the qualitative/quantitative 'divide'. Participations: J. Audience Recept. Stud. **8**(2), 559–593 (2011)

[DES15] Desjardins, D.: The digital-only media consumer: key findings from a conversation with all-digital millennials (2015)

[DIA21] Diamond, S., et al.: Visualizing wellness: the Myant Skiin system connected life app. In: Gao, Q., Zhou, J. (eds.) HCII 2021. LNCS, vol. 12787, pp. 234–250. Springer, Cham (2021). https://doi.org/10.1007/978-3-030-78111-8_16

[DUA20] Duan, H., et al.: Using goal-directed design to create a mobile health app to improve patient compliance with hyper-tension self-management: development and deployment. JMIR Mhealth Uhealth **8**(2), e14466 (2020)

[DUP13] Dupont, N., Augros, J.: Cinema and marketing: when cultural demands meet industrial practices. French J. Media Stud. (3) (2013)

[FAN19] Fancourt, D., Finn, S.: What is the evidence on the role of the arts in improving health and well-being? A scoping review. World Health Organization. Regional Office for Europe (2019)

[FIE17] Fiellin, L., et al.: Video game intervention for sexual risk reduction in minority adolescents: randomized controlled trial. J. Med. Internet Res. **19**(9), e314 (2017)

[HEN15] Hennig-Thurau, T., Wiertz, C., Feldhaus, F.: Does Twitter matter? The impact of microblogging word of mouth on consumers' adoption of new movies. J. Acad. Mark. Sci. **43**, 375–394 (2015)

[HIL10] Hill, K.: The arts and individual well-being in Canada: connections between cultural activities and health, volunteering, satisfaction with life, and other social indicators in 2010. Hill Strategies Research Incorporated (2013)

[HUM19] Humble, A.: Computer-Aided Qualitative Analysis Software. SAGE Publications Ltd. (2019)

[IOR15] Iordanova, D.: The film festival as an industry node. Media Industr. J. **1**(3) (2015)

[ISO10] ISO, B, Standard, B.: Ergonomics of human-system interaction. British Standards Institution (2010)

[JAA17] Jaakonmäki, R., Müller, O., Vom Brocke, J.: The impact of content, context, and creator on user engagement in social media marketing. In: Proceedings of the Annual Hawaii International Conference on System Sciences, pp. 1152–1160 (2017)

[KIM14] Kim, H., Hanssens, D.: Paid and earned media, consumer interest and motion picture revenue. Citeseer (2014)

[KIR16] Kirkpatrick, J., Kirkpatrick, W.: Kirkpatrick's four levels of training evaluation. Association for Talent Development (2016)

[LAR14] Larrazet, C., Rigoni, I.: Media and diversity: a century-long perspective on an enlarged and internationalized field of research. French J. Media Stud. (5) (2014)

[LEH21] Lehdonvirta, V., Oksanen, A., Räsänen, P., Blank, G.: Social media, web, and panel surveys: using non-probability samples in social and policy research. Policy Internet **13**(1), 134–155 (2021)

[LUO19] Lu, K., Wu, J.: Sentiment analysis of film review texts based on sentiment dictionary and SVM. In: Proceedings of the 2019 3rd International Conference on Innovation in Artificial Intelligence, pp. 73–77 (2019)

[MED14] Medhat, W., Hassan, A., Korashy, H.: Sentiment analysis algorithms and applications: a survey. Ain Shams Eng. J. **5**(4), 1093–1113 (2014)

[MEO19] Meo, T., et al.: Aesop: a visual storytelling platform for conversational AI and common sense grounding. AI Commun. **32**(1), 59–76 (2019)

[MIN22] Mind Tools. Kirkpatrick's Model (2022)

[MIP14] Media Impact Project. Offline Impact Indicators (2014)

[NEI21] Neill, R., Blair, C., Best, P., McGlinchey, E., Armour, C.: Media consumption and mental health during COVID-19 lockdown: a UK cross-sectional study across England, Wales, Scotland and Northern Ireland. J. Public Health 1–9 (2021)

[NGU14] Nguyen, C., Romaniuk, J.: Pass it on: a framework for classifying the content of word of mouth. Aust. Mark. J. (AMJ) **22**(2), 117–124 (2014)

[NIE05] Nielsen J. Ten usability heuristics. 2005

[PAR10] Park, M., Oh, H., Park, J.: Measuring the experience economy of film festival participants. Int. J. Tour Sci. **10**(2), 35–54 (2010)

[PER18] Perrier, M.J., Martin Ginis, K.: Changing health-promoting behaviours through narrative interventions: a systematic review. J. Health Psychol. **23**(11), 1499–1517 (2018)

[PHI14] Philanthrophy.com. Index Aims to Measure When Entertainment Leads to Activism. The Chronicle of Philanthropy (2014)

[PLO20] Plothe, T., Buck, A.: Netflix at the Nexus: Content, Practice, and Production in the Age of Streaming Television. International Academic Publishers, Peter Lang Incorporated (2020)

[QUI11] Quinn, N., Shulman, A., Knifton, L., Byrne, P.: The impact of a national mental health arts and film festival on stigma and recovery. Acta Psychiatr. Scand. **123**(1), 71–81 (2011)

[REA14] Rea, L., Parker, R.: Designing and Conducting Survey Research: A Comprehensive Guide. Wiley, Hoboken (2014)

[RIG19] Rigby, J.M., Brumby, D.P., Gould, S.J., Cox, A.L.: Development of a questionnaire to measure immersion in video media: the film IEQ. In: Proceedings of the 2019 ACM Inter-national Conference on Interactive Experiences for TV and Online Video, pp. 35–46 (2019)

[RIV19] Rivard-Boudreau, É.: Developing your audience: going beyond the #Hashtag [Internet]. Canada Media Fund (2019)

[ROC21] Rocklage, M., Rucker, D., Nordgren, L.: Mass-scale emotionality reveals human behaviour and marketplace success. Nat. Hum. Behav. **5**(10), 1323–1329 (2021)

[STO13] Stone, A., Mackie, C.: Subjective Well-Being: Measuring Happiness, Suffering, and Other Dimensions of Experience. National Academies Press (2013)

[STO14] Stone, M.: Big data for media (2014)

[TEL21] Telefilm Canada. Formal Recommendations Pan-Canadian Consultations (2021)

[UNG17] Ungar, T., Norman, C., Knaak, S.: Think you can shrink? a proof-of-concept study for men's health education through edutainment. J. Technol. Behav. Sci. **2**, 71–76 (2017)

[VER14] Verboord, M.: The impact of peer-produced criticism on cultural evaluation: a multi-level analysis of discourse employment in online and offline film reviews. New Media Soc. **16**(6), 921–940 (2014)

[WAL16] Walmsley, B.: From arts marketing to audience enrichment: how digital engagement can deepen and democratize artistic exchange with audiences. Poetics **58**, 66–78 (2016)

[WAR21] Ware, C.: Visual Thinking for Information Design. Morgan Kaufmann (2021)

[WES18] Weston, A., Diamond, S., Kumar, R., Royen, D.V., Gordon, M., et al.: Culture creates bonds (2018)

Discussion of User Experience for Streaming Platform by Using Mouse Trajectory

Shih-Yun Lu[1]([⊠]) [iD], Wei-Her Hsieh[2] [iD], and Chang Yuan Ku[3]

[1] Department of Fine Arts, National Taichung University of Education, No. 140, Minheng Rd., West Dist., Taichung City 403454, Taiwan (R.O.C.)
lucia@mail.ntcu.edu.tw

[2] Department of Fashion Design and Management, National Pingtung University of Science and Technology, No. 1, Shuefu Road, Neipu, Pingtung 91201, Pingtung County, Taiwan (R.O.C.)
weiher@mail.npust.edu.tw

[3] Department of Digital Content and Technology, National Taichung University of Education, No. 140, Minsheng Rd., West Dist., Taichung City 403454, Taiwan (R.O.C.)

Abstract. Live streaming is one type of indispensable entertainment in our life due to technology development. Users could interact with streamers on the live streaming platform that they form an individual social group. Various live streaming platforms are now available on the market. It makes it crucial to study the user interface design of the platform based on an evaluation of user experience.

This research studies two of the largest companies, Nonolive and King Kong, together with Twitch, an almost-10-year-old company in this industry. The consideration is based on the average spending time of users, company development, and popularity. The purpose of this research is to compare these three companies and discuss:

1. User habits and needs while using the video game streaming platform.
2. Differences in the user interface design.
3. Interface design principles and finalize the guidelines for future reference.

The researcher looks into five aspects principles of Nielsen across Twitch, Nonolive, and King Kong by applying the mouse tracking technology, questionnaire, and interviews for qualitative and quantitative results. The researcher summarizes that the fundamental functions of live streaming platforms are: search, follow, sort by, night mode, streamer information, and notification. In addition, coherence, clarity, and color are needed. The researcher suggests including these elements to help to improve the five aspects of the user interface in the future.

Keywords: streaming platform · user experience · interface design · mouse trajectories

1 Introduction

1.1 Research Motivation and Purpose

This research looks into mouse trajectories on Twitch, Nonolive, and King Kong to summarize interface design guidelines to cater to users' needs. In brief, the purpose of this research is to: (1) discuss key elements of designing a live streaming interface; (2) discuss the difference between mouse movement and trajectory chart when users watching live streaming and; (3) summarize interface design guidelines of a user-friendly platform to improve users' satisfaction.

2   Literature Review

2.1   Mouse Trajectory and Behavior

Researchers use various methods to analyze the process of decision making. The eye-tracking and mouse-tracking technology are the two examples. The former mainly focuses on analyzing users' gazes, while the latter tracks mouse movement paths by giving two options in a relative position (Fig. 1). This is done by specific software (Zgonnikov et al. 2017).

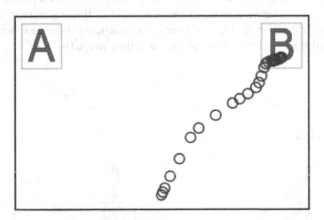

Fig. 1. Mouse-Tracking Analysis (Zgonnikov et al. 2017)

Ahmed and Traore (2007) categorize two sampling methods for mouse trajectories: active and passive. The active sampling method collects mouse movement paths to develop applications so that the users could interact with the program. By which means, the data is collected. However, users have to be in the program. In contrast, the passive sampling method uses a mouse tracker to collect mouse-related data at the same time when users use their mouse. Users would not be interrupted.

2.2   Mouse Trajectory Analysis

According to AAE Ahmed and I Traore (2007), mouse tracking analysis includes Mouse Dynamics and Histogram of Mouse Trajectory.

1. Mouse Dynamics: It is an approach to collect data of the mouse trajectory when users use their mouse. The trajectory refers to a path from a preset starting and ending point. The data is collected to calculate kinetic energy such as distance, speed, and click. The result is then used to identify users. Gamboa and Fred (2004) applied this

Fig. 2. Game Interface (left), Mouse Trajectory (right) (Gamboa and Fred 2004)

approach to gather trajectories when users play games and interact with the interface. With the collected data, they could identify each of the users (Fig. 2).

I. Histogram of Mouse Trajectory: This approach saves the mouse trajectory patterns in a certain unit time for researchers to study samples. Ahmed and Traore (2007) took the distance of movement paths as the amount of time users took to review the difference and distribution (Fig. 3). There is a significant difference between user 1 with 35% and user 2 with 23% under the same time range 0–0.5 s.

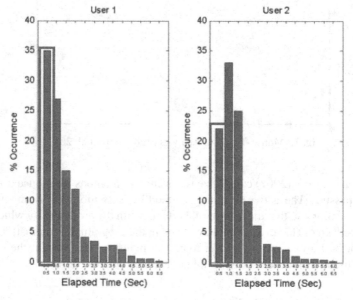

Fig. 3. Bar Chart of User 1 and 2 (AAE Ahmed and I Traore 2007)

According to the above statement, this research will utilize an open-source software Ogama for tracking mouse trajectory data and adopt the active sampling method for accuracy. The researcher will give users assigned tasks to complete. The mouse trajectory data will be saved after each task. It is because users might finish all tasks without stopping, and the researcher has to interrupt. Lastly, Histogram of Mouse Trajectory will be applied to gather the distance of mouse movement paths as well as the node amount in order to calculate the efficiency.

2.3 Usability Evaluation

Utilizing QUIS (Questionnaire for User Interface Satisfaction) in this research is to understand users' satisfaction, feedback, and situation when using Twitch, Nonolive, and King Kong. The questionnaire is designed based on nine aspects with Likert Scale: (1) screen; (2) terminology and system feedback; (4) learning; (5) system capability; (6) on-line tutorials; (7) multimedia; (8) teleconferencing and (9) software installation. However, the research will adjust the content suitable for this research. The score is from 1 the lowest to 9 the highest. The higher the score, the more satisfied the users think about the webpage.

3 Research Method

This research aims to discuss users' satisfaction toward the user interface and their willingness to the platform. The five usability principles of Nielsen (1993), learnability, efficiency, memorability, error, and satisfaction, are the foundation for analysis. The result will be the reference to finalize interface design guidelines for the streaming platform.

3.1 Usability Task Design

This experiment includes a behavior test and a mouse trajectory test. After the both tests, there will be a questionnaire to fill and an interview to complete. With the collected data, the researcher will analyze the result for usability, issue questions, and suggest improvements.

Typical Tasks. In line with sample analysis, the researcher integrates the "live streaming watching procedure" with the internet environment to design typical tasks and scenario stimulation of usability evaluation. The researcher observes the real situation, movement, and problem while the tasks are being carried out.

(a) Designing typical Task: There are two movements among users: purposive browsing and unpurposive browsing. Purposive browsing refers to users who watch live streaming through functions of notification, searching, category, recommendation, and follow. As for unpurposive browsing, users watch via the category and recommendation function. However, both types of movements have the same functions: follow, chat, interaction, information, setting, notification, and so on. Therefore, tasks are designed based on the users' movement as well as the interface function.

(b) Scenario simulation: It is a simulation of the actual platform environment and real-world events. It enables the researcher to discover users' behavior. Each scenario contains several tasks for usability, in which subjects will feel the reality.

3.2 Tool and Environment for Experiment

Subjects. There is a total of 31 subjects, and all of them from ages 20 to 30. This research focuses on users' experience toward video game streaming platform, therefore, having the related experience is crucial as part of the data.

Method. It is a one-to-one experiment, which the subjects will enter the platforms and complete the tasks first on Twitch, followed by Nonolive, and the on King Kong. The tasks are the same across the three platforms. The subjects could ask the researcher questions if they have. Upon the accomplishment on each platform, the subjects need to fill a questionnaire. Besides, the researcher will carry out a semi-instructed interview at the end of the entire experiment.

Ogama is an open source software designed by Voßkühler of Freie Universität Berlin (Fig. 4). It analyzes such as slides and videos via eye or mouse trajectory data or both at the same time. The software use dots and attentionmap to record eye gaze and the amount of mouse click. The researcher will use this software and defined AOI for analysis and discussion.

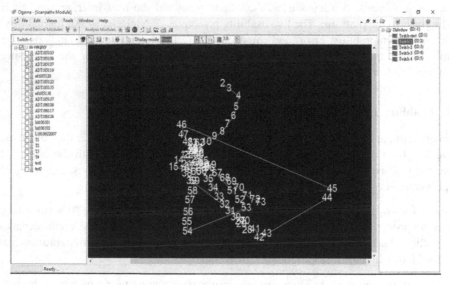

Fig. 4. Ogama, an open source software.

3.3 Analysis

Five aspects of Nielsen are taken into account in this research to understand the usability of the three major streaming platforms. The researcher collects data through mouse-tracking technology, questionnaire, semi-structured interview, and analyzes the result of Learnability; Error; Efficiency; Memorability; Satisfaction for questions and suggestions. The Semi-instructed interview will be conducted after they fill out the QUIS questionnaire. The questions are about the function, operation, visual impact, and overall satisfaction. It helps the researcher to apprehend their actual feeling concerning the streaming platforms.

4 Analysis and Discussion

4.1 Learnability Data Analysis

It focuses on reviewing the time subjects spend on tasks and actual situations. On the other hand, the interview helps the researcher to understand detailed information on usability so that the researcher could suggest improvements.

The frequency distribution and average task time for Twitch and King Kong are 25–125 s with 367.56 s, and 330–550 s with 333.94 s. There is a huge difference between both platforms. On the other hand, Nonolive has a 250–500 s frequency distribution with 534.56 average task time. The difference is comparatively small (Table 1).

Table 1. Frequency distribution - task 1.

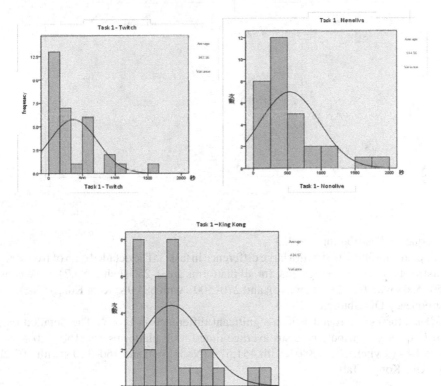

1. Frequency Distribution - Task 2

   All platforms are found with a large difference in task 2. The frequency for Twitch is distributed predominately among 180–500 s. Though the average time of accomplishment is 464.53 s, many people finished the task after 500 s. As for Nonolive and King Kong, the former is with is 100–200 s frequency distribution with a 284.34 s average time while the latter is 100–250 s with 383.94 s (Table 2).

Table 2. Frequency distribution - task 2.

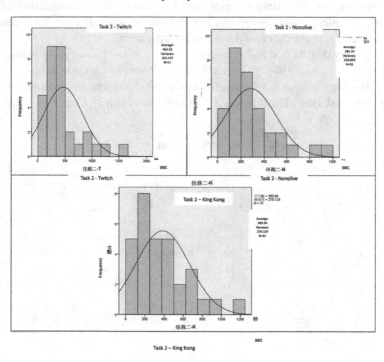

2. Frequency Distribution - Task 3

   All platforms are found with a large difference in task 3. The detailed data of frequency distribution versus average time for all platforms are 0–250 s with 385.71 s (Twitch); 50–500 s with 651.4 s (Nonolive); and 270–500 s with 684.9 s (King Kong) (Table 3).

3. Frequency Distribution - Task 4

   All platforms are found with a significant difference in task 4. The detailed data of frequency distribution versus average time for all platforms are: 160–320 s with 494.04 s (Twitch); 220–380 s with 451.57 s (Nonolive); and 160–320 s with 502.22 s (King Kong) (Table 4).

Table 3. Frequency distribution - task 3.

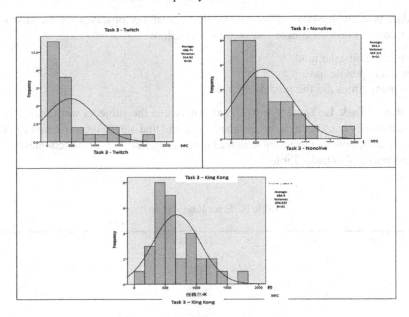

Table 4. Frequency distribution - task 4.

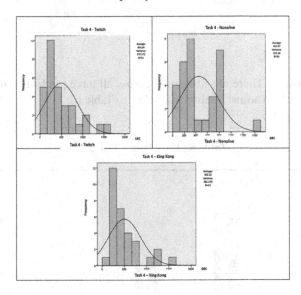

4.2 Error Data Analysis

Error data is about mistakes during tasks. The researcher observes on the side when subjects conduct tasks and note following information:

- What is the mistake made?
- How many people have it?
- How many times did the mistake happen?

Error Rate - Task 1. There is a low error rate when the subjects were using Twitch which means they could search the assigned game and find out the most-viewed streamer. Nonolive, on the opposite, is found with the highest error rate. Subjects encountered many problems during this task (Table 5).

Table 5. Error Rate - Task 1

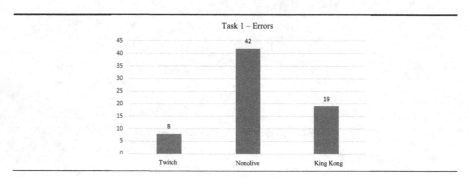

Error Rate – Task 2. There are few errors across all three platforms. It means that it was easy for subjects to adjust quality and volume (Table 6).

Table 6. Error Rate - Task 2

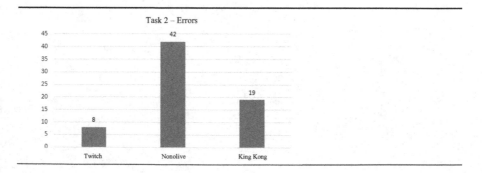

Error Rate - Task 3. Twitch has the lowest error rate; however, the result does not show the same in the number of people who have errors. It is uneasy for the subjects to check streamers' information and their previous videos on Twitch. Nonolive has the highest amount of people who made errors even its error rate is low. It explains that the subjects managed to correct them quickly, but the platform is not easy for them to use in the first place. The highest error rate goes to King Kong, which means the platform is uneasy to tackle this task (Table 7).

Table 7. Error Rate - Task 3

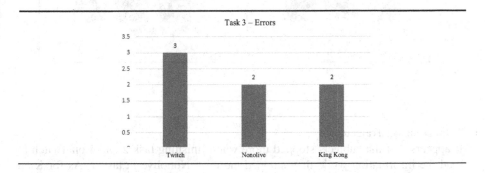

Error Rate - Task 4. Errors across all platforms are low. This information shows that the subjects could easily save games and recommend streaming channels through provided functions (Table 8).

Table 8. Error Rate - Task 4

Efficiency Data Analysis. It mainly analyzes mouse movement, such as distance of mouse movement and mouse node.

Distance of Mouse trajectory and Mouse Node. Histogram of Mouse trajectories is applied in this research to get the distance of mouse movement paths and nodes on trajectories for efficiency analysis. The longer the distance, the more time the subjects spend on the platform to complete the task. The node means the pause of the mouse onscreen. The more nodes are found; the more time subjects need to understand the information.

Nonolive has the longest distance in total among the three. This result explains that the subjects spent more time to understand the platform and finish tasks. Twitch has the shortest distance except in task 1 when it has a higher result than King Kong. It means that the subjects required more time in task 1 on Twitch. However, the rest of the performance on Twitch is better than the rest two (Table 9).

Table 9. Total distance of mouse movement path.

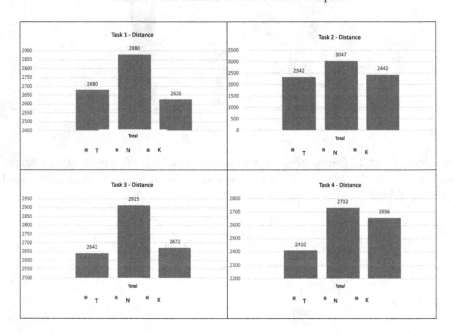

1. Total Node on Trajectories

   It appears that the subjects stopped more when finishing task 2 and 4 on Twitch to read the information while they stopped more on Nonolive in task 1. As for King Kong, they took more time to intake information in task 3 (Table 10).

Table 10. Total mouse node on trajectory.4.4. Memorability Data Analysis

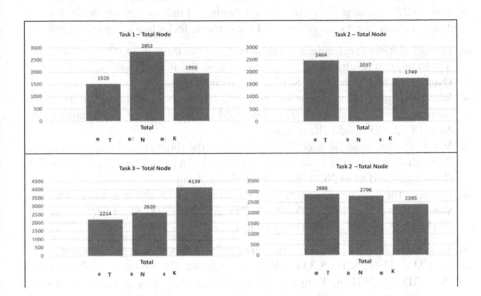

By using the mouse trajectory approach, the subjects are given assignments to complete for the memorability study. It is found that the correct rate of question 1, 3, 5, 6, 7, 9, and 11 are 100%. It is followed by 93% for question 2 and 8. Question 4, 10, and 12 have the lowest rate of 90%. All questions are above 90% correct rate, which evinces that the "search," "follow," "setting" function and the "followed" icon are rememberable.

4.3   Satisfaction Data Analysis

It is aim to analyze satisfaction of subjects to the platforms by conduction a 21-qeuestion survey.

Reliability Test. Reliability Test reviews the reliability, coherence, and stability of a testing tool, or the survey. Devellis divided reliability into four Cronbach's α. When α is between .06-.65, the tool is unadaptable. The minimum acceptable α range is between .65-.70. A good and an excellent too is ranged between .70-.80 and .80-.90 separately. Gay also mentioned that if $\alpha > 0.90$, the reliability is good. Therefore, the survey of this research will be reviewed to ensure its reliability.

Five-Aspect Analysis of Satisfaction. After reviewing the QUIS questionnaire, the results are varied in the five-aspect satisfaction so the researcher utilizes One-way ANOVA to examine the difference between the three samples in five aspect analysis.

1. Descriptive statistic:

   The results of "overall platform performance," "website display," "words and information used," "learning the website," and "website function" are shown in Fig. 13.
   The higher the result, the more satisfied the subjects feel when using the website.

   - Overall platform performance: The average of the three is 34.03, above average.
     The individual result is M = 37.13, SD = 9.64 (Twitch), M = 33.23, SD = 8.36
     (Nonolive), and M = 31.74, SD = 8.89 (King Kong).
   - Website display: The average of the three is 16.49, above average. The individual
     result is: M = 17.81, SD = 5.97 (Twitch), M = 16.26, SD = 5.29 (Nonolive), and
     M = 15.42, SD = 5.51 (King Kong).
   - Words and information used: The average of the three is 22.82, above average.
     The individual result is M = 25.06, SD = 6.32 (Twitch), M = 22.68, SD = 5.38
     (Nonolive), and M = 20.71, SD = 5.76 (King Kong).
   - Learning the website: The average of the three is 17.25, above average. The indi-
     vidual result is M = 18.26, SD = 5.24 (Twitch), M = 17.00, SD = 5.09 (Nonolive),
     and M = 16.48, SD = 4.69 (King Kong).

2. Website function: The average of the three is 28.86, above average. The individual
   result is M = 31.65, SD = 8.33 (Twitch), M = 28.90, SD = 6.08 (Nonolive), and M
   = 26.03, SD = 7.35 (King Kong). 2. In terms of variance analysis, the three variance
   analysis, the three aspects: "overall platform performance," "website display," and"
   learning the website" do not have a significant difference. The F value of each is
   2.978 (p.056 > .05), 1.452 (p.24 > .05), and 1.027 (p.36 > .05) separately. However,
   "words and information used" performs outstandingly with 4.332 (p.16 < .05). It
   means that at least one group of the combinations has a difference in means. Hence,
   the researcher applied Scheffe to find out which two groups of the combinations are
   they.

   According to the Scheffe result tested Post Hoc, there is a significant difference in
   means in the below combinations:

   - Twitch with King, and Twitch > King Kong
   - Twitch with Nonolive, hence, Twitch = Nonolive
   - Nonolive and King, hence, Nonolive = King Kong.

   In summary, Twitch > King Kong, and King Kong = Nonolive. Twitch performs
   the best in the aspect of "words and information used".

   F value of "website function" is 4.572 (p.01 < .05) that is outstanding. Therefore,
   at least one group of combinations perform significantly in mean difference. Hence, the
   researcher applied Scheffe to find out which two groups of the combinations are they.

   According to the Scheffe result tested Post Hoc, there is a significant difference in
   means in the below combinations:

   - Twitch with King Kong, and Twitch > King Kong
   - Twitch with Nonolive, hence, Twitch = Nonolive
   - Nonolive and King Kong, hence, Nonolive = King Kong

   In conclusion, Twitch > King Kong, and King Kong = Nonolive. Twitch performs
   the best in aspect of "website function".

Based on the above results, "overall platform performance", "website display" and "learning the website" are with less difference. Twitch performs better than the other two in aspects of "words and information used" and "website function", which lead to higher satisfaction. The following section will discuss the questionnaire of Twitch.

QUIS Analysis for Twitch. Table 11 shows the result of the analyzed QUIS in nine sections. Following sections are with scores over 6.5: "overall website performance (bad, good)," "overall website performance (low efficiency, high efficiency)," "word and image related to the task," "website smoothness," "speed," "system stability," and "music matches with the website". Subjects not only are satisfied with overall platform performance but also think words and images are easy to understand. They can easily use the website and even rely on it.

Table 11. Analysis of twitch QUIS survey.

Aspect	Question	Average	Variance
Overall Platform Performance	bad and good	6.52	1.81
	difficult and easy	6.00	2.08
	dissatisfied and satisfied	6.06	1.83
	inefficient and efficient	6.55	1.82
	boring and interesting	6.00	1.71
	inflexible and flexible	6.00	1.59
	average	6.19	
Content Displayed	read on the website	6.45	1.93
	content displayed	5.48	2.41
	page layout	5.87	2.32
	average	5.94	
Words and Information Used	words and icons related to tasks	6.55	1.69
	clear terminology	5.87	1.73
	information displayed	5.87	1.73
	website smoothness	6.77	1.86
	average	6.27	
Learning the Website	Learning the website	5.94	1.88
	New function discovered after tries and errors	5.90	1.81
	simple task conducted	6.42	2.01
	average	6.07	

(*continued*)

Sections with scores between 5–6 are: (1) "Content display" and "page layout." It indicates that subjects are not satisfied with the layout on the interface of the platform.

Table 11. (*continued*)

Aspect	Question	Average	Variance
Website Function	speed	6.74	1.79
	system stability	6.74	1.93
	music matches with website	6.68	1.66
	error correction	5.65	1.96
	suitable for new users	5.84	2.41
	average	6.33	

(2) "Specific terminology" and "information displayed." It explains that subjects are unable to understand and use the platforms. (3) "Learning the website," "new function discovered after tries and errors," "error correction" and "suitable for non-experienced." It describes that new users require more time to learn how to use the platform. The subjects will be interviewed once they finish the QUIS questionnaire. It helps the researcher to understand their actual feedback towards the streaming platforms.

5 Conclusion and Suggestion

In line with five-aspect principle, the researcher suggests guidelines for future reference as below:

1. Streaming Platform Function:
   An effective function could allow users to easily operate, and a user-friendly design could increase efficiency. Looking into the result of the survey and interview, the researcher suggests the following function designs.
   (a) Search: The purpose of it is to help users quickly find the information they want. It is not just for finding games or streamers, but a fully developed function to look for such as on-live streamers.
   (b) Follow: Three words: "save," "follow," and "subscribe" confused first-time users. The latter two are keywords. "Follow" is similar to the "my favorite" function of the website, in which users could add their preferred streamers to their list; while "subscribe" is that users support their preferred streamers by donations. There should be a clear definition to separate both to avoid any confusion.
   (c) Sort by: Users can filter the channels based on their need with this function. Despite the popularity, start time, review, and follower could be added to enrich this function. Users are able to find out the streamer that closes to their preference.
   (d) Night mode: Users stare at the screen to watch live streaming. It causes visual fatigue and other eye injuries easily. Allow eyes to rest is one way, but adding the night mode by darkening the platform is also helpful to reduce the exposure under a bright screen.
2. Streamer information: clear streamer information enables users to know streamers better. Apart from Facebook, Instagram, and other social media, designers could also

add streamers' previous videos to make it easy for users to understand streamers' styles.

3. Notification: a notification function could help users when they encounter a problem. To be specific, if there are no words next to the "follow" icon, then when the users stop the mouse on the icon, a notification pops up to tell users what is it about and how to use it.

4. Layout and color:

The visual design of platforms could also affect how users operate. The researcher suggests as following.

(e) coherency: Coherency in standardized process and messages help users to utilize platforms quickly and effectively. At the same time to increase satisfaction.

(f) Clarity: Designers are expected to understand users' needs. A clean interface enables users to learn fast how to operate the platform effectively and properly.

(g) Color Properly using color contrast could stimulate efficiency. Take Nonolive as an example, it applies color contrast in the volume bar so users could accurately adjust it. This is a way to reduce the problem on the users' side.

Acknowledgments. Not applicable.

Author Contributions. Conceptualization, S.Y.L. and W.H.H.; data curation, C.Y.K.; formal analysis, C.Y.K.; funding acquisition, none; investigation, C.Y.K.; methodology, S.Y.L. and W.H.H.; project administration, S.Y.L.; resources, C.Y.K.; software, C.Y.K.; supervision, S.Y.L.; validation, S.Y.L., W.H.H. and C.Y.K.; visualization, C.Y.K.; writing – original draft, C.Y.K.; writing – review & editing, C.Y.K.

Funding. This research received no external funding.

Data Availability Statement. Data generated at a central, large-scale facility, available upon request. Raw data were generated at National Taichung University of Education, Department of Digital Content and Technology, Taiwan (R.O.C.). Derived data supporting the findings of this study are available from the corresponding author Prof. Hsieh on request.

Conflicts of Interest. None.

References

Zgonnikov, A., Aleni, A., Piiroinen, P.T., O'Hora, D., di Bernardo, M.: Decision landscapes: Visualizing mouse-tracking data. Royal Soc. Open Sci. **4**, 170482 (2017)

Ahmed, A.A.E., Traore, I.: A new biometric technology based on mouse dynamics. IEEE Trans. Dependable Secure Comput. **4**, 165–179 (2007)

Gamboa, H., Fred, A.: A behavioral biometric system based on human-computer interaction. In: Biometric Technology for Human Identification, International Society for Optics and Photonics, Defense and Security, Orlando, Florida, United States, vol. 5404, pp. 381–393 (2004)

Nielsen, J.: Usability engineering. Elsevier, Academic Press, Inc., Harcourt Brace & Company, San Diego, USA (1993)

DeVellis, R.F.: Applied social research methods series. In: Scale Development: Theory and Applications. Sage Publications, Inc., vol. 26 (1991)

Feasibility Study on Touch Screen Interaction Technology Based on "The Sword of King Goujian" Exhibit

Yuanyuan Song[✉]

Wuhan University of Technology, 122 Luoshi Road, Wuhan, Hubei, People's Republic of China
805763149@qq.com

Abstract. Museums, as important carriers of historical cultural relics, can provide more innovative and attractive viewing experiences to attract more visitors while a wide range of interactive technologies are developed nowadays. As we all know, the traditional exhibition format mainly relies on text, pictures and physical displays to convey information. However, this approach may not be able to provide visitors with sufficiently detailed and in-depth information, resulting in a limited cognitive understanding of the exhibits. This study focuses on how the Hubei Provincial Museum's exhibit "The Sword of Yue Wang Goujian" uses touch screen interactive technology to present more detailed exhibit content and interactive game experience on the display glass to carry out the corresponding interactive design research. The Sword is not only a valuable heritage of ancient Chinese sword-making craft, but also an important window for people to explore and understand ancient history. This study is based on the application of touch-screen interaction technology to the exhibit "the Sword of King Goujian " on the protective glass screen of the exhibit, aiming to make the connotation of the important historical relics represented by "the Sword of King Goujian" more deeply understood and the history and culture of the exhibit have a stronger dissemination power. In conclusion, the application of touch screen interactive technology for the Hubei Provincial Museum emphasises the enhancement of visitors' interactivity and a more detailed understanding of history and culture, and provides useful exploration and practice for the cultural communication and digital construction of the museum.

Keywords: Touch Screen Interaction · Museum User Experience · the Sword of Goujian

1 Introduction

In order to enhance audience participation and promote learning and understanding, museums introduce some simple interactive methods to promote the interaction between the audience and the exhibition. This kind of participatory experience can increase the interest and attention of the audience, make them more engaged in understanding the exhibits and related knowledge, and at the same time, they can understand the background

M. Rauterberg (Ed.): HCII 2024, LNCS 14717, pp. 90–98, 2024.
https://doi.org/10.1007/978-3-031-61147-6_7

and story of the exhibits more deeply, thus deepening their knowledge of culture, history, science and so on. In the museum field, the design of exhibitions and displays is increasingly centered on the audience's personal and autonomous interactive experience, so as to enable the audience to actively explore historical, artistic and social knowledge. However, domestic museums in China still favor the traditional way of displaying exhibits by visiting them first and then reading a short textual explanation. Therefore, this study is a feasibility study based on the principle of user-centered design, and by exploring the feasibility of transparent touch screen interactive technology on the display of cultural relics can stimulate the audience's curiosity and desire for exploration, prompting the audience to understand the story behind the relics in greater depth, and achieve the important significance of promoting the dissemination and inheritance of culture.

2 Limitations of Traditional Museum Display Methods

Most of the domestic museums in China still focus on traditional interaction methods, including voice recognition and intelligent guide and scanning QR code, while novel interaction methods such as somatosensory interaction or projection interaction are superficial and lack of interest. According to the analysis and visits, the limitations of the domestic museum display methods are as follows:

First of all, traditional museum displays are usually based on physical exhibits, supplemented by simple text descriptions and pictures. This form of display is relatively single, and it is difficult to provide audiences with comprehensive and in-depth knowledge of cultural and historical background. This leads to the fact that most of the audience's understanding and knowledge of the exhibits only stays on the surface. Most of the viewers watch the exhibitions offline and then read the written descriptions, receiving very limited information about the cultural relics. '

Secondly, the audience's participation is not high: on the display of traditional museums, the audience can only passively watch the exhibits and read the explanations. This kind of display cannot fully mobilize the audience to participate in the enthusiasm, so that the audience is easy to fatigue and boredom in the process of visiting. Finally, the audience has certain limitations: due to the different historical and geographical conditions, economic development, education system and resources and other factors, resulting in a certain degree of cultural differences among people. Usually, the content of the display is inclined to be academic, and many professional terms appear on the introduction of the exhibits, but this only allows professional scholars and highly educated people to understand better, while other people with less than medium level of education only stay in a short understanding, which makes it difficult to satisfy the needs of the audience with different educational backgrounds in viewing the exhibition.

3 The Application of Touch Screen Interaction Technology in Display

3.1 Principle of Transparent Touch Screen Interaction Technology

Domestic museums in the use of interaction is relatively single, the application scene is also very monotonous, but this also shows that the development of new interactive technology in the museum has a huge space potential.

OLED transparent touch display splicing screen is a new type of display technology, which utilizes the most advanced OLED technology and touch technology to splice multiple displays into a specific shape, which not only displays video information, but also supports touch interaction, combining visual effects, touch sensing, interactive experience, and can provide high-definition large-screen playback, low-latency control, seamless dual-screen according to different scenes. It can provide HD large screen playback, low latency control, seamless dual screen splicing and other effects according to different scenes.

The basic principle of transparent screen touch interaction technology is to integrate touch sensors on the transparent display, so that the display can detect the user's touch operation while displaying images. The touch sensor can recognize the contact between the user's finger or other touch devices and the screen surface, and transfer the contact position information to the processor, thus realizing the interactive function, and it is also able to support the touch interaction function, which combines the visual effect, touch sensing, and interactive experience, and it can provide the effects of high-definition large-screen playback, low-latency control, and seamless splicing of dual-screens, etc. according to different scenarios.

However, there are some difficulties and obstacles that may be faced in the process of combining transparent touch screen interactive technology with museum displays. Firstly, the high cost of the technology may make it difficult for some museums to afford it at the initial stage. Secondly, the maintenance and updating of transparent touch screen interactive technology requires regular inspections by professional technicians, which will increase the economic costs of museums. In addition, the audience's acceptance of the new technology also affects the actual effect of the transparent touch screen interactive technology in the museum application. Museums need to provide some operational reminders so that visitors can be better integrated into the touch screen interaction.

3.2 Comparison Between Traditional Touch Screen and New Transparent Screen

In contrast to traditional touch screens, this new all-in-one no longer requires a limited touch area, but instead applies touch functionality directly to the entire transparent screen. This means that users can operate the device by touching anywhere on the transparent screen, whether it's swiping, clicking or zooming.

The use of OLED Transparent Touch Display Splice Screen technology for museum display credentials can also provide a more immersive interactive experience for the audience. When users interact with the OLED transparent touch all-in-one machine, they can see the artifacts or scenes behind them, creating a realistic combination of reality and reality. This immersive experience not only enhances user participation, but also makes the artifacts more vivid, deepening the user's understanding and viewing experience.

3.3 Transparent Touch Screen Interaction Technology Brings Immersive Change of Viewing Experience

Immersive interaction is a kind of interaction mode, which enables users to interact with the virtual world more deeply and feel the rich virtual content through multiple senses. This research wants to enhance the immersive experience of the viewer through transparent touchscreen interaction. The main purpose of this interaction is to enable users to experience the virtual world more deeply, to help them better understand the knowledge of cultural artifacts, and to be able to interact with the virtual world in a more intuitive and vivid way.

Transparent touch screen interactive technology, as an advanced display and interactive technology, has brought about a change in the immersive viewing experience for the museum and exhibition field. Firstly, it is the combination of transparent display and physical exhibits. The high transparency of the transparent touch screen interactive technology makes the audience obtain relevant information and animation through the transparent screen while enjoying the physical exhibits. This combination of transparent display and physical exhibits allows the audience to better understand the background, history and value of the exhibits in the process of viewing the exhibition, and improves the quality of viewing the exhibition.

At the same time, the transparent touch-screen interactive technology provides the audience with an intuitive interactive experience, enabling them to interact directly with the display content while viewing the exhibits. Visitors can independently select the information and content they are interested in by clicking, sliding and other operations, which further enhances the degree of participation and immersion in the exhibition.

Transparent touchscreen interactive technology has revolutionized the immersive viewing experience in the museum and exhibition field and has made this research feasible. This feasible approach improves audience participation, interest and satisfaction through the combination of transparent display and physical exhibits, intuitive interactive experience, multi-level information display, flexible display form and immersive experience that integrates virtual and reality. With the continuous development and application of transparent touch-screen interactive technology, the future exhibition experience will be richer and more diversified.

4   Touch Screen Interactive Technology Based on the "the Sword of King Goujian" Display Program Design

4.1   Background of the Case

Hubei Provincial Museum is located in Wuhan, Hubei Province, China. Founded in 1953, the museum mainly collects, researches and displays historical relics and natural specimens in Hubei, aiming to promote the excellent traditional culture of the Chinese nation, disseminate scientific knowledge and improve people's cultural quality.

The Sword of King Goujian(see Fig. 1) is a cultural relic of great historical, cultural and artistic value. It was unearthed in December 1965 in Hubei Province. After more than 2,500 years, it still has clear and exquisite decorations, glittering cold light and no rust, and is regarded as "the first sword in the world". It witnessed the history of the Spring and Autumn and Warring States Periods, reflecting the political, economic and social conditions at that time. By studying and learning about this sword, the audience can understand the historical background and cultural traditions of that time, and also have a deeper understanding of the customs, beliefs and values of the ancient Chinese

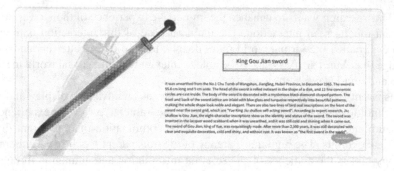

Fig. 1. The King Gou Jian sword

society, so as to deepen their knowledge of and respect for Chinese culture, and at the same time attract a large number of domestic and international tourists to come to visit the site, which provides tourists with a window to understand Chinese culture.

4.2 Research Steps

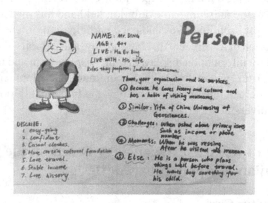

Fig. 2. Museum visitors' persona arrangement

This study uses observation and user interviews to conduct a case study of the Hubei Provincial Museum to further identify design opportunities to enhance interaction. The steps of the study are as follows. First, the researchers conducted more than 10 on-site surveys at the Hubei Provincial Museum between May and June 2022 to learn about the case-related data and information such as tourists' visiting behaviours, museum services and facilities, and interactive information in the exhibition halls through the observation method (e.g., Fig. 2). Secondly, according to the research theme, 20 visitors to the Hubei Provincial Museum were interviewed and semi-structured interviews were conducted, which were mainly based on the experiential experience of visiting the Hubei Provincial Museum, including different feelings and experiences during the pre-, mid-, and post-periods of the visit. The advantage of the semi-structured interviews is that they provide a deeper understanding of the real thoughts of visitors to the Hubei Provincial Museum, and the number of interviewees is random in terms of age and occupation. The experiences of the interviewees ranged from first-time visitors to those who had visited several times. Thirdly, the researchers collected the maximum amount of data and materials such as information about the services and activities carried out by the museum through the official website of the museum and on-site visit surveys, and analysed the data and materials based on the generalisation of the above data (e.g. Figs. 3 and 4). Fourthly, based on the results of the analysis, the feasibility analysis and improvement study of the Sword of King Goujian Exhibition Hall is carried out.

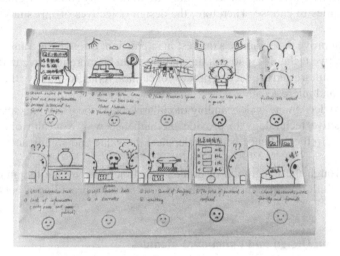

Fig. 3. User visit mood

Fig. 4. User visit experience map

4.3 Result Analysis and Design Objectives

According to the results of the analysis, Hubei Provincial Museum, as one of the important museums in China, is not satisfactory in terms of user experience. Before visiting, users do not know what exhibitions are in the museum, and the flow of information is not clear enough; when arriving at the museum, visitors think that the guide is not clear, and there is no guide map that can provide help when visiting different exhibition halls. When visiting the cultural relics, visitors think that the museum provides too little information about the relics, and the information they know is very limited and imperfect, so they can only rent additional interpretation equipment, but it is very inconvenient to wear and there is no clear guide to help rent equipment. Finally, there is a souvenir shop at the main entrance of the museum when you are ready to return from your visit, but the location is very poorly arranged. At the same time, the museum's souvenirs are few in number and not creative enough, so visitors who want to buy some souvenirs have very few opportunities to choose. Therefore, the design objectives of this study have three main directions:

First, to improve the audience's interest in interaction: through the transparent touch screen interactive technology, so that the audience can be more intuitive understanding of the history, culture and production process of cultural relics, to improve the audience's participation and interest.

Second, to deepen the understanding of cultural relics: the use of transparent touch-screen interactive technology to provide the audience with a wealth of educational resources to help the audience better understand the value and significance of cultural relics.

Third, through the integration of guided tour function, provide the audience with real-time exhibition information and guided tour service, providing a better viewing experience.

4.4   Interaction Design and Functional Modules

In terms of interaction design, intuitive touch operations such as clicking, sliding, zooming and other interactive gestures are used to ensure that viewers can interact easily and conveniently. And the visual presentation uses high-quality pictures and visual effects to show the details and features of The Sword of King Goujian. At the same time, keep the interface design simple and consistent to improve the audience's visual experience. Besides, the interactive interface should reasonably use animation and transition effects to enhance the attractiveness and interest of the display content. In the function module is mainly divided into two, display module and interactive module. The display module includes the detailed introduction of the historical background, production process and cultural value of cultural relics, as well as high-definition pictures and other multimedia materials. And the interactive module will provide interactive games related to the exhibits such as The Sword of King Goujian to increase audience participation.

5   Conclusion

5.1   Research Results and Contributions

Based on the research of transparent touch screen interactive technology and the program design aspects, this study explores whether the new interactive technology can be used in museums, and simulates the display case of The Sword of King Goujian to show the feasibility of the study (see Fig. 5). The significance of transparent touch screen interactive technology in museum display is mainly reflected in the fact that it provides richer display methods. The transparent touch-screen interactive technology adopted by the museum combines multimedia technology and virtual reality technology, which can provide a more intuitive and vivid experience for the audience by building virtual exhibition halls, digital exhibition boards, touch-screen guides and other methods. The touch screen technology protects, preserves and passes on the museum's precious items, reduces the risk of possible damage to physical cultural relics, and guarantees the safety of cultural heritage, while allowing visitors to continue to learn about cultural relics. By studying the Hubei Provincial Museum's design attempts to improve visitors' visiting experience in terms of user experience and interactive services, design ideas that can be drawn upon are proposed.

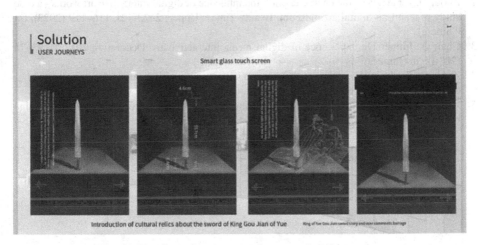

Fig. 5. Simulate transparent touch screen glass interaction

5.2 Future Research Directions and Prospects

The future development of the display field, in addition to touch screen interaction technology, can also explore the integration of sound, gesture, eye tracking and other diversified interaction methods into the display program to further enrich the audience's interactive experience. In addition, it is possible to study how to leverage social media, online communities and other platforms to inspire visitors to interact with others and share their feelings and insights during the viewing process, realizing a social and collaborative display strategy.

The current era is an ever-evolving digital economy, where digital technology is penetrating into all levels of society and public life, and the cultural heritage field, with museums at its core, is moving towards a new stage of development. By introducing more touch-screen interactive technologies into museums, digital museums can utilize the data collected to present their collections more vividly and convey the cultural heritage and essence of museums to a wider social group. In conclusion, the future research direction and outlook can be expanded from integrating new interaction technologies, the use of artificial intelligence in display strategies, multimodal interaction and other levels. In the face of the future, museums should make full use of the advantages of data resources, integrate artificial intelligence and other emerging technologies to provide services for realizing the digital transformation and innovative development of museums, and explore more interactive modes of museums in the context of new technologies.

References

1. Wang, X.: The impact of interactive gestures on user emotion cognition from the perspective of embodied cognition. Packag. Eng. **43**(24), 153–158 (2022). (in Chinese)
2. Zhou, M.: Analysis of the characteristics and influence of digital interactive art works - a case study of teamLab digital art museum. Beauty Times (Upper) **2023**(12), 116–119 (2023). (in Chinese)
3. Chai, Q.: Immersive experience of digital media interactive art. Decoration **2012**(2), 73–75 (2012). (in Chinese)
4. Zhou, C.: Exploring the experience design to improve user visit in museums - a case study of the National Museum of Korea. Beijing Cult. Creat. **2023**(4), 12–17 (2023). (in Chinese)
5. Leiting, P., Wanna, L.: Research on optimizing museum visitor experience services in China based on IPOP theory. Chin. Mus. **03**, 68–74 (2020). (in Chinese)

Exploring User Behavior Based on Metaverse: A Modeling Study of User Experience Factors

Siqin Wang[1] and Sunghee Ahn[2]([✉])

[1] International Design School for Advanced Studies, Hongik University, Seoul 04068, Republic of Korea
[2] School of Design Convergence, Hongik University, Sejong 30016, Republic of Korea
sahn2002@hongik.ac.kr

Abstract. The metaverse plays a significant role in breaking through the limitations of time and space in the real world, better using current digital intelligence, and presenting new insights visually that might otherwise be buried. Nevertheless, as of now, users' use of the metaverse is more based on experimentation, and how users can engage with it is very limited. Accordingly, this paper proposes a User Experience Factor Model, based on UGC creation, digital economy, and leisure interaction as the main elements, which can realize the experience of immersion and belongingness for users and analyzes the cyclic facilitation between the details and the reasonableness of the model using structural equation modeling and quantitative data. Furthermore, this study optimizes the model based on the analysis results to realize the metaverse design cycle of immersion and belonging. It proposes that the model can be used as a paradigm for overlapping interactions between the physical and virtual worlds. The paradigm presented in this paper can help metaverse development and investment companies understand user needs more effectively and provide a paradigm that can be referenced to attract user engagement and retention.

Keywords: Emotional Design · User Experience · UGC · Metaverse · Participatory Design · User Research · HCI

1 Introduction

While the mass adoption of the metaverse is still questionable, the adoption of virtual and augmented reality technologies has expanded. A survey by IDC shows that about 20% of companies plan to improve customer experience by investing in augmented reality and virtual reality technologies [1]. Mystakidis (2022) posits that the metaverse is predicated upon the convergence of multifarious technologies, which facilitate immersive interactions with virtual environments, digital entities, and individuals [2]. The term "metaverse" is employed to denote a virtual realm that coexists alongside the physical world, and its evolution has transitioned from a conceptual framework to practical implementations within the domain of virtual reality gaming [3]. Concurrently, metaverse technology transcends temporal and spatial constraints, affording users a novel dimension of experiential freedom.

© The Author(s), under exclusive license to Springer Nature Switzerland AG 2024
M. Rauterberg (Ed.): HCII 2024, LNCS 14717, pp. 99–118, 2024.
https://doi.org/10.1007/978-3-031-61147-6_8

The Metaverse is a large-scale, interoperable meta-ecosystem [4]. It can be experienced synchronously and continuously by an unlimited number of users and consumers, and the co-creation of creatively guided goods managed by coordinators and supported by platform owners increases the user experience. Meta-innovation presents promising prospects for digital advancement beyond the confines of conventional social media or computer gaming, thereby establishing novel foundations for further innovation across the entirety of the digital economy landscape.

The metaverse incorporates multifaceted technological integration, fosters social interconnectedness, and transcends conventional temporal and spatial constraints [5]. It introduces an expansive three-dimensional virtual realm, effectively liberating users from the constraints of real-world temporal and spatial limitations. The metaverse has inherent attributes [6]. The practical potential of the metaverse resides in its capacity to harness existing digital intelligence more effectively and to manifest latent insights in a visually accessible manner that might otherwise remain obscured [7]. This technological innovation holds the promise of facilitating the resolution of real-world issues while fostering the development of a more ecologically sustainable, inclusive, and sophisticated societal milieu.

However, users now use the metaverse more on an experimental basis. Most of the metaverse's content and outcome creation comes from industry experts and companies with strengths. Users participate in the metaverse only as a novel game with a different way of accessing it, primarily by experiencing it. Users become more of a "player" and less of a "personified citizen." As a result, the metaverse still needs to be seen as an area of low retention and a small audience.

Therefore, this paper proposes a metaverse user experience research based on emotional design, verifies the metaverse user experience of immersion and belongingness, proposes a User Experience Factors Model centered on leisure interaction-digital economy-UGC creation, and puts forward better initiatives for the subsequent development and research of metaverse. This study consists of three parts. First, this study attempts to develop a complete User Experience Factors Model of the metaverse. Second, the developed user experience model is analyzed by quantitative research to determine the correlation between its key factors and immersion and belongingness. Finally, optimization of the User Experience Factors Model, metaverse user retention growth, and further development possibilities are discussed.

2   Factors of User Experience in Metaverse

Immersive three-dimensional virtual environments, wherein users engage with both fellow users represented by avatars and projected object identities, are experiencing a growing surge in popularity. Moreover, these spaces are in a continuous state of evolution, progressively maturing into highly interactive, cooperative, and commercially oriented cyber domains [8]. The emerging virtual worlds provide unprecedented opportunities for enterprises to collaborate with co-creation users. Nevertheless, pioneering enterprise co-creation systems have failed to attract satisfactory levels of participation and engagement [9]. While previous studies on user experience in the metaverse have laid the groundwork for this work, the tangible contribution these studies have made to how to efficiently improve user retention and expand the user base in the metaverse is limited from the current perspective. Based on the arguments of this study, it will be proposed to present models that help to utilize the metaverse to effectively improve user experience.

2.1 User Experience Factor Model

The presentation of the Metaverse is accomplished through the utilization of Extended Reality, often referred to as Cross Reality (XR). XR serves as an overarching concept that encompasses a diverse spectrum of immersive technologies, data representations, and digitally projected environments. Within the XR framework, one finds Virtual Reality (VR), Augmented Reality (AR), and Mixed Reality (MR) [10]. It represents an inclusive term encompassing an array of immersive technologies and digital environments designed for the representation and projection of data. Their interrelationships are shown in Fig. 1. Where AR presents the virtual in the real world, while VR tends to recreate characters in the virtual world [11]. The emergence of virtual languages and avatar-based platforms underscores the escalating importance of creating and sustaining digital environments that facilitate collaboration and communication [12].

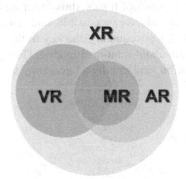

Fig. 1. Relationships of Digital Construction Techniques

Kim (2015) proposed a framework for categorizing individual experiences from different perspectives [13], such as experiences gained through personal sensory experiences and interactions and experiences in the physical space in which an individual is located by analyzing previous studies that explored experiences from a philosophical perspective, as shown in Fig. 2.

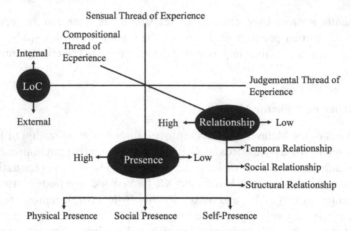

Fig. 2. Personal Experience Categorization Framework [13]

Based on Kim's Personal Experience Categorization Framework, the user's experience comes from empiricism and sensationalism, acquiring a deep binding of personal and social relationships. Prior research findings indicate that forthcoming inquiries should encompass a broad spectrum of topics, thus fostering the formulation of sound methodologies for creating an inclusive, accessible, and secure metaverse that ensures both equity and diversity [14]. Consequently, the key to the user experience model of this study is leisure interaction about relational linking, User-generated content (UGC) creation about self-actualization, and the digital economy that binds them as shown in Fig. 3.

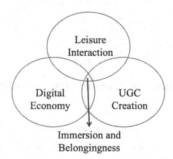

Fig. 3. User Experience Factor Model

2.2 Leisure Interaction Factor

As the most enjoyable user experience, leisure interaction can inspire more creativity. In addition, users purchase the work of others, including those created by others, or learn skills from others, creating a closed loop of the digital economy. The resulting system is also communal and social, leading to a cycle of belongingness.

In the metaverse, users can create an avatar [15]. An avatar represents some sort of ideal appearance, whether it reflects the real-life self or a different identity, which can lead to content creativity for the user detached from the real world. The metaverse also reshapes social relationships between people to emphasize more human involvement. Communities form organically around shared interests and creations, further enhancing belongingness in the virtual world.

Furthermore, immersive authenticity and empowerment are the most apparent demand realization and value creation perceived by the user. The emergence of digital life in the metaverse is expected to break down these boundaries further and create new scenarios for social experiences in virtual space [16]. Users can create virtual communities based on shared interests and communicate via text, voice, and video in real time. Some metaverse platforms also allow for the creation of virtual events, such as parties or gatherings, which can bring people together from all over the world. The social metaverse represents the convergence of social virtual reality and social applications [17].

In addition, virtual worlds are reorganizing how we design and deliver learning [18]. This opens a learning transition that builds on the concept of immersive learning rather than a collection of knowledge passed between tutor and learner. The development and utilization of virtual environments encompass a multitude of scenarios. Enhancements to digital learning ecosystems can be achieved by thoroughly investigating user behavior and engagement metrics within educational virtual realms [19]. It has been shown that UGC is prompted during leisure interaction based on the infinite creativity of users. These usually include UGC providing new interaction paths, generating activity content without users changing the original model and ground rules, and generating resource files that can be shared [20]. Based on the contribution of leisure interaction to UGC creation, this paper proposes Hypothesis 1.

- Hypothesis 1. The degree to which users experience leisure interaction is directly proportional to the degree of UGC creation in the metaverse.

2.3 UGC Creation Factor

UGC production and all its aspects, enabling user-created, user-owned, decentralized, assetable content, is the essential difference that distinguishes the consumer metaverse from the current consumer internet. The Metaverse allows consumers to adapt UGC exposure to their needs and desires [21]. UGC also is significant in its ability to ignite creativity and diversity in the digital realm, allowing users to contribute their unique ideas, designs, and content. This diversity of creative expression enriches the virtual landscape and promotes deeper user engagement and immersion. When users can create, modify, and personalize their virtual experiences, they become more emotionally invested in the metaverse, resulting in more profound and lasting interactions.

Currently available research discusses the metaverse design [23]. For instance, Second Life represents an early endeavor to establish fully realized virtual realms wherein participants can establish a virtual existence. Within this virtual environment, players exercise control over their avatars, enabling a wide range of creative activities, including customizing their surroundings [24]. Linden Dollar, a virtual currency exchangeable for real-world currency, underpins the in-game economy of Second Life. Today, the knowledge of co-creative design and construction of online worlds still needs to improve [25]. To support the active participation of users in the design and evaluation of web applications, the digital economy system of the metaverse encourage non-specialized users to become active producers and designers.

Meanwhile, Non-Fungible Tokens (NFT) represent distinct digital assets within the virtual communal expanse of the metaverse, encompassing domains such as virtual real estate, in-game artifacts, and collectible items. Existing research has found that the metaverse enables the separation of the cornerstones of neoliberal production and consumption through cryptocurrencies, algorithmic collectibles, and NFTs [26]. This engenders a digital economy where these assets can be transacted, exchanged, and traded akin to tangible assets.

UGC presents economic opportunities as users can create and sell virtual goods, services, and experiences, fostering an emerging digital economy in the metaverse. Within the context of the Metaverse's mobile edge network, users assume the role of creators for virtual assets, including but not limited to videos, music, and profile pictures, thereby shifting the traditional responsibility from platform developers/operators to end-users who can offer these assets in the marketplace [27]. Furthermore, UGC has the potential to be stored within distributed cloud systems and edge servers. For instance, Decentraland is a virtual platform constructed upon the Ethereum blockchain, facilitating the storage of UGC and its subsequent monetization through NFTs [28]. Therefore, based on the contribution of UGC creation to the digital economy, this study proposes Hypothesis 2.

- Hypothesis 2. The degree of UGC creation is directly proportional to the degree of user experience digital economy in the metaverse.

2.4 Digital Economy Factor

The digital economy system of virtual currency and traceable transactions is the neural network that enables the world of consumer metaverse to function, adding the value system of the virtual world to the value system of the consumer Internet and integrating and interoperating between the value systems of the virtual world and the real world [29].

The Metaverse Economy represents a novel iteration of the digital economy that distinguishes itself from its predecessors under the advent of digital currencies, the evolution of digital fiat currencies, and the proliferation of innovative production and business paradigms centered around digital assets. Introducing new digital asset forms, such as NFTs or Non-Fungible Resources (NFRs), underpinned by distributed ledger technology, is poised to engender a transformative impact upon diverse business models. This transformation will significantly perturbate production, circulation, and consumption paradigms [30]. The convergence of digital and physical assets will create an entirely novel economic landscape. In a Metaverse economy where value is recognized as determining value, cultural, historical, and aesthetic values can be harnessed through technology, generating a more diverse economy, and expanding the global economy.

The advancement of the digital economy within the metaverse era is propelled by the digital transformation of industries and the digitization of user demands [31]. A notable distinction setting the virtual universe apart from other digital platforms is its heightened realism and the consequent expansion of economic exchange possibilities. Consequently, the formation and progression of digital economic transactions within this sphere offer abundant prospects for retailers.

Within this context, three distinct areas of opportunity materialize, namely value exploration, value exchange, and value valuation, each cultivated through the amplification of touchpoints encompassing digital economy exchanges. Based on digital economy-driven consumer behavior, the metaverse dimension amplifies three user touchpoints (digital economic exchange, complex social relationships, and direct environmental interactions) in the digital experience of the three primary stakeholders of any transaction [32]. Therefore, based on the role of the digital economy in driving consumption and generating leisure interactions in virtual worlds, this study proposes Hypothesis 3.

• Hypothesis 3. The degree of user experience leisure interaction is directly proportional to the degree of user experience digital economy in the metaverse.

2.5 Immersion and Belongingness

The metaverse constitutes a digitized environment characterized by embodied presence, wherein individuals engage through technologies facilitating bodily presence, thereby engendering a novel mode of interaction and socialization. Emotional design establishes user expression and expresses the user's identity or personality [33]. The inherent interplay between cognition and emotion, a fundamental facet of human consciousness, must be thoughtfully acknowledged [34]. This interconnectedness holds particular significance in its capacity for emotional processes to bolster and maintain cognitive operations, including the central mechanisms underlying user experience.

Norman's (2004) Emotional Design Model explains how different aspects of a product affect emotions [35]. The Emotional Design Model scrutinizes how a product's characteristics evoke emotional reactions in users, encompassing sensations of comfort, ease, and enjoyment while using an interactive product. According to Norman (2004), the affective design model divides the user's mental processing into three levels: heartfelt, behavioral, and reflective. Users' perception of UGC can be explained by the concept of "emotion as information" [36], and the "halo effect" as an emotional response extends to the perception of the entire metaverse [37]. Following the affective-informational framework, emotional states serve as informative signals to individuals concerning their present circumstances, subsequently provoking either approach or avoidance behaviors [38].

The metaverse is a conduit that connects the knowledge and proficiency associated with the design of physical realms, encompassing structures, communities, cities, and facilitating human interactions. One of the keywords that designers will need to ensure is crucial is immersion and belongingness. Designers must create appropriate interaction systems that protect users' freedom to socialize and create boundaries to define what is real and what is not [39]. These boundaries will help people because certain things will not just happen in both worlds in one but affect both, which is why users are willing to commit to it, to experience the metaverse immersivity, and to develop a sense of belongingness to the metaverse. Further, immersive experiences are advantageous for broad user engagement based on the directionality of perception to behavior [40].

Therefore, the following hypotheses are proposed based on this model which suggests that leisure interaction, UGC creation and digital economy fulfill the immersion and belongingness of user experience.

- Hypothesis 4. The degree to which users experience leisure interaction is directly proportional to the degree to the degree of user immersion and and belongingness in the metaverse.
- Hypothesis 5. The degree of UGC creation is directly proportional to the degree of user immersion and belongingness in the metaverse.
- Hypothesis 6. The degree of user engagement digital economy is directly proportional to the degree of user immersion and and belongingness in the metaverse.

And considering that users will increase retention and loyalty in the metaverse when immersion and belongingness based on user experience is satisfied, this study therefore proposes Hypothesis 7.

- Hypothesis 7. The degree of user immersion and and belongingness is directly proportional to the degree of user experience in the metaverse.

3 Methods

3.1 Hypothesis and Research Model

Based on the literature and case studies, the user experience model of the metaverse needs to be further validated through quantitative analysis. Based on the main factors of the model, the key to justifying the UX model in this study is to demonstrate the correlation between leisure interaction, UGC creation, and digital economy, their correlation with immersion and belongingness, and the correlation between immersion and belongingness correlation with the degree of experience. Therefore, the specific research model is shown in Fig. 4 below.

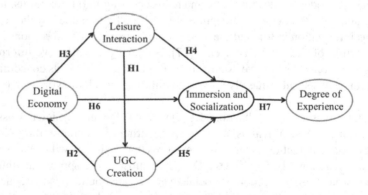

Fig. 4. The Research Model

3.2 Participants and Questionnaire

This study collected data through an online survey. Participants who confirmed experiencing the metaverse were first asked questions about their user experience in the fifteen dimensions of the metaverse. Following this, participants rated the Adaptation About Immunity and Belongingness Scale and provided information about their demographics and experience level. This survey was advertised on several metaverse-related online forums, and 360 volunteers were recruited to participate in this study. This study ultimately yielded 316 valid data. In this study, a questionnaire was designed by reviewing relevant literature and experiences collected from users. All the user experience questions were asked using a five-point Likert scale.

3.3 User Experience Measurement in Metaverse

Based on the proposed conjecture, the user experience degree about the metaverse based on immersion and belongingness is formed as in Table 1.

Table 1. Variables and Measurement Items

Variables	Number	Measurement Items	Number of Questions	Source
Leisure Interaction	LI 1	Break the physical communication barrier	5	Mogaji et al. (2023) [41] Yeh et al. (2011) [42] Cheng (2023) [43]
	LI 2	Experience novel virtual interactions		
	LI 3	Experience virtual world services		
	LI 4	Make new friends		
	LI 5	Create or join metaverse communities		
Digital Economy	DE 1	Have more of a desire to express myself	5	Papagiannidis et al. (2008) [44] Xu et al. (2022) [45] Neustaedter & Fedorovskay (2009) [46]
	DE 2	Expand my fanbase		
	DE 3	Create more personalized works		
	DE 4	Recreate real world works		
	DE 5	Increate my own virtual space		
UGC Creation	UC 1	Gain by creating or managing	5	Xu et al. (2022) [45] Gonzalez-Rodriguezet al. (2021) [47] Zivlak et al. (2020) [48]

(*continued*)

Table 1. (*continued*)

Variables	Number	Measurement Items	Number of Questions	Source
	UC 2	Get rewards for completing system tasks		
	UC 3	Get advertising revenue		
	UC 4	Convert virtual earnings into real earnings		
	UC 5	Complete transactions in the metaverse		
Immersion and Belongingness	IB 1	Feel safe	5	Xiao et al. (2022) [59] Berthon et al. (2019) [50] Zhang et al. (2022) [51]
	IB 2	Want to return to the metaverse when I'm in the real world		
	IB 3	Get more friends into the metaverse		
	IB 4	Don't want to leave the metaverse		
	IB 5	Invest more time in the future		
Degree of Experience	DE 1	Average time spent	3	Raudenbush & Liu (2001) [52]
	DE 2	Average number of times		
	DE 3	Average number of programs		

4   Results

4.1   Descriptive Analysis

In this paper, a total of 316 valid samples were collected to describe and analyze the basic situation of the respondents in terms of gender, age, and education, respectively. Among them, the number of male respondents is much higher than that of females, with 180 people (57%), and the age of respondents is concentrated between 26 to 33 years old (38%) and 34 to 41 years old (32.3%), which may be due to male users in the interval having sufficient interest, time, and financial resources to explore and try the metaverse. In this survey, most respondents have received good education, with 82.3% having a bachelor's degree or above.

4.2   Reliability Analysis

To ensure the validity of the user experience dimension measurement questions, questions with factor loadings below 0.8 were removed. In general, Reliability Analysis (RA) uses Cronbach's Alpha reliability coefficients to check the degree of consistency of the questionnaire study variables across the measurement questions [53]. For a variable to have good reliability, it is generally accepted that Cronbach's Alpha coefficient must be greater than 0.8. As shown in Table 2 below, the Cronbach's Alpha coefficients of the variables are more significant than the criterion of 0.8, which indicates that the variables have good internal consistency reliability.

Table 2. Reliability Analysis

Variable	Cronbach's Alpha	N of Items
Leisure Interaction	0.910	5
Digital Economy	0.913	5
UGC Creation	0.916	5
Immersion and Belongingness	0.906	5
Degree of Experience	0.801	3

4.3 Validation Factor Analysis

To rigorously assess the questionnaire's validity, this study employs AMOS 24.0 to perform a validation factor analysis. This analysis entails an exploratory factor analysis to scrutinize the scale's validity, focusing on evaluating combined reliability (CR) and convergent validity (AVE).

Table 3. Goodness-of-fit Test Results

CMIN	DF	CMIN/DF	IFI	TLI	CFI	RMSEA
278.841	220	1.267	0.988	0.986	0.988	0.029
___	___	< 3	> 0.9	> 0.9	> 0.9	< 0.08

The Table 3 Presented above reveals specific fitness indices for the model. The CMICMIN/DF ratio is calculated at 1.267, falling below the established threshold of 3. Additionally, the indices IFI, TLI, and CFI surpass the stipulated threshold of 0.9, while RMSEA registers at 0.029, well below the 0.08 threshold. These findings collectively align with the typical standards applied in empirical research, suggesting that the model exhibits a satisfactory fit.

As evident in the preceding Table 4, the standardized factor loadings for each measurement surpass the threshold of 0.6 or higher. Furthermore, the component reliabilities (CR) all exceed 0.7, and the average variance extracted (AVE) exceeds 0.5 for each variable [54], affirming the convergent solid validity of all variables under consideration.

Table 4. Convergent Validity Test Results

			Estimate	CR	AVE
LI1	←	LI	0.773	0.912	0.675
LI2	←	LI	0.925		
LI3	←	LI	0.801		
LI4	←	LI	0.785		
LI5	←	LI	0.814		
DE1	←	DE	0.737	0.915	0.683
DE2	←	DE	0.853		
DE3	←	DE	0.768		
DE4	←	DE	0.874		
DE5	←	DE	0.889		
UC1	←	UC	0.774	0.918	0.693
UC2	←	UC	0.756		
UC3	←	UC	0.877		
UC4	←	UC	0.846		
UC5	←	UC	0.900		
IB1	←	IB	0.858	0.908	0.664
IB2	←	IB	0.772		
IB3	←	IB	0.819		
IB4	←	IB	0.780		
IB5	←	IB	0.842		
DOE1	←	DOE	0.725	0.801	0.573
DOE2	←	DOE	0.796		
DOE3	←	DOE	0.748		

4.4 Relevant Analysis

The preceding section established the structure of dimensions and their corresponding questions through a rigorous assessment of validity and reliability. To derive a representative score for each dimension, the average of the scores of its constituent questions was calculated. Subsequently, a correlation analysis was executed. This analysis primarily investigates the interrelationships among the variables, with correlation coefficients ranging from −1 to 1. The magnitude of the absolute value of these coefficients reflects the strength of the associations between the variables.

This study will proceed to examine the correlations between variables in accordance with these criteria. The specific findings are detailed in Table 5 below:

Table 5. Correlations

	Mean	SD	Gender	Age	Education	SLI	SDE	SUC	SIB	SDOE
Gender	1.57	0.496	1							
Age	2.60	0.995	-0.089	1						
Education	2.76	1.109	-0.003	-0.075	1					
SLI	3.4753	1.05097	0.054	-0.030	-0.097	1				
SDE	3.6367	0.84428	.162**	-0.005	-0.031	.502**	1			
SUC	3.7975	1.06404	0.010	-0.029	-0.121	.443**	.499**	1		
SIB	3.7968	0.88220	.155**	-0.032	0.097	.354**	.366**	.367**	1	
SDOE	3.6688	1.03518	0.031	0.053	0.028	.429**	.410**	.410**	.381**	1

**. Correlation is significant at the 0.01 level (2-tailed)

4.5 Structural Equation Model

Structural Equation Modeling (SEM) is a statistical approach that investigates the relationships among variables by examining their covariance matrices, a characteristic that gives rise to the name "covariance structural analysis" [55]. SEM employs a posteriori reasoning to assess the model's viability. It scrutinizes the overall model fit and examines the significance of individual paths within the model after its construction. Subsequently, SEM systematically evaluates the influence of independent variables on the dependent variable, one at a time. This study utilized AMOS 24.0 to execute the calculations using the maximum likelihood method to obtain the following Fig. 5 and Table 6.

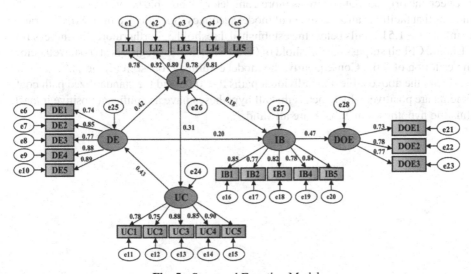

Fig. 5. Structural Equation Model

Model fit is the most critical indicator in structural equation modeling. The fit index is a metric for gauging the extent of congruence between the hypothetical, theoretical

Table 6. Degree of Model Fit

CMIN	DF	CMIN/DF	IFI	TLI	CFI	RMSEA
337.215	223	1.512	0.977	0.973	0.977	0.04
_____	_____	< 3	> 0.9	> 0.9	> 0.9	< 0.08

Table 7. Path Factor

			STD Estimate	Estimate	S.E	C.R	P
IB	< ---	LI	0.184	0.157	0.059	2.68	0.007
IB	< ---	UC	0.218	0.196	0.063	3.127	0.002
IB	< ---	DE	0.201	0.239	0.086	2.764	0.006
DOE	< ---	IB	0.467	0.497	0.072	6.902	***
UC	< ---	LI	0.315	0.298	0.065	4.572	***
DE	< ---	UC	0.433	0.329	0.051	6.51	***
LI	< ---	DE	0.418	0.582	0.093	6.253	***

model, and empirical data. A higher model fit index corresponds to more excellent concordance between the theoretical model and the observed data [56]. The fit index determines whether the designed model is reasonable and can explain the correlation between the original data matrices more completely. The table above presents a set of fit indices that facilitate an assessment of model adequacy. Specifically, the CMIN/DF ratio, computed at 1.512, falls below the established threshold 3. Furthermore, the indices IFI, TLI, and CFI all surpass the threshold of 0.9, while RMSEA registers at 0.04, well below the criterion of 0.08. Consequently, the model exhibits a robust fit (Table 7).

From the above table, the individual paths $P < 0.05$ and the standardized path coefficients are positive, which means that all hypotheses have a significant positive impact, thus the hypotheses in Table 8 are all valid.

Table 8. Verification results of hypotheses.

Hypothesis	Content	Result
Hypothesis 1(H1)	The degree to which users experience leisure interaction is directly proportional to the degree of UGC creation in the metaverse	Valid
Hypothesis 2(H2)	The degree of UGC creation is directly proportional to the degree of user experience digital economy in the metaverse	Valid
Hypothesis 3(H3)	The degree of user experience leisure interaction is directly proportional to the degree of user experience digital economy in the metaverse	Valid
Hypothesis 4(H4)	The degree to which users experience leisure interaction is directly proportional to the degree to the degree of user immersion and and belongingness in the metaverse	Valid
Hypothesis 5(H5)	The degree of UGC creation is directly proportional to the degree of user immersion and belongingness in the metaverse	Valid
Hypothesis 6(H6)	The degree of user engagement digital economy is directly proportional to the degree of user immersion and and belongingness in the metaverse	Valid
Hypothesis 7(H7)	The degree of user immersion and and belongingness is directly proportional to the degree of user experience in the metaverse	Valid

5 Discussion

The social experience in the metaverse is a unique, dynamic experience that evolves with technology and user behavior. It allows users to explore various social interaction, communication, and even commerce possibilities. The metaverse can become a powerful tool for social connection and communication. Therefore, based on UGC creation, digital economy, and leisure interaction as the main elements, which have been proven in H1-H8, the User Experience Factor Model was improved to realize an immersive and belongingness metaverse design cycle, presented in Fig. 6.

Based on the model, it is evident that in addition to the facilitation generated between the elements, users develop loyalty to the metaverse based on higher digital economy participation and leisure interaction experiences. Assembly of users can gain fan traffic based on experience and re-creation. Additional digital economy benefits can also be gained through UGC creation that the system rewards.

Furthermore, the Improved User Experience Factor Model can exist as an overlapping space between the physical and virtual worlds, as shown in Fig. 7. Users can realize the currency exchange with the physical world through the revenue gained from the metaverse and purchase more advanced interface devices for a better interaction experience. In addition, users can also generate a fan economy by gaining a real-world following through content creation. The resulting external economic cycle can be an interactive link between the virtual and the real.

Nevertheless, the optimized research model still has deficiencies that need to be improved in practice. Firstly, the audit of UGC in the two-dimensional world requires

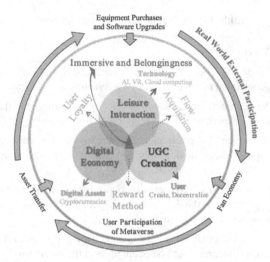

Fig. 6. Improved User Experience Factor Model

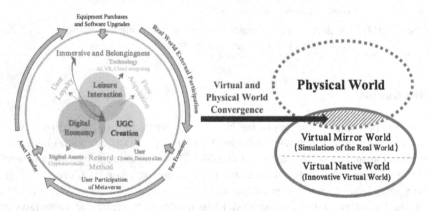

Fig. 7. Virtual and Physical World Convergence

the system to pay a considerable amount of arithmetic power to the extent that some content needs to be manually involved so that the audit difficulty will be further increased in the three-dimensional world. Secondly, certain risk loopholes have led to some countries' resistance to the digital economy in recent years. How to avoid financial risks and establish sound legal rules is a huge challenge. Then, the appropriateness of the content of the user's leisure experience for all people and how to formulate and fulfill the rating restriction policy for teenagers and children is worth considering. Finally, users gain immersion and belongingness in the virtual world, and there is a possibility that psychological problems may arise that need to be solved in cooperation with a more specialized team in addition to the development of rules, such as users' rejection of the physical world or difficulty in distinguishing what constitutes the physical world.

Undoubtedly, the metaverse presents an exciting future worthy of more user participation, but maintaining a favorable environment for participation requires more careful designers.

6 Conclusion

User participation has been shown to be beneficial in developing functional and usable systems [57]. Applying participatory design to the metaverse is working with social and design research methods. Participatory design (PD) has begun to explore ways to help users overcome differences, support mutual learning, and find common ground between participants [58]. Based on the development of a metaverse facilitated by users' Outside-In and Bottom-Up UGC under the theory of Participatory Design, it can form a circular ecology being considered for attracting more users and retaining stable users.

In the virtual world, users prefer more natural and realistic products, while content created by the users themselves will be more favorable to them. Participatory design is a great way to create a metaverse. Technology enterprises hold elevated anticipations regarding the metaverse market, driven by the escalating investments in this domain and the concurrent advancement of cost-effective, high-performance hardware and software infrastructure [41]. Concurrently, consumer-oriented brands are actively vying for their digital assets, responding to a growing demand for experiences that transcend the boundaries of the physical realm. Hence, active engagement with the populace within this platform is pivotal for all stakeholders.

User participation in the design of the metaverse is imperative because it ensures that the virtual environment is aligned with its potential inhabitants' diverse needs, preferences, and expectations. User participation fosters a sense of ownership and empowerment among users, increasing their investment in the metaverse and promoting its long-term success. Ultimately, incorporating user input enhances the metaverse's capacity to serve as a compelling, immersive, and inclusive digital realm that effectively complements the physical world.

The tendency for metaverse development to become oriented towards user participation can also create challenges for user involvement. Defining principles and practices to design a good Metaverse is extremely important. The User Experience Factor Model is to provide a referenceable paradigm for the participatory design of the Metaverse. These exemplary practices serve as the foundational framework for constructing a narrative, fostering interactive dialogue, generating innovative inquiries, and ultimately arriving at the solutions for designing the metaverse as a realm that augments rather than substitutes the physical world.

References

1. Metaverse - Starting with a Customer Immersion Experience. https://www.idc.com/getdoc.jsp?containerId=prCHC49304522
2. Mystakidis, S.: Metaverse. Encyclopedia 2(1), 486–497 (2022)
3. Njoku, J.N., Nwakanma, C.I., Amaizu, G.C., Kim, D.S.: Prospects and challenges of metaverse application in data-driven intelligent transportation systems. IET Intel. Transport Syst. 17(1), 1–21 (2023)

4. Schöbel, S.M., Leimeister, J.M.: Metaverse platform ecosystems. Electron. Mark. **33**(1), 12 (2023)
5. Ning, H., et al.: A survey on the metaverse: the state-of-the-art, technologies, applications, and challenges. IEEE Internet Things J. (2023)
6. Wang, Y., et al.: A survey on metaverse: fundamentals, security, and privacy. IEEE Commun. Surv. Tutorials (2022)
7. Veeraiah, V., Gangavathi, P., Ahamad, S., Talukdar, S.B., Gupta, A., Talukdar, V.: Enhancement of metaverse capabilities by IoT integration. In: 2022 2nd International Conference on Advance Computing and Innovative Technologies in Engineering (ICACITE), IEEE, pp. 1493–1498 (2022)
8. Tikkanen, H., Hietanen, J., Henttonen, T., Rokka, J.: Exploring virtual worlds: success factors in virtual world marketing. Manag. Decis. **47**(8), 1357–1381 (2009)
9. Kohler, T., Fueller, J., Matzler, K., Stieger, D., Füller, J.: Co-creation in virtual worlds: the design of the user experience. MIS Quart. 773–788 (2011)
10. Milgram, P., Takemura, H., Utsumi, A., Kishino, F.: Augmented reality: a class of displays on the reality-virtuality continuum. Telemanipulator Telepresence Technol. **2351**, 282–292 (1995)
11. Bolter, J.D., Engberg, M., MacIntyre, B.: Reality media: augmented and virtual reality. MIT Press (2021)
12. Rejeb, A., Rejeb, K., Treiblmaier, H.: Mapping metaverse research: identifying future research areas based on bibliometric and topic modeling techniques. Information **14**(7), 356 (2023)
13. Kim, J.: Design for experience: where technology meets design and strategy. Springer (2015)
14. Zallio, M., Clarkson, P.J.: Designing the metaverse: a study on inclusion, diversity, equity, accessibility and safety for digital immersive environments. Telematics Inform. **75**, 101909 (2022)
15. Park, J., Kim, N.: Examining self-congruence between user and avatar in purchasing behavior from the metaverse to the real world. J. Global Fashion Market. 1–16 (2023)
16. Allam, Z., Sharifi, A., Bibri, S.E., Jones, D.S., Krogstie, J.: The metaverse as a virtual form of smart cities: opportunities and challenges for environmental, economic, and social sustainability in urban futures. Smart Cities **5**(3), 771–801 (2022)
17. Zytko, D., Chan, J.: The dating metaverse: why we need to design for consent in social VR. IEEE Trans. Visual Comput. Graph. **29**(5), 2489–2498 (2023)
18. de Freitas, S., Rebolledo-Mendez, G., Liarokapis, F., Magoulas, G., Poulovassilis, A.: Developing an evaluation methodology for immersive learning experiences in a virtual world. In 2009 Conference in Games and Virtual Worlds for Serious Applications, IEEE, pp. 43–50 (2009)
19. Cruz-Benito, J., Therón, R., García-Peñalvo, F.J., Lucas, E.P.: Discovering usage behaviors and engagement in an Educational Virtual World. Comput. Hum. Behav. **47**, 18–25 (2015)
20. Duan, H., Huang, Y., Zhao, Y., Huang, Z., Cai, W.: User-generated content and editors in video games: survey and vision. In 2022 IEEE Conference on Games (CoG), IEEE, pp. 536–543 (2022)
21. Daugherty, T., Eastin, M.S., Bright, L.: Exploring consumer motivations for creating user-generated content. J. Interact. Advert. **8**(2), 16–25 (2008)
22. Hisrich, R.D., Soltanifar, M.: Unleashing the creativity of entrepreneurs with digital technologies. Digital Entrepreneurship: Impact Bus. Soc. 23–49 (2021)
23. Volk, D.: Co-creative game development in a participatory metaverse. In Proceedings of the Tenth Anniversary Conference on Participatory Design 2008, pp. 262-265 (2008)
24. What Comparisons Between Second Life and the Metaverse Miss. https://slate.com/techno logy/2022/02/second-life-metaverse-facebook-comparisons.html

25. Obrist, M., Geerts, D., Brandtzæg, P.B., Tscheligi, M.: Design for creating, uploading and sharing user-generated content. In: CHI 2008 Extended Abstracts on Human Factors in Computing Systems, pp. 2391–2394 (2008)
26. Belk, R., Humayun, M., Brouard, M.: Money, possessions, and ownership in the metaverse: NFTs, cryptocurrencies, Web3 and Wild Markets. J. Bus. Res. **153**, 198–205 (2022)
27. Karunarathna, S., Wijethilaka, S., Ranaweera, P., Hemachandra, K.T., Samarasinghe, T., Liyanage, M.: The role of network slicing and edge computing in the metaverse realization. IEEE Access. **11**, 25502–25530 (2023)
28. Goanta, C.: Selling LAND in Decentraland: the regime of non-fungible tokens on the Ethereum blockchain under the digital content directive. Disruptive Technol. Legal Innov. Future Real Estate 139–154 (2020)
29. Carlsson, B.: The Digital Economy: what is new and what is not? Struct. Chang. Econ. Dyn. **15**(3), 245–264 (2004)
30. Yuan, Y., Yang, Y.: Embracing the metaverse: mechanism and logic of a new digital economy. Metaverse **3**(2), 15 (2022)
31. Cheng, X., et al.: Exploring the metaverse in the digital economy: an overview and research framework. J. Electr. Bus. Digital Econ. (ahead-of-print) (2022)
32. Yoo, K., Welden, R., Hewett, K., Haenlein, M.: The merchants of meta: a research agenda to understand the future of retailing in the metaverse. J. Retail. (2023)
33. Ho, A.G., Siu, K.W.M.G.: Emotion design, emotional design, emotionalize design: a review on their relationships from a new perspective. Des. J. **15**(1), 9–32 (2012)
34. Plass, J.L., Kaplan, U.: Emotional design in digital media for learning. In: Emotions, Technology, Design, and Learning, pp. 131–161(2016)
35. Norman, D.A.: Emotional Design: Why We Love (or Hate) Everyday Things. Civitas Books (2004)
36. Lindgaard, G., Dudek, C., Sen, D., Sumegi, L., Noonan, P.: An exploration of relations between visual appeal, trustworthiness and perceived usability of homepages. ACM Trans. Comput.-Hum. Inter. (TOCHI) **18**(1), 1–30 (2011)
37. Kim, E., Tadisina, S.: A model of customers' initial trust in unknown online retailers: an empirical study. Int. J. Bus. Inf. Syst. **6**(4), 419–443 (2010)
38. Pengnate, S.F., Sarathy, R.: An experimental investigation of the influence of website emotional design features on trust in unfamiliar online vendors. Comput. Hum. Behav. **67**, 49–60 (2017)
39. Crumlish, C., Malone, E.: Designing social interfaces: Principles, patterns, and practices for improving the user experience. O'Reilly Media, Inc. (2009)
40. Wang, S., Chen, S., Nah, K.: Exploring the mechanisms influencing users' willingness to pay for green real estate projects in Asia based on technology acceptance modeling theory. Buildings **14**(2), 349 (2024)
41. Mogaji, E., Wirtz, J., Belk, R.W., Dwivedi, Y.K.: Immersive time (ImT): conceptualizing time spent in the metaverse. Int. J. Inf. Manage. **72**, 102659 (2023)
42. Yeh, N.C., Chuan-Chuan Lin, J., Lu, H.P.: The moderating effect of social roles on user behaviour in virtual worlds. Online Inf. Rev. **35**(5), 747–769 (2011)
43. Cheng, S.: Metaverse and Social View. In: Metaverse: Concept, Content and Context, pp. 107–122. Cham: Springer Nature Switzerland (2023)
44. Papagiannidis, S., Bourlakis, M., Li, F.: Making real money in virtual worlds: MMORPGs and emerging business opportunities, challenges and ethical implications in metaverses. Technol. Forecast. Soc. Chang. **75**(5), 610–622 (2008)
45. Xu, M., et al.: A full dive into realizing the edge-enabled metaverse: visions, enabling technologies, and challenges. IEEE Commun. Surv. Tutorials (2022)
46. Neustaedter, C., Fedorovskaya, E.A.: Presenting identity in a virtual world through avatar appearances. Graph. Inter. 183–190 (2009)

47. Gonzalez-Rodriguez, M.R., Diaz-Fernandez, M.C., Bilgihan, A., Shi, F., Okumus, F.: UGC involvement, motivation and personality: comparison between China and Spain. J. Destin. Mark. Manag. **19**, 100543 (2021)
48. Zivlak, N., Zhang, S., Shi, Y.: Digital marketing in China-Weibo and fan economy. In: Industrial Innovation in Digital Age. Cham: Springer International Publishing, pp. 185–192 (2020)
49. Xiao, R., Wu, Z., Hamari, J.: Internet-of-gamification: a review of literature on IoT-enabled gamification for user engagement. Int. J. Hum.-Comput. Inter. **38**(12), 1113–1137 (2022)
50. Berthon, P., Pitt, L., Campbell, C.: Addictive de-vices: a public policy analysis of sources and solutions to digital addiction. J. Public Policy Mark. **38**(4), 451–468 (2019)
51. Zhang, G., Wu, J., Jeon, G., Chen, Y., Wang, Y., Tan, M.: Towards understanding metaverse engagement via social patterns and reward mechanism: a case study of nova empire. IEEE Transact. Comput. Soc. Syst. (2022)
52. Raudenbush, S.W., Liu, X.F.: Effects of study duration, frequency of observation, and sample size on power in studies of group differences in polynomial change. Psychol. Methods **6**(4), 387 (2001)
53. Churchill, G.A., Iacobucci, D.: Marketing research: methodological foundations. New York: Dryden Press. 199, No. 1 (2006)
54. Kamis, A., Saibon, R.A., Yunus, F., Rahim, M.B., Herrera, L.M., Montenegro, P.: The Smart-PLS analyzes approach in validity and reliability of graduate marketability instrument. Soc. Psychol. Educ. **57**(8), 987–1001 (2020)
55. Ullman, J.B., Bentler, P.M.: Structural Equation Modeling. Handbook of Psychology, Second Edition. 2 (2012)
56. Barrett, P.: Structural equation modelling: adjudging model fit. Personality Individ. Differ. **42**(5), 815–824 (2007)
57. Kujala, S.: Effective user involvement in product development by improving the analysis of user needs. Behav. Inf. Technol. **27**(6), 457–473 (2008)
58. Slingerland, G., Murray, M., Lukosch, S., McCarthy, J., Brazier, F.: Participatory design going digital: challenges and opportunities for distributed place-making. Comput. Support. Coop. Work (CSCW) **31**(4), 669–700 (2022)

Research on AR Cultural Heritage Museum Application Design Driven by User Demands

Kexin Yi[1] and Yongkang Chen[2($\boxtimes$)]

[1] Guangzhou Maritime University, Guangzhou 510725, China
[2] College of Design and Innovation, Tongji University, Shanghai 200092, China
ekexin33work@163.com

Abstract. In the context of the extensive integration of cultural heritage digitization and virtual augmented reality (AR) technology development, the purpose is to better promote the inheritance of cultural heritage, meet user needs, and enhance the user experience of AR cultural heritage museum apps. The method employed a user-driven product design approach, conducting a comprehensive study and analysis using Kano, Analytic Hierarchy Process (AHP), and Quality Function Deployment (QFD) methods. Firstly, user requirements were obtained through preliminary research using observation and interviews, and Kano was used for attribute classification. Secondly, AHP was utilized to calculate the weight values of different attributes of user requirements. Thirdly, the QFD method was applied to transform user requirements into quality characteristics and calculate their relative importance. Finally, clear design strategies were proposed based on the results. The results indicate that intuitive high-definition user interfaces, QR code-scanning AR entry points, comprehensive museum tour guides, virtual exhibit animations, and distinguishing modes for AR both inside and outside the museum are relatively important design features that should be prioritized in the design process. In conclusion, this study thoroughly explores user requirements and, based on the analysis of these requirements, maps them into concrete design strategies. The scientifically designed AR cultural heritage museum app provides guidance and valuable insights for subsequent related design research.

Keywords: User demands driven · Cultural Heritage · Augmented Reality · Museum · Application Design

1 Introduction

Cultural heritage digitization and dissemination, hereafter referred to as cultural heritage (CH) digital dissemination, have been widely recognized as a global trend. Augmented Reality (AR) technology enhances user experiences by overlaying computer-generated information onto the real environment [1]. Users can immerse themselves in cultural artifacts and heritage in a novel way [2], making AR widely applicable in the field of CH [3]. Moreover, numerous studies have confirmed the effectiveness of AR in disseminating CH [4–6]. For CH museums, touch-based interaction plays a crucial role in engaging users with historical artifacts [7]. Currently, an increasing number of CH museums in China are promoting and supporting users to download applications on mobile electronic devices to experience AR. Although this enhances the digital display and interactivity of museums to some extent, such applications (hereafter referred to as apps) also face several issues. These include a heavy focus on improving navigation systems and developing cultural and creative products [8], often from the perspective of CH institutions themselves and relying on qualitative research methods, while lacking user-centered qualitative and quantitative comprehensive studies. Therefore, applying a user-driven approach to the design and research of AR CH museum apps holds significant practical significance for enhancing CH visiting experiences and promoting the widespread adoption of AR technology in museum apps.

2 Research Method

User-driven innovation refers to a type of driving force in innovative design, primarily focusing on utilizing user needs as the primary driver for product innovation [9]. The Kano model, hereafter referred to as Kano, is a tool that captures the nonlinear relationship between product performance and user satisfaction based on user feedback [10]. While this model emphasizes methods for classifying product quality attributes and qualitative descriptions, it does not explicitly specify the priority order of satisfaction and importance of quality attributes within the same category [11]. Hence, it is necessary to combine other methods or tools to comprehensively understand and evaluate the depth and priority of user needs. Analytic Hierarchy Process (AHP) is a multi-criteria decision-making analysis method that assigns weight indices to each requirement by scoring the decision-making process, aiding in determining priorities and making optimal decisions [12]. After applying Kano to classify user requirements, AHP is utilized to analyze the weights of these requirements to ensure that the weight calculation of each requirement accurately reflects its relative importance in the overall user requirements structure. However, the combination of Kano and AHP still cannot address the specific issue of obtaining design features related to design suggestions and user needs. Quality Function Deployment (QFD) is a quantitative research method for quality management and product development that translates customer needs into specific features of products or services [13]. The user satisfaction model of Kano can be optimized and combined with QFD to obtain design features. The prerequisite for combining Kano and QFD is to determine the hierarchical structure and priorities of user requirements in advance [14]. Therefore, the comprehensive research method combining Kano, AHP, and QFD helps ensure that the design process fully considers user expectations, identifies key design features, aids in rational product solution decisions, and ensures the scientific integrity of the development process. This study will adopt the combined research method of Kano, AHP, and QFD to conduct qualitative and quantitative user requirement studies, proposing scientifically sound design strategies for AR CH museum apps. The design method process is illustrated in Fig. 1.

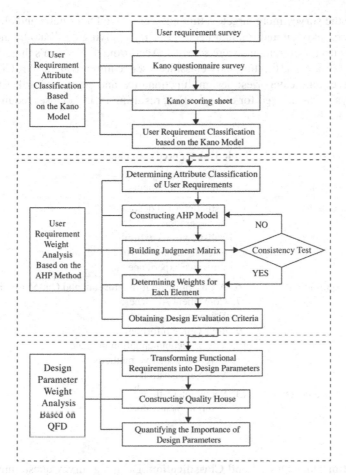

Fig. 1. Integrated KANO-AHP-QFD design process

3 Combining Kano-AHP-QFD in the Design Research Process of AR CH Museum Apps

3.1 User Requirement Classification Based on Kano

Acquisition of User Requirements. User requirements were acquired through desktop research, surveys, and in-depth user interviews. In this study, data from 65 individuals who had used AR applications related to CH were randomly sampled for analysis and statistics. It was found that the main audience consisted of young people who were eager to experience new things and had a strong interest in CH and virtual digital technology, making them potential primary users. Therefore, this study targeted young people aged 18 to 35 who frequently visit such museums. This group exhibited the following characteristics: (1) a strong interest in CH learning, with an average frequency of visiting offline museums of no less than once a week, indicating high visitation rates; (2) experience with AR CH applications and a willingness to engage with virtual digital technology.

To make the survey more targeted, this study employed interviews and observations to obtain users' explicit and implicit needs [15]. By applying the Kano method to user research, key user requirements were selected. According to Norman's three-level hierarchy theory of needs [16], this study classified user requirements for AR CH museum apps into three main categories: design, functionality, and emotion. Furthermore, card sorting analysis was utilized for classification, resulting in 14 key user requirements as shown in Table 1.

Table 1. User need extraction

Experience Element	Emotional Requirements
Design Requirements	1. Aesthetic visual design 2. Easy operation 3. Realistic virtual exhibits 4. Dynamic display of virtual exhibits 5. Immersive experience
Functional Requirements	6. AR usability both In-Museum and Out-Museum (O3) 7. Convenient AR access 8. Voice explanations 9. Tour Guide Information 10. Visitor recommendation guidance 11. Diverse interactive methods 12. Video explanations
Emotional Requirements	13. Social interaction 14. Entertainment value

Kano Questionnaire Design and Classification. Design a survey questionnaire based on the identified key user requirements. The questionnaire follows the Likert 5-level format, with questions posed in both positive and negative directions, as shown in Table 2. Based on the questionnaire results, refer to the Kano evaluation criteria, as shown in Table 3. This model categorizes product and service quality characteristics into different types, such as Must-Be Quality (M), Attractive Quality (A), Indifferent Quality (I), Reverse Quality (R), and One-Dimensional Quality(O). User requirements are classified according to the Kano model's attribute division.

Analysis of Kano Questionnaire Results. A total of 119 questionnaires were distributed in this survey, targeting young people aged 18 to 35 who had experienced AR CH museum applications. A total of 110 valid questionnaires were collected. The captured user requirements were analyzed using the SPSS statistical analysis tool and classified into different requirement attributes, as shown in Table 4. Among these 14 requirements, each corresponds to one of the four Kano orientations: Must-be (M), One-dimensional (O), Attractive (A), and Indifferent (I). Requirements numbered 10 and 12 were classified as Indifferent (I), indicating that whether these two requirements are met or not will not

Table 2. KANO level 5 likert questionnaire

If this requirement is met, your attitude is (Positive)						If this requirement is not met, your attitude is (Negative)				
5	4	3	2	1	User Requirements for AR CH Museum Applications	5	4	3	2	1
					Easy operation Realistic Virtual Exhibits Dynamic Display of Virtual Exhibits Immersive Experience AR usability both In-Museum and Out-Museum Convenient AR access Voice explanations					

Table 3. Table of KANO evaluation

Positive Statement		Negative Statement				
		Not at all dissatisfied (5)	Slightly dissatisfied (4)	Moderately dissatisfied (3)	Very dissatisfied (2)	Extremely dissatisfied (1)
	Extremely satisfied (5)	Q	A	A	A	O
	Very satisfied (4)	R	I	I	I	M
	Moderately satisfied (3)	R	I	I	I	M
	Slightly satisfied (2)	R	I	I	I	M
	Not at all satisfied (1)	R	R	R	R	Q

significantly affect users. Therefore, these two types of user demands will not appear in the subsequent design process.

There are three Must-be attributes: Easy operation, Convenient AR access, and Tour guide information. Failure to meet these requirements would result in significant dissatisfaction, but meeting them would not increase satisfaction. Therefore, they should be satisfied but do not need to be excessively optimized. There are four One-dimensional attributes: AR usability both indoors and outdoors, Authentic virtual exhibit effects, Attractive visual design, and Voice explanations. Meeting these expectations will not cause surprise to users, but failing to meet them will lead to dissatisfaction. Therefore, efforts should be made to meet these requirements as much as possible to improve user satisfaction. There are five Attractive attributes: Dynamic display of virtual exhibits, Entertainment value, Immersive experience, Diverse interactive methods, and Social interaction. Emphasizing these features in the design can not only exceed user expectations but also create a more satisfying and enjoyable virtual exhibition experience. Therefore, they should be given special consideration in the design process.

Table 4. KANO Questionnaire Results Analysis

Demand Number	Percentage(%)						Kano Positioning	Better Coefficient	Worse Coefficient
	A	O	M	I	R	Q			
1	13.3	41.6	35.0	10.0	0.0	0.0	O	55.0	−76.6
2	0.0	0.0	63.3	20.0	3.3	13.3	M	0.0	−76.0
3	23.3	30.0	26.6	15.0	1.6	3.3	O	56.1	−59.6
4	55.0	0.0	0.0	21.6	20.0	3.3	A	71.7	−0.0
5	53.3	8.3	5.0	33.3	0.0	0.0	A	61.6	−13.3
6	23.3	35.0	25.0	16.6	0.0	0.0	O	58.3	−60.0
7	0.0	0.0	46.6	23.3	3.3	26.6	M	0.0	−66.6
8	11.6	35.0	28.3	25.0	0.0	0.0	O	46.6	−63.3
9	0.0	0.0	51.6	21.6	6.6	20.0	M	0.0	−70.4
10	0.0	0.0	0.0	50.0	46.6	3.3	I	0.0	−0.0
11	50.0	0.0	0.0	36.6	13.3	0.0	A	57.6	−0.0
12	0.0	0.0	0.0	61.6	38.3	0.0	I	0.0	−0.0
13	41.6	0.0	0.0	40.0	16.6	1.6	A	51.0	−0.0
14	48.3	0.0	0.0	23.3	23.3	5.0	A	67.4	−0.0

3.2 Based on AHP, User Requirement Weight Calculation and Analysis

To clarify the priority of each requirement, a structured decision framework was generated using AHP based on the Kano analysis results, systematizing user requirements and conducting hierarchical decomposition at different levels, and finally obtaining weight values through quantitative calculations [17]。

Construction of AHP Model. Based on the analysis results of the positional attributes of user requirements for AR CH museum applications in Table 4, the overall objective layer of the Analytic Hierarchy Process (AHP) model was determined, which is the design scheme. The criteria layer includes the Kano attributes: Must-be attributes (M), One-dimensional attributes (O), and Attractive attributes (A). The sub-criteria layer involves the decomposition of user requirements, totaling 12 aspects. Thus, the AHP model was constructed, as shown in Fig. 2.

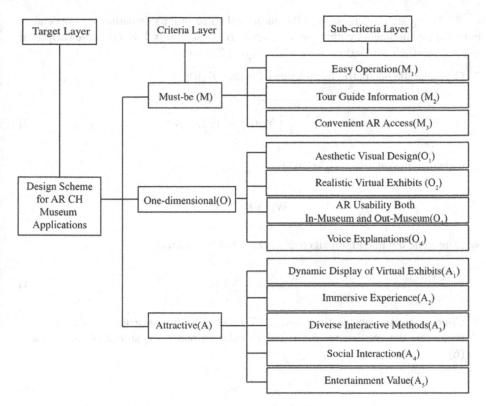

Fig. 2. Hierarchical Analysis Model of AR CH Museum App

Calculation of User Requirement Weights. To ensure the professionalism and usability of the weight results, 12 experts related to the design of AR CH museums were invited to fill out the AHP questionnaire. The construction of the expert judgment matrix involved 3 professors specializing in interaction design, 2 professors specializing in CH, 3 interaction designers, 2 AR designers, and 2 museum staff members. Experts compared and scored the importance of each level of requirement in pairs using a 1–9 scale, and the arithmetic mean was used as the basis for weight calculation, thus obtaining judgment matrices for each level. The geometric mean method was used to calculate the weight coefficients for each level, and the final weights of user requirements were obtained. The weighted results are calculated as follows:

1. Construction of judgment matrices

$$Y = \left(y_{ij}\right)_{n\times m} = \begin{bmatrix} y_{11} & y_{12} & \cdots & y_{1n} \\ y_{21} & y_{22} & \cdots & y_{2n} \\ \vdots & \vdots & \ddots & \vdots \\ y_{n1} & y_{n2} & \cdots & y_{nm} \end{bmatrix} \tag{1}$$

In the equation, y_{ij} represents the numerical value of the comparison of importance between two indicators within the same level. Because matrix Y is a positive reciprocal matrix, $y_{ij} > 0$, yii $= 1$, and $y_{ij} \cdot y_{ji} = 1$, where($i, j=1, 2, \cdots, n$).

2. Calculate the geometric mean value of matrix Y (ti):

$$t_i = \sqrt[n]{\prod_{i}^{n} Y_{ij}} (i, j = 1, 2, ..., n) \tag{2}$$

3. Calculate the relative weights(W_i):

$$W_i = t_i / \sum_{i=1}^{n} t_i \tag{3}$$

4. Determine the maximum eigenvalue (λ_{max}) of the matrix:

$$\lambda_{max} = \frac{1}{n} \sum_{i=1}^{n} \frac{Y_{Wi}}{W_i} \tag{4}$$

5. Conduct consistency testing, where CI represents the consistency index and CR represents the consistency ratio. The calculation method is shown in Eqs. (5) and (6).

$$I_{CI} = \frac{\lambda_{max} - n}{n - 1} \tag{5}$$

$$I_{CR} = \frac{I_{CL}}{I_{CR}} \tag{6}$$

Usually, if ICR ≤ 0.1, the consistency test is considered passed. If not, the judgment matrix must be reconstructed. The results show that all ICR values are less than 0.1, meeting the consistency test criteria, as shown in Tables 5 and 6. Based on the calculation results in Table 5, it can be seen that the design of AR CH museum apps should not only meet the essential requirements such as easy operation, convenient AR access, and tour guide information but also focus on the top-ranked expectations and attractive requirements, such as authentic virtual exhibit effects, dynamic display of virtual exhibits, and attractive visual design.

Table 5. Criterion level weight

Main Indicators	M	O	A	Weight Value	I_{CR}
M	1	2	3	0.5390	0.0088
O	1/2	1	2	0.2973	
A	1/3	1/2	1	0.1638	

Table 6. Sub-criterion level weight

Primary Indicator	Secondary Indicator	Judgment Matrix					Weight	Relative Weight	I_{CR}
Must-be (M)	Easy Operation(M_1)	1	3	2	x	x	0.5390	0.2905	0.0088
	Easy Operation(M_1)	1	3	2	x	x	0.5390	0.2905	
	Convenient AR Access (M_3)	1/2	2	1	x	x	0.2973	0.1602	
One-dimensional (O)	Aesthetic Visual Design (O_1)	1	1/2	2	3	x	0.2727	0.0810	0.0558
	Realistic Virtual Exhibits (O2)	2	1	3	4	x	0.4569	0.1358	
	AR Usability Both In-Museum and Out-Museum (O_3)	1/2	1/2	1	2	x	0.1766	0.0525	
	Voice Explanations (O_4)	1/3	1/4	1/2	1	x	0.0937	0.0278	
Attractive (A)	Dynamic Display of Virtual-Exhibits (A_1)	1	2	3	5	3	0.4188	0.0685	0.0137
	Immersive Experience (A_2)	1/2	1	1/2	4	2	0.2155	0.0352	
	Diverse Interactive Methods (A_3)	1/5	1/4	1/2	1	1/3	0.0660	0.0108	
	Social Interaction (A_4)	1/3	1/2	1	2	1/2	0.1216	0.0199	
	Entertainment Value (A_5)	1/3	1/2	2	3	1	0.1781	0.0291	

3.3 Design Feature Analysis Based on QFD Method

QFD is an essential method in the product design process for realizing the transformation of requirements. Constructing a House of Quality (HOQ) model is the core tool of the QFD method. Obtaining the relative importance of design requirements through the construction of the HOQ model is a crucial prerequisite [18]. After determining the weight values of each user requirement and the overall weight value through AHP, it is necessary to transform them into design features using the QFD method and ultimately calculate the weights of design elements.

Conversion of User Requirements into Design Characteristics. In the application of QFD, design characteristics are crucial components in constructing the House of Quality model. Therefore, before using QFD, it is necessary to transform user requirements into specific design characteristics. This study will utilize a combination of literature review and case analysis methods to obtain more scientifically reasonable design characteristics.

Firstly, through the method of literature review, a large amount of relevant literature and materials will be consulted to preliminarily obtain design characteristics. For example, Tang et al. [19] combined paper-based books of Cantonese furniture with AR applications using two browsing modes, namely, three-dimensional models and video animations. Xu et al. [7] designed postcard AR and CubeMuseum AR based on the characteristics of cultural relics in CH museums, and these applications had a positive impact on users' motivation and participation in learning CH through gamified AR interfaces. Cecilia Maria et al. [20] provided visual comparisons of different periods of CH park sites in Milan, Italy, through holographic AR stereoscopic images, facilitating interactive exploration of CH sites. Paliokas et al. [21] implemented various features such as virtual projection marking of artifacts, treasure hunting games, and completion of visiting quizzes in AR museum applications to encourage visitors to spend more time interacting with the exhibits.

Secondly, the case analysis method will be employed to select the top ten AR CH museum apps in mobile app stores for comparison and analysis. For instance, the German Ceramic Museum utilizes AR to display artifacts with subtle animations and dynamic maps for artifact exploration. AR-T Museum motivates visitors to scan world-famous paintings into their living scenes using AR technology. The Jiaozuo Museum designs games based on different venue characteristics and promotes user interaction through panoramic immersive AR mode. Detailed analysis is shown in Table 7.

Finally, to ensure the inferred design characteristics are objective, authoritative, and comprehensive, the Delphi method will be used on the basis of literature review and case analysis. Two professors specializing in interactive design, five interactive designers, and four professors in the CH field will be invited to provide feedback on the inferred design characteristics. Through three rounds of expert interviews, the design characteristics will be organized and summarized until consensus among experts is reached, achieving theoretical saturation. The final confirmed design characteristics are presented in Table 8.

Building the House of Quality. After extracting the design features, it is necessary to establish the House of Quality to clarify the weights and priorities of each parameter. The House of Quality provides a more intuitive and precise method to express the relationship between user requirements and design elements, thereby prioritizing the design elements [22]. As shown in Table 8, among the 12 requirements and 11 design elements of the AR CH museum app, each requirement is compared with each design element and represented by symbols: ● indicates strong correlation, ◎ indicates moderate correlation, △ indicates weak correlation, and blank indicates no correlation, corresponding to values of 1.5, 1.2, 1, and 0, respectively.

The various user requirements from Table 6 along with their respective combined weight values are imported into the left wall of the House of Quality (for ease of calculation, the values are multiplied by 10 and rounded to two decimal places); the design features extracted based on user requirements as shown in Table 8 are imported into the ceiling to complete the construction of the House of Quality. Subsequently, five interaction designers with over five years of experience are once again invited to fill in symbols

Table 7. AR CH Museum Case: Requirements Analysis and Design Features

App Icon	Museum	User Requirements	Design Features
	Heikantien Museum	① Fun Guided Tour② Intuitive and Clear Interface ③ Immersive Browsing	① Dynamic Interface② AR Exhibit Animation Display
	Jiaozuo Museum	① Immersive Virtual Experience② AR Experience in Different Scenes③ Regional Feature Design ④ Educational and Interactive	① In-museum and Off-museum Modes ② Panoramic Virtual Museum Interface ③ Guided Tour with Games
	Shanghai Museum	① AR Experience in Different Scenes② Real-world Guidance③ Detailed Artifact Display	① AR Experience and Direct Browsing Modes ② Panoramic 3D Exhibition Display③ 3D Structural Exhibition Videos
	Russian Museum	① Clear Guided Tour② Visit Guidance	① Recommended Guided Tour② AR Operation Guidance
	Macau Museum	① Multiple Guided Tour Modes② Self-guided Tour	AR, VR, QR Tour Modes
	National Palace Museum, Taipei	① Emphasis on Learning Experience② Easy Operation	① Random Quiz Setup ② AR Operation Guidance
	Sichuan Museum	① Simple Interface ② Easy AR Operation Control③ Scene Animation	① AR Animation Display② Single Main Interface
	Comprehensive Museum Platform	Getting Close to World Famous Paintings	AR Application Integrated into Daily Life Scenes
	Kaifeng Museum	① Integration of Display and Interactive Functions② Historical Environment Restoration ③ Immersive Experience of Song Dynasty Tea Culture	① Real-world Scanning ② Panoramic Virtual Immersive Game Interaction
	Comprehensive Museum Platform	① Compatible with Multiple Museums② Visit Guidance	Comprehensive Guided Tour Guidance

to assess the correlation, thus establishing the correlation matrix of the House of Quality, as illustrated in Fig. 3.

Design Feature Weight Calculation and Analysis. By assessing the correlation between user requirements and design features, corresponding weights of secondary indicators can be obtained. Using the symbol F_j to represent the importance of design features, W_i to represent the weight value of the i th user requirement, and R_{ij} to represent the strength of the relationship between them. The calculation of this relationship strength follows the formula (7) as follows:

$$F_j = \sum_{i=1}^{n} W_i \times R_{ij} (i, j = 1, 2, ..., n) \qquad (7)$$

Table 8. Mapping of User Requirements to Design Parameters

Category	Number	User Requirement	Design Parameter
Design	O_1	Aesthetic Visual Design	Consistent Design Style and Theme (DP_1)
	M_1	Easy Operation	Intuitive and High Definition User Interface (DP_2)
	O_2	Realistic Virtual Exhibits	
	A_1	Dynamic Display of Virtual Exhibits	Dynamic Presentation of Virtual Exhibits (DP_3)
	A_2	Immersive Experience	Panoramic Scene Design (DP_4)
Functional	O_3	AR Usability Both In-Museum and Out-Museum	In-Museum and Out-Museum AR Mode Differentiation (DP_5)
	M_3	Convenient AR Access	QR Code Scanning for AR Access (DP_6)
	O_4	Audio Guide	Audio Guide (DP_7)
	M_2	Tour Guide Information	Comprehensive Tour Guide (DP_8)
	A_3	Diverse Interactive Methods(	Various Interaction Methods (DP_9)
Emotional	A_4	Social Interaction	Social Media Sharing and Posting Functionality (DP_{10})
	A_5	Entertainment Value	AR Interactive Game for Fun (DP_{11})

The calculated design feature weight values are normalized, and the priority ranking of design features is shown in Fig. 4. From Fig. 4, it is evident that DP2, DP6, and DP8 should be prioritized as Must-be Quality. DP3 and DP5 perform well in user experience and functional implementation, making them key design features for AR CH museum apps. Therefore, continuous reinforcement and optimization should be carried out in subsequent designs. Additionally, DP1, DP4, DP11, and DP7 also have relatively high scores, indicating their importance in overall user satisfaction and system functionality. Hence, they require careful consideration and attention during the design process. Although DP10 and DP9 have lower scores, their potential value and importance should not be overlooked. Further analysis of the limitations and potential optimization points of these features may be necessary to ensure comprehensive and holistic design.

4   User-Driven Design Strategies for AR CH Museum Apps

Based on the conclusions drawn from the methods mentioned above, the design strategies for AR CH museum apps are outlined as follows:

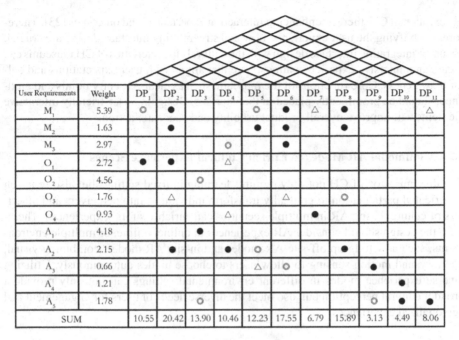

User Requirements	Weight	DP₁	DP₂	DP₃	DP₄	DP₅	DP₆	DP₇	DP₈	DP₉	DP₁₀	DP₁₁
M_1	5.39	○	●			○	●	△	●			△
M_2	1.63		●			●	●		●			
M_3	2.97				○		●					
O_1	2.72	●	●		△							
O_2	4.56			○								
O_3	1.76		△				△		○			
O_4	0.93				△			●				
A_1	4.18			●								
A_2	2.15		●		●	○			●			
A_3	0.66					△	○			●		
A_4	1.21										●	
A_5	1.78			○						○	●	●
SUM		10.55	20.42	13.90	10.46	12.23	17.55	6.79	15.89	3.13	4.49	8.06

Fig. 3. Quality House

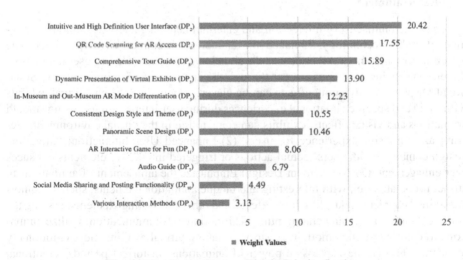

Fig. 4. User Design Feature Weight Priority Sorting

4.1 Streamline Interface Interaction, Emphasize Core Functions

The product interface serves as the primary means through which users experience the product. A clear interface navigation in AR applications contributes to users' understanding of the interface, their tasks, and fosters embodied experiences and reflective observation of CH, thereby enhancing interaction experiences and outcomes [23]. Therefore, simplifying the user experience flow and streamlining interface design are crucial. Visually, integrating interface design with the cultural characteristics of CH museums can create an immersive experience atmosphere that aligns with user expectations and cultural awareness. Core functions of the museum, such as clear AR entry points and guidance, should be prominently placed in the interface. Designing user-friendly interactive elements will improve overall product usability and user satisfaction.

4.2 Multimodal AR Modes to Enrich Cultural Experience Scenes

The dissemination of CH not only requires learning in fixed settings but also relies on experiential participation to gradually transform individuals into perceivers and inheritors of culture. Using AR in multiple scenarios can enrich visitors' experiences. Therefore, the design should consider AR experiences in online, offline, or multiple environments, such as setting up off-site AR modes and in-site AR modes, combining visual, auditory, and motion sensing to allow users to choose modes autonomously. Utilizing diverse experience modes in different environmental settings can not only provide a broader cultural perception but also meet the diverse needs of users for engagement and personalized experiences.

4.3 Strengthening Exhibit Interaction and AR Animation to Enhance Entertainment

Leverage the multisensory interaction and entertainment characteristics unique to augmented reality technology. Enhance the animation design of virtual exhibits. The dynamic presentation of AR enhances the situational awareness during user interaction, thereby enhancing user engagement through the amusement of animations. (1) Situational Display: AR dynamic effects can be cleverly applied to present virtual exhibits with vivid and specific situational experiences during user interaction. By using smooth animations and visual effects, exhibits can come to life in the virtual environment, creating an immersive experience for users. (2) Enhanced User Interaction: Animation design combined with users' actual actions or triggered interactive elements enhances user engagement. (3) Amusement Design: Emphasize the amusement of animations to attract users' attention with interesting and unique animation elements, such as humorous animal characters, dazzling light effects, and other captivating elements, making the entire exhibition lively and entertaining. (4) Emotional Communication: Utilize animations to convey specific emotions or stories, making virtual exhibits more emotionally resonant. Through the expressive power of animations, historical periods' emotional atmosphere can be portrayed, or the stories behind cultures can be presented, prompting audience reflection and emotional resonance.

4.4 Immersive Panoramic Design to Deepen Cultural Experiences

The unique immersive experience provided by AR technology can give participants a sense of presence, as if they are placed in historical cultural scenes. Therefore, AR CH museum apps should focus on embodying immersion. (1) Panoramic Gaming Interface: Expand the perception range of cultural experiences by combining panoramic gaming interfaces with virtual reality technology, achieving profound emotional resonance. By cleverly integrating AR interactive gaming elements into cultural historical scenes, participants can immerse themselves. By presenting virtual reproductions of historical events or figures, participants can experience and understand the rich connotations of culture. (2) Combination of Reality and Virtuality to Stimulate Exploration Desire: Utilize AR technology to hide puzzles, treasure hunts, or puzzle-solving elements in the exhibition space to stimulate participants' desire for exploration. By completing tasks or challenges, participants can not only gain deeper insights into the cultural representations of exhibits but also experience the vividness of history through interaction.

4.5 Implement Feedback Mechanisms to Enhance Interaction Experience

To further enhance user interaction experience, the design should consider introducing effective feedback mechanisms. By establishing immediate and emotionally rich feedback systems and introducing various interaction methods, the user's interaction experience with the AR CH museum app can be enhanced. (1) Immediate Guidance and Rewards: Timely guidance and reward mechanisms during user interaction can enhance user motivation. For example, when users successfully complete a task or unlock specific information, positive feedback can be provided promptly through animations, sound effects, or text prompts, along with corresponding rewards such as virtual medals or achievement badges, to stimulate users' learning interests. (2) Emotional Feedback Design: Consider introducing emotional feedback design to convey emotions through virtual characters, expressions, or sounds, allowing users to experience a richer immersive experience. For example, when users interact with virtual exhibits, the exhibits can convey emotions such as joy or surprise through expressions or sounds, enhancing users' emotional resonance.

5 Conclusion

This study, based on a user-centered design philosophy, adopted a comprehensive model of user-driven design methods to derive feasible solutions for AR CH museum apps by classifying and weighting user needs attributes and prioritizing design elements. The design method integrated Kano, AHP, and QFD methods for qualitative and quantitative research, possessing advantages of comprehensive systematic and scientific nature compared to single research methods. This method not only guided precise decision-making centered around users but also provided research and reference value for design strategies in related fields.

References

1. Aggarwal, R., Singhal, A.: Augmented Reality and its effect on our life[C].2019 9th International Conference on Cloud Computing, Data Science & Engineering (Confluence). IEEE, pp. 510–515 (2019)

2. Bekele, M.K., Pierdicca, R., Frontoni, E., Malinverni, E.S., Gain, J.: A survey of augmented, virtual, and mixed reality for cultural heritage. J. Comput. Cult. Heritage (JOCCH) **11**(2), 1–36 (2018)
3. Boboc, R.G., Băutu, E., Gîrbacia, F., Popovici, N., Popovici, D.M.: Augmented reality in cultural heritage: an overview of the last decade of applications. Appl. Sci. **12**(19), 9859 (2022)
4. Pedersen, I., Gale, N., Mirza-Babaei, P., Reid, S.: More than meets the eye: the benefits of augmented reality and holographic displays for digital cultural heritage. J. Comput. Cult. Heritage (JOCCH) **10**(2), 1–15 (2017)
5. Okanovic, V., et al.: Interaction in extended reality applications for cultural heritage. Appl. Sci. **12**(3), 1241 (2022)
6. Bachiller, C., Monzo, J.M., Rey, B.: Augmented and virtual reality to enhance the didactical experience of technological heritage museums. Appl. Sci. **13**(6), 3539 (2023)
7. Xu, N., Li, Y., Wei, X., Xie, L., Yu, L., Liang, H.N.: Cubemuseum Ar: a tangible augmented reality interface for cultural heritage learning and museum gifting. Int. J. Hum.–Comput. Inter. 1–29 (2023)
8. Hu W.Y.: Research on Digital Display Design of Cultural Heritage Based on Augmented Reality-Taking Shandong Museum as an Example. Shandong University (2020). (in Chinese)
9. Hu J., Chen Source, Operating Mechanism, and Evaluation of Innovative Design. Packag. Eng. **41**(18), 60–70 (2020). (in Chinese)
10. Xu, Q., Jiao, R.J., Yang, X., Helander, M., Khalid, H.M., Opperud, A.: An analytical Kano model for customer need analysis. Des. Stud. **30**(1), 87–110 (2009)
11. Zhang, D.J., Hou, Z.X., Huang, L., Zhao, Y.H.: Research on the product demands configuration method based on user satisfaction. J. Graph. **41**(4), 649 (2020). (in Chinese)
12. Nukman, Y., Ariff, H., Salit M.: Use of analytical hierarchy process (AHP) for selecting the best design concept. J. Teknol. **49**(A), 1–18 (2009)
13. Herrmann, A., Huber, F., Braunstein, C.: Market-driven product and service design: bridging the gap between customer needs, quality management, and customer satisfaction. Int. J. Prod. Econ. **66**(1), 77–96 (2000)
14. Griffin, A., Hauser, J.R.: The voice of the customer. Mark. Sci. **12**(1), 1–27 (1993)
15. Wang, Y.F.: Observation And Interviewing Method In User Research.Wuhan University of Technology (2009). (in Chinese)
16. Norman, D.A.: Design psychology 3: emotional design. Xiaomei He, Qiuxing Ou, Zhongxin Edition Group **84** (2015)
17. Li, R., Chau, K., Zeng, F.: Ranking of risks for existing and new building works. Sustainability **11**(10), 2863 [Z] (2019)
18. Li, H., Wang, S.Y., Li, J.L.: Research on human-machine interface evaluation method based on QFD-PUGH. J. Graph. **42**(6), 1043 (2022). (in Chinese)
19. Tang, X.Y., Ou, X.L., Xie, D.N.: Design application and research of "museum on paper" of Cantonese furniture based on AR technology. Packag. Eng. **39**(4), 115–122 (2018). (in Chinese)
20. Bolognesi, C.M., Sorrenti, D., Bassorizzi, D.: Utilizing stereography to compare cultural heritage in the past and now: an interactive AR application. Appl. Sci. **13**(15), 8773 (2023)
21. Paliokas, I., et al.: A gamified augmented reality application for digital heritage and tourism. Appl. Sci. **10**(21), 7868 (2020)
22. Hauser, J.R., Clausing, D.: The House of Quality (1988)
23. Wang, M., Tan, P., Ji, Y.: Interaction design of cultural heritage type augmented reality application based on experiential learning theory. Packag. Eng. **42**(4), 97–102 (2021). (in Chinese)

Technology, Art, and Culture

Studying the Usability of the Yunlin Puppet Theater Website

Hsiu-Ching Laura Hsieh and Tsu-Chi Shen[✉]

National Yunlin University of Science and Technology, 123 University Road, Section 3, Douliou, Yunlin 64002, Taiwan, R.O.C.
laurarun@yuntech.edu.tw, chenzuqi21@gmail.com

Abstract. Puppetry is part of Taiwan's rich cultural heritage. Passed down from generation to generation, it has become a performing art form that carries historical, religious, and traditional values. Yunlin Puppetry Theater is located in the birthplace of puppetry, and it is an important venue for inheriting puppetry culture. The theater's website contains articles and photos documenting the history of puppetry culture and this venue. Puppetry is facing a transformation and is expected to become more aligned with modern trends. From traditional stages to online platforms, website usability will be the key to understanding and promoting puppetry and its venues. However, there is currently no review of existing Yunlin puppetry. Drama culture should conduct usability research on the website.

This study aims to: 1) test the usability of the existing Yunlin Puppet Show website using the SUS (System Usability Scale) and interview data; 2) analyze the website's usability based on the results; 3) propose a design basis for modifying the website based on the test results.

This study's research methods were as follows: 1) collecting information on the Yunlin Puppet Theater website; 2) recruiting users to participate in the test; 3) collecting user feedback and making recommendations for improvement.

This research aims to improve the usability of the Yunlin Puppet theater website. Through this usability test, we can provide people with a better user experience and enable them to visit the physical venue after browsing the website. To gain a deeper understanding of how various age groups utilize this website, we will expand the collection of user feedback. We expect that design researchers and government departments can continue to optimize the website based on the user feedback recommendation from this study to enhance the user experience.

Keywords: usability · website · puppet show · Yunlin Puppet Theater

1 Introduction

Puppet theater has a long history and rich artistic value. In recent decades, puppet theater has become a traditional art form and a symbol of Taiwanese culture and identity (Huwei's Puppet Theater Heritage, 2023; Wang & Tseng, 2023). Yunlin is considered the birthplace of puppet theater (Huwei's Puppet Theater Heritage, 2023). Yunlin Puppet Theater is Taiwan's puppet theater-themed venue. Establishing Yunlin Puppet Theater

M. Rauterberg (Ed.): HCII 2024, LNCS 14717, pp. 137–149, 2024.
https://doi.org/10.1007/978-3-031-61147-6_10

was a major milestone regarding Taiwan's cultural preservation. The Yunlin Puppet Theater regularly holds several related activities and is essential for promoting the puppet theater. A website with sufficient information has been established online. However, there is still a lack of research on the Yunlin Puppet Theater website's usability.

Based on the above, the present study has explored the usability of the Yunlin Puppetry Museum website, collected user feedback, and proposed design modifications to enhance users' experiences while promoting puppetry culture.

2   Literature Review

This article explores the following five aspects of the meaning of puppet show; an introduction and description of the Yunlin Puppet Opera Museum website; the definition of usability; the evaluation and improvement of website usability.

2.1   The Meaning of the Puppet Show

Puppet Plays, also known as Puppet Plays, Palm Plays, Xiaolong, and other names, originate from Quanzhou and other places in southern Fujian, China. They later became popularized in Taiwan. The puppet heads are hollow figures carved from wood. In addition to the puppet's head, hands, and feet, its torso and limbs are made of cloth. During performances, gloves are inserted into puppet costumes to perform puppeteering. A large cloth bag is used to store props during performances. This bag can be used as a curtain to cover the body of the protagonist during the performance, leaving a distinct visual impression on the audience. Therefore, it has been called "Puppet Opera", also known as Palm Opera (Xintianren Chinese Language Network, 2023).

Local Taiwanese people's opinions of Taiwan's puppet shows include several aspects. Watching it in temples can connect residents' emotions. When puppet shows gradually appeared on TV and later in movies, this representation of Taiwanese culture attracted much attention from local people. It is hoped that traditional culture can continue to be preserved (Wu & Wu, 2018). Through innovation and development, the Taiwan Puppet Show Club combines traditional culture with modern elements to cater to the needs of modern audiences (Li & Huang, 2012). However, the puppet show is no longer limited to these previous impressions, such as fixed scripts and temple stages. Online audio and video technology can also introduce people to innovative puppet show culture (Huagang Radio, 2023).

Based on the above, puppetry has a long history and is transforming into a digital form. Currently and in the future, websites will be an important medium for people to understand puppetry.

2.2   Yunlin Puppet Theater Website Introduction and Description

The Yunlin Puppet Theater website is not only a display platform for the puppetry industry but also provides various historical information and photos related to puppetry and the Yunlin Puppetry Hall. It is also committed to promoting the development of the art of puppetry.

Regarding the Yunlin Puppet Theater website, four characteristics are evident: layout, hyperlinks, visuals, and multimedia:

1. Layout: This website is responsive with a Z-shaped layout. The list at the top of the page is marked with the latest news, visits, understanding of the puppet show hall, activity overview, and the source and transportation of the puppet show. Each page has a large picture at the top, along with the title and page content, which can be scrolled with the mouse. The puppet show is supplemented by pictures and texts combined with Chinese and English. Relevant reference materials are recorded.
2. Hyperlinks: A hyperlink back to the homepage is located in the upper left. Each option in the list above has a large amount of information.
3. Visuals: There is a large picture related to the puppet theater at the top of each page. The above list is superimposed with white text. The background colors of the text are white, off-white, and gray, and the text is black and white.
4. Multimedia: Currently, only photos exist, and the video type is an external link.

2.3   Definition and Evaluation of Website Usability

The research scope is to explore this website's usability. Usability is important to ensure that users can use products or services efficiently and effectively and to improve user satisfaction. Based on Nielsen's (1993) definition, usability has five main attributes. (1) Learnability: How easy it is for a user to complete a basic task when challenged for the first time; (2) Efficiency: Once the user understands the design, efficiency is the speed with which they perform tasks; (3) Memorability: When users return to the design after not using it for a period of time, how easily can they re-establish proficiency? (4) Errors: What mistakes did the user make, and could they recover from making them? (5) Satisfaction: The degree of enjoyment in using the design.

Regarding website evaluation tools, Nielsen's (1993) five usability attributes are compared with various interface design patterns and other usability assessment methods for application in the changing socio-technical environment (Nielsen, 1993). The present study used SUS measurements to evaluate the usability of the Yunlin Puppet Show website. System Usability Scale (SUS). This scale can be used to evaluate a website platform's usability by users. It is a streamlined reliable tool (Bouraghi et al., 2022; Brooke, 2013; Farzandipour et al., 2022; Lee, 2019). Ahmad et al. (2021) found that usability evaluation is a key activity that helps improve user experience standards. Appropriate usability evaluation enhances the user experience.

Based on the above, the present study adopted the five attributes of usability defined by Nielsen (1993) as the basis and the SUS scale as the measurement tool.

2.4   Related Research on Improving Website Usability

Improving website usability provides users with a good experience while also achieving its intended effects. By analyzing the following literature, we can gain a deeper understanding of the advantages elicited through improving usability.

Fantoni, Stein, Bowman, and Reference Falk (2009) identified five characteristics for visiting museums and other cultural organizations, integrating five main motivations:

1) planning a visit to a museum; 2) looking for specific information for research or professional purposes; 3) looking for specific information that matches personal interests; 4) casual browsing without looking for specific content; 5) to conduct transactions on the website.

By tracking users' online behavior, research suggests that various users plan to visit museums, seek specific information for research or professional purposes, and seek specific information that matches their personal interests. People with these three types of motivations have a higher probability of visiting the venue after browsing online (Fantoni, Stein, Bowman, 2012).

Findings on the high usability of museums, which can attract new visitors who have never been to a physical museum or existing visitors who have already been there, should encourage museums to improve their websites' usability and appearance. If a company wants to expand its audience and media, their website should not just provide information but also include multimedia and aesthetic interfaces (Pallud & Straub, 2014).

3   Methodology

The research process was divided into three steps: 1) ask the testers to use the Yunlin Puppet Show website according to its specific operations; 2) ask the testers to complete the SUS scale questions; 3) since the SUS scale results indicate poor usability, interviews were used to provide further understanding. We compiled recommendations based on the positive and negative experiences and difficulties users encountered.

3.1   Research Subjects

This study recruited 10 subjects aged 19–28 to participate in the usability questionnaire and interview test of the Yunlin Puppet Opera website in Taiwan. Among them, five were male and five were female. Five participants were university graduates and five were graduate students. There are ten people, all of whom are currently students.

3.2   Research Tools

The SUS Scale. The System Usability Scale (SUS) used in the present study is a system usability scale initially compiled by Brooke (1986). The scale contains 10 questions, each of which is rated on a 5-point scale. Half of the questions are positive narratives, and the other half are negative narratives. By evaluating these 10 sets of questions, a SUS score can finally be calculated, which can be used for subsequent system usability analysis (Alfred, 2023)

Interviews. The researcher of this study developed assessment methods, operations, and interviews, as shown in Appendix 2. This was based on Hong (2014) while adopting Nielsen's (1993) five major usability attribute development interface elements

4   Result and Discussion

4.1   SUS Score Results

Bangor, Kortum, and Miller (2009) found that people's feelings about products are closely related to SUS. Thus, they divided the scores into six levels: Worst Imaginable, Poor, Ok, Good, excellent, and Best Imaginable (Alfred, 2023).

U stands for user, and the SUS score is as follows (Fig. 1):

User	SUS score	Adjective ratings	Acceptability ranges
U1	48	OK	Not Acceptable
U2	46	OK	Not Acceptable
U3	62	GOOD	Marginal
U4	62	GOOD	Marginal
U5	54	GOOD	Marginal
U6	18	WORST IMAGINABLE	Not Acceptable
U7	66	GOOD	Marginal
U8	54	GOOD	Marginal
U9	60	GOOD	Marginal
U10	60	GOOD	Marginal

Fig. 1. SUS test results

4.2   Interview Results

Since the scores were found to be unacceptable, critical, or below OK, the researcher collected feedback from testers through development questions. Figure 2 presents a summary of user feedback.

Problem Item	No.	User Feedback
Classification	U6Q1	Too many categories.
Information	U1Q4	Some information needs to be omitted, such as traffic information.
Hyperlink	U6Q5, U2Q5	Page links are irrelevant to the content and should be independent. The button to return to the homepage needs to be more obvious. Frequently used functions should be placed on the homepage.
Layout	T7Q5	The large picture in the above list should be made smaller.
Homepage (latest news)	U1Q3 U2Q3 U3Q4 U4Q3 U6Q2 U8Q3 U10Q3 U10Q4 U10Q5	The activity information pictures and fonts on the homepage (latest news) are too small. The latest information is the same as the homepage. The activity information of the latest information is not linked to the calendar.
Event calendar	U3Q3, U8Q3	The event calendar page needs to be enlarged. The homepage's infographics are more memorable, but the calendar format is difficult to remember.
Theme	U4Q4, U3Q5, U7Q4	No puppet show features.
Interactivity	U8Q5	The interactivity is not enough; I hope there can be interactive games or animation.
Responsiveness	U1Q5	The main image of the mobile version will be cut off.

Fig. 2. Summary of user feedback

5   Conclusions and Suggestions

Yunlin Puppetry Theater is located in the birthplace of puppetry and carries the unique cultural essence of Taiwan. This study is committed to improving the usability of the Yunlin Puppetry Theater website and increasing people's willingness to visit cultural venues while promoting puppetry culture. This study used the SUS (System Usability Scale) to evaluate the usability of the Yunlin Puppet Theater website. We proposed design modification suggestions based on the feedback gathered through interviews. The SUS scale results show that the website's usability is between unacceptable and critical. Time, with an OK below. After the interviews, the researcher found that the positive feedback indicated that the data was quite sufficient. After organizing the negative feedback, the four recommendations are as follows: layout, hyperlinks, visuals, and multimedia:

- Layout:
  1. The homepage should be independent.
  2. The classification and information should be simplified For example, with the introduction of puppet theater and puppetry, the classification can be reduced, and the transportation information can be simplified.
  3. The large picture listed above should be reduced.
  4. Please consider the size of the large picture listed on the mobile phone board.
- Hyperlinks:

1. The homepage's color and size button should be changed to make it eye-catching and make people aware of its function.
2. The event information on the homepage should be linked to the calendar.

- Visuals:

1. Add puppet show elements to enhance the theme.
2. The homepage's activity information graphics and fonts can be enlarged or presented so that users can click to enlarge.
3. The event calendar font should be enlarged.

- Multimedia: The website lacks interactive items. Audio and video materials, animations, or games could be added.

In the future, we will expand the collection of user feedback and conduct in-depth research on the experiences of different age groups. We hope that government departments can draw upon this literature and use these suggestions to continue to optimize the website, improve usability, and increase people's willingness to visit the Yunlin Puppet Theater to promote puppetry culture.

Appendix

Appendix 1: The SUS Scale

The SUS scale items are as follows:
Q1. I think that I would like to use this website frequently.
Q2. I found the website unnecessarily complex.
Q3 I thought the website was easy to use.
Q4. I think that I would need the support of a technical person to be able to use this website.
Q5. I found the various website functions were well integrated.
Q6. I thought that this website had too much inconsistency.
Q7. I imagine that most people would learn to use this website very quickly.
Q8. I found the website very awkward to use.
Q9. I felt very confident using the website.
Q10. I needed to learn a lot of things before I could use this website.

Appendix 2 User Interview Questionnaire

Usability calibration	Evaluation elements	Assessment method	Operation	Interview
Learnability	Layout	1. You can find it on the homepage	Please find the date of 2024 Yunlin Puppet Show Day?	Q1. Do you think this layout makes it easy for you to find it?

(continued)

(*continued*)

Usability calibration	Evaluation elements	Assessment method	Operation	Interview
		2. You can find it in the branch on the homepage	Where can I see the development and changes of Taiwan's puppet theater?	
Efficiency	hyperlink	1. You can find it on the homepage	What are the opening and closing times of Yunlin Puppet Theater?	Q2. Do you think it is efficient to find this information?
		2. You can find it on the homepage	Where can I see the Yunlin Puppet Theater Museum?	
Memorability	Vision	You can find it on the homepage	What activities will be held in January 2024?	Q3. Is this information memorable?
			What kind of activities will be held during the Spring Festival in 2024?	
Errors	Multimedia	Therefore, the website does not have this element, and the conclusion will be drawn based on the usage of the previous question		
Satisfaction	Overall	Overall feelings and opinions		Q4. How do you feel about the overall website?
				Q5. What suggestions are there for visuals, layout, and links?

Appendix 3 Interview Feedback

Usability calibration	Interview	Positive feedback	Negative feedback
Learnability	Q1. Do you think this layout akes it easy for you to find it?	U1Q1 is not bad	U6Q1 has too many categories and can be sorted again
		U3Q1 is clearly classified and you can see where to find the information	
		U4Q1 can	
		U5Q1 can	
		U7Q1 can do it, and will subconsciously look at the list above	
		U8Q1 is pretty easy	
		U9Q1 is pretty easy	
		U10Q1 can, the above list is detailed	
Efficiency	Q2. Do you think it is efficient to find this information?	U3Q2 is efficient	U6Q2 takes a little longer to display directly on the homepage (latest news)
		U4Q2 does not use it	
		U5Q2 does not	
		U7Q2 does not need it, it is efficient	
		U8Q2 is very efficient	
		U9Q2 does not	
		U10Q2 can	
Memorability	Q3. Is this information memorable?	U3Q3 remember	The event information pictures and fonts on the U1Q3 homepage (latest news) are too small
		U6Q3 forgets about it immediately and will not look for it from the homepage, but from the event calendar. The activity information pictures on the homepage are arranged in weird categories	The activity information picture on the U2Q3 homepage (latest news) should be larger
		U7Q3 will	The 3Q3 event calendar page needs to be enlarged

(*continued*)

(*continued*)

Usability calibration	Interview	Positive feedback	Negative feedback
		U9Q3 is fairly easy to find	U4Q3 will not know how to go back to the homepage. The way to go back to the homepage is not obvious. The latest information is the same as the homepage
			The U8Q3 poster will be more memorable, but the calendar format is difficult to remember
			The font size of U10Q3 is too small, and the activity information picture on the homepage cannot be enlarged when clicked
Errors	Therefore, the website does not have this element, and the conclusion will be drawn based on the usage of the previous question	1. The activity data of the latest information is not linked to the calendar. Eight out of ten people will search for activities in the calendar during the operation of the Q3 question. However, the font of the calendar interface is small. Although they can interpret and complete the operation. Researchers need to be reminded that the latest information is available	
		2. People do not know how to go back to the homepage. The function of returning to the homepage must be made more eye-catching	
Satisfaction	Q4. How do you feel about the overall website?	U5Q4 has everything it needs	1Q4 There are too many unnecessary things, such as traffic information
		U6Q4 is an ordinary website with no theme, and other contact information is arranged in a messy fashion and should be at the bottom of the homepage	U2Q4 is very detailed but requires more time to become familiar with it

(*continued*)

(*continued*)

Usability calibration	Interview	Positive feedback	Negative feedback
		U9Q4 is clear and has sufficient information	U3Q4 The homepage event information graphics are a bit too small and need to be scaled
		U10Q4 is quite clear	U4Q4 Taiyangchun, there are too few puppetry elements, and the architectural photos lack the characteristics of puppetry
			The U7Q4 homepage is rather simple and has no homepage feel or features but sufficient information. T8Q4 has sufficient and clear information and a concise style. T8Q5 is not interactive enough. I hope there can be interactive games
			U10Q4 The homepage activity information picture is too small
	Q5. What suggestions are there for visuals, layout and links?	U1Q5 is visually clean	U1Q5 However, each activity information picture should occupy one page. The main picture of the opening and closing times of the mobile version will be cut off
		U8Q5 are all very good and very intuitive to list	The information U2Q5 needs most should be marked on the homepage

(*continued*)

(*continued*)

Usability calibration	Interview	Positive feedback	Negative feedback
		U9Q5 are all very good, and there are still places to search for them in the above list	U3Q5 is very ordinary and has no characteristics. If it is a local cultural heritage, the website should have more characteristics
			The U4Q5 homepage should be thematic
			The U6Q5 homepage link is not relevant to the content. The information on other websites is arranged in a messy fashion
			The large picture in the upper list of U7Q5 can be smaller, and the picture below can be centered, with space on the right
			U10Q5 Homepage activity information picture: I hope the pilot can go in and enlarge it

References

Ahmad, N.A.N., Hamid, N.I.M., Lokman, A.M.: Performing usability evaluation on multi-platform-based application for efficiency, effectiveness and satisfaction enhancement. Int. J. Interact. Mob. Technol. **15**(10), 103–117 (2021)

Alfred, C.J.J.: Understanding usability assessment: a brief discussion of the SUS Scale and its application. https://medium.com/@alfredcjj/%E6%B7%BA%E8%AB%87%E5%8F%AF%E7%94%A8%E6%80%A7%E9%87%8F%E8%A1%A8-sus-%E8%88%87%E7%9B%B8%E9%97%9C%E6%87%89%E7%94%A8-1ac1e02422e0. Accessed 16 Mar 2023

Bangor, A., Kortum, P., Miller, J.: Determining what individual SUS scores mean: adding an adjective rating scale. J. User Exp. **4**(3), 114–123 (2009)

Bouraghi, H., Rezayi, S., Amirazodi, S., Nabovati, E., Saeedi, S.: J. Educ. Health Promot. 30(11), Article 182 (2022)

Brooke, J.: SUS: a retrospective. J. Usabil. Stud. **8**(2), 29–40 (2013)

Fantoni, S.F, Stein, R, Bowman, G.: Exploring the relationship between visitor motivation and engagement in online museum audiences. Museuma and Web site (2016)

Farzandipour, M., Nabovati, E., Sadeqi Jabali, M.: Comparison of usability evaluation methods for a health information system: heuristic evaluation versus cognitive walkthrough method. BMC Med. Inform. Decis. Making **22**, 157 (2022)

Hong, H.D.: Exploring the effect of cultures on the web design based on Taiwanese and Australian cultures. In: Hsiu-Ching, H. (2014)

Huwei's PUPPET THEATER HeritageYunlin International Puppets Arts Festival (2023). https://eng.taiwan.net.tw/m1.aspx?sNo=0002019&lid=080937

Lee, C.W., Jalin, K.H.: Action design in cultural creativity media-a study of interactive puppetry display. J. Cult. Creat. Industr. Res. **2**(1), 85–97 (2012)

Nielsen, J.: Usability Engineering. Harcourt Brace & Company, San Diego (1993)

Pallud, J, Straub, D.W.: Effective website design for experience-influenced environments: the case of high culture museums. Inf. Manage. **51**(3) (2014)

PeoPo Citizen Journalism. https://www.peopo.org/news/634592. Accessed 6 May 2023

Will you still only do SUS and usability testing? Interface design evaluation methods you should consider: 5Es, NPS and Kano analysis (2019). https://medium.com/ux-plus/interface-design-evaluation-5es-nps-kanomodel-ed27dd7af302

Wu, S.M., Ward, S.: A preliminary study of local people's views on Taiwan hand puppet theater in the context of its modern evolution. Art Vision J. **15**, 1–16 (2014)

Xinterra (2023). https://xinterra.com/

Construction of Immersive Art Space Using Mirror Display and Its Evaluation Through Heart Rate Measurements

Go Kazawa(⊠), Naoko Tosa, and Ryohei Nakatsu

Kyoto University, Kyoto, Japan

`kazawa.gou.62x@st.kyoto-u.ac.jp, tosa.naoko.5c@kyoto-u.ac.jp`

Abstract. This study, conducted at Kyoto University, explores the construction of an immersive art space using a mirror display and evaluates its impact through heart rate measurements. The research integrates Naoko Tosa's media art, which captures the hidden beauty in nature, into an immersive space surrounded by mirrors. This unique setting aims to blur the boundaries between art and viewer, offering a more natural and less device-dependent immersive art experience.

The study involved 43 Kyoto University students, with ECG data collected during normal and art viewing states. Using Poincaré plots, the study analyzed changes in heart rate variability and other physiological markers. The results showed significant emotional and physiological changes in viewers, with approximately half experiencing clear immersion in the art pieces.

This research contributes to the field of immersive art experiences by employing Naoko Tosa's unique aesthetic and scientific approach to art and using innovative mirror display technology. It offers insights into the psychological and physiological effects of art on viewers, with potential applications in various fields. However, the study acknowledges the need for caution in generalizing results and the importance of further research in diverse settings.

Keywords: Immersive Art · Mirror Display Technology · Heart Rate Variability (HRV) · Physiological Data Analysis · Art and Emotion · ECG (Electrocardiogram) Data · Poincaré Plots · Viewer Immersion Experience, · Art and Technology Integration

1 Introduction

1.1 Research Background

In contemporary immersive art experiences, advanced technologies such as virtual reality (VR) and augmented reality (AR) enable artists to access new creative methodologies beyond traditional physical constraints. Utilizing such technologies, the form of art expression transforms into multidimensional, dynamic, and interactive modalities.

However, implementing immersive art experiences using VR and AR necessitates the use of specific devices, which can be obtrusive and restrict movement, requiring a

M. Rauterberg (Ed.): HCII 2024, LNCS 14717, pp. 150–166, 2024.
https://doi.org/10.1007/978-3-031-61147-6_11

degree of acclimatization to the devices for a truly immersive experience. Therefore, we hypothesize that spaces themselves, transformed by art, can more naturally blur the boundaries between space and individuals. Such spaces, diminishing the demarcation between art and the viewer, become a crucial element in fostering new forms of art and expanding the horizons of creativity. Immersive art experiences are believed to initiate a new wave of creativity in the realm of art, offering innovative experiences for both artists and observers.

Furthermore, immersive art experiences hold various significant social implications. For instance, in educational settings, utilizing such experiences enables learners to engage in experiential learning, which is not achievable through traditional textbooks and lectures. This approach can enhance motivation for learning, deepening understanding of art and stimulating interest in culture and history. Immersive art experiences are also beneficial in promoting cultural inclusivity. They provide new forms of art access to people from diverse cultural backgrounds, facilitating shared experiences that transcend cultural barriers and deepen cross-cultural understanding.

However, to apply these immersive art experiences to solve societal challenges, more participant data is needed. This study creates a unique space using a mirror display to facilitate immersive art experiences for participants, collecting and analyzing their physiological data.

The art content utilized in this research is the media art of Naoko Tosa. Tosa's art, known for capturing the hidden beauty in nature and providing viewers with a sense of infinite space, is considered highly suitable for creating the desired immersive art experience. Through this study, we aim to analyze the changes in states experienced by viewers during immersive art experiences compared to normal conditions. Anticipating the potential changes in viewers, we aspire to contribute to applications in various fields.

1.2 Outline

In this study, Sect. 2 will delve into Tosa Art, recent research on immersive art experiences, physiological data analysis of art experiences, and the relationship between art and emotions. It will discuss how this research addresses existing gaps in the literature and aims to provide new insights. Section 3 will touch upon the research methodology. This includes details about the mirror display used in the experiments, the experimental procedures, information about the participants, the data collected, and the methods used for data analysis. Section 4, the results section, will present the data, perform statistical analysis, and discuss the observed trends and patterns. Section 5 is the discussion part, where the interpretation of results, their relation to the literature review, and the significance and impact of the research will be explored. Finally, Sect. 6, the conclusion part, will discuss the study's main findings, limitations, and proposals for future research.

2 Literature Review

2.1 Tosa Art

One of the authors, Naoko Tosa, is renowned for her creation of media art utilizing cutting-edge technology. Her works specialize in capturing the hidden beauty within natural and physical phenomena using high-speed cameras (Tosa, 2016). She has a particular interest in the behavior of fluids, visualizing movements not typically visible to the naked eye by capturing their dynamics with high-speed cameras. This field, known as fluid dynamics, has been the subject of extensive academic research. The visualization of fluid motion fascinates many due to its beautiful movements, attracting attention not only from a scientific perspective but also an artistic one (Tosa, 2023; Pamg, 2017).

Tosa's work distinguishes itself from the broader research in fluid dynamics. While general studies on fluid visualization focus on capturing stable fluid behavior, Tosa challenges herself to capture the art in unstable and unpredictable fluid movements. Through this approach, she provides viewers with a novel visual experience, expressing the deep beauty and complexity hidden in fluid motions. Her work blurs the boundaries between science and art, demonstrating how these two fields can interact.

The reason for selecting Naoko Tosa's media art in this study is due to the unique aesthetic and scientific background of her work, which we believe is highly suitable for research in immersive art experiences. Her work captures the beauty hidden in natural phenomena, offering viewers a sense of infinite space and deep emotion. These characteristics play a crucial role in the creation of immersive art experiences that this study aims to achieve. Through Tosa's work, viewers can discover new aspects of natural phenomena and enjoy a unique experience born from the fusion of art and science. Such experiences are thought to expand viewers' perceptions and deepen the understanding of the impact of immersive art experiences.

2.2 Immersive Art Experience

Immersive art experiences refer to situations where viewers deeply interact with artworks and exhibitions. This field, situated at the intersection of art, technology, and psychology, has evolved significantly with recent technological advancements. This section explores prior research on immersive art experiences, elucidating their historical development and significance in research. The concept of immersive art experiences is believed to have originated from installation art in the 1960s. Kaprow (1966) explored the immersive aspects of art experiences through 'Happenings' that emphasized the interaction between the environment and the viewer (Kaprow, 1966). These early experiments aimed to remove physical barriers between the artwork and the viewer, integrating the viewer into the art. Entering the 1990s, with technological advancements, the concept of immersive art took on a new dimension. Marín-Morales (2019) notes that with the introduction of virtual reality (VR) technology, artists could immerse viewers in entirely different environments (Marín-Morales, 2019). This transition allowed art experiences to evolve from purely visual to multisensory. The new concept of immersive art is considered to have a significant impact on individuals, and since then, psychological aspects of how immersive art experiences affect viewers' cognition and emotions have been actively studied. Grau (2003) researched how VR-based artworks alter viewers' emotional responses, showing that immersive art evokes strong emotional reactions in viewers (Grau, 2003).

Currently, immersive art experiences are becoming even more diverse. Recent studies incorporate augmented reality (AR) and interactive installations, allowing viewers to interact more dynamically with artworks. Guerra-Tamez (2023) discovered that interactive artworks stimulate viewers' creativity and inquisitiveness. The research on immersive art experiences goes beyond traditional understandings of art, delving deeply into the impacts of art on human emotions, cognition, and society (Guerra-Tamez, 2023). This field, promoting the fusion of art and science, holds the power to fundamentally change our perception of art by exploring new creative possibilities (Guerra-Tamez, 2023). However, there are still many challenges in providing pure immersive art experiences. One such challenge is the constraints associated with device wear. The use of VR or AR devices can affect viewers' movements and sensory experiences. Ito (2021) studied the physical discomfort and unease felt by viewers when wearing head-mounted displays (HMDs), noting how this can impact the quality of immersive experiences (Ito, 2021). The weight, size, and the hassle of wearing these devices can also act as barriers to immersive experiences. Kim & Lee (2019) state that first-time users of VR devices need time to become accustomed to the operation, and initial discomfort during this phase can degrade the quality of the experience (Kim & Lee, 2019). This acclimatization process is an important consideration when using such devices. The ongoing trial and error in modern technology to achieve complete immersive art experiences is noteworthy. Pyun (2022) is advancing research to improve the quality of immersive experiences through the development of lighter and more comfortable devices and interface improvements. Research is also being conducted on alternative methods to realize immersive experiences without devices, with the hope that more natural immersive experiences will be possible in the future (Pyun, 2022). This study addresses gaps in existing research on immersive art experiences with our newly developed device. We analyze the impact of the immersive space created using the mirror display on viewers, contributing to the realization of complete immersive art experiences and their application in various fields.

2.3 Analysis of Physiological Data

The analysis of physiological data is a crucial means of quantitatively assessing the impact of immersive art experiences. This analysis can elucidate how viewers' experiences affect them psychologically and physiologically. However, collecting and analyzing physiological data presents challenges due to its complexity and the precision required. Particularly, time-series analysis is essential for accurately capturing data variations and understanding the dynamic changes in viewers' responses. Collecting physiological data is one of the more challenging aspects of research due to its complexity and the precision required. According to Smith et al. (2018), physiological data such as heart rate and skin conductance can vary significantly due to environmental factors and the individual's physiological and psychological state (Smith et al., 2018). Therefore, rigorous experimental design and advanced measurement techniques are essential for accurate data collection and analysis. In this study, we conducted advanced ECG (Electrocardiogram) measurements with the cooperation of Shimadzu Corporation. Shimadzu is a company highly regarded in the field of precision measurement instruments, and its technological expertise greatly contributed to the accuracy of our research. Specifically, Shimadzu's ECG measuring instruments can capture minute changes in electrocardiograms with high precision, making them ideal for tracking in detail how participants respond to immersive art experiences. The use of these advanced measuring instruments allowed us to capture participants' psychological and physiological responses more accurately, unaffected by environmental changes or individual differences. On the other hand, time-series analysis of physiological data is crucial to capture the dynamic changes in psychological and physiological responses of viewers and to understand how these changes relate to specific elements of the experience. For instance, a study by Matthews et al. (2016) used HRV analysis to track the autonomic nervous system's responses of viewers when they were in specific stress or emotional states over time. This research clarified how viewers' emotional responses and stress levels are related to particular elements of their experience. While time-series analysis can reveal the relationship between specific elements and changes in viewers, it also presents difficulties in handling due to the complexity, diversity, noise, and the amount of data involved. Moreover, physiological data are susceptible to influences from stress, emotional states, physical activity, and even daily activities like sleep and diet, requiring careful analysis to accurately discern the dynamic changes in psychological and physiological responses of viewers in relation to specific elements of the experience. In this study, we chose to use Poincaré plots to comprehensively analyze the RRI (R-R interval, i.e., the interval between heartbeats) as time-series data.

2.4 Identifying Research Gap

Based on the foregoing, this study addresses gaps in previous research in the following ways. Primarily, by utilizing the media art of Naoko Tosa, we focus on filling the gaps in research on immersive art experiences. Tosa's work is known for capturing the hidden beauty in natural phenomena, providing viewers with a sense of infinite space and profound emotion, playing a vital role in creating immersive art experiences. Previous studies have lacked research on immersive experiences using art with such unique aesthetics and scientific background. Additionally, in response to the challenges of realizing complete immersive art experiences with modern technology, this study employs a newly developed mirror display space. Using this innovative device adds a new dimension to the research on immersive art experiences and allows for a comprehensive analysis of the impact on viewers. This contributes to a deeper understanding of how art experiences affect viewers' psychological and physiological responses, aiming to expand the potential applications of immersive art experiences. Furthermore, in the analysis of physiological data, we conduct a comprehensive analysis of time-series data, keeping in mind the complexities, diversity, and noise issues associated with such data. Using Poincaré plots for the time-series analysis of the R-R intervals (RRI), we aim to understand the physiological responses of viewers. Thus, this study overcomes the gaps in research on immersive art experiences, aiming to provide new insights.

3   Methodology

3.1   Research Design

This study analyzes the changes that occur in viewers undergoing immersive art experiences compared to their normal state, using ECG (Electrocardiogram) data. We proceeded with the analysis under the hypothesis that significant changes would be observed in the viewers' heart rate and ECG data during the immersive art experience compared to their normal state.

In this study, we opted to avoid the use of common headsets in VR or AR, and instead employed a mirror display space to provide a deeper immersive art experience. To further explore the potential of creativity in art, we developed a special immersive space surrounded by mirrors. The mirror display, which combines the functions of mirrors and display screens, has been commercialized by several companies. The one we used is developed by AGC Inc. And commercialized under the name "Mirroria" [Mirroria]. A key feature of this display is its use of the company's glass manufacturing technology to achieve a half-mirror reflectance rate of about 65%, equivalent to that of a regular mirror. Part of this space functions as a display screen. As shown in Fig. 2, this hexagonal space is fitted with three sets of opposing mirrors, creating the illusion of infinite reflections. Covering the ceiling and floor with mirrors further amplifies this effect. The six main mirrors installed in this space have the capability to display images, and as shown in Fig. 2, their vertical length exceeds the actual display area. By adjusting the display position, it is possible to prevent overlapping of images while maintaining the illusion of infinite reflections. Initially, data was collected during a normal three-minute period, followed by a three-minute viewing of Tosa Art within this space, and ECG data was measured for each period (Fig. 1).

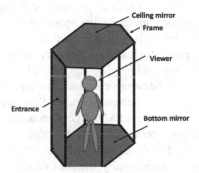

Fig. 1. Conceptual diagram of immersed space

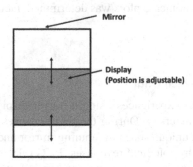

Fig. 2. Configuration of indivisual mirror displays

3.2 Data Collection Method

In this study, we collected Electrocardiogram (ECG) data from 43 students at Kyoto University. The process involved data collection in two different states for each participant: a normal state (baseline) and while viewing an art piece. Data collection for each state lasted for three minutes, meticulously recording variations in heart rate and ECG.

During the data collection process, participants were fitted with ECG measuring devices, and data was gathered in a relaxed environment to capture physiological responses both during baseline and while observing the art piece. Careful preparation and meticulous measurement were conducted to ensure the comfort of the participants and the accuracy of the data.

After data collection, an analysis based on the quality, completeness, and reliability of the data revealed that the data from 22 out of the 43 participants were accurate and analyzable. Therefore, the final analysis was conducted based on the ECG data of these 22 participants.

3.3 Analytical Method

In this study, RRI (R-R Interval) data were extracted from the collected ECG data, and the initial step involved creating Poincaré plots. In these plots, RRI_i (the R-R interval at a given time point) was plotted on the x-axis, and RRI_{i+1} (the R-R interval at the next time point) on the y-axis. This method was applied to the entire dataset. For this analysis, instead of using statistical methods like t-tests on the entire dataset, we focused on classifying and observing trends based on individual data characteristics. This approach was chosen because physiological data can vary significantly due to individual characteristics, health status, age, and gender, making it challenging to adequately consider these personal differences when analyzing the entire dataset collectively. Therefore, detailed analysis was conducted on each participant's Poincaré plot. Initially, SD1 (the standard deviation of the short axis) and SD2 (the standard deviation of the long axis) were calculated, indicating short-term heart rate variability and long-term variability, respectively, and are associated with parasympathetic activity and autonomic nervous system regulation capabilities. Additionally, measures such as variance (X-axis), variance (Y-axis), density, central position, and branching structure were calculated. These metrics were evaluated based on the rate of change relative to the resting (rest) state, from which the state of the Poincaré plots was determined, facilitating the classification and interpretation of results.

4 Result

4.1 Presentation of Collected Data

In this study, immersive art experiences using a mirror display were conducted with 43 students from Kyoto University. During these experiences, participants viewed art pieces by Naoko Tosa in a unique space combining mirror and display functionalities. To measure participants' physiological responses, ECG (electrocardiogram) data were recorded for 3 min each during both rest and viewing periods. From this data, an analysis was conducted to determine how participants' physiological states changed during the immersive art experience.

Upon data validation, it was found that only ECG data from 22 participants were suitable for analysis due to issues such as noise. Particularly, the analysis focused on RRI (R-R interval), which represents the time interval between R waves, the most prominent part of the ECG waveform, indicating cardiac contractions (the heart pumping blood throughout the body).

RRI variability, also known as heart rate variability (HRV), is widely used as an indicator of autonomic nervous system balance. High HRV generally indicates a healthy autonomic nervous system, while low HRV suggests stress. Given that this characteristic aligns with the objectives of this study, RRI was adopted as the focus of analysis.

As a result, RRI data were obtained for 22 participants for both rest and art viewing periods, each lasting 3 min, as depicted in Fig. 3.

4.2 Statistical Analysis and Visualization

In this study, we utilized Poincaré plots to analyze the nonlinear characteristics of RRI (R-R interval). While Poincaré plots have limitations in capturing dynamic changes at specific time points or direct associations with specific elements of an experience, they are highly effective in interpreting particular shapes or patterns of heart rate variability. Moreover, this method enables analysis that accounts for individual differences among participants. The collected RRI data from 22 participants were transformed into Poincaré plots, as shown in Fig. 4, and the results were analyzed accordingly.

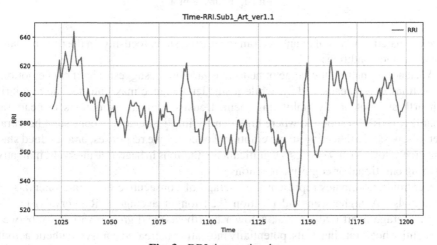

Fig. 3. RRI time series data

The data extracted from Poincaré plots of each participant in this study encompassed eight parameters: SD1 (standard deviation of short-axis) reflecting short-term fluctuations of heartbeats predominantly influenced by parasympathetic activity, SD2 (standard deviation of long-axis) indicating longer-term variations in heartbeats primarily representing autonomic regulatory capacity, variance (X-axis), variance (Y-axis), density, centroid position (x-coordinate & y-coordinate), and branching structure. These metrics

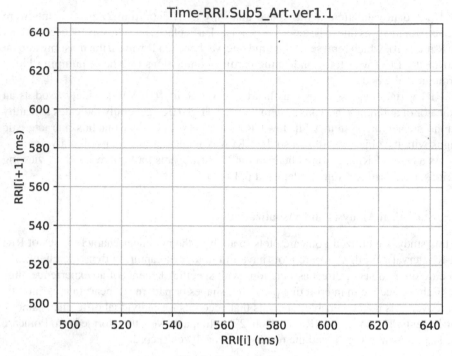

Fig. 4. Poincaré plot

were evaluated in terms of changes from the resting state, focusing on the rate of change from baseline conditions.

Variance, depicting the range of heart rate variability, suggests significant emotional fluctuations if it spreads widely, while a smaller variance may enhance the regularity of heartbeats, potentially stabilizing them. Density indicates variations in heart rate variability (HRV) responses, where high density implies relatively consistent heart rate intervals, possibly reflecting stable emotional or cognitive responses, or a subdued state. Conversely, low density suggests significant fluctuations in heart rate intervals, indicative of strong emotional or cognitive reactions.

Centroid coordinates represent the average of consecutive heart rate intervals (R-R intervals). A higher centroid position (i.e., longer average R-R intervals) implies longer average heart rate intervals (slower heartbeats) and greater variability between consecutive heart rate intervals, potentially indicating increased parasympathetic activity reflective of relaxation or a relaxed state. Conversely, a lower centroid position (shorter average R-R intervals) implies shorter average heart rate intervals (faster heartbeats) and reduced variability between consecutive heart rate intervals, suggesting increased sympathetic activity.

Lastly, an increase in branching structure on the Poincaré plot (i.e., more diverse points appearing) signifies increased complexity in heart rate variability, potentially indicating heightened emotional responses or mental activity. Conversely, a decrease in branching structure on the Poincaré plot (i.e., fewer different points appearing) suggests a relaxing effect and increased regularity in heart rate, possibly reflecting a state of relaxation.

Figures 5, 6, 7, 8, 9 and 10 depict the rate of change from the resting state for each parameter across all participants. Scatter plots were utilized for variance and centroid coordinates, showing the x-coordinate and y-coordinate relationships, respectively.

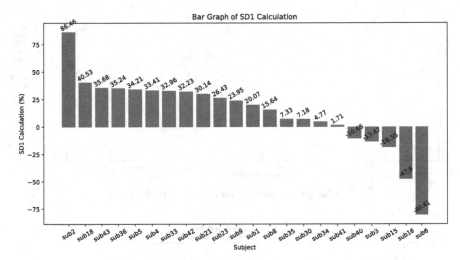

Fig. 5. Change in SD1 from Rest to Art Observation

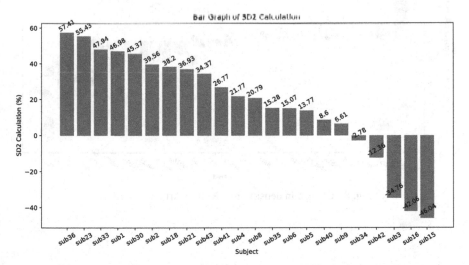

Fig. 6. Change in SD2 from Rest to Art Observation

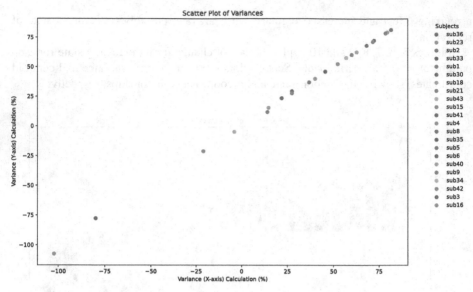

Fig. 7. Change in variances from Rest to Art Observation

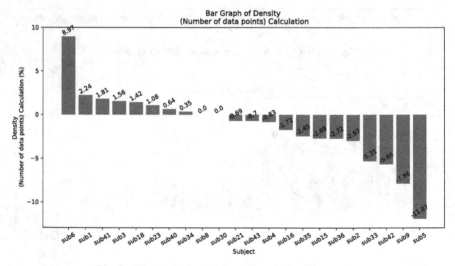

Fig. 8. Change in density from Rest to Art Observation

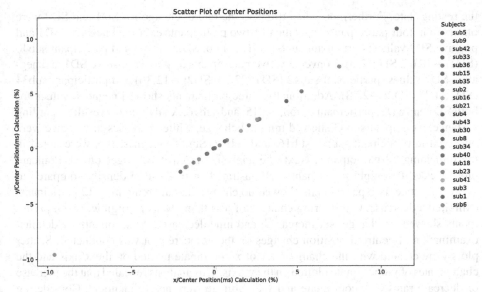

Fig. 9. Change in Center Positions from Rest to Art Observation

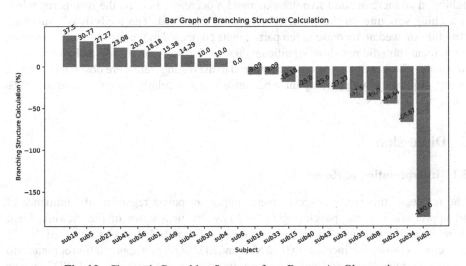

Fig. 10. Change in Branching Structure from Rest to Art Observation

4.3 Description of Observed Trends and Patterns

As a general trend, it cannot be denied that various factors such as the psychological state and physical characteristics of individual participants, personal preferences and experiences with art, as well as the daily physiological and mental state, may influence the outcomes. However, notable differences were observed in the comparison between the resting state (rest) and the art appreciation state (art). Specifically, for instance, in both SD1 and SD2, 15 out of the total 22 participants showed an increase compared to the resting state. Furthermore, distortions in the rate of change for SD1 and SD2 were observed in four participants. Specifically, two participants exhibited negative SD1 and positive SD2 values: participant sub6 (SD1: −47.6, SD2: 15.07) and participant sub40 (SD1: −10.65, SD2: 8.6). Conversely, two participants displayed positive SD1 and negative SD2 values: participant sub42 (SD1: 32.23, SD2: −12.36) and participant sub34 (SD1: 4.77, SD2: −2.78). Additionally, three participants showed negative values for both SD1 and SD2: participants sub3, sub15, and sub16. Analyzing the results regarding variance, participant sub43 showed minimal change, while decreases in variance were observed in participants sub3, sub16, and sub42. Significant increases were noted in the remaining 18 participants. Next, the analysis of density changes on the Poincaré plot revealed that eight participants demonstrated an increase in density compared to the resting state, two participants showed no change, and the remaining 12 participants exhibited a decrease. Considering changes of less than 1% as negligible, seven participants showed no change, six increased, and nine decreased. Subsequently, a detailed examination of centroid position changes on the Poincaré plot was conducted. Scatter plots were created with the change rates of x-coordinate plotted on the x-axis and the change rates of y-coordinate plotted on the y-axis. This analysis revealed that the increase or decrease rates of x-coordinate and y-coordinate were nearly identical. Considering changes of less than 1% as negligible, eight participants showed minimal change, nine exhibited an increase, and five demonstrated a decrease. Finally, the results regarding branching structure on the Poincaré plot were examined. The analysis of branching structure showed an increase in ten participants compared to the resting state. However, participant sub6 did not show significant changes between the resting and art appreciation states. Furthermore, decreases compared to the resting state were observed in eleven other participants, with participant sub2 showing a particularly large decrease of -180% compared to others.

5   Discussion

5.1   Interpretation of Results

The results of this study suggest several important points regarding the influence of art appreciation on the psychological and physiological states of the viewers. First, focusing on the indices of heart rate variability, SD1 and SD2, it was observed that 15 participants showed an increase in both SD1 and SD2 during art appreciation compared to the resting state. SD1 represents short-term fluctuations in heart rate, while SD2 reflects the magnitude of long-term heart rate variability. This suggests that approximately 68% of the participants exhibited strong emotional responses such as joy, surprise, excitement, or anxiety to artworks both in the short and long term. Furthermore, three participants who showed negative values for both SD1 and SD2 were found to be relaxed both in the short and long term during art appreciation. Additionally, among the four participants where distortions in the rate of change for SD1 and SD2 were observed, those with positive SD1 and negative SD2 tended to be relaxed in the long term despite experiencing intense emotions in the short term, while those with negative SD1 and positive SD2 tended to be relaxed in the short term but experienced intense emotions in the long term.

Regarding the changes in variance on the Poincaré plot, which indicates the spread of RR interval (RRI) data and helps understand the characteristics of heart rate variability, an increase in variance was observed in 18 participants. These viewers may be showing strong emotional reactions to artworks or being emotionally aroused. On the other hand, three participants (sub3, sub16, sub42) showed a decrease in variance, indicating that their RR interval data points were relatively concentrated on the Poincaré plot, suggesting minimal heart rate variability and implying emotional stability or a relaxed psychological state while appreciating art. These participants exhibited negative values for both SD1 and SD2, supporting the notion of a relaxed state during art appreciation.

Concerning changes in density, high density suggests relatively constant heart rate intervals and stable emotional and cognitive responses, while low density implies significant fluctuations in heart rate intervals and intense emotional or cognitive responses. When considering changes of less than 1% as negligible, seven participants showed no change, six increased, and nine decreased in density. Notably, participants with increased density, especially participant sub6, exhibited a significantly large increase. This suggests a relaxed state during art appreciation, as evidenced by a substantial decrease in SD1, representing short-term heart rate variability, compared to other participants.

Conversely, the decrease rate showed greater changes than the increase rate, indicating that artworks may induce strong emotional or cognitive responses. Particularly, those who experienced a decrease in density suggested significant emotional or cognitive fluctuations during art appreciation, implying that artworks may evoke profound emotional experiences in viewers.

Regarding changes in the centroid position on the Poincaré plot, it was evident that the change rates of x-coordinate and y-coordinate were nearly identical. This suggests a consistent influence of art appreciation on the balance of heart rate variability. Specifically, when the centroid position moves to the upper right on the scatter plot, indicating longer average heart rate intervals (slower heart rate) and larger differences in consecutive heart rate intervals, viewers may be relaxed but experiencing emotional responses or short-term stress reactions simultaneously. Conversely, moving the centroid position to the lower left suggests shorter average heart rate intervals (faster heart rate) and smaller differences in consecutive heart rate intervals, indicating that viewers may feel stressed and excited but exhibit relatively little short-term heart rate variability, suggesting emotional stability. Analyzing the scatter plot positions, eight participants showed minimal change, while nine moved to the upper right and five moved to the lower left. Particularly, participants with a significant decrease in density (e.g., sub5, sub9, sub42) moved significantly to the upper right, indicating large momentary emotional fluctuations.

Finally, the analysis of branching structure on the Poincaré plot suggests that complex branching structures indicate diverse and unpredictable changes in heart rate intervals. Such complexity may imply healthy cardiac function and adaptive autonomic nervous system responses. The presence of complex branching structures during art appreciation suggests that viewers may exhibit emotionally rich responses and vigorous cognitive activities, reflecting deep emotional experiences or immersion induced by artworks. Conversely, participants with simple or linear branching structures may indicate relatively regular and predictable heart rate variability, suggesting a relatively stable emotional state or consistent emotional responses during art appreciation. Among the 22 participants, 10 showed an increase in branching structures compared to the resting state, while 11 showed a decrease, with participant sub2 exhibiting a particularly significant decrease compared to others. These results serve as important indicators of immersion experience, suggesting that immersion in Tosa art with its intricate movements induces diverse emotional fluctuations. In just three minutes of art appreciation, nearly half of the participants experienced an increase and complexity in branching structures, indicating that the mirror display space created in this study could provide an excellent immersive experience (Table 1).

Table 1. Summary Table of Paticipant's State Changes Due to Art Observation

subject	immersive experience	emotional condition	emotional stability	SD1	SD2	Variances	Density	Center Position
sub1	Immersion	Excited	Stable	Increase	Increase	Increase	Increase	left-lower
sub2		Excited	Stable	Increase	Increase	Increase	Decrease	right-upper
sub3		Relax	Fluctuating	Decrease	Decrease	Decrease	Increase	left-lower
sub4	Immersion	Excited	Stable	Increase	Increase	Increase	Almost no change	Almost no change
sub5	Immersion	Excited	Stable	Increase	Increase	Increase	Decrease	right-upper
sub6		Excited	Stable	Decrease	Increase	Increase	Increase	left-lower
sub8		Excited	Stable	Increase	Increase	Increase	Almost no change	Almost no change
sub9	Immersion	Excited	Stable	Increase	Increase	Increase	Decrease	right-upper
sub15		Excited	Fluctuating	Decrease	Decrease	Increase	Decrease	right-upper
sub16		Relax	Fluctuating	Decrease	Decrease	Decrease	Decrease	right-upper
sub18	Immersion	Excited	Stable	Increase	Increase	Increase	Increase	Almost no change
sub21	Immersion	Excited	Stable	Increase	Increase	Increase	Almost no change	Almost no change
sub23		Excited	Stable	Increase	Increase	Increase	Increase	left-lower
sub30	Immersion	Excited	Stable	Increase	Increase	Increase	Almost no change	Almost no change
sub33		Excited	Stable	Increase	Increase	Increase	Decrease	right-upper
sub34		Relax	Fluctuating	Increase	Decrease	Decrease	Almost no change	Almost no change
sub35		Excited	Stable	Increase	Increase	Increase	Decrease	right-upper
sub36	Immersion	Excited	Stable	Increase	Increase	Increase	Decrease	right-upper
sub40		Excited	Stable	Decrease	Increase	Increase	Almost no change	Almost no change
sub41	Immersion	Excited	Stable	Increase	Increase	Increase	Increase	left-lower
sub42	Immersion	Relax	Fluctuating	Increase	Decrease	Decrease	Decrease	right-upper
sub43		Excited	Stable	Increase	Increase	Increase	Almost no change	Almost no change

The experiment using the artworks of Naoko Tosa provided important insights into the changes in emotions and immersion states among the participants. While individual differences were observed, it was confirmed that the majority of participants experienced significant emotional changes. This indicates the profound emotional impact that Tosa's artworks have on the viewers. Furthermore, the analysis of branching structures based on the Poincaré plot revealed that approximately half of the participants were in a clear state of immersion. This suggests that participants were deeply immersed in the artworks and strongly responsive to the emotional and cognitive fluctuations induced by the artworks. Such immersion underscores the depth of influence that the unique aesthetics and expressive power of artworks exert on the psychological and physiological responses of viewers, providing valuable insights into research on immersive art experiences. Overall, this study offers a new perspective for understanding the impact of art appreciation on the emotions and psychological states of viewers, potentially serving as a valuable foundation for future research and applications in the field of art experiences.

5.2 Relation of Results to the Literature Review

This study makes significant contributions to addressing gaps in previous research on immersive art experiences in the following ways. Firstly, by utilizing the media art of Naoko Tosa, this research offers a novel perspective to the study of immersive art experiences by employing Tosa's artworks, which capture the hidden beauty within natural phenomena, thereby filling a gap in research that has overlooked experiences involving such unique aesthetics and scientific background. This approach sheds light on the process by which viewers deeply immerse themselves in artworks and the emotional impact thereof. Secondly, the use of the newly developed mirror display space addresses technical challenges towards achieving a fully immersive art experience, thereby adding a new dimension to the research. By employing this device, comprehensive analysis of viewers' emotional and physiological responses was facilitated, demonstrating technological advancements in the study of immersive art experiences. Furthermore, the application of time-series analysis of physiological data enhanced understanding of viewers' physiological responses by utilizing Poincaré plots on the time-series data of heart rate intervals (RRI). This deepened understanding of the influence of art appreciation on viewers' psychological and physiological states, thereby expanding the potential applications of immersive art experiences. Through these elements, this study overcomes gaps in previous research on immersive art experiences and offers a profound understanding of the impact of art appreciation on viewers, along with new possibilities for application.

6 Conclusion

This study provides important insights into the psychological and physiological effects of immersive art experiences using the media art of Naoko Tosa. Specifically, it was found that the majority of participants experienced significant emotional changes in response to the art pieces, with approximately half experiencing a clear state of immersion. Furthermore, the use of a newly developed mirror display space was shown to be effective in deeply exploring viewers' emotional and physiological responses. Additionally, the application of time-series analysis of heart rate intervals using Poincaré plots allowed for a more detailed understanding of the stability and variability of viewers' emotions. However, as this study is based on specific art pieces and a limited participant pool, caution is needed in generalizing the results. Moreover, the evaluation of emotional changes and immersion status relies on subjective interpretation, highlighting the need for further development of objective measurement methods. Additionally, the research setting and cultural background may influence the results, warranting additional studies in different environments and cultures. Future research should aim to generalize the results of this study by including various art pieces and participants with different cultural backgrounds. Moreover, the development and application of more objective and precise measurement methods are necessary for evaluating emotional changes and immersion status. Further research is also needed to deepen understanding of how the characteristics of art pieces and individual differences in viewers may influence emotional and physiological responses. This broader understanding could lead to the development of new applications for art experiences.

References

Cristobal Rodolfo Guerra-Tamez: The impact of immersion through virtual reality in the learning experiences of art and design students: the mediating effect of the flow experience. Educ. Sci. **13**(2), 185 (2023)

Grau, O.: Virtual Art: From Illusion to Immersion. MIT Press, Cambridge, MA (2003)

Ito, K., Tada, M., Ujike, H., Hyodo, K.: Effects of the weight and balance of head-mounted displays on physical load. Appl. Sci. **11**(15), 6802 (2021). https://doi.org/10.3390/app11156802

Kaprow, A.: Assemblages, Environments, and Happenings. Harry N. Abrams Inc, New York (1966)

Kim, J., Lee, S.: A study on the immersive experience in virtual reality: focused on the first time user. Int. J. Virtual Reality **19**(1), 65–74 (2019)

Marín-Morales, J., et al.: Real vs immersive-virtual emotional experience: analysis of psychophysiological patterns in a free exploration of an art museum. PLoS ONE **14**(10), e0223881 (2019). https://doi.org/10.1371/journal.pone.0223881

"Mirroria."AsahiGlassPlaza". https://www.asahiglassplaza.net/products/mirroria/

Nakatsu, R., Tosa, N., Niiyama, S., Kusumi, T.: Evaluation of the effect of art content on human psychology using mirror display with AR function. In Nicograph International **2021**, 54–61 (2021)

Nakatsu, R., et al.: Construction of immersive art space using mirror display and its preliminary evaluation. In: Brooks, A.L. (ed.) Proceedings of International Display, vol. 565, pp. 781–784. Springer, Cham (2023). https://doi.org/10.1007/978-3-031-55312-7_22

Nakatsu, R., et al.: Construction of immersive art space using mirror display and its evaluation by psychological experiment. In: Brooks, A.L. (ed.) ArtsIT 2023. LNICS, vol. 565, pp. 290–304. Springer, Cham (2023). https://doi.org/10.1007/978-3-031-55312-7_22

Nakatsu, R., et al.: Construction of immersive art space using mirror display and its preliminary evaluation. In: Proceedings of the 27th World Multi-Conference on Systemics, Cybernetics and Informatics (WMSCI 2023), pp. 434–439 (2023)

Nakatsu, R., Tosa, N., Takada, H., Kusumi, T.: Psychological evaluation of image and video display on large LED displays and projections. J. Soc. Art Sci. **20**(1), 45–54 (2021)

Pang, Y., Zhao, L., Nakatsu, R., Tosa, N.: a study of variable control of sound vibration form (SVF) for media art creation. In: Proceedings of the 2017 International Conference on Culture and Computing (2017)

Pyun, K.R., Rogers, J.A., Ko, S.H.: Materials and devices for immersive virtual reality. Nat. Rev. Mater. **7**(11), 841–843 (2022). https://doi.org/10.1038/s41578-022-00501-5

Smith, J.L., et al.: Measuring physiological responses to sensation in typical adults. Psychophysiol. **55**(3), e13025 (2018)

Tosa, N., Nakatsu, R.: Creating Japanese culture through the fusion of art and technology. J. Inst. Electron. Inf. Commun. Eng. **99**(4), 295–302 (2016)

Tosa, N., et al.: Creation of Fluid Art 'Sound of Ikebana' under Microgravity Using Parabolic Flight. Leonardo/ISAST, MIT Press (2023). https://doi.org/10.1162/leon_a_02360

Color Constancy Assuming Viewing Works Using a Display

Meeko Kuwahara[1]([⊠]), Hiroki Takagi[1], and Masaki Hayashi[2]

[1] Meisei University, 2-1-1 Hodokubo Hino, Tokyo, Japan
meeko.kuwahara@meisei-u.ac.jp
[2] Uppsala University, Cramérgatan 3, 621 57 Visby, Sweden

Abstract. This paper reports on the differences in color constancy from the real world that occur when viewing a work of art in the virtual world on a display screen.

Keywords: Color constancy · Virtual Museum · Lighting in the virtual

1 Introduction

There are increasing opportunities to view artworks that exist in a virtual space using a display. Virtual spaces, such as the Metaverse, are expected to be accessed on a wide variety of devices. In a virtual space, lighting can be freely manipulated without the physical constraints of the real world (except for technical issues that will surely be resolved eventually). However, given that viewers still inhabit the real world, unless they utilize highly immersive devices such as head-mounted displays (HMDs), it is rare for the lighting conditions in the virtual space to align with those of the viewer. In such cases, color constancy would be lower and color perception would differ from reality, affecting the impression of artworks. This paper reports color constancy when viewing works of art in a virtual space such as a metaverse space or a virtual museum when the lighting is changed, assuming that the artworks are viewed on a display screen. This study will used data on public domain paintings published by the owning museums. The lighting consisted of main lighting and spotlights illuminating the paintings, assuming a virtual museum exhibition room that imitated an actual museum. Its main lighting and spotlights were adjusted and changed to study the impression of the paintings. The outcome will be the creation of user-friendly virtual museums, facilitating easy digital enjoyment of artworks and enhancing the overall experience for people.

2 Effects of Lighting (Illuminance and Color Temperature)

2.1 Lighting Impressions

Color exerts a significant influence on our psychology, and one of the most well-known distinctions is between warm and cold colors. This classification is not dependent on the actual physical temperature of an object. Colors in the red-orange range are associated with warmth, while those in the blue-blue-purple range evoke a sense of coldness. This represents a synesthetic experience. Light with a high color temperature creates a clean and lively impression, and it also stimulates the sympathetic nervous system within the autonomic nervous system, contributing to mental and physical excitement. Conversely, light with a low color temperature has a calming effect, inducing a sense of relaxation in both the body and mind. There have been studies exploring the extent and nature of the impact that lighting can have on the impression of a painting. From the perspective of the impression of artworks, there are studies suggesting a preference for higher illuminance lighting, with paintings being evaluated as more beautiful, dynamic, and attractive [1–3]. In a study by Nishikawa and Kitaoka that aimed for a more realistic exhibition environment, it was found that paintings were perceived as more beautiful, pleasant, dynamic, likable, exciting, warm, joyful, and reassuring under illuminances of 1350 lx compared to 50 lx and 150 lx. Conversely, evaluations of the scariness, eeriness, and loneliness of paintings tended to be higher under relatively dim lighting conditions [4].

2.2 Lighting for Artworks

The lighting of exhibition spaces in museums and galleries depends on the content of the exhibit and its purpose. For art exhibits, the primary objective is appreciation.

If the objective is not to observe or conduct research on artworks, but rather to appreciate them, an ideal and comfortable display is more desirable than achieving precise accuracy in perceiving the shape, color, and texture of the artworks. Furthermore, unlike standard lighting, it is crucial to implement measures to pre-vent damage caused by lighting in museums and galleries. Typically, curators are responsible for lighting design, and it is uncommon for museums to have a dedicated lighting design team [5].

The illumination level on the exhibition room is set to create a comfortable and less tiring lighting environment for visitors to view and observe. Many museums recommend a low level of illumination, as higher than necessary illumination levels not only inhibit good viewing, but also cause damage to the artwork due to radiation and heat. For exhibits that are very sensitive to light (textiles, watercolors, drawings, printed matter, botanical specimens, etc.), it is recommended by ICOM (International Council of Museums) that the illuminance be kept below 50 lx (as low as possible) and the correlated color temperature at 2900 K [6, 7]. Given that the illuminance in everyday living spaces is around 500–1000 lx, many exhibitions room employ relatively dim lighting. As a result, many people have the impression that the lighting in museums is dark. Light with high color rendering properties is easy to distinguish in terms of color. Therefore, in the case of high color rendering light, the intended lighting effect is likely to be achieved even if the illuminance of the exhibits is reduced, and it is important to select a light source with high color rendering from the standpoint of protecting exhibits.

2.3 Color Constancy

Color constancy is a visual function in which human unconsciously try to compensate for the color effects of light when they see things. Even when illuminated by the orange light of a light bulb or the bluish-white light of a fluorescent lamp, human can perceive object colors without being affected by the color of the light.

On the other hand, it has long been known that in the case of photographs and illustrations, lighting conditions may not be accurately perceived, leading the brain to incorrectly compensate for them. This phenomenon is referred to as the color constancy illusion [8]. The same effect occurs when viewing images through display monitors. Figure 1 illustrates the color constancy illusion. Each figure in Fig. 1 consists of large and small concentric circles, where the large circle is filled with gray (RGB 120 α 50%), and the small circle is filled with white (RGB255 α 50%). Within that small white circle, there are two even smaller circles symmetrically positioned on the right and left of the center. For these two circles in the leftmost two figures, the fill color is red (R 255, G 0, B 0, α 50%), for the middle two figures, the fill color is green (R 0, G 255, B 0, α 50%), and for the rightmost figure, the fill color is blue (R 0, G 0, B 255, α 50%). In the second, fourth, and sixth figures from the left, the filter color, which is gray (RGB 120 α 50%) when overlapped with the color of the smallest circle, is applied to the left half and the small circle on the right. Specifically, in the second figure, it is filled with cyan (R102 G 255 B 255 α 50%), in the fourth figure with magenta (R 255 G 102 B 255 α 50%), and in the sixth figure with yellow (R 255 G 255 B 102 α 50%). In the second, fourth, and sixth figures from the left, the small circle on the right appear as gray to many people. However, despite this perception, many people judge the second small circle on the left as red, the fourth as green, and the sixth as blue. To demonstrate that the fill colors of the small circles on the left and right are indeed identical, a gray horizontal line runs through the center of each figure in Fig. 2. The small circles on the left and right match the color of the gray horizontal line, confirming that their fill colors are indeed the same. The gray opaque horizontal line overlaps other colors at the frontmost layer. Therefore, it does not blend with other colors, but some people perceive it as gray, while others perceive it as the color before overlaps.

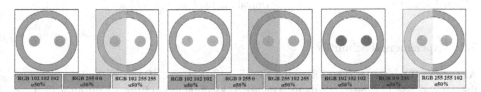

Fig. 1. Ex: color constancy illusion (Color figure online)

Fig. 2. Ex: color constancy illusion (Color figure online)

3   Experimental Stimulus

3.1   3D Virtual Space

In the experiment, a 3D virtual space was constructed to replicate a real museum [9, 10], and images from the art museum, published into the public domain or open access, were utilized (Fig. 3). As depicted in Fig. 3, the space simulating a museum is a rectangle measuring 20 m in length and width, with a height of 4 m. The paintings are installed on the inner walls of this rectangle, centered at a height of 150 cm from the floor. The lighting setup includes general lighting and spotlights. The general light is positioned 500 cm from the wall, while the spotlight is placed 200 cm from the wall, exclusively illuminating the artworks.

The camera was positioned at a height of 150 cm from the floor and 100 cm from the wall. Unreal Engine 5 was employed to construct the environment for the experiment, and the variations in color temperature using Unreal Engine 5 are illustrated in Fig. 4.

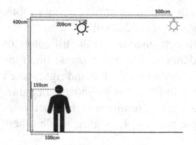

Fig. 3. Experimental environment (3D Virtual Space)

Fig. 4. The variations in color temperature using Unreal Engine 5

3.2   Experimental Stimulus

Artworks (Original). The following Fig. 5, 6, 7, 8, 9 and 10 shows digital images of the artwork used in the experiment. The artworks depicted in Figs. 11 through 17 were chosen for a preliminary experiment by selecting paintings primarily featuring orange and blue colors. These colors were chosen due to their susceptibility or resistance to the influence of orange, representing the color of the light bulb. The selected artworks were sourced from museums with collections available in the public domain. The preliminary experiment involved testing these artworks under illuminance levels ranging from 50 lx to 100 lx and color temperatures of 3000 K and 6000 K.

Fig. 5. Sunflowers, The Metropolitan Museum of Art, New York, USA [11], Date: 1887, Medium: Oil on canvas, Dimensions: 43.2 × 61 cm

Fig. 6. Improvisation No. 30 (Cannons), The Art Institute of Chicago, Chicago, USA [12], Date: 1913, Medium: Oil on canvas, Dimensions: 111 × 111.3 cm

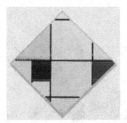

Fig. 7. Lozenge Composition with Yellow, Black, Blue, Red, and Gray, The Art Institute of Chicago, Chicago, USA [13], Date: 1921, Medium: Oil on canvas, Dimensions: 60 × 60 cm (Color figure online)

4 Experimental

Artworks (in 3D Virtual Space). The digital images described in the previous section were imported into a 3D virtual space replicating a real museum, with the color temperature and illuminance of the general lighting and spotlights adjusted. Figures 11, 14, 15, 17 and 18 showcase the images under the configured lighting environment. Each of Figs. 11, 14, 15, 17 and 18 are grounded in real museum lighting configurations, featuring an illuminance of 50 lx and color temperatures of 3000 K, 5000 K, and 6000 K, starting from the left-most figure. Due to the extensive range of devices employed for accessing virtual museums and metaverses on the Internet, the survey requested feedback on these images presented in a format that displayed them sequentially on a display monitor. 16 subjects were surveyed, 7 on desktop PC monitors and 9 on smartphone monitors.

Fig. 8. Cypresses, Artist: Vincent van Gogh, The Metropolitan Museum of Art, New York, USA [14], Date: 1889, Medium: Oil on canvas, Dimensions: 93.4 × 74 cm

Fig. 9. Hydrangea and Swallow, from an untitled series of large flowers, Artist: Hokusai Katsushika, The Art Institute of Chicago, Chicago, USA [15], Date: 1833/34, Medium: Color woodblock print; oban, Dimensions: 26.1 × 38.5 cm (Color figure online)

Fig. 10. Hydrangea and Swallow, from an untitled series of large flowers, Artist: Hokusai Katsushika, ADACHI HANGA, Tokyo, Japan (Color figure online)

The respondents were instructed to rate their level of agreement or disagreement with the question using a 5-point scale. It is a five-point rating scale where '1' corresponds to 'strongly disagree' and '5' corresponds to 'strongly agree'. The common questions addressed in each figure are as follows:

- Q1: Does the color appear to change from original?
- Q2: Has the impression changed from original?

In Table 1 below, the evaluation scores for Fig. 11 are presented. The results indicate that there are noticeable changes in impression and color perception at lower color temperatures. At 6000K, the majority of respondents indicated that there was not much difference from the original. As shown in Fig. 12, some people perceive the center of the sunflower as light blue-green and others perceive the background as dark blue-green, even though the 3000K figure is composed primarily of orange and brown tones. Figure 13 shows the illuminance of the lighting in Fig. 10 increased to 1300lx. In each figure, it can be seen that the illusions affected by color temperature are less likely to occur. Previous research has shown that an illuminance of 1350lx is the illuminance that makes paintings look attractive.

Fig. 11. Sunflowers (Fig. 5) (Color figure online)

Table 1. Figure 11 Q1 and Q2

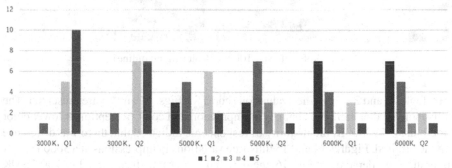

Fig. 12. Color constancy illusion (Color figure online)

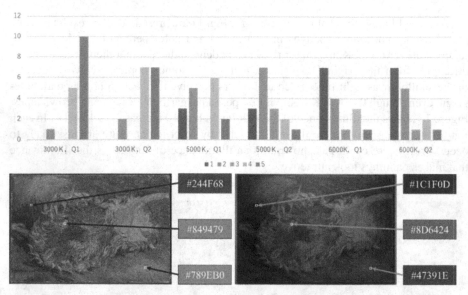

Fig. 13. Sunflower, 1000l× (Color figure online)

In Tables 2 and 3 below, the evaluation scores for Figs. 14 and 15 are presented. The results indicate that there are changes in impression and color perception at lower color temperatures. At 3000K, the majority of respondents indicated that there was difference from the original. Figures 14 and 15 illustrate variations in impressions at a 5000 K color temperature. As depicted in Fig. 16, the dark blue color transforms into black at 5000K in Fig. 15. Despite the noticeable change in color, over half of the respondents perceived no difference in impression during their evaluations. When asked if they could see these dark blue-turned-black colors and imagine that the original color was blue, most said it was difficult.

Fig. 14. Improvisation No. 30 (Cannons) (Fig. 6) (Color figure online)

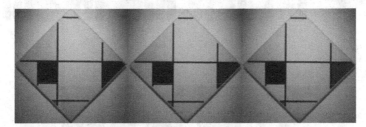

Fig. 15. Lozenge Composition with Yellow, Black, Blue, Red, and Gray (Fig. 7) (Color figure online)

Table 2. Figure 14 Q1 and Q2

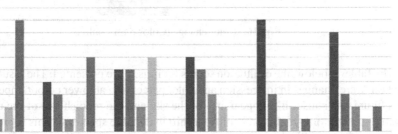

Table 3. yFigure 14 Q1 and Q2

Fig 14, Question1, 2

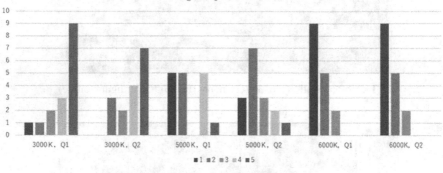

3000K, Q1   3000K, Q2   5000K, Q1   5000K, Q2   6000K, Q1   6000K, Q2

■1 ■2 ■3 ■4 ■5

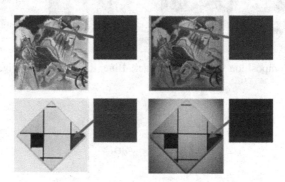

Fig. 16. Color change (Color figure online)

In Tables 4 below, the evaluation scores for Figs. 8 are presented. The results indicate that there are changes in impression and color perception at lower color temperatures. In this figure, the sunset-like appearance of the sky and the reddish hue of the trees result from a stronger orange tint, rather than a shift in the blue spectrum. This is probably due to a color contrast illusion.

Fig. 17. Cypresses (Fig. 8) (Color figure online)

Table 4. Figure 16 Q1 and Q2

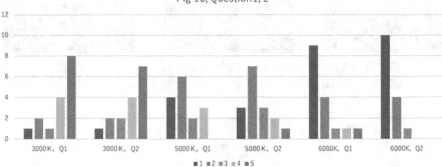

Figures 18 also shows a change in impression at lower color temperatures, like the figure described in the previous section. Ukiyo-c is greatly affected by deterioration due to light, and many of the works in museums and other collections are tanned. As evident in Figs. 9 and 10, hydrangea colors typically include light blue and light peach. However, in all three images of Fig. 19, a considerable number of individuals perceived the light peach color as white. Remarkably, some observers interpreted the tanning of the paper in Fig. 9 as a change in color temperature. This could be attributed to the prevalence of light yellow, a main background color in Ukiyo-e. Figure 19 shows a comparison of the data with the newly printed Ukiyo-e data. This may be due to the discoloration of the paper due to the color of the tanning process, which is orange or brown in color, and the fading of the color. However, we also considered the influence of the light-yellow background to be significant, since the muse-um collection piece also appears to be light pink flower in another work that uses color.

Fig. 18. Hydrangea and Swallow, from an untitled series of large flowers (Fig. 9) (Color figure online)

Fig. 19. Hydrangea and Swallow, from an untitled series of large flowers (Fig. 9 and 10) (Color figure online)

4.1 Discussion

The experimental results indicate that under low illuminance and low color temperature conditions, the impression is significantly influenced by the color composition of the painting. These effects are not solely attributed to the overlapping of lighting colors but also include the illusions of color constancy and color contrast. The experiment results revealed that artworks undergo changes in color and are prone to be perceived differently from their original colors and impressions, which may be unintended. While the setting within the virtual space allows for freedom, and individual preferences play a role, curating artwork necessitates a lighting design distinct from that of a physical museum, even though it is not constrained by physical limitations.

5 Conclusions

In this paper, we report on color constancy when the lighting is varied, assuming that the viewer is viewing a work of art on a display screen in a virtual space such as a metaverse space or a virtual museum. In this study, we used public-domain painting data available from museums. The lighting was assumed to be a virtual museum exhibition room that imitated an actual museum, and consisted of a main light that illuminated the paintings and spotlights. The main lighting and spotlights were adjusted and changed to investigate the impression of the paintings. As a result, color constancy is unlikely to occur when viewing a work of art in the low illumination and low color temperature of a virtual space viewed on a display monitor. It was also found that even when the illusion of color constancy did occur, the same impression. As a future issue, although the data in this study was photographed, all works of art have texture, which is greatly affected by light. Therefore, we believe it is necessary to take them into account.

This is expected to result in the creation of a user-friendly virtual museum, which will allow people to easily enjoy works of art digitally and improve their overall experience.

Disclosure of Interests. The authors have no competing interests to declare that are relevant to the content of this article.

References

1. Loe, D.L., Rowlands, E., Watson, N.F.: Preferred lighting conditions for the display of oil and watercolour paintings. Light. Res. Technol. **14**, 173–192 (1982)
2. Nakajima, Y., Fuchida, T.: Study of museum lighting: optimum lighting and color environment (3)-new calculation method of color quality index for museum lighting-. J. Illum. Eng. Inst. Japan **99**(5), 263–269 (2015)
3. Nakajima, Y., Fuchida, T.: Study of museum lighting: optimum lighting and color environment (2)-color evaluation structure for low illuminance level-. J. Illum. Eng. Inst. Japan **99**(2), 74–82 (2015)
4. Megumi, N., Akiyoshi, K.: Impressions of paintings modulated by lighting. J. Color Sci. Assoc. Japan, JCSAJ **44**(3) (2020)
5. Panasonic Lighting Design Support Site P.L.A.M. (Japanese). Accessed Jan 2024
6. Japanese Industrial Standards, General rules of recommended lighting levels, JIS Z 9110:2010 (Japanese)
7. CIE 157 "Control of damage to museum objects by optical radiation
8. KITAOKA A. A brief classification of colour illusions. Talk in the 11th Congress of the International Colour Association (AIC) 2009
9. Takumi, F.: Lighting Handbook for Curators in the Museum, Kodansha, 2014. (Japanese)
10. Panasonic museum solution (Japanese) https://www2.panasonic.biz/jp/solution/museum/. Accessed Jan 2024
11. van Gogh, V.: Sunflowers. Public Domain, The Metropolitan Museum of Art, New York (1887)
12. Kandinsky, V., No, I.: 30 (Cannons). The Art Institute of Chicago, Chicago (1913)
13. Mondrian, P.: Lozenge Composition with Yellow, Black, Blue, Red, and Gray. The Art Institute of Chicago, Chicago (1921)
14. van Gogh, V.: Cypresses. The Metropolitan Museum of Art, New York (1889)
15. Hokusai Katsushika, Hydrangea and Swallow, from an untitled series of large flowers, The Art Institute of Chicago, Chicago, 1833/34
16. Hokusai Katsushika, Hydrangea and Swallow, from an untitled series of large flowers, ADACHI HANGA. https://store.adachi-hanga.com/products/uk_hokusai118. Accessed Jan 2024

Application of Interactive Installation Art Design Based on Generalization Theory

Lin Liu, Yue Mi[✉], Xinyi Cheng, and Yu Shi

Hubei University of Technology, Wuhan 430070, China
747894020@qq.com

Abstract. This paper combines the theory of empathic design to explore the new ideas of interactive installation art design with the theme of natural environment. Through the discussion on the development of interactive installation art, we analyze the necessity of integrating the theory of empathy, and secondly, we use the theory of empathy combined with emotional design to construct an interactive installation art design model, and combine it with the design practice of the Lake Island in Zhongshan Park, Wuhan, to verify its feasibility. Through the practice of this project, it is concluded that the interactive installation based on the empathic theory and the emotional communication between people is two-way, which can more effectively give the experiencer a rich sensory experience, and with the help of the empathic experience to expand and deepen the perceptual dimensions, and obtain a deep emotional experience, which has feasibility and practicality.

Keywords: Synaesthesia Theory · Interactive installation art · Emotional Design · Ecological · Human-Computer Interaction

1 Introduction

Against the backdrop of an increasingly deteriorating global environment, more and more artists have begun to utilize this theme to explore the relationship between human beings and nature in a variety of artistic forms. As an emerging form of art creation, interactive installation art, through the form of interaction to increase the bond between the audience and the work, in order to enhance the dissemination of art information, to demonstrate a higher emotional value, has gained the favor of many art creators and experiencers. This paper is oriented to the realization of the emotional value of the experiencer, and proposes to build a design theoretical model based on the theory of empathy and apply it to the design of interactive devices, using multi-sensory stimulation and psychological resonance to enable the audience to further communicate with the works in depth, and bring a richer emotional interactive experience to the experiencer, and to provide a new perspective for the contemporary design of interactive device art.

© The Author(s), under exclusive license to Springer Nature Switzerland AG 2024
M. Rauterberg (Ed.): HCII 2024, LNCS 14717, pp. 180–195, 2024.
https://doi.org/10.1007/978-3-031-61147-6_13

2   Interactive Installation Art Concept and Development

Interactive installation art is a kind of art form that can interact with the audience by utilizing multimedia technology and the combination of ready-made products. With the change of technology, it has gradually evolved into an art form that combines interactive technology and art creation. Through computer graphics, information acquisition and processing, and arithmetic and other ways of inputting and outputting all kinds of data, and displaying them in the space through carriers, it allows the audience to interact with the works and get a richer, more vivid and real experience. Interactive installation art can not only stimulate the audience's imagination and creativity, but also promote people's understanding and awareness of art, science and technology and culture. It is an art form that crosses over the interactive field and the art field, and has a strong synthesis.

2.1   International Development of Interactive Installation Art

Interactive installation art originated in the early 19th century as ready-made art, and through the development of light art, performance art, etc., it became a popular art form in the Western art world in the 1990's. With the advancement of technology, more and more designers connect interactive installation art with nature to create art. With the advancement of technology, more and more designers are linking interactive installation art with nature to create art.

For example, "Sense Energy" is a "fantasyland" to be created in 2022 by the international design and creative firm CRA-Carlo Ratti Associati in collaboration with the architect Italo Rota, utilizing 500 m of digitally curved copper tubes, photovoltaic electricity, and a large number of other materials. The designers used 500 m of digitally curved copper tubing, photovoltaic panels, and synthetic materials to create an interactive sensory path, and the whole installation is intended to use the game to demonstrate the connection with the world of energy, and through the interaction between people and the installation to stimulate thinking about the efficiency of energy use in the real world. London-based architectural and creative firm ecoLogicStudio created the world's first microalgae air-purification biotechnology playground in Warsaw, using wood, glass and algae reactors. The shape of the building is predominantly wood, wrapped in an ETFE membrane to protect the algae reactors, creating an algae greenhouse, while the space is used as a playground and outdoor classroom, providing a place for people to have fun and relax. From the above cases, it can be seen that the development of interactive installation art is more mature, beginning to break away from the constraints of indoor space to the development of public space, with multi-level sensory communication and the combination of the surrounding environment, to build a new sensory experience for the experience of the person in order to obtain a richer emotional connotation.

2.2 Development of Interactive Installation Art in China

The development of installation art in China is relatively short. Especially influenced by the American Pop artist Rauschenberg, it was only recognized and emerged in the 1980s. in August 1985, the famous American Pop artist Rauschenberg held an exhibition of installation art using readymade products at the National Art Museum of China, which aroused Chinese artists' understanding of and concern for installation art. With the passage of time and the progress of art development, interactive installation art has continued to develop and grow in China, and become a form of art creation respected by artists. The work "Urban Breathing", presented at the 9th Architecture Biennale, focuses on the carbon cycle of the city in the form of an installation. It utilizes four balloon columns made of semi-transparent film and a built-in fan to form "exhalation" and "inhalation", simulating the process of carbon cycle. At the same time, short films of urban life, music sampling urban noise, and sounds of nature were played on a loop to create an immersive experience.UK Studio created an interactive bamboo installation - Tree of Life with bamboo, a natural material, to show the power of nature to the world. The entire installation uses bamboo and ropes to connect with a towering tree, making the tree also a part of the installation and providing shade and resting places. The entire installation uses bamboo and ropes to connect with a towering tree, making the tree also a part of the installation and providing shade and rest places. The audience can get a situation similar to an outdoor bonfire and establish a harmonious relationship between humans and nature.

From the above analysis of China's interactive installation cases, it can be seen that China's installation art development time is relatively short, the entire interactive installation art is based on visual expression, relatively single, less interactive, difficult to evoke the audience's deep emotional cognition, while the western countries have long been the development of the installation art as a kind of "multi-sensory art", which strengthens the deeper connection between the experiencer and the work, and better expresses the creator's intent This reflects the fact that Chinese installation art still has a long way to go. This reflects that Chinese installation art still has a lot of room for progress and development potential.

3 Overview of Relevant Theories

Under the wave of experience economy, people are more in favor of those products that can touch their emotions, and the combination of emotional design and generalization theory can make the design have stronger perceptual functions, thus triggering multi-level experiences for users, and creating a design product that combines memories, products, and experiences for users. In the following subsections, this paper will provide an overview of the General Sense Theory and Emotional Design, which will provide theoretical support for the design thinking model of this paper.

3.1   Overview of Generalization Theory

Synesthesia, also known as alliance or transference, is a cross-modal sensory experience in which stimuli from different senses merge to produce different cognitive experiences [1]. The study of synesthesia can be traced back to the ancient Greek period, when philosophers were investigating whether the color of music was a quantifiable physical quality. It was later formalized in the 17th century by Wendt of the German school of linguistic psychology, and translated into English as "Synesthesia", an extension of the Greek word meaning "a joint expression of the senses". In 1945, Merleau-Ponty developed a new interpretation of synesthesia, and in his book Phenomenology of Perception, he emphasized that the commonality of the body's synesthesia is based on the sensory perception of the body's illustrations, and that synesthesia is the superimposition of the body's organs on each other by means of arousal in order to achieve the purpose of perception [2], for example, when people see different colors, they will have a different emotion for the color or the perception of the temperature. Sensory interoperability is based on the cognitive foundation of human beings, processing the acquired external information and combining it with human beings' own past experiences and emotions to achieve diversified experiences, and it is a conscious and spontaneous perceptual activity of human beings.

China's research on the theory of synesthesia was firstly put forward by Qian Zhongshu in his book "Synesthesia" and applied to the field of literature, which believes that "human synesthesia is based on association", "the senses of sight, touch, hearing, taste and smell can often be connected with each other, and the domains of the eyes, ears, tongue, nose and body can not be separated from each other. The fields of each organ can be divided into no boundaries, such as color can have temperature, sound can have image, warmth and cold can have weight, and smell can have sharpness, etc." [3]. The characteristic of the sense is to deepen from shallow to deep, superficially speaking, it is to stimulate the occurrence of another sense by one sense, and in-depth exploration is to achieve the mutual transformation and projection of each sense through the multiple perceptual images caused by external stimulation, so as to form the experience of "through". According to Chen Yude's methodology in The Spiritual Heart of Wonderful Enlightenment - A Treatise on Artistic Communication, communication can be categorized into three main types, namely, sensory displacement, superimposition of multiple senses, and interoperability of imagery [4]. Sensory displacement belongs to the shallowest level of perceptual experience, i.e., after the senses are stimulated by the outside world, they are able to trigger the combination of another or more than one type of sensory stimulation, which is the most basic perception and lacks a deeper emotional experience. Multi-sensory superposition is a multidimensional experience that integrates multi-sensory perception and perceptual cognition on the basis of mutual perception and combination of senses, and at the same time triggers a chain reaction of perceptual cognition, such as imagination, association, and so on. Imaginary intercommunication belongs to abstract experience, which is a kind of through-sense experience that integrates subjective emotion on the basis of perceptual cognition, rational cognition and cognition of objective things, so that the outside and the inside can be integrated with each other and obtain high-level feelings. Through the analysis of the literature above, it can be seen that empathy is a way of perceiving the external world, and it guides people's daily life by the mutual influence of each organ of perception, so the theory of empathy is not only a specific field of a single discipline, but also the use of integrated disciplines (Figs. 1).

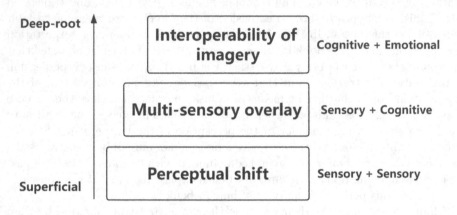

Fig. 1. Three levels of Synesthesia

3.2   Overview of Emotional Design

Emotional design was firstly proposed by Donald A. Norman, a famous American scholar, in the book "Design Psychology: Emotional Design", which refers to the design theory that while maintaining rationality and scientificity in the design process, it is also necessary to add certain emotional factors in order to satisfy the psychological needs of users [5]. The book points out that human brain activity is mainly divided into three levels: instinctive layer, behavioral layer and reflective layer. The instinctive layer is the user's direct perception of the product's appearance. Behavioral layer is the user's feeling of the practicality of the product, and reflective layer is the user's overall feeling of the product, including the product experience, self-feeling and so on. The three levels from shallow to deep bearing progressive relationship, the three interrelated, from the instinctive layer of visual stimulation and then triggered by the behavioral layer of interaction, through the behavioral guidance of the product, the user in the use of the process of obtaining the product experience to stimulate emotional resonance. Emotional design not only provides a solid theoretical foundation for product design and other design fields, but also provides a complete theoretical framework for many design researchers (Fig. 2).

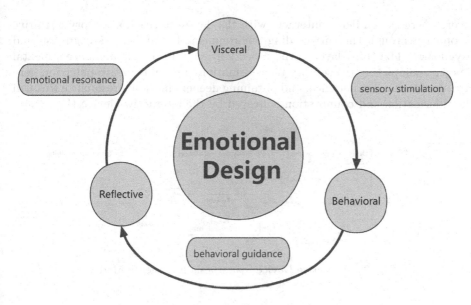

Fig. 2. Three Levels of Emotional Design

4 Interactive Installation Design Practice of "or Symbiosis, or Imbalance"

4.1 Interactive Device Design Method Based on Generalization Theory

This paper combines the theory of empathy and emotional design to construct an overall model for the design of the interactive installation with the theory of empathy as the main focus and emotional design as the supplement. Supported by the theory of empathic transformation, it determines the three levels of empathy, i.e., sensory displacement, multi-sensory superposition, and inter-operability of imagery, and on the basis of which it establishes that this installation is presented in an interactive way. At the same time, combined with the emotional design, from the three perspectives of instinctive layer, behavioral layer, and reflection layer, we establish the modeling, material, structure, site selection, and interactive mode of the installation, combining the above analysis with the three levels of flux, respectively, from the "superposition of the senses transformation", "combination of senses and association, cognition ", "the combination of sensation and association, cognition", "the combination of cognition and emotion" are transformed to the interactive device, using the three levels of empathic experience and the three levels of emotional design theory to carry out different experience design for the interactive device. The first layer of the interactive device is the instinctive layer, mainly through the device modeling, materials, structure to give a certain degree of users and the device to achieve visual stimulation of the sensory experience. The second layer is the behavioral layer, where the audience interacts with the device to reach a sensory cognitive resonance through the surrounding environment, the audience's cognition and psychology. The third layer is the reflection layer, using the audience's mental imagery, completing the sensory transformation in the interactive behavior, generating emotional experience, and obtaining deeper emotional resonance through the information and connotation conveyed by the interactive device (Fig. 3).

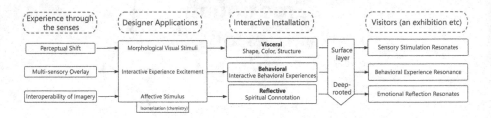

Fig. 3. Interactive Device Synesthesia Experience Model

4.2   Pre-scenario Research

Project Site Selection. This project is based on the principle of proximity to the project site selection, from the geographic location of Wuhan Zhongshan Park is surrounded by man-made buildings, and Zhongshan Park has an ecological environment that makes its existence more like the only "natural purity" in the downtown area, the front of the park is the main entrance, the number of people visiting the park is higher. However, as the visual center of the front area, the lake island is the area with the least number of visitors in the landscape part of the whole front area. From a spatial point of view, it is surrounded by water, but it is poorly connected to the surrounding environment, which makes it impossible to realize a more complete functional zoning plan. Through the field study of the island, from the functional point of view, there is only a Chinese traditional hexagonal wooden brick pavilion for passers-by to rest, and the landscape plants for ornamental use have not played their ornamental effect. In general, the island has a good shade and rest, summer function, but compared to other parts of the landscape tends to be ordinary, can carry out a single activity, stopping the crowd is small, so that this piece of "visual center" is buried. In addition, the existence of the island in the center of the lake is more like an isolated island that has not been overly interfered by man, and still retains part of its original appearance, so the island in the center of the lake was chosen as the placement area for this installation design.

Crowd Analysis. Before carrying out the main body of the landscape planning and design installation of the lake island, this project carries out a preliminary analysis of the crowd activities around Zhongshan Park. In order to make the analysis more authentic and effective, this paper conducted a field study, mainly at 9:00 a.m., 3:00 p.m. and 6:00 p.m., and randomly selected a total of 100 tourists in the park in the form of questionnaires to understand the basic information of the park tourists and tour preferences, such as the number of times a week for the tourists to visit the park, the sightseeing time period, and so on. Through the field research and questionnaire survey, it can be seen that the largest number of tourists in Zhongshan Park are middle-aged and elderly people aged 51–60 and over 60, and the occupation of the crowd is mostly retired people, followed by people aged 26–30, and the occupation of the crowd is mostly full-time housewives, and due to the special nature of the occupation of the full-time housewives, they need to lead the children to do outdoor activities, and they also become the main group of tourists in Zhongshan Park. From the viewpoint of visitors' trajectory of action in the three tour areas, the number of tourists in Zone 1 is medium, but Zone 1 is mainly a landscape area, almost no amusement facilities, and lack of attraction for the lower age groups. Therefore, in the design process, it is necessary to increase the interactive features as the main focus, so as to increase the number of low-age people, increase the vitality of the lake island and the whole Zhongshan Park Zone 1 (Fig. 4).

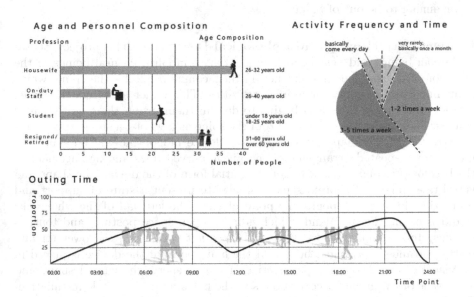

Fig. 4. Crowd Analysis Chart

4.3   Project Planning

Thematic Orientation. This paper explores the relationship between human beings and the natural environment as the theme of the current relationship between nature, nature is the basis for human survival and development, however, with the rapid development of human economy, resulting in serious damage and pollution of the natural environment. Countries around the world have also actively launched policies to respond to this change. In 2015, the 193 member states of the United Nations formally adopted 17 Sustainable Development Goals (SDGs) at the summit, of which the 15th development goal, terrestrial ecology, was proposed to protect, restore and promote the sustainable use of terrestrial ecosystems. Echoing this call, this project takes the relationship between human and nature as its theme, and uses installation as the main body of the design, utilizing the interactivity and strong visual impact of installation art to awaken people to re-examine nature and their own behavior.

The relationship between humans and nature is broadly categorized into two types in the creative theme:

1. To divide nature roughly into three major categories, human-animal-plant, and to maintain harmony and balance among the three, so as to achieve the great harmony of nature and harmonious coexistence between human beings and nature.
2. Nature and human beings are in a state of confrontation, and human behavioral activities continue to devour nature, and human beings and nature are beginning to be out of balance.

Element Extraction and Morphological Derivation. This project focuses on human beings and vertebrate animals that symbolize natural beings in the selection of design elements, extracting their common point - the spine, which is an important support for animal activities. This paper abstracts the spine, extracts the curved lines and begins to deform them, using them as the outer contour lines of the main device. From the spine as a whole, a single spine bone is extracted as the shape structure of the device monolithic will be simplified into a box, repeated arrangement, see Fig. 5. curved lines and arrangement of the box for the combination, to get the initial form of the device, the shape and vertebrate spine and thorax is more similar to present a state of support and protection. From the topographic point of view, the left half of the whole lake island is facing the mainland, which is in an open space posture, and tourists are easy to concentrate here, and the upper left corner is in a lower terrain, so the entrance is arranged here, and the main body of the device is placed in its visual center. From the perspective of the greenery, the curved shape and amplitude of the greenery corresponds to the flat lines of the whole installation. The form of the installation presented by the irregular lines and the continuous frame organized by the ring beams form a unique monumental nature, which as a geometric form becomes the starting point of the whole design: the dialogue between man and nature.

Interaction Modes and Material Selection. The constructive nature of the installation is reflected in the assembly and articulation, with all components prefabricated and connected by high-strength bolts and mortise-and-tenon joints, the materials of which are shown in Fig. 6. The columns of the installation have a maximum height of 3.8 m and a minimum height of 2 m. The beams are articulated with rectangular square tubes, which form a solid enclosure in a triangular

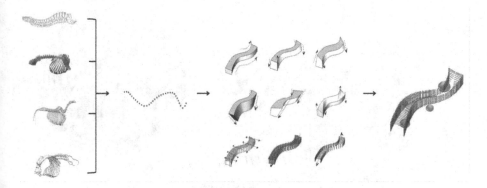

Fig. 5. Abstraction, Simplification and Derivative Molding

arrangement. The beams are articulated with rectangular square tubes, which are arranged in a triangular shape to form a solid enclosure. Architectural device entrances and exits reserved structural openings, up and down customized barge parts hinged fixed, device monolithic maximum 3.9 m, where a single arrangement of frame beams and columns in the combination of part of the choice of mortise and tenon inlay structure, the beams and columns embedded in the assembly. The beam tube is divided into two parts, the front beam tube is solid, smaller than the rear beam tube, which can be indented into the rear beam tube, and the rear beam tube is hollow. This project arranges 65 single units in a path array in the center of the lake island. The whole main device is made of rich materials, no interactive columns of brushed stainless steel, interactive columns and beams of galvanized sheet metal, beams inside the retractable inner tube is made of hose, wrapped in mirror material is able to reflect the surrounding things. When the mirror on the main device maps the surrounding landscape, from the appearance of more like nature as a coat for the package, into the surrounding natural landscape, to achieve harmony between nature and artificially created objects, to create an environment that allows the audience to immersive experience.

The interactive mode of this device selects stepping as the main, the workflow is shown in Fig. 7, and the interactive mode is shown in Fig. 8. 4 irregularly sized circular load-bearing sensing devices are placed under the main device, the built-in load cell is connected to the arduino sensing device, and the maximum weighing limit of 240 kg ($\approx$ 4 adult weights) is set up in advance, when the load-bearing capacity of the circular load-bearing device reaches the limit, the load-bearing information is transferred to the sensing device. When the load-bearing capacity of the circular load-bearing device reaches its limit, the load-bearing information will be transmitted to the inductor, and the inductor will receive the information so that the beams of the main device above will start to fall down and shrink the inner tube, and when the weight is less than the

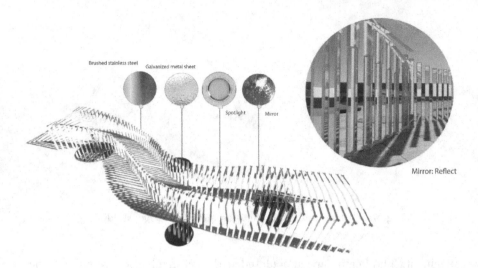

Fig. 6. Material Selection

maximum weighing limit of the load-bearing device, the deformed main device will restore the original, and the beams and tubes will rise up and extend outward. The deformation pattern of the whole device is a metaphor for the way man and nature get along with each other, when human behavior is excessive, nature will begin to lose its original balance. When human behavior is moderate, nature will maintain the balance, at the same time, the falling beam tube will produce a certain degree of visual oppression, the broken device to "prick" visual stimulation to stimulate people to the "pain" of the tactile sensory experience, to complete the visual experience to the tactile experience of the visual experience to the tactile experience is completed, and the most basic sensory transfer is achieved. At the same time, the combination of the visual stimulation of sharp "thorns" and the tactile stimulation of "pain" triggers the audience's further association and cognition - that is, the instinctive fear and repulsion of human beings towards sharp objects, so as to obtain a multi-sensory experience. The combination of visual stimulation and tactile stimulation triggers further associations and perceptions - the instinctive fear and rejection of sharp objects, thus obtaining a multi-sensory overlay. The realization of the two experiences and the combination with the entire landscape environment to achieve the highest level of empathetic experience - imagery interoperability, by the joint role of the device and the surrounding landscape will be implanted into the audience's heart the concept of symbiosis between man and nature, to achieve emotional resonance. The final effect is shown in Fig. 9.

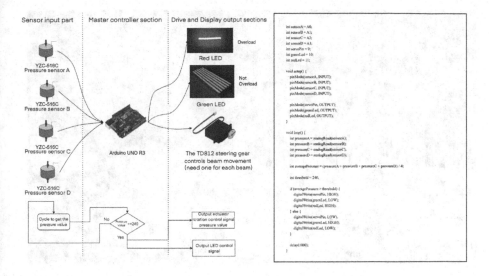

Fig. 7. Workflow and part of the running code

4.4   Design Effectiveness Verification

In order to verify whether the interactive installation "Or Symbiosis, or Imbalance" meets the audience's perceptual experience, the project presents the artwork to the audience by means of a scale questionnaire, and uses 100 audience members as the sample to measure their satisfaction with the installation.

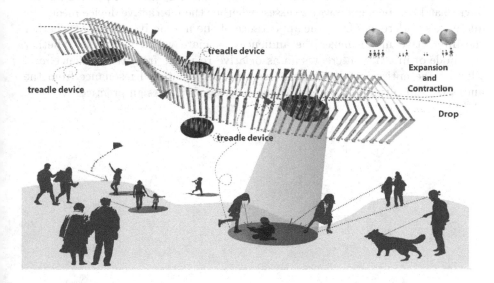

Fig. 8. Specific Display of Interaction Mode

Fig. 9. Final rendering

The questionnaire consists of 10 questions, including 3 questions on appearance impression, 2 questions on interactive experience and 5 questions on emotional resonance, which can effectively measure the audience's immediate satisfaction with the work and their willingness to experience the installation. The questionnaire adopts a 5-level scale, and the respondents need to evaluate the device from very dissatisfied to very satisfied according to their feelings after watching the demo animation, which is a complete linear evaluation process for the device, and can be a good way to assess whether the interactive device meets the audience's preferences from the appearance of the interactive device, or whether the interactive mode makes the audience associate with the device. Whether the mode of interaction creates an associative response from the audience, and whether the entire installation inspires a deeper emotional resonance from the audience, will ultimately determine the success of this design practice.

Table 1. Cronbach's reliability analysis

Questionnaire	Correction term total correlation (CITC)	Deleted α coefficients for item	Cronbach's α coefficient
From the looks of it I would love and want to experience the "or symbiosis, or imbalance" interactive installation	0.622	0.874	0.886
I think the use of materials and the design of the shape of this interactive installation make it look harmonious with its surroundings	0.625	0.874	
I think the "or symbiosis, or imbalance" interactive installations are designed to meet my daily park needs	0.655	0.887	
Watching the demo animation, I could clearly understand the operation mechanism of the interactive installation	0.554	0.892	
While watching the demo animation, I was very satisfied with the interactive experience of the interactive installation	0.728	0.866	
While watching the animation of the deformation of the device triggered by the interactive location, from the visual perception, I felt nervous and uneasy about the shape of the device that deformed after triggering the interaction	0.599	0.876	
While watching the interactive location-triggered device morphing animation, the descending and retracting metal tube triggers a response in my tactile senses (e.g., pain, etc.)	0.611	0.875	
When I watched the demo animation, the device that restored the original state at the end of the interaction gave me a feeling of ease in my heart	0.54	0.88	
When watching the animated presentation, I can understand the theme that this installation is trying to convey about the relationship between human beings and nature	0.609	0.875	
After watching the presentation animation, I was thinking seriously about the current unbalanced relationship between man and nature (e.g., I feel that current human behavior is destroying the natural environment while also destroying itself)	0.637	0.873	

The Cronbach's coefficient is used to evaluate the internal consistency and stability of multiple items in the questionnaire, and the formula for calculating the coefficient is as follows:

$$\alpha = \frac{K}{K-1}\left(1 - \frac{\sum_{i=1}^{K}\sigma_{Y_i}^2}{\sigma_x^2}\right) \tag{1}$$

Table 2. Cronbach's reliability analysis

KMO and Bartlett's test	
KMO value	0.899
Bartlett Sphericity Check approximate chi-square (math.)	393.737
df	45
p-value	0.000

In the formula, K is the number of test questions, represents the variance of the total test results, and represents the variance of the test of the current observation sample. The Cronbach's alpha coefficient test was performed on the scales in the questionnaire using SPSS statistical analysis software. From the test table, it can be seen that the Cronbach's coefficient is 0.886, which is greater than 0.8; the KMO value of the questionnaire is 0.899, which is greater than 0.8; and the P-value of the Bartlett's sphericity test is much less than 0.05, as shown in Table 1 and Table 2. Combining the above two indicators, it can be seen that this questionnaire has good reliability and validity. After organizing and analyzing, the audience's satisfaction with the appearance impression of this interactive installation work is 78%, the interactive experience is 76%, and the emotional resonance is 73%. The results show that the audience has a good overall satisfaction with the interactive installation "Coexistence or Imbalance".

5   Conclusions

This project is based on the development trend of the relationship between humans and nature, using synesthesia theory as the basis, and interactive installation art as the carrier, simplifying the complex interrelationships in the entire natural world, and proposing a possibility for the future of mankind - human beings' evil deeds against nature will eventually backlash on themselves. Through the consideration, application and practice of design methods, interactive installation art design based on synesthesia experience can not only bring more diverse interactive experience modes to the audience, but also strengthen the emotional connection between the installation and the audience, enabling designers to more effectively convey their design concepts to others. It also obtains a design thinking model that combines synesthesia theory with emotional design, providing new ideas for future interactive installation art design. However, this article has insufficient experience in the combination of thinking and methods, and the design practice is not perfect. In the future, we need to continue to explore better ways to combine synesthesia theory with emotional design, optimize it, and find more effective and reasonable design methods.

References

1. Zhang, B., Chen, X., Han, D.: Sound scene interaction design based on synesthesia theory of Meidai Zhao. Packag. Eng. 44(S1), 15–23 (2023). https://doi.org/10.19554/j.cnki.1001-3563.2023.S1.003
2. Merleau-Ponty, M.: The World of Perception. Routledge, London (2004)
3. Qian, Z.-S.: Seven Patches [M]. Beijing: Life · Reading · New Knowledge Joint Publishing Company (2019)
4. Chen, Y.-D.: Spiritual Insight and Wonderful Realization - Art Synesthesia Theory. Anhui Education Press, Hefei (2005)
5. Norman, D.A.: Emotional Design [M]. Q.-F. Fu and J.-S. Cheng, Trans. Beijing: Electronic Industry Press (2005)

6. Song, X., Gu, Y.: Research on art design of digital media interactive installation based on green design. In: International Symposium on Robotics, Artificial Intelligence, and Information Engineering (RAIIE 2022). SPIE, vol. 12454, pp. 15–20 (2022)
7. Zhou, L., Xie, F.: Welcome to Heshan: an installation to create immersive and entertaining experiences with local art through interactive media technologies. In: Rau, P.L.P. (ed.) HCII 2022. LNCS, vol. 13312, pp. 304–317. Springer, Cham (2022). https://doi.org/10.1007/978-3-031-06047-2_22
8. Zhong, M., He, R., Zhao, D., et al.: Design of interactive devices based on synaesthesia experience. Packag. Eng. **42**(4), 109–114 (2021). https://doi.org/10.19554/j.cnki.1001-3563.2021.04.014
9. Liu, J.: Science popularization-oriented art design of interactive installation based on the protection of endangered marine life-the blue whale. In: Journal of Physics: Conference Series. IOP Publishing, vol. 1827, no. 1, p. 012116 (2021)
10. Liu, W., Li, Z., Guo, Q., et al.: Research on cultural and creative product design based on the emotional needs of generation Z. Packag. Eng. 1-17 (2023) [Online]

Effect of Art's Increasing Human Creativity and Motivation When Viewed in an Immersive Environment

Ryohei Nakatsu[1]([✉]), Naoko Tosa[1], Yunian Pang[1], Satoshi Niiyama[2],
Yasuyuki Uraoka[3], Akane Kitagawa[3], Koichi Murata[3], Tatsuya Munaka[3],
Yoshiyuki Ueda[1], Masafumi Furuta[3], and Michio Nomura[1]

[1] Kyoto University, Sakyo, Kyoto 606-8317, Japan
nakatsu.ryohei@gmail.com, {tosa.naoko.5c,pang.yunian.2c,
ueda.yoshiyuki.3e,nomura.michio.8u}@kyoto-u.ac.jp
[2] AGC Inc., Yokohama, Kanagawa 230-0045, Japan
satoshi.niiyama@agc.com
[3] Shimadzu Corporation, Seika-cho, Soraku-gun, Kyoto 619-0237, Japan
{uraoka-y,kitagawa.akane.5jf,murata.koichi.9ar,munaka,
m_furuta}@shimadzu.co.jp

Abstract. How art appreciation affects the human mind is an interesting question. Several studies have already been conducted on art's calming and inspiring effects on the human mind. As an extension of this, whether art can enhance people's creativity is a fundamental and interesting question. If art appreciation can enhance people's creativity, a new function of art will be discovered. It is well known that displaying media art, such as video art, in an ample space can provide a deeply immersive experience, as with projection mapping. A deep sense of immersion can contribute to enhancing creativity. Therefore, it is desirable to research to evaluate whether creativity is aroused by displaying and viewing media art in an ample space. One way to make a small space look vast is to construct a space using mirrors. We have designed and constructed an immersive space surrounded by mirror displays with the functions of both a mirror and a display. Firstly, this paper describes the specific method. In addition, using art created by one of the authors, we conducted a psychological experiment using 40 subjects to compare her art and geometric figures displayed in the space. The results show that the immersive space and art combination have characteristics that motivate people's minds and arouse creativity.

Keywords: Immersive Space · Mirror Display · Psychological Evaluation · Creativity

1 Introduction

Art can enrich people's minds, heal their hearts, and inspire them [1, 2]. Art can be considered the ultimate VR with the power to immerse people. Much emphasis has been placed on technological research to give people a sense of immersion in VR. However,

M. Rauterberg (Ed.): HCII 2024, LNCS 14717, pp. 196–213, 2024.
https://doi.org/10.1007/978-3-031-61147-6_14

more research needs to be conducted on designing and constructing immersive spaces that combine art and VR and their evaluation.

We designed and constructed an immersive space suitable for art content to evaluate how art content affects the human mind. The video art of Naoko Tosa (hereafter "Tosa art"), one of the authors, was used as art content. As described later, Tosa art uses technology to extract the beauty hidden in natural phenomena and transform it into video art characterized by its abstract and organic forms. Many people who have viewed Tosa art have commented that they feel like they are in outer space or feel a sense of floating. Therefore, the characteristics of Tosa art are best expressed when viewed in a vast space. To give viewers the feeling of being in an infinite space, we conceived the idea of constructing a space surrounded by mirror displays that function as both a mirror and a display and having viewers appreciate Tosa art in that space.

This paper describes the design and construction method of an immersive space constructed using a mirror display. In addition, we evaluated how combining the immersive space and Tosa art would affect people's minds through a psychological experiment.

2 Related Studies and Activities

2.1 Research on Immersive Spaces in VR

The purpose of VR is to create a space different from reality and to give people an immersive feeling as if it were reality [3, 17]. VR space can be constructed by projecting images into an actual space using a projector or displaying images on an HMD (Head Mounted Display). In both cases, there is much research on adding the senses of touch, taste, and smell to increase the sense of presence. As these are primitive human senses, however, there is a problem: Research progress takes time [4].

2.2 Fusion of VR and Art

Attempts to fuse art and VR occurred with the advent of VR and have continued until now. For example, William Latham of Goldsmiths, University of London, has been actively creating an art-expressed artificial life form called "Mutator VR" [5]. In the 1990s, there were many attempts to create an immersive space (CAVE is a typical example of such an immersive space [6]) using projectors, etc., and to display art in the space.

2.3 Construction of Immersive Space Using Mirrors

Mirrors are often used in art expression because it is relatively easy to create a seemingly endless space by using mirrors. One well-known example is Yayoi Kusama's "Infinity Mirror Room," in which she installed her art in a mirrored space [7].

3 Digital Art "Sound of Ikebana"

3.1 Concept of "Sound of Ikebana"

One of the authors, Naoko Tosa, discovered that by applying sound vibrations to a fluid such as paint and photographing it with a high-speed camera, the fluid creates a shape similar to that of a flower arrangement. Tosa further edited the resulting video to match the colors of the Japanese seasons and created a digital artwork called "Sound of Ikebana." Fig. 1 shows a scene from the work. For the details of the art creation process, please refer to [8, 9, 13]. Although there has been various research on the visualization of sound, called "Cymatics" (for example [18]), this is another way of sound visualization.

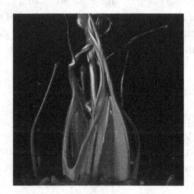

Fig. 1. A scene from "Sound of Ikebana."

3.2 Effects of "Sound of Ikebana" on Human

When Tosa exhibited her digital art around the world with a focus on the "Sound of Ikebana," many overseas art professionals pointed out that "Tosa's digital art, which expresses beauty latent in physical phenomena in an abstract form, expresses beauty previously unnoticed by Westerners, and this is Japan's consciousness and sensitivity."

Since then, "Sound of Ikebana" has taken on challenges in new directions, such as attempting to create new shapes by using the birth cries of newborn babies and the voices of Olympic athletes as sound sources and attempting to create art in the space age by creating works under microgravity [9]. Many people who have viewed Tosa art have commented that they feel their creativity is enhanced. A stimulating new art effect can be found if art appreciation enhances the viewer's creativity. Such effects are apparent in a space with infinite expansion. This also led us to design and construct a space that gives a sense of infinite expansion and have visitors view Tosa art in that space to see if it improves creativity.

4 Design and Construction of Immersive Spaces Using Mirror Displays

4.1 Mirror Display

As mentioned in Sect. 2.3, using mirrors is appropriate for constructing a system that gives the impression of being in an infinite space. Here, we decided to use a "mirror display" with the functions of both a mirror and a display.

We used a mirror display developed by AGC Corporation and commercialized under the name "Mirroria" [10]. The feature of this display is that it achieves a half-mirror reflectance of approximately 65%, the same level of reflectance as that of an ordinary mirror, by utilizing the company's glass manufacturing technology.

4.2 Design and Construction of Immersive Spaces

Several psychological experiments have confirmed that art content positively affects the human mind [11, 12]. Art content was displayed on large LED and mirror displays in these experiments. To take this further and confirm whether art content is effective in improving people's creativity, placing people in a more immersive environment would be effective.

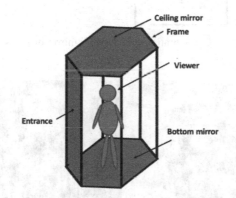

Fig. 2. Conceptual diagram of immersed space.

Therefore, we construct an environment in which the space is surrounded by mirrors and part of the mirrors are used as mirror displays to display art contents. First, a hexagonal space surrounded by rectangular mirrors is constructed. The concept is shown in Fig. 2, where the hexagonal space comprises three sets of two mirrors facing each other. It is well known that mirrors create an infinite number of images by mutually reflecting each other. By having three sets of mirrors, the person inside feels as if he/she is surrounded by countless mirror images of himself/herself. Furthermore, by using the ceiling and floor as mirrors, one feels as if one is surrounded by an infinite number of images of oneself, both above and below.

The six mirrors that make up this hexagonal space are mirror displays and can display images. Since the vertical length of the mirrors is longer than the vertical length of the display, the display on which the images are shown forms part of the mirrors. At the same time, the position of the display is variable in the vertical direction (Fig. 3). This makes it possible to shift the position where the six mirrors display the image. Suppose the mirrors facing each other have the same position for displaying the images. In that case, the respective images will interfere with each other, reducing the sense of an endless series of images. Thus, by shifting the position of the image display, it is possible to create the effect of an endless series of images without having each image interfere with the other.

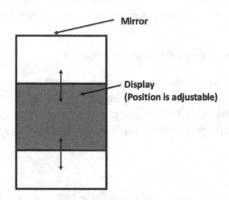

Fig. 3. Configuration of individual mirror displays.

Fig. 4. Exterior view of the immersed space (left: exterior view, right: door open).

The appearance of the constructed immersive space is shown in Fig. 4. Inside this device, even simple shapes can generate an environment of beauty by continuing back and forth, left and right, and up and down indefinitely (Fig. 5). Figure 6 shows several scenes where Tosa art is shown as an example of art content.

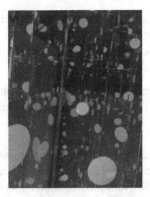

Fig. 5. Geometric figure (circle) displayed in the immersed space.

Fig. 6. Example of displaying Tosa Art in the immersive space.

In this immersive space, preliminary experiments have confirmed that people can experience a sense of floating and liberation. Since a sense of liberation and floating are linked to creativity, people's creativity is expected to be aroused when art content is displayed in this immersive space. Then, we can set the following hypothesis.

Hypothesis. The combination of the immersive space and Tosa art increases human creativity.

Next, we conduct psychological experiments to check this hypothesis.

5   Evaluation of Immersive Space by Psychological Experiments

5.1   Evaluation Concept

We evaluated the constructed immersive space. This immersive space gives people inside it the feeling of being in an infinitely expanding space. Therefore, evaluating art in it is considered a good match with contemporary art, such as video art and media art. As mentioned earlier, there have been many attempts to combine VR and art, but art content can only demonstrate its actual value if viewed in a space suitable for it.

To evaluate this immersive space, we conducted a psychological experiment to compare and evaluate the impression subjects receive when art content and comparison content are displayed. As for the art content, we decided to use Tosa art. The reasons for this are as follows.

1. As mentioned, Tosa art is created by filming fluid phenomena with a high-speed camera. This indicates that Tosa art is based on physical phenomena. Therefore, it is more compatible with the scientific evaluation method compared with art created by another artist.
2. Since it is based on fluid phenomena, various variations can be created by changing parameters, such as the type of fluid and the type of sound. In this respect, it is also compatible with the scientific evaluation methods under different conditions.

5.2 Contents Used in the Experiments

1. Art Content

For the reasons stated above, we decided to use Tosa art. Specifically, we used a 3-min video with the "Sound of Ikebana" as its primary content.

2. Comparative Content

When conducting evaluation experiments using art content, preparing comparison content is essential. We used simple geometric figures such as circles and squares as comparison contents. We conducted a preliminary experiment and evaluated several geometric figures through psychological experiments to determine the geometric figures to be compared with the art contents. The following three types of geometric figures were used in the preliminary experiment.

- Geometric Fig. 1: The shape is a circle and only the color changes with time.
- Geometric Fig. 2: The shapes change to circles and squares in sequence along with the colors.
- Geometric Fig. 3: The shape is a square, and the square rotates. The colors change with time, as in Geometric Figs. 1 and 2.

Here, the colors were set to be the same as the representative color of the art content, in synchronization with the time variation of the color of the art content, to create a similar impression as the art content. Preliminary experiments showed no significant differences among the three types of geometric shapes. As the degree of change for Geometric Fig. 2 is in the middle among the three types, we decided to use Geometric Fig. 2 (hereafter referred to as "Figure") for comparison with the art content. The details of the preliminary experiments are described in the literature [13] and can be found there.

5.3 Evaluation Items

Regarding the evaluation items, first, an evaluation item, "Impression factor," was established to determine what impression the subjects had. This has been used in several psychological experiments such as [14–16] and used by us for art evaluation.

In addition, since one of the purposes of this evaluation is to assess whether the combination of "immersive space + art content" arouses people's creativity, we decided to add an evaluation item regarding how it affects people's minds. As a result of discussions led by one of the authors, Michio Nomura, who specializes in psychology, we decided to evaluate the content in terms of whether it relaxes people's minds ("Relaxation factor"), whether it inspires people's minds ("Motivation factor"), and whether it arouses people's creativity ("Creativity factor"). Specific evaluation items are shown in Table 1 below. Overall, there are 24 evaluation items, which is done on a 7-point scale. The difference in meaning between "immersed," one in the Motivation factor, and "immersive," one in the Creative factor, is subtle, but "immersed" corresponds to logical brain processing, such as "immersed oneself in studying." In contrast, "immersive" corresponds to sensory brain processing, such as "listening to music makes me immersive."

Table 1. Evaluation Items

1. Impression factor (9 items)	**3. Motivation factor (5 items)**
Comfortable - Uncomfortable	Enthusiastic – Not enthusiastic
Friendly - unfriendly	Immersed – Not immersed
Beautiful - Not beautiful	Curious – Not curious
Calm - Restless	Motivated – Not motivated
Interesting - Boring	Aroused – Not aroused
Warm - Cold	**4. Creativity factor (5 items)**
Changeable - Not changeable	Associate – Do not associate
Luxury - Sober	Immersive – Not immersive
Individual – Ordinary	Activated – Not activated
2. Relaxation factor (5 items)	Inspired – Not inspired
At ease – Not at ease	In the zone – Not in the zone
Secure – Not secure	
Pleasant – Not pleasant	
Relaxed – Not relaxed	
Healed – Not healed	

5.4 Participants

Forty students (32 males and eight females) in their first through fourth year at Kyoto University participated in the experiment.

5.5 Experimental Procedure

Below is the process of the experiment.

1. First, after briefly explaining the purpose and content of the experiment, the participant signed a consent form.
2. The participant moved into the immersive space.

3. Then, the participant performed an initial evaluation before viewing Content 1 ("No content" condition). The participant brought his/her smartphone into the space, and the evaluation was done using Google Forms.
4. Before Content 1 was displayed, a resting period (3 min) was taken to reset the participant's psychological state. During this time, the display was kept black.
5. Contents 1 was displayed (3 min).
6. After viewing Content 1, the participant was asked to complete a second evaluation.
7. Before Content 2 was displayed, a resting period (3 min) was taken to reset the participant's psychological state. During this time, the display was kept black.
8. Contents 2 was displayed (3 min).
9. After viewing Content 2, the participant was asked to complete a third evaluation.
10. Then, the participant exited the immersive space.

Regarding the order of presentation of art and geometric figures, to ensure that order effects did not affect the results, the order was controlled for each participant so that the total order of art → geometric figures and geometric figures → art was 20, respectively.

6 Evaluation Results

6.1 Results for Each Evaluation Factor

The average evaluation scores of 40 subjects for each Impression, Relaxation, Motivation, and Creativity factor are shown in Figs. 7, 8, 9, and 10, respectively. In these figures, the graphs show the differences in the evaluation scores for three different contents: while the display was kept black ("No content"), after viewing the geometric figures ("Figure"), and after viewing the art content ("Art"). Also, the results of the analysis of variance (ANOVA), which will be described later, are overlapped on these figures.

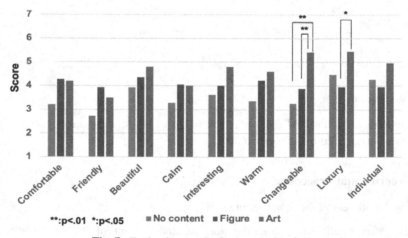

Fig. 7. Evaluation results for Impression factor.

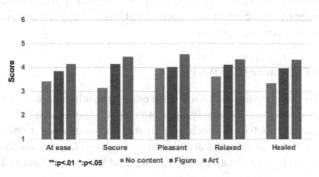

Fig. 8. Evaluation results for Relaxation factor.

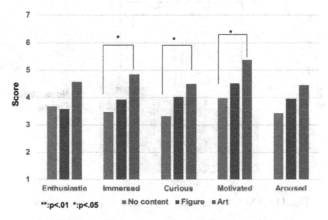

Fig. 9. Evaluation results for Motivation factor.

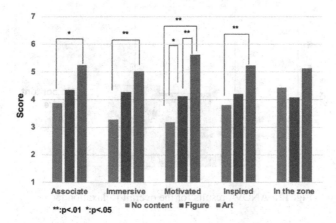

Fig. 10. Evaluation results for Creativity factor.

In the individual evaluation results, for many of the evaluation items, the results were higher in the order of "No content < Figure < Art," indicating the effectiveness of the "immersive space + Tosa art" approach.

6.2 Analysis of Variance (ANOVA)

In order to verify the significance of the differences in evaluation scores between each content in 6.1, we calculate the averaging score of each Impression, Relaxation, Motivation, and Creativity factors for each participant, and conducted a one-way analysis of variance (ANOVA). The results are shown in Fig. 11 (Impression factor), Fig. 12 (Relaxation factor), Fig. 13 (Motivational factor), and Fig. 14 (Creativity factor).

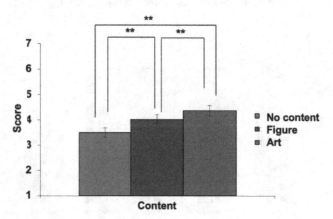

Fig. 11. ANOVA results for the overall Impression factor.

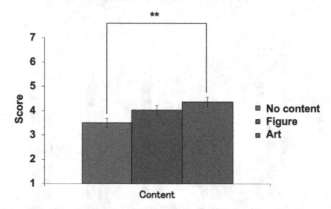

Fig. 12. ANOVA results for the overall Relaxation factor.

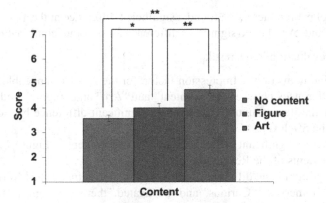

Fig. 13. ANOVA results for the overall Motivation factor.

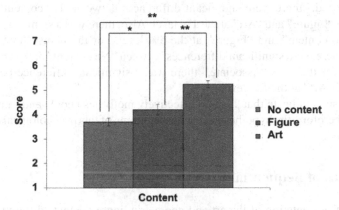

Fig. 14. Analysis of variance results for the overall Creativity factor.

6.3 Considerations

1. ANOVA results

A one-way ANOVA was conducted on the overall Impression, Relaxation, Motivation, and Creativity factors. The results showed that, except for the Relaxation factor, there were significant differences among "No content," "Figure," and "Art" (Figs. 11 through 14). Specifically, for the Impression factor, there was a significant difference at the 1% level among each combination of "No content," "Figure," and "Art" (Fig. 11). As for the Motivation and Creativity factors, there was a significant difference at the 1% level between "No content" and "Art" and between "Figure" and "Art." Also, there was a significant difference between "No content" and "Figure" at the 5% level (Figs. 13 and 14).

For the Relaxation factor, we found a significant difference at the 1% level between "No content" and "Art" but no significant difference for the other combinations (Fig. 12).

2. Individual evaluation items results

For the nine items on the Impression factor, for the item "Changeable," there were significant differences between "No content" and "Art," and "Figure" and "Art" at the 1% level. For the item "Luxury," there was a significant difference between "Figure" and "Art" at the 5% level.

There were no significant differences among "No content," "Figure," and "Art" on any of the five items of the Relaxation factor.

There was a significant difference for three of the five items on the Motivation factor. For the items "Immersed," "Curious," and "Motivated," there were significant differences between "No content" and "Art" at the 5% level.

There were significant differences for four items on the Creativity factor. For the item "Motivated," there were significant differences between "No content" and "Art" and between "Figure" and "Art" at the 1% level. Also, there was a significant difference between "No content" and "Figure" at the 5% level. For the items "Immersive" and "Inspired," there were significant differences between "No content" and "Art" at the 1% level. Also, for the item "Associate," there was a significant difference between "No content" and "Art" at the 5% level.

These results indicate that Tosa art effectively motivates people and improves their creativity. Therefore, the hypothesis set at the beginning of this psychological experiment was supported.

7 Analysis of Sequential Effects

The order of presentation of the art and geometric figure contents differed among the participants: Order 1 (Figure, then Art) was 20 participants, and Order 2 (Art, then Figure) was 20 subjects. Determining whether this difference in presentation order affects the evaluation results is crucial.

Therefore, an analysis of variance was conducted. This evaluation experiment consisted of two factors: order (Order 1/Order 2) and content (Figure/Art). In addition, the participants are different in Order 1 and Order 2. Therefore, a two-factor ANOVA (between-participant factor x within-participant factor) was conducted for each evaluation factor. The results are shown in Figs. 15 (Impression factor), 16 (Relaxation factor), 17 (Motivation factor), and 18 (Creativity factor).

Each case had no significant difference concerning the main effect on order. This indicates that the evaluation results are the same concerning the order of viewing geometric figures first or art first.

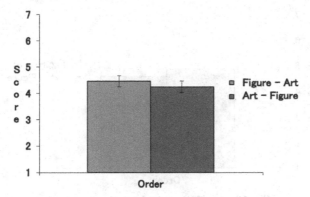

Fig. 15. ANOVA results for Impression factor.

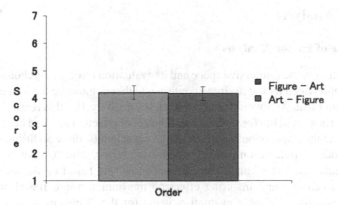

Fig. 16. ANOVA results for Relaxation factor.

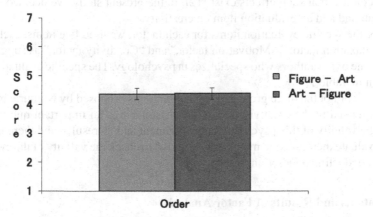

Fig. 17. ANOVA results for Motivating factors.

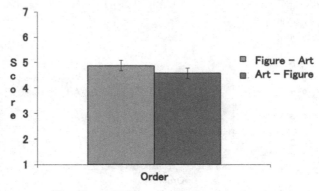

Fig. 18. ANOVA results for Creativity factor.

8 Factor Analysis

8.1 Purpose of Factor Analysis

The construction of the immersive space and its evaluation through psychological experiments were motivated by the desire to confirm whether combining the immersive space and art content (Tosa Art) would arouse people's creativity. For this reason, in addition to the nine evaluation items for impressions (Impression factor) that had been used in the past to evaluate the impressions received by the participants, three additional evaluation items were added: "Relaxation factor," "Motivation factor," and "Creativity factor."

The "Relaxation factor" and "Motivation Factor" are based on the authors' belief that art has a calming and inspiring effect on the human mind. Based on this idea, the authors established simple evaluation items for the "Relaxation Factor" and the "Motivation Factor" and conducted psychological experiments using these evaluation items to confirm that such effects exist [12]. In the present study, we decided to revise the content and add an evaluation item on creativity.

As for the specific evaluation items for each factor, we used five items, each related to the "Relaxation factor," "Motivation factor," and "Creativity factor," as suggested by Nomura, one of the authors who specializes in psychology. The specific evaluation items are shown in Table 1.

Whether or not the three groups of evaluation items proposed by Nomura, including the items related to the creativity factor, are reasonable is an important question concerning the validity of this psychological experiment and its results, and there is a great need to evaluate them. As one method, we decided to check the validity of the evaluation items by conducting a factor analysis.

8.2 Contents and Results of Factor Analysis

A factor analysis was conducted to compare the above groupings of evaluation items with actual data. The results of the factor analysis for the evaluation of art content are shown in Table 2.

Table 2. Results of factor analysis of art content

Item	Factor1	Factor2	Factor3	Communarity
At ease	.961	.085	-.057	.964
Relaxed	.873	.016	.041	.779
Healed	.790	.249	.020	.795
Pleasant	.693	-.015	.121	.509
Secure	.690	-.500	-.025	.543
Curious	-.007	.816	-.271	.702
Enthusiastic	.343	.726	-.143	.770
Immersive	.089	.707	.104	.565
Aroused	-.266	.667	.192	.468
Immersed	.041	.634	.234	.497
Motivated	.069	.098	.780	.649
Inspired	-.047	.007	.775	.595
Activated	-.128	.038	.770	.591
In the zone	.271	-.198	.622	.489
Associate	.093	.204	.429	.266

Table 2 shows the factor analysis results using the maximum likelihood Promax method with three factors since the scree plot indicated that three factors were appropriate. The grouping of the three factors corresponds to the "Relaxation Factor," "Motivation Factor," and "Creativity Factor," each of which consists of the five items described above. In some cases, "more motivated" in the "motivational factor" and "immersed" in the "creativity factor" are interchanged, but this is considered reasonable. Therefore, it was shown that the three factors (Relaxation Factor, Motivation Factor, and Creativity Factor) and the evaluation items that make up each factor are almost confirmed for the actual data. When conducting similar psychological experiments in the future, it would be appropriate to use the following evaluation items, replacing "more motivated" in the "motivational factor" and "immersed" in the "creativity factor."

- Relaxation factor: restful, reassuring, comfortable, pleasant, soothing
- Motivators: enthusiastic, immersed, curious, immersed, aroused
- Creativity Factor: associative, more motivated, activated, inspired, in the zone

9 Conclusion

Previous studies have shown that art has a calming and inspirational effect on the human mind [1, 2]. Through several psychological experiments, we have also found that art has a relaxing and inspiring effect on the mind [12, 13]. In addition to this, we hypothesize that art has the effect of increasing a person's creativity. This is because when we exhibited video art created by Naoko Tosa, one of the authors, in various places of the world, many people commented that "We felt Japanese beauty." In addition, many others said "We felt a sense of levitation" and "Our creativity was aroused." If art appreciation increases people's creativity, then a new benefit of art can be found. This study was conducted to confirm this through a psychological experiment.

In this paper, we first described designing and constructing an "immersive art space" suitable for art appreciation. The fact that projection mapping using art images is used in many situations means that displaying art in a vast space increases the sense of immersion. In this study, we proposed and constructed a hexagonal immersive space using a mirror display that functions as both a mirror and a display to create a sense of being in a vast space. In this space, three sets of mirrors facing each other create the impression of an infinite space. By displaying art images in the mirrors, it is possible to give people the feeling of being in an infinite space surrounded by art images.

In the latter half of this paper, we described the results of an experiment to confirm whether displaying art in the constructed space enhances creativity through psychological evaluation. The art used for the evaluation was the video art by Naoko Tosa. Geometric figures were used as the content to be compared with the art content. Based on the results of an experiment to compare multiple types of geometric figures with different shapes and movements [13], one of them was selected and used in this study.

We asked 40 participants to rate on a 7-point scale how they felt when viewing the three types of content, "No content," "Figure," and "Art," using 24 evaluation items in four groups related to "Impression," "Relaxation," "Motivation," and "Creativity." The results revealed the following.

First, a two-way ANOVA was used to test whether there were statistically significant differences between the ratings of the three types of content for the four groups of "Impression," "Relaxation," "Motivation," and "Creativity." The results showed that the main effects of content were significant in "Impression," "Motivation," and "Creativity," indicating that there were differences among "No Content," "Figure," and "Art." For "Relaxation," the main effect of content was significant only between "No content" and "Art."

The analysis on each evaluation item showed significant differences between the contents for two of the nine "Impression" items. Regarding "Motivation," three out of five items showed significant differences among the contents. In addition, significant differences were found in 4 out of 5 items for "Creativity." Among the "Creativity" items, significant differences were found for "Motivated" in all combinations of "No content," "Figure," and "Art" among the contents. These results indicate that combining "immersive art space" and "Tosa art" contributes to creativity.

In addition, to confirm whether the order in which figures and art were presented affected the results, an ANOVA was conducted to determine whether there was a difference in results between participants with "Figure to Art" order and those with "Art to Figure" order. The results showed no significant differences between these two orders. In addition, a factor analysis was conducted to determine whether the evaluation items used in the Relaxation, Motivation, and Creativity factors were reasonable. As a result, the 15 evaluation items were correctly classified into the three factors except for one item, and it was confirmed that the proposed evaluation items were reasonable.

There are several possible directions for future research. One is to see if the results of this study are generalizable by using art other than Tosa art as content. Another is to reveal what happens in our body and mind during the art appreciation by measuring physiological indices during the evaluation.

References

1. Winner, E.: How Art Works: A Psychological Exploration. Oxford University Press, Oxford (2018)
2. Renee, L.: Beard, "art therapies and dementia care: a systematic review." Dementia **11**, 633–656 (2012)
3. Greensgard, S.: Virtual Reality. The MIT Press, Cambridge (2019)
4. Jones, L.: Haptics. The MIT Press, Cambridge (2018)
5. William Latham. (https://en.wikipedia.org/wiki/William_Latham_(computer_scientist))
6. Cave automatic virtual environment. (https://ja.wikipedia.org/wiki/Cave_automatic_virtual_environment)
7. Yayoi Kusama: Infinity Mirror Rooms (https://www.tate.org.uk/whats-on/tate-modern/yayoi-kusama-infinity-mirror-rooms)
8. Pang, Y., Zhao, L., Nakatsu, R., Tosa, N.: A study of variable control of sound vibration form (SVF) for media art creation. In: 2017 International Conference on Culture and Computing (2017)
9. Tosa, N., et al.: Creation of Fluid Art 'Sound of Ikebana' under Microgravity Using Parabolic Flight," Leonard/ISAST, MIT Press (2022). https://doi.org/10.1162/leon_a_02360
10. Mirrors. https://www.asahiglassplaza.net/products/mirroria/
11. Nakatsu, R., Tosa, N., Niiyama, S., Kusumi, T.: Evaluation of the Effect of Art Content on Human Psychology Using Mirror Display with AR Function. Nicograph Int. **2021**, 54–61 (2021)
12. Nakatsu, R., Tosa, N., Takada, H., Kusumi, T.: Psychological evaluation of image and video display by large-screen LED display and projection. Trans. Soc. Art Sci. **20**(1), 45–54 (2021)
13. Nakatsu, R., et al.: Development of Immersive Art Space Using Mirror Display and Its Preliminary Evaluation. In: WMSCI 2023 (2023)
14. Flynn, J.E., Hendrick, C., Spencer, T., Martyniuk, O.: A guide to methodology procedures for measuring subjective impressions in lighting. J. Illum. Eng. Soc. **8**, 95–110 (1979)
15. Loe, L., Mansfield, K.P., Rowlands, E.: Appearance of lit environment and its relevance in lighting design: experimental study. Light. Res. Technol. **26**, 119–133 (1994)
16. Oi, N.: The difference among generations in evaluating interior lighting environment. J. Physiol. Anthropol. Appl. Hum. Sci. **24**(1), 87–91 (2005)
17. Bowman, D.A., McMahan, R.P.: Virtual reality: how much immersion is enough. Computer **40**(7), 36–43 (2007)
18. Misseroni, D., Colquitt, D.J., Movchan, A.B., Movchan, N.V., Jones, I.S.: Cymatics for the cloaking of flexural vibrations in a structured plate. Sci. Rep. **6**(1), 23929 (2016)

Data Shed: Interactive Art in the Service of Data Fluency

Adit Verma[✉], Sara Diamond, and Alexis Morris

OCAD University, 100 McCaul Street, Toronto, ON M5T 1W1, Canada
{aditverma,sdiamond,amorris}@ocadu.ca

Abstract. As data continues to permeate all aspects of our lives, the need for data fluency becomes paramount. The "Data Shed" project explores the intersection of interactive art, machine learning, and data visualization to facilitate experiential learning about data and its pervasive influence in our digital age. Grounded in the metaphor of shedding, akin to a snake's skin, the installation portrays the implicit generation and shedding of latent data in our digital interactions. The paper delves into related work, emphasizing the accelerating role of algorithms, motivated by the challenges posed by data misuse and potential for bias. It draws on the concepts of data fluency and critical data studies, exploring the paradox of privacy in the face of increasing concerns about data handling by organizations. The study reviews generative artworks and human-AI collaboration before addressing the ability of machine learning to address surveillance and data-shedding concerns. The paper details research creation, the development methodology, and highlights gaps where the "Data Shed" approach can bring focus to these issues. Evaluative insights are provided, emphasizing technical goals, interactivity levels, and assessment of achievement of data fluency objectives. The research underscores the importance of interactive art works, user engagement, and ethical considerations, in fostering a deeper understanding of data in our digital landscape. The project invites users to reflect on the shaping influence of data in our lives and its potential impact on our collective future.

Keywords: Data Collection · Data Ownership · Latent Data · Data Shedding · Machine Learning · Generative Art · Interactive Installation

1 Introduction

The interactive art installation, "Data Shed," is designed to facilitate understanding and experiential learning about data. It conceptualizes data shedding as a "natural" process, drawing an analogy from the shedding of a snake's skin. This representation captures the implicit generation and shedding of latent data in our digital interactions. Data shedding occurs in various interactions with technology or even when we are near it, from location tracking, sensor systems, facial recognition, search engines, to online shopping.

As data has become ubiquitous in our lives; data are all around us, and we constantly generate data without even realizing it. The rapid progress in artificial intelligence and

M. Rauterberg (Ed.): HCII 2024, LNCS 14717, pp. 214–232, 2024.
https://doi.org/10.1007/978-3-031-61147-6_15

machine learning, fueled by data, has given rise to new algorithms and technologies that are accelerated by the rapid breakthroughs in the field. Despite having all these data and access to powerful tools we understand so little about how data is collected and how data directs our decisions and choices in this well woven digital environment and economy. Data fluency is the key to unlocking knowledge and understanding how data has become the main ingredient of the digital age.[1]

Data are used to make many of our day-to-day activities easier. For instance, a person purchasing a transit ticket in many places around the world provides the data from the station they are boarding and the destination station. The data trade-off gives insights such as identifying the stations that see higher footfall, which can then be used to design stations and transit schedules, responding to the footfall at different stations. This is an example of how a small interaction can lead to data generation in an implicit manner, where the users are not aware they generated data through their interactions. These examples can be described as **latent data** that exists around the user without them knowing about it.

As more organizations start collecting personal data, there is a growing need for people to understand this hidden force acting on their behalf, making decisions for them, and how all this data is being collected with the use of new algorithmic systems.

Given this context it is essential for us to seek more ethical and conscientious methods of utilizing the vast amount of data collected. "Data Shed" fills this gap in knowledge by actively addressing the imperative for ethical data practices. "Data Shed" responds to the call for ethical data practices by empowering users with insights into the often-unnoticed world of data shedding, thereby contributing to a more informed and responsible approach to data utilization.

2 Related Work

The literature review draws on a wide range of sources, including studies on data collection, algorithmic bias, and critical data studies to form the foundation for understanding the multifaceted landscape of data in our digital age. The exploration extends to the rise of machine learning, addressing concerns related to surveillance and data shedding. Related work includes generative artworks and human-AI collaboration, contributing to the theoretical groundwork for understanding the intersections of technology, art, and data. This theoretical framework forms the backdrop against which the "Data Shed" project unfolds.

2.1 Navigating Data's Dominance in the Modern Age: Algorithms, Acceleration and Data Shedding Dynamics

In the past decade, the world has seen a tremendous increase in the use of artificial intelligence (AI). AI systems are evolving so fast that it has become increasingly possible to build an intelligent computer system that is programmed to do a single task. For

---

[1] Haksar, Mr Vikram, et al. Toward a Global Approach to Data in the Digital Age. International Monetary Fund, 2021.

example, a camera can extract data regarding what people are wearing to analyze the number of people who wear a tie during the day. Intelligent machines accelerate the data collection process several folds, often automatically, creating a gap in the knowledge of the data being generated, collected, and analyzed. Efficiency and quantity push data to the forefront of our digital economy as "The amount of data in the world doubles every two years" [1]. Clive Humby's statement "Data is the new oil" has echoed relentlessly in recent years as people have started to harness and understand the value of data [2, 3]. Traditionally, one way of using this data was to sell more things through targeted advertisements [4]. Unrefined data is meaningless; it makes sense when connected and analyzed [5], which makes it very crucial to start looking at data as a system [6, 7].

Algorithms within the field, like computer vision, can produce data from multimedia which can be used for object recognition, facial recognition, and motion recognition. In addition, these algorithms can filter data and find the needed information quickly. Although latent to us, data with the help of algorithms are making decisions for many of our day-to-day activities [8].

2.2 Data Bias

Modern algorithmic systems are plagued by bias, as these systems are actively trained on historical data to help the algorithm understand context based on historic decisions [9]. The datasets often contain data that is biased, compounded by bias that engineers bring to choices in the data that they use to solve questions, giving rise to discrimination in algorithms [10]. Cathy O'Neil scrutinizes the ways that algorithmic decision making can worsen existing inequalities and keep them in place [11]. As these systems are built for predicting outcomes, they are more likely to give biased predictions due to the nature of dataset used to train them. As Julia Angwin proves risk scores in states such as Florida discriminate against people by race and label those with higher scores as being more likely to be criminals when empirical evidence contradicts machine learning outcomes [12].

The more data these algorithms access, the more accurate they can be in their predictions. Yet this has not been the case. Rather, as Wendy Hui Kyong Chun demonstrates, it is "slippery identifications-mis-and missed identifications- that form the basis for recognition and correlation" [13, pg. 228]. Bias in datasets can arise from various sources, including historical inequalities, under representation of certain groups, or systemic prejudices embedded in the data collection process [14]. Thereby these models do not work well with outliers, eliminating small data sets, or with data that was not widely available to the model in the first place while training, which further adds to the problem of data bias in such systems [15].

"Data Shed" is motivated by this growing recognition of data biases. As we are working with vision-based ML (Machine Learning) models, it becomes important to establish that these models are not perfect and that they can be biased. "Data Shed" is a real-time system that does not directly address the issue of data bias, but grapples with it indirectly through interactive artworks to raise awareness of latent data.

2.3   Data Fluency and Critical Data Studies

Data fluency is the ability to understand structural meaning of data and be able to comprehend and explain data through a more granular level of detail [16]. It involves being able to recognize patterns and connections between data to make better decisions and translate these to others [17]. Although many people have become more concerned about how their data is handled, managed, and used by organizations, their behavior still does not reflect this concern as individuals continue to tick consent boxes as though they do not matter [18]. This behavior is known as the "Privacy Paradox" [19].

The privacy paradox can be attributed to lack of understanding of data-driven systems compounded by the limitation of services if individuals do not comply and share data. The organizations that hold data are an integral part of daily life and have few incentives to offer control to their users to control their own data and even if they do, it is buried under the many layers of settings that an average user is not aware of. Technology users struggle to comprehend data and protect their privacy.

One can say, "Data is intangible" and "We are data," as anything that users do online generates data. Data subtly influences recommendations and decisions, often operating beneath users' explicit awareness. [18]. The revelation of these concealed data points is vividly demonstrated through targeted advertisements. An illustrative example is presented in the New York Times article "These Ads Think They Know You," which scrutinizes ads from a data-centric perspective, unraveling how user data triggers specific advertisements [20]. Examining a sample ad reveals a keen understanding, stating, "This ad thinks you're trying to lose weight but still love bakeries," drawing insights from the user's browsing and credit card history.

As data has become building blocks of everyday life, Dalton and Thatcher advocate for a critical perspective on the overwhelming dominance of data in modern society [21, 22]. This dominance has given rise to "Algorithmic Culture" where human thoughts are expressed through big data and computation [23]. It has become complicated for individuals to analyze and interpret data in a meaningful way, as there is a divide between the person that is generating the data and the person that is reading the data [21, 22]. Dalton and Thatcher argue that data production is place-dependent, giving rise to data biomes and illustrating the challenge of accurately reading big data sets out of context, compounded by missing data. Available data could not portray the full picture to the reader who might be unknowingly making decisions at some remote location.

The whole data generation and collection process is often seen as a flat process that does not take into consideration the other hidden aspects that influence data production; there is a growing business and institutional faith in 'big data' as a solution for all problems and that data is the key to unlocking human understanding. Data's role in targeted marketing and the surveillance state are clear, but what other purposes could it serve?" [21, 22]. Can this data help us to understand people through artworks and artifacts, but how does this data relate to people in real life?

2.4 Rise of Machine Learning and Artificial Intelligence in Addressing Surveillance and Data-Shedding Concerns

The rapid advancement of machine learning and artificial intelligence has ushered into a transformative era, impacting various facets of society, with particular significance in the context of surveillance and challenges surrounding data-shedding. The ability to detect, classify and analyze complex data is often enabled by classifier systems, predictive models like linear regression, decision trees, random forests, gradient boosting, and neural networks in machine learning algorithms. As these systems become more common and complex, the associated risks and impacts will increase significantly making it possible for malicious actors to access both the entire model and the training datasets, through a malicious ML provider posing a significant security concern [24].

Classification without permission, location data being shared to advertisers, geolocation services used to track users in the real world, user profiling and aggregation of data without user consent are all examples of privacy concerns arising from the increased reliance on these technologies [25–28].

Facial Recognition Technology has integrated itself into the fabric of our lives as it is so widely used and scalable, living in a time where we are constantly being monitored and tracked using CCTV's and other surveillance cameras [29]. A byproduct of these systems are people losing their sense of privacy; trying to figure out how to evade these technologies to avoid being identified or misidentified. In 2019 Hong Kong police used face detection technology to identify protestors against a controversial extradition bill [30]. Facebook used facial recognition to track users based on the pictures they posted but then later removed this feature, reflecting an acknowledgment of the privacy implications associated with classifying individuals without their explicit consent [31]. This feature could have been used to protect users' privacy by limiting the impersonation of users on Facebook. Apple introduced Face ID in 2017 as a replacement to the fingerprint scanner on the iPhone X which holds biometric data that includes depth mapping of a user's face and infrared images of their face [32]. Grave damage to users could occur in a data breach, as a face cannot be changed as opposed to passwords that can be changed.

This context sets the stage for the significance of "Data Shed," which addresses the ethical dimensions of data use and sheds light on the implications of unconstrained data collection. It serves as a proactive response to the growing concerns outlined in the literature review, offering an interactive platform to educate users about the intricacies of data dynamics and encouraging responsible data practices.

2.5 Exploring User Understanding: Generative Artworks and Human-AI Collaboration

Human and Artificial Intelligence Collaboration has ushered in a new era of creativity, where the synergy between human ingenuity and advanced AI technologies fosters unprecedented innovation. As AI systems evolve, their integration with human capabilities forms super teams, transforming traditional workflows. This collaboration yields unique expressions and innovative creation methods. One example is the Casual Creator, an interactive system promoting fast and joyful exploration of creative possibilities, resulting in the generation of artifacts that instill pride and creativity in users [33].

The synthesis of workflows between tools and artists has given rise to systems like Midjourney[2] and Dalle[3], enabling artists to co-create with AI. This collaborative approach varies, with artists either inputting parameters or the AI system leading the creation process. Examples such as "Move Mirror" and "Body, Movement, Language: AI Sketches With Bill T. Jones" showcase diverse collaborative workflows, blending human expression with AI capabilities to produce engaging and boundary-pushing content. Defining collaboration in the realm of human-AI interaction may be nuanced, but the potential for exciting possibilities in creativity remains a constant driving force for both sides.

In the ever-evolving landscape of technology and human interaction, the realm of generative artworks stands as a captivating and relevant piece with immense potential for further exploration. Parikh's study indicates predictability in user preferences through choices made while creating interactive generative art as subtle interactions with generative art can unveil unforeseen data regarding user preferences [34]. In the synergy of generative art and AI, "Data Shed" facilitates interaction between the AI-driven generative art and the audience by intentionally releasing and utilizing data. This intentional sharing of data contributes to a continuous feedback loop, allowing the generative art to adapt and evolve based on user interactions. The collaboration becomes an iterative exchange where data shed refines the creative potential, ensuring the artworks resonate meaningfully and personally with the audience.

2.6 Related Works

The works discussed in this study seek a common goal of visualizing latent data in a visual format. These works played a crucial role in conceptualizing ideas for an interactive installation, focusing on interactivity, data fluency, live data, and the interplay of artwork with dynamic data. "Data Shed" builds on precedents such as "Thermal Drift Density Map" which uses thermal data as a metaphor for life force and military precision technologies (Lozano-Hemmer, 2022), "How Normal am I" which compares and distorts facial data (Schep, 2020), "Herald/ Harbinger" that draws real time bedrock data from the Bow Glacier to create an interactive sound and image work in Calgary, the Centre of Canadian extraction industries (Ruben & Thorp, 2018) and lastly "Visualizing Algorithms" which slows down algorithmic processing to indicate data flow in decision tree classifiers (Catherine Griffiths, 2020). These are interactive artworks that display and analyze data in experiential and moving ways, and at the same time encourage audiences to think critically about the sources of data behind these works.

Through a comparative analysis, the table below indicates levels of interactivity, intention to address data fluency, approaches to data and algorithms, and approaches to interactive media art (Table 1).

---

[2] Midjourney, www.midjourney.com/home?callbackUrl=%2Fexplore. Accessed 1 Feb. 2024.

[3] Betker, James, et al. "Improving image generation with better captions." Computer Science. https://cdn.Openai.com/papers/dall-e-3. Pdf 2.3 (2023).

Table 1. Analyzing Contextual Works: Exploring Similarities and Differences, Anchored by the Artwork 'Data Shed.

Conceptual Works	Interactivity	Data Fluency	Dynamic Data	Artwork	Installation
Thermal Drift Density Map (Lozano-Hemmer, 2022)	✓	✓	✓	✓	✓
How Normal Am I? (Schep, 2020)	✓	✓	✓	✓	
Visualizing Algorithms (Catherine Griffiths, 2020)	✓	✓		✓	
Herald/Harbinger (Ruben & Thorp, 2018)			✓	✓	✓
Data Shed	✓	✓	✓	✓	✓

2.7 Gap in the Study and Need for "Data Shed."

The literature review underscored critical gaps in understanding and addressing the profound implications of big data, particularly in the context of surveillance and decision-making trades offs. While the increasing reliance on machine learning algorithms and artificial intelligence has accelerated data collection, there is a notable lack of awareness among individuals regarding the depth and breadth of data capture. The privacy paradox, as discussed in the literature, highlights the inconsistency between concerns about data handling and the actual behavior of individuals who may unwittingly sacrifice privacy for convenience. Additionally, the literature points out that the overwhelming dominance of data in modern society, often viewed as a solution to various problems, tends to oversimplify the complex nature of data generation and collection. The challenge lies in recognizing the inherent biases in datasets, the limitations of data fluency among users, and the potential societal implications of surveillance technologies. Thus, literature emphasizes the need for a critical perspective on data, fostering awareness of the trade-offs involved in decision-making processes influenced by vast and often indiscriminate data capture.

All the above concerns point towards a need for an interactive installation that educates about data by combining elements of interactivity, data fluency, and live data, addressing a space where these aspects are not fully explored or integrated in existing works. The comparative analysis of contextual works emphasizes this opportunity for a unique approach to teaching about data through an engaging and interactive installation.

3 Methodology

3.1 Process Overview

The creation of "Data Shed" adopted Research-Creation as the chosen methodology, a practice-based method that intertwines artistic creation with research. The interactive installation becomes the canvas, providing a unique space to explore and visualize the intricate dynamics between data, algorithms, and their societal repercussions.

Challenging the assumption that knowledge is primarily conveyed through verbal or numerical means, "Data Shed" employs data visualization techniques to transcend these conventional boundaries [35].

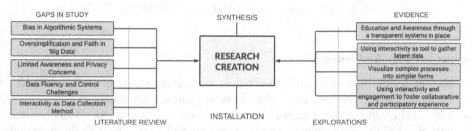

Fig. 1. The conceptual framework to apply Research Creation to create an interactive installation.

The interactive installation serves as a tangible and immersive experience, offering the audience an opportunity to actively engage with and contribute to generative artworks using their pose data (Fig. 1).

3.2 User Engagement and Interaction

Movement-sensing installations engage audiences in actively influencing computer-generated images and sounds through natural movement. These interactive setups require no special training, fostering collaborative and participatory experiences [36]. This unique dynamic leads to a greater acceptance and ownership of the creative results by the participants. In addition, these types of installations can be embedded into environments, making them a promising tool for educational purposes.

User engagement and interaction with the installation is the central aspect of the process as the more engagement the user has with the installation the more information, that is data, they can provide to the underlying models to improve the accuracy of the models and algorithms. The goal is to make the processes more visible to the user and aid the audience in gaining a deeper understanding of the workings of the digital environment through interaction, building upon the taxonomy from "A Common Framework for Audience Interactivity" paraphrased below [37].

Observe Passively:

- At the foundational level, users may choose to observe passively, merely taking in the visual stimuli of the installation without actively participating.

- Passive observation allows individuals to absorb the atmosphere and artistic elements without direct involvement, providing a space for initial comfort and exploration (Fig. 2).

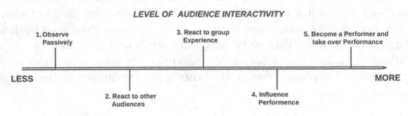

Fig. 2. Levels of audience interactivity, adapted from [37]

React to Other Audiences:

- Moving a step beyond passive observation, users may engage in a reactive mode, responding to the presence and actions of other audience members.
- This level of interaction creates a dynamic environment where individuals become part of a collective experience, sharing reactions and responses with those around them.

React to Group Experience:

- As user engagement deepens, participants may collectively react to the group experience, forming a shared response to the installation.
- This level fosters a sense of community and shared connection, as individuals synchronize their reactions based on the overall atmosphere created by the group.

Influence Performance:

- At a more involved stage, users may actively influence the installation's performance through direct input or manipulation of elements.
- This level empowers individuals to shape the artistic output, allowing for a personalized and co-creative experience that blurs the lines between audience and performer.

Become a Performer and Take Over Performance:

- The highest level of audience interactivity occurs when participants transition from observers to performers, taking over aspects of the installation's performance.
- Users, in this scenario, become active contributors, directly shaping the narrative or visual elements of the installation, transforming the space into a collaborative and participatory platform.

The goal of "Data Shed" is to encourage audience experiences that encompass all these levels of interactivity.

3.3 Data Visualization

Data Visualization plays a fundamental role in data collection by transforming raw and complex datasets into accessible and interpretable visual representations. In the modern era of information overload, where massive amounts of data are generated daily, visualization serves as a powerful tool to distill intricate patterns, trends, and insights from the data. In this way, complicated data relationships and data-driven insights are communicated in an easily comprehensible manner. Moreover, interactive visualization enhances transparency and accessibility, making data-driven insights more comprehensible to a wider audience, thereby fostering a deeper understanding of the underlying information, and promoting data fluency in various fields [38]. While building a data visualization system, several factors are necessary to ensure a user-centered design approach be it diverse types of visualization or approaches to presenting data [39].

Individuals increasingly learn about themselves through mobile telephones and personal informatics, which visualize the user's data [40]. A goal of "Data Shed" was to arrange the data collected and its analysis to help the audience understand the essence of their data in an artistic format of color and shapes rather than the algorithmic outputs of numbers and statistics. The visualization was designed into two stages: (1) data collection and classification and (2) the analysis and visualization of the collected data. The abstract visual language of the system is intended to promote self-discovery in understanding the meaning of the data collected and the abstractions derived from the data [34].

4 Prototypes

Iterative incremental prototyping was used to design and improve the artifact and the interaction with the audience based on their feedback. Prototyping allowed different ideas to be tested, as well as the feasibility and functionality of the technology.

Prototype 1 tested different machine learning models combined with different visualization generation techniques. The basic technology deployed for this prototype were web-based machine learning libraries and P5.Js[4] to visualize an interface deployed in a web browser. A small web application in a browser started latent data collection culled from interaction with an interactive artwork that appeared on a large screen.

Prototype 2 extended functionality and complexity leveraged from the framework of the first prototype and incorporating a LED (Light Emitting Diode) array-based installation that would allow the user to not only interact with the installation but also have a richer visual experience. The second prototype moved from a simple web-based approach to the use of VVVV[5], a visual scripting tool based on.NET platform.

For audience privacy, the artifacts never used cloud-based solutions to compute audience data. All captured data were processed locally and not stored. They were solely used to create artworks displayed on an LED wall. The artifacts from the interaction ensure no disclosure of confidential information or profiling, capturing only non-intrusive data points without facial profiling or unnecessary retention.

---

[4] "Hello!" Home | P5.Js, p5js.org/. Accessed 1 Feb. 2024.

[5] Group, Vvvv. "VVVV - Visual Live-Programming for.NET." Vvvv - Visual Live-Programming for.NET, visualprogramming.net/. Accessed 1 Feb. 2024.

4.1 Prototype 1 Details

The emphasis was on collecting latent user data, exploring the method of implicit data collection through sensor and machine learning interactions. Implicit collection involves observing user interactions and engagements with artifacts. The choices contribute to building a decision table, covering aspects like color preferences and user curiosity during interactions. The sketches were built with P5.Js and incorporated PoseNet[6] to detect the user's face and the body moment data to make interactions possible and collect latent data.

Color Preference. The first artwork was designed around a preconfigured scheme of color swatches. The interaction involves three phases: idle, where the artwork waits for someone to enter the interaction parameters; change, triggered by clapping within the interaction parameter, leading to a shift in color scheme; and engage, where continuous engagement generates a series of artworks based on the chosen color scheme, creating a new artwork every second of the interaction (Fig. 3).

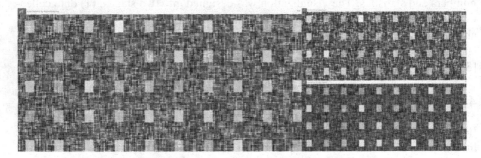

Fig. 3. Generative Artworks for Interaction with Color

Left-Right Preference. The second artwork was centered around creating bold circles with varying weights. The interaction involves three phases: Idle, where circles move randomly on the screen, and new weights are assigned to each circle, generating a new artwork every second; Left Push, where the user uses their left hand to arrange circles based on weights, with higher weights on the left; and Right Push, where the user uses their right hand to arrange circles with higher weights on the right. Both interaction states result in a visually distinctive presentation of circles based on the applied weights (Fig. 4).

---

[6] Papandreou, George, et al. "Personlab: Person pose estimation and instance segmentation with a bottom-up, part-based, geometric embedding model." Proceedings of the European conference on computer vision (ECCV). 2018.

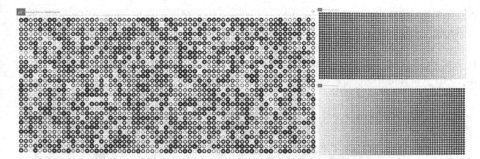

Fig. 4. Generative Artwork for interaction with weight

Prototype 1 provided valuable insights into the interplay of generative art, AI, and data shedding. Users were observed to actively shape their preferences through interactions with the generative artworks, often without conscious awareness. Simultaneously, users also displayed an understanding of the underlying interactivity that played a crucial role in molding their overall experience. The intentional release and use of data in the generative art process highlights the potential for dynamic and engaging interaction between the system and the audience. Prototype 1 set the stage for further exploration and refinement, emphasizing the promising avenues for creative collaboration and innovation at the intersection of technology and human interaction.

4.2 Prototype 2 Details

At this stage of prototyping the emphasis was on creating a functional but visually rich interaction which demonstrated the concept of collecting data and projecting them in a visual way. Prototype 1 focused on simple interactions which could be used to generate latent data by the user. Prototype 2 developed the visual design of the final installation; the LED curtain made a dynamic and responsive output. As LEDs (Light Emitting Diode) can be controlled and adjusted individually these display different animations and visuals with specific brightness patterns and colors. The curtain was made up of two parts with the first part being the curtain wall and the second part being the LEDs scattered on the ground. The interface was divided into different interactions and animations. The first part contained data visualizations that were generated from the user's movement and other data (such as clothing) while the second part of the curtain contained the visuals and animations that showed the flow of latent data shed in response to the user's movements.

The installation was built with VVVV, visual programming software, to develop the software and hardware solutions for our installation. VVVV enabled the use of different.NET libraries and custom code to implement machine learning models and data visualization techniques. ArtNet[7], a protocol for data transmission over Ethernet controlled the LED strips that form the main visual element of the installation. Microsoft

---

[7] "Art-Net." ArtNet, 1 July 2020, art-net.org.uk/.

Azure Kinect DK[8] was chosen as the sensor, as it provides a wide range of features such as depth, RGB and infrared cameras, and a 7-microphone array. These features captured various data points from the user, such as pose, body index, segmentation, point cloud, IR and RGB data. Machine learning algorithms processed and analyzed these data using them to generate the visual output on the LED wall (Fig. 5).

Fig. 5. Photos of the prototype 2 with viewers engaging with it.

Prototype 2 marks a significant advancement in the exploration of generative art, AI collaboration, and data shedding in this research project. The integration of a LED wall appeared to empower users to play a more active role in shaping the evolving artwork. The technical goals were met. The user experience appeared to be seamless and immersive. Challenges occurred in achieving a balance between user influence and showing the underlying layers of data shedding in a simplified manner. Prototype 2 served as a steppingstone for continued exploration in the creation of a final installation and exhibition of "Data Shed".

5   Installation

The final iteration of the installation was developed to house a data double of the person derived from interaction. The visual output was dynamic and responsive to the user's movements. The system housed more refined models and algorithms to differentiate

---

[8] "Azure Kinect DK – Develop AI Models: Microsoft Azure." – Develop AI Models | Microsoft Azure, azure.microsoft.com/en-us/products/kinect-dk. Accessed 1 Feb. 2024.

between the user who was interacting and the audience in the scene. The installation also included a UI (User Interface) to allow the user to interact with a secondary display that acted as an output for the data that was being read by the machine learning algorithms. The users could select and play with the data to view and experiment with the data in a unique way by changing the values or disabling different data streams to create different or broken visualizations. Viewers were encouraged to understand the data collected and its representation by clicking a picture of the artwork they created while collaborating with the installation (Fig. 6).

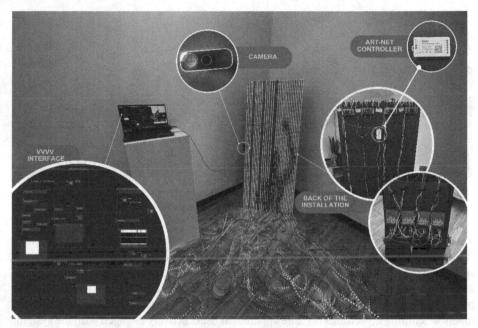

Fig. 6. Photo of the final" Data Shed" installation, including the labeled hardware and software; latent data is captured and presented within the piece dynamically.

Building upon the successes and lessons from previous prototypes, the final version presented a refined experience for users. Users engaged with the installation in playful ways and sought to manipulate patterns on the LED curtain. However, most audience members, while aware of their role in driving the installation did not perceive that their data was captured, analyzed, and were moving the images on the LED curtains. Only those who engaged with the data display and algorithm visualization monitor and the LED curtain fully understood the lessons of "Data Shed." Refinement of the installation would provide a larger role for the data and algorithm capture display.

6 Evaluation, Conclusions and Future Work

6.1 Evaluation

The evaluation was an Observational study, a method for meticulously observing the behavior of individuals within a specific environment [41, pg. 86]. This approach was chosen to gain insights into user interactions with the "Data Shed" installation, ensuring a comprehensive understanding of how participants engaged with the project's technical features and interactive elements (Fig. 7).

Fig. 7. Photo of a people engaging with the installation

Technical Goals. The observational study provided a firsthand opportunity to scrutinize the effectiveness of technical functionalities, specifically the integration of the Microsoft Azure Kinect DK sensor and machine learning algorithms. The sensor captured diverse data points such as poses, body indices, and segmentation precisely, acknowledging its pivotal role in the project's functionality. The real-time processing and adaptability of machine learning algorithms became apparent as users actively engaged with the system, ensuring a responsive and dynamic user experience.

Interactivity Goals. "Data Shed" was designed to offer a spectrum of interactive engagement drawing from Strincr et. al.'s (2015) Common Framework for Audience Interactivity, ranging from passive observation to active participation, fostering a diverse and immersive user experience. Observations during the interactive sessions highlighted the success of distinct levels of interactivity. Users, at the passive observation level, absorbed the visual and auditory stimuli without active engagement, highlighting the installation's ability to captivate audiences even in a non-interactive mode. Moving up the interactivity spectrum, users reacted to other audience members, adjusting their interactions based on the collective experience. As the interactivity levels progressed, participants actively engaging with a group experience, collaborating with others to shape the overall performance expressed by LED visualizations. Users actively influenced the visual and auditory outputs, taking on a more participatory role. Some audience members realized that the system was blind to certain colors and returned over several days to test its response to their clothing. The take-over level allowed users to become performers themselves, exercising full control over the interactive elements, indicating the project's versatility in accommodating varying degrees of user agency, manipulating the data and algorithmic screen.

Data Fluency Goal. The data fluency goal of "Data Shed" aimed to enhance users' understanding of their personal data by translating complex data concepts into visually accessible and comprehensible forms. The project partially met its data fluency goal. Users engaged with dynamic visualizations that represented latent data shedding processes, offering a tangible and intuitive representation of how data is generated and interacted with in the digital realm. While some played with the installation to manipulate its images, they did not necessarily understand the connection between the data that they shed and the machine learning algorithms driving the images. ML (Machine Learning) Future iterations of the installation would provide a large screen display of data collection and algorithms at work to emphasize the path between the user's data, ML (Machine Learning) algorithm, and LED display.

6.2 Conclusions

- "Data Shed" was designed to encourage users to understand this data with the help of computer vision machine learning models and data visualization through interactive installation. The installation's aim was to encourage users to take control of their data and understand how the system in place collects it. Below are further takeaways:
- Interdisciplinary Collaboration: The project underscores the importance of interdisciplinary collaboration in creating meaningful and impactful work. Artists, data scientists, and engineers can work together to create installations that are not only aesthetically powerful but also informative and thought-provoking.
- User Engagement: The interactive nature of the installation can lead to higher user engagement. It shows that when users are actively involved in the process, they are more likely to understand and appreciate the underlying message and reflect on the future of data and the ways it shapes our lives.
- Ethical Considerations: The project serves as a reminder of the ethical considerations in data collection and usage. It highlights the need for transparency and consent in all stages of data handling.
- Public Education: Installation art can be an effective tool for public education and can be used to communicate complex concepts in a simple and engaging manner.
- Innovation in Art: The project shows how modern technologies like machine learning and computer vision can be used in art to create innovative and exciting new forms of expression.

6.3 Future Work

The future stages of the installation are:

- Future development would program machine learning models and algorithms to respond to the interactions triggered by the users and not just the automatic collection of data. These would give the user the ability to choose the models and algorithms that they want to learn about. For example, if the user wants to learn about the voice models the install should be able to trigger the specific voice model and present to the user the information.

- Adding more visuals and graphical representations of the data as a second screen or set of annotations to help the user understand their data shedding process.
- Theoretical research in Human Computer Interaction to better understand the ways that interactions as a framework combined with artworks and machine learning models represent a novel approach to design learning experiences that allow people to explore and gain a deeper understanding of data through interaction.

In summary, this work has presented "Data Shed" as an approach toward raising awareness of the latent data dynamic, by leveraging interactive art exhibition, machine learning, generative design, and physical LED visualizations. It is hoped that such an approach can become a catalyst to shift perspectives on this central aspect of modern life.

Disclosure of Interests. The authors have no competing interests to declare that are relevant to the content of this article.

References

1. Call for Code. "The amount of data in the world doubles every two years." Medium, vol. 7 October 2020. https://medium.com/callforcode/the-amount-of-data-in-the-world-doubles-every-two-years-3c0be9263eb1
2. Hirsch, D.D.: The glass house effect: big data, the new oil, and the power of analogy. Me. L. Rev. **66**, 373 (2013)
3. Beath, C., et al.: Finding value in the information explosion. MIT Sloan Manag. Rev. **53**(4), 18 (2012)
4. Johnson, J.P.: Targeted advertising and advertising avoidance. RAND J. Econ. **44**(1), 128–44 (2013). JSTOR, http://www.jstor.org/stable/43186411
5. Fiaz, A.S., et al.: Data visualization: enhancing big data more adaptable and valuable. Int. J. Appl. Eng. Res. **11**(4), 2801–2804 (2016)
6. Deolalikar, V.: How valuable is your data? A quantitative approach using data mining. In: 2015 IEEE International Conference on Big Data (Big Data), IEEE (2015)
7. Short, J., Todd, S.: What's your data worth? MIT Sloan Manag. Rev. **58**(3), 17 (2017)
8. Rand, L., et al.: Computer vision. In: Emerging Technologies and Trade Controls: A Sectoral Composition Approach, Center for International & Security Studies, U. Maryland, pp. 68–86 (2020). JSTOR, http://www.jstor.org/stable/resrep26934.9. Accessed 31 Jan 2024
9. Ntoutsi, E., et al.: Bias in data-driven artificial intelligence systems—an introductory survey. Wiley Interdisciplinary Rev. Data Min. Knowl. Disc. **10**(3), e1356 (2020)
10. Ghosh, D.: Terms of disservice: How Silicon Valley is destructive by design. Brookings Institution Press, pp. 127–62 (2020)
11. O'Neil, C.: Weapons of Math Destruction: How Big Data Increases Inequality and Threatens Democracy. Crown (2016)
12. Angwin, J., et al.: Machine bias. In: Kirsten, M. (ed.) Ethics of data and analytics. Auerbach Publications, pp. 254–264 (2022)
13. Chun, W.H.K.: Discriminating Data: Correlation, Neighbourhoods, and the New Politics of Recognition. MIT Press, Cambridge, p. 228 (2021)
14. Pitoura, E.: Social-minded measures of data quality: fairness, diversity, and lack of bias. ACM J. Data Inf. Q. **12**(3), 1–8 (2020). https://doi.org/10.1145/3404193

15. Bommasani, R., et al.: On the Opportunities and Risks of Foundation Models. ArXiv, /abs/2108.07258 (2021)
16. Gemignani, Z., et al.: Data Fluency: Empowering Your Organization with Effective Data Communication. Wiley, Incorporated, ProQuest Ebook Central (2014). https://ebookcentral. proquest.com/lib/oculocad-ebooks/detail.action?docID=1810510
17. Herzberg, B.: Data fluency: empowering your data-driven organization - IRM connects, by IRM UK, IT Blog. Irmconnects, 11 Jan 2022. https://www.irmconnects.com/data-fluency-empowering-your-data-driven-organization/#:~:text=Data%20fluency%20is%20the%20a bility%20to%20understand%2C%20interpret%2C,it%20into%20a%20story%20that%20e veryone%20can%20understand
18. Chakravorti, B.: Why it's so hard for users to control their data Hbr, 30 Jan 2020. https://hbr. org/2020/01/why-companies-make-it-so-hard-for-users-to-control-their-data
19. Naughton, J.: The privacy paradox: why do people keep using tech firms that abuse their data? The guardian, 5 May 2019. https://www.theguardian.com/commentisfree/2019/may/ 05/privacy-paradox-why-do-people-keep-using-tech-firms-data-facebook-scandal
20. Thompson, S.A.: Opinion, these ads think they know you - the New York Times Nytimes, 30 Apr 2019. https://www.nytimes.com/interactive/2019/04/30/opinion/privacy-targeted-advert ising.html
21. Dalton, C., et al.: what does a critical data studies look like, and why do we care? Soci-etyandspace, vol. 12, May 2014. https://www.societyandspace.org/articles/what-does-a-cri tical-data-studies-look-like-and-why-do-we-care
22. Dalton, C., et al.: Critical data studies: a dialog on data and space. Big Data Soc. (2016). https://doi.org/10.1177/2053951716648346
23. Striphas, T.: Algorithmic culture. Eur. J. Cult. Stud. **18**, 395–412 (2015). https://doi.org/10. 1177/1367549415577392
24. Song, C., Thomas, R., Vitaly, S.: Machine learning models that remember too much. In: Proceedings of the 2017 ACM SIGSAC Conference on Computer and Communications Security (2017)
25. De Cristofaro, E.: An overview of privacy in machine learning. arXiv preprint arXiv:2005. 08679 (2020)
26. Liu, B., et al.: When machine learning meets privacy: a survey and outlook. ACM Comput. Surv. (CSUR) **54**(2), 1–36 (2021)
27. Claypoole, T., Richard, C.B.: Privacy considerations limit geolocation technologies. Bus. Law Today **March**(2012), 1–4 (2012). JSTOR http://www.jstor.org/stable/businesslawtoday. 2012.03.02
28. Schiaffino, S., Amandi, A.: Intelligent user profiling. In: Bramer, M. (eds.) Artificial Intelligence An International Perspective. LNCS, vol. 5640, pp. 193–216. Springer, Berlin (2009). https://doi.org/10.1007/978-3-642-03226-4_11
29. McClellan, E.: Facial recognition technology: balancing the benefits and concerns. J. Bus. Tech. L. **15**, 363 (2019)
30. Adams, R.: Hong Kong protesters are worried about facial recognition technology. But there are many other ways they're being watched. BuzzFeed News, BuzzFeed News, 17 Aug 2019. www.buzzfeednews.com/article/rosalindadams/hong-kong-protests-paranoia-fac ial-recognition-lasers
31. What is the face recognition setting on Facebook and how does it work? Facebook help center. What Is the Face Recognition Setting on Facebook and How Does It Work? Facebook Help Center. www.facebook.com/help/122175507864081. Accessed 27 Jan 2024
32. About face ID advanced technology. Apple Support, support.apple.com/en-la/102381. Accessed 27 Jan 2024
33. Compton, K., Michael, M.: Casual creators. In: International Conference on Innovative Computing and Cloud Computing (2015)

34. Parikh, Devi. "Predicting A Creator's Preferences In, and From, Interactive Generative Art." ArXiv, 2020, https://doi.org/10.48550/arXiv.2003.01274
35. Smith, H., (ed.) Practice-led research, research-led practice in the creative arts. Edinburgh University Press, Edinburgh (2009)
36. Winkler, T.: Audience participation and response in movement-sensing installations. In: Proceedings of the International Computer Music Conference (2000)
37. Striner, A., Sasha, A., Chris, M.: A common framework for audience interactivity. arXiv preprint arXiv:1710.03320 (2017)
38. Weissgerber, T.L., et al.: From static to interactive: transforming data visualization to improve transparency. PLoS Biology 14(6), e1002484 (2016)
39. Sinar, E.F.: Data visualization. Big Data at Work. Routledge, pp. 115–157 (2015)
40. Li, I., Anind, D., Jodi, F.: A stage-based model of personal informatics systems. In: Proceedings of the SIGCHI Conference on Human Factors in Computing Systems (2010)
41. Hevner, A.R., et al.: Design science in information systems research. MIS Quart. 28(1), 75–105 (2004). JSTOR, https://doi.org/10.2307/25148625. Accessed 2 Feb 2024

The (Un)Answered Question: A Data Science Powered Music Experiment

Lynn von Kurnatowski[1](✉)(iD), Benjamin Wolff[1], Sophie Kernchen[1](iD),
Adriana Klapproth-Rieger[1](iD), David Heidrich[1](iD), Carina Haupt[1](iD),
Andreas Schreiber[1](iD), Thoralf Niendorf[2,3](iD), Andreas Kosmider[4],
Marcus Lobbes[5], and Martin Hennecke[6]

[1] German Aerospace Center (DLR), Institute for Software Technology,
Linder Höhe, 51147 Cologne, Germany
`lynn.kurnatowksi@dlr.de`
[2] Max Delbrueck Center for Molecular Medicine (MDC), Berlin Ultrahigh Field
Facility, 13125 Berlin, Germany
[3] Experimental and Clinical Research Center (ECRC), 13125 Berlin, Germany
[4] Falling Walls Foundation gGmbH, 10969 Berlin, Germany
[5] Academy for Theatre and Digitality, 44137 Dortmund, Germany
[6] Saarländisches Staatstheater, 66111 Saarbrücken, Germany

Abstract. This paper describes the intentions, setup, and live performance of a musical experiment that explores the complex intersection of human-technology interactions, music, and data collection. It brings art and data science together through a novel experimental music installation. The interdisciplinary project "The (Un)Answered Question: A Data Science Powered Music Experiment" explored integrating data science and biomedical imaging techniques with theatrical and compositional ideas. This combination leads to the creation of interactive music. Gestural interfaces and sensory input devices translate physiological behavior into music through digital signal processing. Ralph Waldo Emerson's poem "The Sphynx" and Charles Ives' composition "The Unanswered Question" serve as foundational elements to create a live remix of the original music using biometric data from performers and an audience of 180 people. The audience became a powerful instrument of musical expression. Each live performance was experiential and unique, depending on the different people involved.

Keywords: Peroforming Arts · Music · Data Science · Biometrics

1 Introduction

For centuries, arts and sciences have been in fruitful dialogue. The cross-fertilization between art and science is rooted in the exchange of ideas, techniques, and methods between these two fields of science. Leonardo da Vinci and others combined scrupulous anatomic studies and examination of biological structures with artistic work. The potential of this exchange has reached a

M. Rauterberg (Ed.): HCII 2024, LNCS 14717, pp. 233–246, 2024.
https://doi.org/10.1007/978-3-031-61147-6_16

whole new level with the emergence of digital technology, which has created new possibilities for artists and scientists to collaborate and create works that bridge the gap between their respective domains.

The theater is a form of performing arts [2] that has been particularly affected by the cross-fertilization of art and science, especially in the digital age. Digital technology has allowed theater to explore new forms of storytelling and push the limits of what is possible on stage. For example, digital projections and interactive technologies can be used to create immersive environments that enhance the audience's experience of a performance. Moreover, advances in computer graphics, animation, and special effects have made it possible to create virtual worlds that can be integrated into live performances. This has opened up new possibilities for theatrical productions, allowing them to incorporate elements of science, such as astronomy, biology, or physics, into their narratives.

Scientific breakthroughs, on the other hand, are also often motivated by technological advancements that enable new experiments and data collection and visualization methods, as well as novel experimental setups. The advances in modern methods and technologies in information and data science have pushed the reachable scientific frontiers tremendously, with the vector space of explorable phenomena constantly expanding.

We are both explorers — artists and scientists. Driven by curiosity, the quest for new ways of approaching the world, by the fascination with a particular structure or phenomena, and by the toying around with new ideas, always in search of new answers, or even more, new questions.

"The (Un)Answered Question: A Data Science Powered Music Experiment" is an interdisciplinary project that aims to artistically make the field of data science accessible to the public.

The basic idea was to create a unique remix of the piece "The Unanswered Question" by the American composer Charles Yves[1]. The remix is based on biometric data recorded from the audience. The goal is to create a new remix every night based on the emotional responses of the audience. Regarding the technical setup, there were two main challenges:

1. How to create music from biometric data?
2. How to distribute the generated score in real-time to the musician?

In this paper, we describe the modes of cooperation, shared methods, technology, and the initial results of the first prototypical work.

2   Technical Setup

The goal of the project was to use gesture interfaces and sensory input devices to translate physiological behavior into music through digital signal processing. The first step was to create an interface between the audience and the technology. Sensors and surveys were used to collect both objective and subjective data from

---

[1] https://www.youtube.com/watch?v=kkaOz48cq2g.

the audience. The second step was to process this data using methods from the field of data science. This data would be used as input to render a unique remix of Charles Yves' "The Unanswered Question" and to develop a visualization of the input data.

2.1 Data Acquisition

Nowadays, a wide range of sensors are available to record human physiological behavior [8], such as *Electroencephalography* (EEG), heart rate monitors, or surveys. Therefore, an integral part of the project was to determine which techniques could be used to record humanoid data. The project should be performed live in a theater with an audience of 180 people, therefore some external conditions had to be taken into account.

Due to the substantial size of the audience of 180 participants and the spatial situation of a large theater hall, we decided to conduct a survey, and when selecting suitable sensors, we decided to record *heart rate* frequency using wearable fitness trackers [1] and *emotions* using automatic recognition of facial expressions [6,14].

Emotion — Cameras. A pair of cameras is used to capture the emotional expression of each person in the audience. Therefore, two cameras are strategically placed in front of the stage, one to capture the left half and the other to capture the right half of the audience (Fig. 1). Each camera acts as an input source for the emotion analysis software. The reason for using two cameras was to get a more frontal view of the faces from the audience for better analysis. One camera was controlled by a Dell Latitude 7400 and the other by a Dell XPS 13 notebook.

To analyze the emotions of the audience, software was developed in Python to identify and categorize facial expressions. The framework Retinaface [16] was one of the components used to recognize the faces of each person. Retinaface uses an edge-based recognition technique that is highly accurate even in large crowds and provides box coordinates and orientation points for each identified face. To analyze the facial emotion, components and models of Deepface [15] are used. Deepface is a framework developed for both face recognition and analysis.

The result is an assignment to each identified face in the audience with the percentage of the emotions anger, disgust, fear, happiness, sadness, surprise, and neutrality. For example, one person could be 60% happy and 40% neutral. The results are summarized in a CSV file containing one line per face identified with the corresponding percentages of the seven emotions. In order to capture possible changes in the audience's emotions during the playing of the original piece, a snapshot of the input stream was recorded and analyzed at regular five-second intervals.

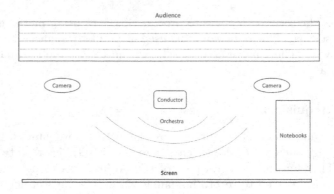

Fig. 1. Set-up of the stage.

Heart Frequency — Fitness Tracker. The MiBand 5 fitness tracker[2] was used to track the heart rate of the audience, with each MiBand measuring and logging the heart rate locally every minute. Once all data was collected locally, the MiBand logs were collected using a Dell Latitude 7400 and a Dell Latitude E7 notebook. The advantage of using two computers is that each computer can cover half of the audience, speeding up the collection process.

To record the local MiBand protocols using the two computers, Python software was developed. The software is based on the MIBAND 4 Python library [7]. This library requires the bluepy Python package [10] to access the Bluetooth interface of the device. The MIBAND 4 Python Library communicates with the MiBand via this interface and receives its responses. Some outdated functions had to be adapted. For example, the activity log has been migrated to MiBand 5 and replaces outdated dependencies.

The developed software connects to each MiBand, extracts the heart rate data from the MiBand protocol, and disconnects from the MiBand. This step takes some time due to the limitations of Bluetooth. A computer can only connect to seven MiBands at the same time. The MiBands are, therefore, processed using a queue. In the end, all the values from all the MiBands were written to a CSV file. As the heart rate recording, like the emotion recording (Sect. 2.1), was intended to record the changes in the audience's values during the performance of the original piece, the values from the MiBands were written to the CSV file at one-minute intervals.

Empathy — Questionnaire. In addition to the objective data of the audience, such as heart rate and emotions (Sect. 2.1), subjective data was also collected. For this purpose, we measured individual personality aspects of the visitors based on the global dimensions of personality — the so-called "Big Five" [4,5] — which include neuroticism, extraversion, openness to experience, agreeableness, and conscientiousness. To reduce the number of questions, we only focused on

---

[2] https://www.mi.com/global/miband/.

the *agreeableness* dimension. As the heart plays a central role in our play, we used the agreeableness dimension as a metaphorical measure for magnanimity (the German translation "Großherzigkeit" literally means "big-heartiness"). Our questions were based on the agreeableness dimension of the German NEO-FFI short version [11]. Due to the concerns of the organizers, however, we modified some questions to make them sound more positive to preserve the positive mood at the beginning of the play. Thus, the survey consisted of the following four questions:

1. I am empathetic and warm-hearted.
2. I have the ability to ignore the idiosyncrasies and mistakes of others.
3. I am helpful and selfless.
4. I am always determined to help others in case of an accident.

Each of these questions could be rated on the following scale: (1) *Disagree at all*, (2) *Rather disagree*, (3) *Partly*, (4) *Tend to agree* and (5) *Totally agree*. The questionnaire included an additional question on the position of the chair (left vs. right). The visitors were instructed to complete the digital questionnaire before the musical performance started. For this, we placed QR codes in the room that the visitors could scan with their phones and then fill out.

Heart Frequency — Cardiac MRI. In addition to the data collected from the audience during the live performance, *cardiac Magnetic resonance imaging* (MRI) data [3] from an actor's heart was collected beforehand while reciting Ralph Waldo Emerson's poem "The Sphynx". The actor without any known history of cardiac disease was included after approval by the local ethical committee[3]. Informed written consent was obtained from the volunteer prior to the study. MRI was conducted on a 7.0 T whole-body MRI scanner [12][4] equipped with an 8 kW RF power amplifier[5] and a gradient system (maximum slew rate = 170 mT/m/ms, maximum gradient strength = 38 mT/m). For radiofrequency excitation and signal reception a 32 channel self-grounded bow-tie transceiver array was used [9]. 2D CINE FLASH imaging of the heart was performed to obtain short axis (SAX), two-chamber (2CV), three-chamber (3CV), and four-camber views (4CV) of the human heart (spatial resolution = $(1.1 \times 1.1 \times 2.5)$ mm^3, echo time TE = 2.09 ms, repetition time TR = 4.55 ms, parallel imaging acceleration GRAPPA R = 2, views per segment = 10, number of cardiac phases = 30, receiver bandwidth = 446 Hz/Px, nominal flip angle = 22°). For retrospective cardiac gating and prospective cardiac triggering *electrocardiogram* (ECG) electrodes and an MR stethoscope[6] were placed between the transceiver array and the anterior chest wall. An average heart rate of 55 bpm was observed. The

---

[3] registration number EA1/256/19, Ethikkommission, Ethikausschuss am Campus Charité - Mitte, Berlin, Germany.
[4] MAGNETOM, Siemens Healthineers, Erlangen, Germany.
[5] RFPA, Stolberg HF-Technik AG, Stolberg-Vicht, Germany.
[6] EasyACT, MRI.TOOLS GmbH, Berlin, Germany.

overall image quality provided ample blood-myocardium contrast and enabled the visualization of fine subtle anatomic structures including the compact layer of the right ventricular free wall and the remaining trabecular layer. Pericardium, mitral, and tricuspid valves and their associated papillary muscles, and trabeculae are identifiable.

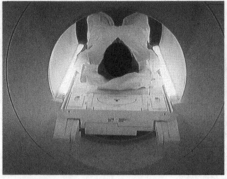 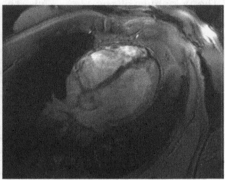

(a) Actor in MRI scanner while reciting the poem and images of his heart are taken.   (b) MRI image of the actor's heart.

Fig. 2. MRI data of the actor's heart was recorded before the performance (Images: Max Delbrück Center for Molecular Medicine in the Helmholtz Association (MDC).

2.2 Data Processing

After all the data from both the actor and the audience had been recorded, they needed to be processed. The goal was to avoid a linear correlation between the audience and performer data and the music. For example, emotions should not directly influence the strings, and the rhythm should not be synchronized with the audience's heart rate. To prevent this, we used clustering techniques to modify certain aspects of the musical composition. We merged the heart frequency data from the actor's MRI data with the audience's heart frequency data in one CSV file and the facial recognition data with the survey values. We perform a *K-means clustering* [17] for each collected timestamp. The center point of each cluster was then determined, which was used as input to generate a new score.

2.3 Score Remix and Score Distribution

We decided to use Inscore (v1.31)[7] as an environment for the design of interactive, augmented, dynamic musical scores. Inscore is an open-source software that was initiated by Dominique Fober and the Interlude project. It is based on

---

[7] https://inscore.grame.fr/.

the GUIDO Engine, so it works natively with Guido Music Notation (GMN)[8]. GMN is a formal language designed to create musical scores that are readable by machines and humans.

Our technical setup consists of internal developer software (*ScoreMaker*) and *Inscore*. The ScoreMaker processes the clustered audience data (Sect. 2.2) and creates a remix, presented as a musical score in GMN-Format. The ScoreMaker was developed in Python and communicates with Inscore via the Open Sound Contol (OSC) protocol [18]. The Center of Music and Film Informatics at Detmold University of Music[9] provided valuable information on several digital score viewing software. However, the combination of ScoreMaker, INScore, and Guido seemed to be most promising, especially in terms of how quickly a music score could be instantly remixed. Moreover, Inscore offers its own script language (*Inscore Script*), which enables dynamic score augmentations.

In a preceding step, we analyzed the original score of Charles Yves and decided to cut the score into semantic pieces (i.e., phrases and motifs), to provide meaningful musical sequences. Based on the provided clustered audience data, ScoreMaker selects semantic musical pieces, rearranges them, and performs several transformations like (Fig. 3):

- rhythmic variations
- transpositions
- stretching and shrinking phrases

For musicians, we decided to use Lenovo Chromebook tablets (in total, 35 tablets). We decided to use Chromebooks because the screen dimensions are similar to a sheet of music. Moreover, Chromebook allows one to run Android and Linux simultaneously in containers. For the visualization of the gmn-scores, we used Inscore Viewer. After rendering the full score, it is separated into single-part scores. These are then distributed to the 35 musicians' tablets. The tempo is indicated by a synchronized cursor above the notes (Fig. 4). In addition to the new score for the musicians, certain parts of the poem are triggered by cluster data via OSC over a time series into Ableton Live, using a python-based OSC-Player. The cluster controls which verse of the poem is included in the remix on any random day. Important tools proved to be Pythonosc and Guidolib. In addition, the sound of certain sections of the orchestra is manipulated electronically. The woodwinds and trumpet are being picked up by microphones, and their signal is being altered using a video mapping of the MRI-heart to control parameters and faders in Ableton. This was archived by existing max4live devices.

---

[8] https://guidodoc.grame.fr/.
[9] http://www.cemfi.de/.

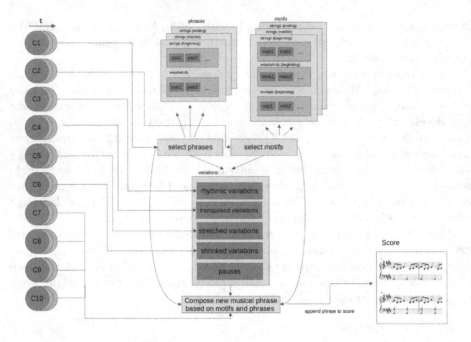

Fig. 3. Workflow to create a new remix based on the cluster files.

2.4 Visualization

The visualization was implemented using Unity 2D and consists of oval-shaped emoticons, the beating MRI image of the heart in the center of the image, and a point for each spectator in the audience (Fig. 5). Each dot flashes in rhythm with the measured pulse and moves from emoticon to emoticon. Since it was not possible to assign each person exactly the emotion and pulse rate, this was done randomly. Another reason why an explicit assignment was not possible was the wearing of face masks against COVID-19 in the audience, so that for some people no emotion data could be collected. Another reason was the wiring of people. For a concrete assignment of the pulse, cables would have been better, but it was also a public artistic performance and not a laboratory set-up.

The goal of the visualization is to convey to the audience what data have been recorded, an understanding of the collective and individual influence on the orchestra remix, and to put the poem The Sphynx and the composition The Unanswered Question into a common context. A constantly evolving image with a timeline and constant update represents the process and evolution through simple tools. The blue background color was a suggestion from the organizers, as this color is meant to convey a scientific image [13]. The beating heart is placed in the center of the screen for the connection of the individual elements of conception, the poem "The Sphynx".

Fig. 4. The new scores were distributed to the orchestra's tablets.

Assuming a faster perception through images, emoticons were used in addition to the text ("neutral", "happy", etc.) to represent the emotions. In addition, emoticons create a more exciting and less static image, so aesthetics also plays a formative role in this decision. The arrangement resulted from different test runs, which resulted in the emotions'neutral' and'happy' being particularly frequently accessed. To avoid creating a one-sided moving image, they were arranged (after evaluating the prototype performance) in such a way that the dots move across the entire screen as far as possible. Again, aesthetics and dramaturgy were decisive factors. The color of the emoticons is the matched complementary color to the background color to create a visually pleasing composition.

3   Live Experiment

Based on the composition "*The Unanswered Question*" (1908) by the American composer Charles Ives (1874–1954), a performance was realized at the Saarländisches Staatstheater in which biometric data of the participants (audience and performer) were processed in video projections and live orchestral remix.

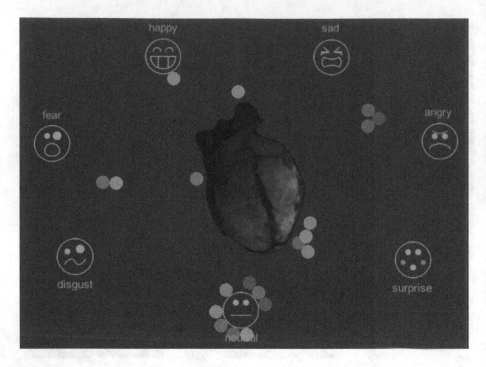

Fig. 5. Visualization of the recorded data of the audience and the actor, heart frequency, emotion and magnanimity.

The composition "The Unanswered Question" refers to the poem "The Sphynx" by Ralph Waldo Emerson[10] and addresses the riddle of the Sphynx from the Oedipus legend. Often described as philosophical "programm music," Ives describes the basic idea of his composition as a debate about the "eternal question of existence". In an increasingly complex world characterized by artificial intelligence and the advancing digitalization of all areas, this question is posed in a new context. The aim of the project was to investigate the relationship between humans and technology, music, and data science, using a musical-digital experimental set-up: Can data science help to turn the "unanswered question" into an "answered question?"

The experience of a concert, the interaction between orchestra and audience, is a unique live artistic experience. With methods and techniques from the field of data science (Sect. 2), it has been possible to turn every evening into a unique experience that depends on the different people involved in the audience.

The live performance at the Saarländisches Staatstheater, consisted of the following three parts:

---

[10] https://poets.org/poem/sphinx.

Part 1: Recitation. In the first part of the live performance, an actor recited the poem "The Sphynx". During recitation, synchronized visualization (Sect. 2.4) of the heart MRI data (Fig. 6), which was previously recorded during the actor's recitation (Section. 2.1).

Fig. 6. Visualization of the heart MRI data during the recitation.

Part 2: Orchestra Performance. In the second part of the live performance, the orchestra played Charles Ives' "The Unanswered Question". Meanwhile, the MiBand fitness tracker track the heart frequency, and the facial recognition tracks the emotions of the audience with 180 members.

Pause. During the pause, all the time series data recorded in part two had to be processed and the notes for the remix generated. To do this, the data from the MiBand fitness tracker first had to be transferred to a CSV file (Sect. 2.1). Then the MRI data was merged with the heart frequency and the survey values with the emotions recognition. The data was clustered (Sect. 2.2), and the resulting clusters were used to generate the score (Sect. 2.3). A remix was rendered into a new score for the left half of the audience and one for the right half of the audience. The new scores were distributed to the 35 tablets of the orchestra.

Part 3: Remix Audition. In the third and final part, the remix was performed live by the Saarländisches Staatstheater Saarbrücken in front of the audience (Fig. 7). First, the newly generated remix from the left half of the audience was played, followed by the remix from the right half of the audience. Meanwhile, the visualization of the data of the audience and the actor was shown synchronously. This made the recorded data audible and visible to the audience. The result was a unique remix of the original composition based on biometric data reflecting the emotional reactions of the audience. This experiment demonstrated the potential synergy between art and science in the creation of interactive musical experiences.

(a) Data processing during the performance.

(b) Orchestra and visualization.

Fig. 7. Live performance at Saarländisches Staatstheater Saarbrücken. While the orchestra is playing, the biometric data is processed and visualized in the background of the stage.

4 Conclusion

Based on Ralph Waldo Emersons's poem "The Sphynx" and the piece "The Unanswered Question" by the American composer Charles Ives, a prototype live performance was developed in which biometric data of the audience and performer, collected via human-machine interfaces, were processed in video projections and live orchestral remixes. In this way, the interdisciplinary project "The (Un)Answered Question: A Data Science Powered Music Experiment" createed an immersive live experience using tools and techniques from the field of data science.

Various biometric data of the audience and the performer, such as heart frequency or facial expression, recorded by fitness tracker or emotion recognition, are decisive for the respective result. An intelligent algorithm collects these various biometric data and processes them into a visualization and a live orchestral remix of the original composition. This remix becomes a new score that is streamed to the musicians' tablets. The result was an immersive and exclusive live performance.

Acknowledgments. We acknowledge the Helmholtz Information & Data Science Academy (HIDA) for providing financial support that allowed a short-term research stay of Martin Hennecke at the German Aerospace Center (DLR) and at the Academy for Theatre and Digitality to work together with researchers from the Institute of Software Technology on the work described in this paper.

Disclosure of Interests. Author Martin Hennecke received scholarship grants from the Helmholtz Information & Data Science Academy (HIDA).

References

1. Albaghli, R., Anderson, K.M.: A vision for heart rate health through wearables. In: Proceedings of the 2016 ACM International Joint Conference on Pervasive and Ubiquitous Computing: Adjunct, UbiComp 2016, pp. 1101–1105. Association for Computing Machinery, New York, NY, USA (2016). https://doi.org/10.1145/2968219.2972715
2. Baumol, W.J.: Performing Arts. In: Eatwell, J., Milgate, M., Newman, P. (eds.) The World of Economics. The New Palgrave. Palgrave Macmillan, London, pp. 544–548 (1991). https://doi.org/10.1007/978-1-349-21315-3_72
3. Bogaert, J., Dymarkowski, S., Taylor, A.M., Muthurangu, V.: Clinical cardiac MRI. Springer Science & Business Media (2012)
4. Borkenau, P., Ostendorf, F.: NEO-Fünf-Faktoren Inventar: Nach Costa u. McCrae; NEO-FFI. Hogrefe, Verlag f. Psychologie (2008)
5. Costa, P.T., McCrae, R.R.: Normal personality assessment in clinical practice: the NEO personality inventory. Psychol. Assess. **4**(1), 5 (1992)
6. Dagar, D., Hudait, A., Tripathy, H.K., Das, M.N.: Automatic emotion detection model from facial expression. In: 2016 International Conference on Advanced Communication Control and Computing Technologies (ICACCCT), pp. 77–85 (2016). https://doi.org/10.1109/ICACCCT.2016.7831605
7. Dhakal, S.: MIBAND 4 - Python Library, October 2022. https://github.com/satcar77/miband4
8. Dzedzickis, A., Kaklauskas, A., Bucinskas, V.: Human emotion recognition: review of sensors and methods **20**(3), 592 (2020). https://doi.org/10.3390/s20030592, https://www.mdpi.com/1424-8220/20/3/592
9. Eigentler, T.W., et al.: 32-channel self-grounded bow-tie transceiver array for cardiac MR at 7.0t. Magnetic Resonance in Medicine **86**, 2862–2879 (2021). https://api.semanticscholar.org/CorpusID:235636158
10. Harvey, I.: bluepy, May 2021. https://github.com/IanHarvey/bluepy
11. Körner, A., et al.: Persönlichkeitsdiagnostik mit dem neo-fünf-faktoren-inventar: Die 30-item-kurzversion (neo-ffi-30). PPmP-Psychotherapie· Psychosomatik· Medizinische Psychologie **58**(06), 238–245 (2008)
12. Niendorf, T., Barth, M., Kober, F., Trattnig, S.: From ultrahigh to extreme field magnetic resonance: where physics, biology and medicine meet **29**(3), 309–311 (2016). https://doi.org/10.1007/s10334-016-0564-1
13. Perra, M., Brinkman, T.: Seeing science: using graphics to communicate research **12**(10), e03786 (2021). https://doi.org/10.1002/ecs2.3786, https://esajournals.onlinelibrary.wiley.com/doi/abs/10.1002/ecs2.3786
14. Rani, J., Garg, K.: Emotion detection using facial expressions-a review. Int. J. Adv. Res. Comput. Sci. Softw. Eng. **4**(4) (2014)

15. Serengil, S.I., Ozpinar, A.: Lightface: a hybrid deep face recognition framework. In: 2020 Innovations in Intelligent Systems and Applications Conference (ASYU), pp. 23–27. IEEE (2020). https://doi.org/10.1109/ASYU50717.2020.9259802
16. Serengil, S.I., Ozpinar, A.: Hyperextended lightface: a facial attribute analysis framework. In: 2021 International Conference on Engineering and Emerging Technologies (ICEET), pp. 1–4. IEEE (2021). https://doi.org/10.1109/ICEET53442.2021.9659697
17. Steinley, D.: K-means clustering: a half-century synthesis **59**(1), 1–34 (2006). https://doi.org/10.1348/000711005X48266, https://bpspsychub.onlinelibrary.wiley.com/doi/abs/10.1348/000711005X48266
18. Wright, M.J., Freed, A.: Open soundcontrol: a new protocol for communicating with sound synthesizers. In: International Conference on Mathematics and Computing (1997). https://api.semanticscholar.org/CorpusID:27393683

Innovations in Digital Cultural Representation

Spatial Interaction Elements in AR-Glasses-Based Touristic Service Scenario Design

Sunghee Ahn[1] , Juhee Lee[1] , Hyungmin Kim[3] , Seong Lee[2] , and Jong-Il Park[3](✉)

[1] HongIk University, Sejong 30016, South Korea
[2] Seerslab, Seoul 06628, South Korea
[3] Hanyang University, Seoul 04763, South Korea
jipark@hanyang.ac.kr

Abstract. This research sets out to explore the sensory elements of user spatial interactions, with a specific focus on the empathic aspects. To achieve this objective, we developed an XR service for touring traditional houses dating back a century. Through the process of designing AR Glass UX scenarios based on the user's spatial interaction experiences during the development of this service, we aim to discern the differences and unique features compared to traditional 2D screen-centric mobile interactions. This study extracts key interaction elements, offering insights into the distinctive characteristics of AR Glasses-based interactions. Anticipated to lay a foundational understanding, this research contribute to the design of future AR Glasses-based services, providing essential groundwork.

Keywords: AR-Glasses-based tour service · Spatial Interaction · Metaverse UX · XR Service Scenario Design

1 Background

1.1 Research Background

According to the Design Proxemics theory introduced by E. Hall, there exists a direct relationship between the physical and social distances of individuals, influencing spatial interactions [1]. This theory elucidates how both "fixed objects" (architectural spaces or stationary objects) and "semi-fixed objects" (humans or mobile objects) can impact understanding of space during human interactions. The theories regarding sensory acceptance and perceptual relationships between physical world elements, which seem outdated, gain renewed significance in the context of AR media, where interactions involving human body movements and spatial dynamics are essential alongside digital screen interactions. Recent studies have progressed to define the mixed reality ecosystem [2], introducing geographic spatial perspectives in AR and implementing the concept of mixed objects, shedding light on changes in spatial and contextual awareness between imagined reality [3] and actual reality. This highlights a fundamental shift in how people perceive visual environments and engage with contextual scenarios. As McLuhan famously

© The Author(s), under exclusive license to Springer Nature Switzerland AG 2024
M. Rauterberg (Ed.): HCII 2024, LNCS 14717, pp. 249–258, 2024.
https://doi.org/10.1007/978-3-031-61147-6_17

predicted, the extension of human senses [4] demonstrates how media fundamentally alters our behaviors and the messages themselves. Emerging services are reshaping how individuals consume and enjoy content, thereby altering the social landscape.

1.2 Research Aim and Object

In the realm of Extended Reality (XR), where virtual and real environments coexist, many areas remain unaddressed by existing interaction theories. A paradigm shift is currently unfolding in XR-based interactions, moving beyond the traditional screen-centric approach and prompting new discussions. Within this evolving discourse, user experience (UX) in XR environments is increasingly shaped by spatial contexts and user body movements.

This study serves as a precursor to content design for spatial interactions, aiming to conduct experimental research on user trajectories and UX based on contextual aspects of space. The ultimate goal is to construct scenarios for an AR-Glasses service and design interface prototypes as outcomes. Given that narrative exploration in XR/AR and AR media is a relatively new area, this experimental research employs a qualitative approach centered on UX methodologies.

The methodology of this experimental study focuses on investigating the relationship between human-AR-glass interaction and space, premised on empirical exploration. The prototype designed for this purpose will be deployed in the field for user testing, allowing for feedback collection and subsequent refinement. This iterative process will inform the future application of the prototype in product development.

2   Design Conditions Process

2.1 Design Background and Conditions

Tour Location. In order to establish the parameters for our spatial design, we conducted research by concurrently employing desk research and user research methodologies, including surveys and interviews, to extract trends and preferences among foreign tourists. Given the nature of AR-Glasses services, catering well to individual travelers, our findings suggest an apt alignment between this technology and the preferences of our target demographic.

Contrary to widespread speculation that the influx of foreign tourists to Korea would be significantly influenced by the global popularity of K-pop acts such as BTS and Blackpink dominating the music scene since 2020, our empirical findings diverge from such expectations. The rankings of motivating factors for foreign tourists visiting Korea, as well as their preferred keywords, revealed a consistent preference for traditional cultural content, with such themes occupying the top positions. Additionally, among the nine key locations in Seoul frequented by foreign tourists, five are associated with Hanok (traditional Korean houses), further indicating a high preference for traditional cultural experiences among this demographic. Consequently, we have selected to focus our spatial study on the traditional Hanok cotage, deemed an appropriate subject for investigating spatial interaction elements within the context of this research.

For our AR content, we have selected two notable examples of national cultural heritage: the Yangban residence from the Joseon Dynasty, designated as National Treasure No. 138, and the Sejong Hong-Panseo[1] House. The latter, in particular, holds significant historical and cultural value as a hanok, and its inclusion is anticipated to not only enhance the tourist experience but also stimulate local economic development by encouraging regional mobility among tourists.

AR-Glasses Product Conditions. The specifications for the AR-Glasses under development have been deliberately chosen to enable mass distribution with relatively modest, mainstream specifications, diverging from the high-end specifications of premium XR glasses such as Microsoft HoloLens. The product's specifications are outlined in Table 1 below.

Table 1. AR-Glasses Product Condition (in display)

Specification	Conditional Description
Display	LCD Display
Resolution	1080p(1920 × 1080pixels)
Field of View (FoV)	About 40 °
Refresh Rate	60 Hz
Connectivity	Bluetooth 5.0, Wifi 802.11ac
Weight	Approx. 250 g
Sound System	Internal/Stero
Operating System	Android-based OS

3 AR-Glasses-Based Contents Design

3.1 Over All Design Concept

Upon examining the current landscape of AR content in domestic contexts, it is evident that AR content at tourist destinations often suffers from limitations associated with the screen size of smartphones or tablets, necessitating users to either zoom in on their mobile devices or seek assistance from staff while navigating the site. Although some famous historical tourist sites have introduced AR content, it predominantly relies on smartphone-based services, primarily focusing either on educational informational content or entertainment-oriented content, thus demonstrating a tendency towards a concentration of content in one of these categories. In light of this, based on the findings of a brief online interview survey, it was decided to incorporate elements preferred by

---

[1] Panseo: It is a Minister level of noble officer's title in Lee Dinesty period, from 15th to 19th cenuty.

foreign tourists, such as Hanok (traditional Korean houses, including palaces) and Hanbok (traditional Korean clothing), into AR content. Furthermore, to differentiate from existing AR content offerings, a fusion approach was adopted, providing content in a ratio of 6 informational pieces to 4 entertainment-oriented ones, with the aim of enhancing user curiosity and accessibility. Additionally, aligning with the evolving trend of personalized travel experiences, the goal was to develop traditional cultural content that could be enjoyed individually or by small groups, catering to diverse preferences and interests (Fig. 1).

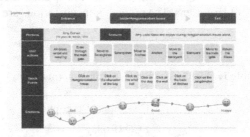

Fig. 1. User Journey Map

3.2 User Experience Design

User Flow. Research on human experience in Augmented Reality (AR) and Mixed Reality (MR) environments focuses onphysacal and emotional abilities to interact with virtual worlds, supported by various functional and control systems [5, 6].

For the design and layout of content provided through AR glasses for tours, this study initially implemented AR service points onto a map of Hong-Pansoe House. Hongpansoedaek, characterized by its unique structure where the Sarangchae and Anchae are interconnected and enclosed by a perimeter wall, necessitated precise prediction of visitor routes due to limited pathways (Fig. 2).

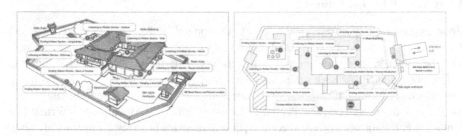

Fig. 2. User (visitors)'s Physical Rout by AR-Glasses in Hong-Panseo House Tour

To achieve this, we adopted the observation method from UX methodologies, observing various experiential routes by physically visiting the site. Among these, the most recurrent routes were hypothesized and established as the "General route" for visitors. Through visualization using floor plans, we focused on designing for user-centric movement convenience, ensuring visitors wearing AR glasses could seamlessly navigate along the content, naturally finding their way, thus enhancing user experience. The following Fig. 3 provides an overview of the user flowchart, illustrating the anticipated trajectory of user engagement with the content rout from entry to exit of the cottage.

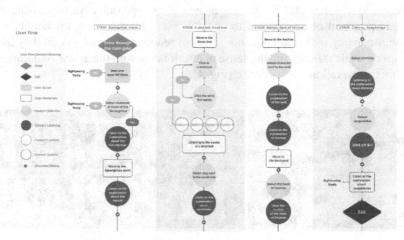

Fig. 3. Flowchat for Hong-Panseo House Tour

Drawing upon the analysis derived from user research, we endeavored to predict the sequence of actions users might undertake and designed the interface accordingly, presenting users with suggested on-screen choices to guide their navigation and facilitate their progression through the content.

In the realm of User Flow Design, this study innovatively derived ideations for trigger points targeting young demographics disinterested in tradition. Firstly, it introduced a "Service Point Guide" providing basic information about Hanok architecture to guide users. Secondly, it sought to enhance familiarity and amusement by imaginatively recreating the childhood scenes of Hongpanseo through "Listening to Hidden Stories via the Youth Character," thereby fostering a sense of intimacy. Thirdly, it incorporated gamification elements by introducing "Discovering Hidden Stories through Motion," adding an interactive layer to the experience. Finally, a small yet intriguing reward mechanism was devised to conclude the user journey.

UI Component Design. One of the most different and yet still unfamiliar interactions for users in AR-glass-based systems is the interaction with virtual objects using hands. This interaction is challenging because it is difficult to feel a response regarding whether contact has been made, and the action of 'contact' is not satisfying. Since digital objects lack substance, we cannot physically touch them, leaving us uncertain and requiring approximate actions through repeated attempts [7].

The UI components presented following Fig. 4 are designed for integration into the AR-Glasses Interface, representing the outcomes of this study. For typographic elements, a neutral and simplistic Pretendard Bold was selected to ensure seamless legibility, even when overlaid on the actual visual landscape visible to users. Additionally, a subdued shade of blue (#2569EC) was chosen as the primary color to facilitate clear differentiation between the components and the background, allowing users to perceive them distinctly without causing visual discomfort in various external and internal environments. Given the potential for excessive components on the screen to obstruct the appreciation of architectural elements or landscapes, care was taken to limit the placement of basic components to less than 20% of the screen area. This approach aims to mitigate visual clutter and potential obstruction of the field of view. Furthermore, the application of partial transparency to the components serves to reduce the visual weight they impose on the screen while minimizing the sense of discordance with the actual landscape, thus enhancing the overall user experience (Fig. 4).

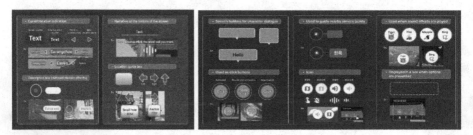

Fig. 4. Component for AR-Glasses Interface for Hong-Panseo House Tour (part)

User Scenario Design. The scenarios are composed of four integrated content types, blending information with entertainment, to provide tourists with an engaging and comprehensive tourism experience. Additionally, five additional pieces of content were created as killer content, focusing on the informational aspect of "listening to hidden stories." The AR content is designed to encompass various features, ranging from typical characteristics of hanoks like the Sarangchae and Anchae to unique elements specific to the Sejong Hongpanseo House such as wells and openings in the walls. Visitors can obtain immersive information about the hanok through the character dialogue of a young nobleman (Hong-Panseo), while the AR-Glasses assist in maintaining focus on the content until the 15-min tour concludes.

The nine content stages that consist the service are as follows: Sarangchae - Daecheongmaru (inside Sarangchae) - Eaves end - Enclosure wall - Well - Anchae - Back of Anchae - Backyard - Chimney - Jangdokdae, with the story unfolding in this sequence. The core content is depicted in the following Fig. 5. This study involved the creation of interface prototypes based on scenarios as a preliminary step towards content service development and release. Subsequent research will involve actual development and on-site User Testing (UT).

Fig. 5. Interface Design (part) for prototype framework for the agent zone scenario

4 Spatial Interaction Element in Designing AR-Glass-Based Service Content

As seen in following Table 2, the first highlighted design element emphasized through this study is 'Subjectivization of Spatial Experience'. Users can design spatial interaction experiences that enhance interest in target spaces for tourism by personalizing and subjectively altering the experience of public spaces through AR glasses, offering a more personalized perspective compared to traditional 2D-based devices.

Table 2. Spatial Interaction elements in Designing AR Glass-Based Contents

User's Spatial Experience	Experience Design Object
Subjective Experiences	Layered Information
Non-Space-based Interaction	Contextual Scenario
Convergence Senses	Multi-modal Media
Spatial Immersiveness	Graphic quality
Pesonalised Interoperability	Sensual trigger
Object Presence and Identity	Imaginative creativity

The second element, 'Non-Space-based Interaction', is pivotal in enabling users to seamlessly transition between the real and virtual worlds. Users should be able to press virtual buttons that exist in empty space and engage with this surreal interaction, facilitated by narrative elements.

This immersion is realized through the third element, 'Integrated Sensory Experience'. Quek [8] argues that interactions between humans and the external physical environment inherently involve multimodal forms. While 2D interactions relied heavily on visual-centric and auditory senses, along with a limited engagement of bodily sensations and spatial awareness, spatial interaction experiences in 3D interactions bring about a more realistic bodily experience, engaging senses like smell, touch, and gravity. By enhancing integrated sensory experiences, the design can shift from a ratio of 1:2:7 (visual:auditory:bodily sensations) to around 2:6:4 (conceptual split), emphasizing a more realistic and blended sensory fusion. If a virtual interface screen, while not physical, maintains contextual coherence within each scene by guiding or recommending interactions that reflect its spatial characteristics, people naturally and validly perceive and accept it. Skarbez et al. [9] refer to this as "coherence," but it may be more appropriately understood as 'Empathic Connectivity'. Furthermore, to support the placement decisions of icons or text on the AR-Glass screen, heuristic factors such as spatial consistency [10], as well as real-world backgrounds [11], and heuristic elements that are not overly heterogeneous should be considered.

The fourth element encompasses the 'Spatial Immersion Experience' facilitated by graphical elements, including interfaces. This involves designing a new consideration in HCI that visually represents information through AR glasses, aligning with human perception of reality through the holistic senses of sight, sound, and interaction. These graphical elements on the screen offer an immersive experience that can lead other experiential elements, integrating them into the design of this study. Integral to user expectations is the level of personalization.

This not only impacts Spatial Immersiveness but is also augmented by the fifth element, 'Interoperability', which delineates the breadth of user choice and decision-making. This proactive environment offers a personalized experience beyond individualization, as it provides a world that is not another person's world nor the same as anyone else's, thus transcending personalization into a hyper-personalized realm.

The sixth element pertains to 'Existential presence and Identity', which goes beyond the phenomenological sense created by human emotions and imagination (Fig. 6).

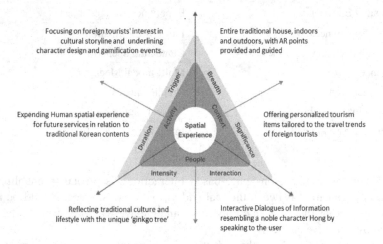

Fig. 6. Spatial design analysis of AR-glass tour service (Revised from Rahimi et. al. [13])

Certainly, while a taxonomy of bodily movement and interaction, akin to Wang et al. [12], should follow in the near future, our study aims to initially propose a preliminary hypothesis regarding the integration rather than fragmentation of interactions since it is about tour activity and interaction.

This aspect is formed not only through physical sensations and interactions but also by the cognitive processes and emotional senses of our brains. The reason why we can feel existence in non-existence and allow for the overlapping of existence lies in our cognitive activity, which integrates various layers of existence. From a design perspective, it is essential to create devices that trigger users' cognitive activities by providing diverse layers of stimuli and experiences.

5 Conclusion

Defining or categorizing emotional exchanges, networks, and interactions offline, outside of Human-Computer Interaction (HCI), presents challenges due to the varying cultural traits and individual lifestyles that influence each situation differently. Consequently, incorporating these nuances into a systematically structured classification within systems is currently deemed difficult. [14] However, failing to engage in research aimed at understanding contextual and integrated changes and advancements in new interactions, diverging from conventional systemic thinking, may hinder the future development of technology in a human-centric direction, making it challenging to provide effective guidelines. Therefore, this study seeks to initiate and define a conceptual approach to interactions between individuals and spaces, albeit qualitatively and somewhat ambiguously, from a user experience perspective.

Ultimately, an AR interface is a form of spatial visualization because it displays information over specific locations in a 3D environment using graphics. [15] Therefore, as mentioned earlier in this study, the design variables and constraints that consider both integrated and contextual positions are provided as constants in the challenging relationship between real-time, real-space, which constantly changes.

The field of Extended Reality (XR) is rapidly evolving, with both software and hardware undergoing updates daily, if not hourly. Presently, the technology falls short of providing users, the humans, with a seamless sensory satisfaction level that completely overlays reality or seamlessly blends virtual and physical worlds. However, the utilization of Augmented Reality (AR) services integrated with physical space environments is anticipated to become a significant content avenue in the near future. This study explores new research methodologies to create technological experiences for content production from a user interaction perspective. Through this research, significant findings emerged, emphasizing the narrative scenarios—i.e., AR content—as the driving force behind dynamic experiences that engage users' physical movements.

Acknowledgments. This work was supported by Korea Radio Promotion Association Grant funded by the Korean Government (MSIT) (No. RNIM20230236).

References

1. Hall, E., et al.: Proxemics and comments and replies. Curr. Anthropol. **9**(2/3), 83–108 (1968)
2. Evangelidis, K., Papadopoulos, T., Sylaiou, S.: Mixed reality: a reconsideration based on mixed objects and geospatial modalities. Appl. Sci. **11**, 2417 (2021)
3. Akins, H.B.; Smith, D.A.: Imaging planets from imaginary worlds. Phys. Teach. **56**, 486–487 (2018)
4. McLuhan, M.: Understanding Media: The Extensions of Man. pp. 7–8, MIT Press, Cambridge (1994). Original work Published 1964

5. Olsson, T.: Concepts and subjective measures for evaluating user experience of mobile augmented reality services. In: Huang, W., Alem, L., Livingston, M. (eds.) Human Factors in Augmented Reality Environments, pp. 203–232. Springer, New York (2013). https://doi.org/10.1007/978-1-4614-4205-9_9

6. Han, D.I., Tom Dieck, M.C., Jung, T.: User experience model for augmented reality applications in urban heritage tourism. J. Herit. Tour. **13**, 46–61 (2018). [CrossRef]

7. Polasek, R.: User Interface Concept for Smart Glasses, University of West Bohemia (2020). https://doi.org/10.13140/RG.2.2.26591.69288/1

8. Quek, F., et al.: Multimodal human discourse: gesture and speech. ACM Trans. Comput.-Hum. Interact. (TOCHI) **9**, 171–193(2002)

9. Skarbez, B., et al.: Immersion and Coherence in a Stressful Virtual Environment, VRST 18 November 29 December 1, 2018, Tokyo, Japan (2018)

10. Ens, B., et al.: Spatial constancy of surface-embedded layouts across multiple environments. In: Proceedings of the3rd ACM Symposium on Spatial User Interaction (Los Angeles, California, USA) (SUI 2015), Association for Computing Machinery, NY, USA, pp. 65–68 (2015). https://doi.org/10.1145/2788940.2788954

11. Saredakis, D., et al.: Factors associated with virtual reality sickness in head-mounted displays: a systematic review and meta-analysis. Front. Hum. Neurosci. **14**, 96 (2020). https://doi.org/10.3389/fnhum.2020.00096

12. Wang, L., et al.: Survey of movement reproduction in immersive virtual rehabilitation. IEEE Trans. Vis. Comput. Graph. (TVCG) (2022). https://doi.org/10.1109/TVCG.2022.3142198

13. Rahimi, B., et al.: Systematic review of the technology acceptance model in health informatics. Appl. Clin. Inf. **9**(3), 604–634 (2018). https://doi.org/10.1055/s-0038-1668091

14. Satkowski, M., Dachselt, R., Investigating the impact of real world environments on the perception of 2D visualizations in augmented reality. In: Proceedings of the 2021 CHI Conference on Human Factors in Computing Systems (Yokohama, Japan) (CHI 2021), Association for Computing Machinery, New York, NY, USA, Article 522, p. 15 (2021). https://doi.org/10.1145/3411764.3445330

15. Lee, B., Sedlmair, M., Schmalstieg, D.: Design patterns for situated visualization in augmented reality. IEEE Trans. Vis. Comput. Graph. (2023). https://doi.org/10.1109/TVCG.2023.3327398

The Inheritance of Traditional Weaving Skills of Indigenous Settlement and the Practice of Micro-industry and the Dream of Weaving Craft Village

Shyh-Huei Hwang[✉] and Hsiu-Mei Huang

Graduate School of Design, National Yunlin University of Science and Technology,
Yunlin 64002, Taiwan
hwangsh@yuntech.edu.tw

Abstract. The subject of this study is the Zhongyuan (ZY) settlement of the Seediq tribe, an Indigenous people in Taiwan, which has recently explored various paths for developing distinctive ethnic weaving craftsmanship. The research **investigates** the challenges and breakthroughs encountered in the inheritance of traditional weaving skills in **the** tribe, the survival strategies of social enterprises with traditional weaving as their theme, and the analysis of the formation and support systems of **an** ideal Weaving Craft Village. The comprehensive conclusions are as follows: 1. The main challenges in the inheritance of weaving skills are the loss of daily life opportunities for traditional weaving, the uncertainty of favorable employment or entrepreneurial **opportunities** through learning traditional weaving, the considerable time required to master traditional weaving, and the difficulty of rapid recovery. 2. Reasons and methods for overcoming inheritance difficulties include the presence of three cultural heritage preservers within the tribe, who offer free or low-cost courses to encourage learning both within and outside the tribe. Additionally, the development of experiential learning activities beyond product creation has created a viable business model. 3. The Weaver's Home Workshop (WH), located in the tribe, adopts a diversified income and service approach to achieve the survival of a social enterprise. 4. The ideal of the ZY settlement Weaving Craft Village has gradually gained recognition and discussion among villagers after undergoing processes such as preserver registration, recognition as a national treasure or important preserver, skill courses, passing down to apprentices, and over four years of investigation by YunTech. The support system is largely self-initiated by the indigenous people, combining through spontaneous collaboration related to weaving, with a practical focus on economic unity and cooperation. Government plans also provide support, and the vision is being implemented step by step through practical actions. 5. Universities with expertise in design and HCI (Human-Computer Interaction) contribute to the electronic processing of tribal resources and innovative designs. Examples include website design for introducing tribal resources, innovative designs for weaving patterns, and electronic books on ethnic plants.

Keywords: Inheritance of Traditional Weaving Skills · Taiwan Indigenous People · Micro-industry · Weaving Craft Village

M. Rauterberg (Ed.): HCII 2024, LNCS 14717, pp. 259–273, 2024.
https://doi.org/10.1007/978-3-031-61147-6_18

1 Introduction

Taiwan has a population of 23.45 million, with approximately 580 thousand individuals belonging to the Indigenous peoples, constituting about 2.47% of the total population. There are officially recognized 16 Indigenous tribes in Taiwan, each with its unique cultural heritage that contributes to the rich diversity of Taiwan. Traditionally, many Indigenous people engage in weaving, particularly using ramie as the primary material for threads. Ramie cultivation, harvesting, and the intricate process of preparing threads through scraping, splicing, boiling, and dyeing are all part of the traditional weaving practice.

Historically, backstrap loom weaving has been the predominant method, where women, bound by a backstrap, sit on the ground to weave. This process is labor-intensive, physically demanding, and restricts mobility, as depicted in Fig. 1. Weaving is also influenced by factors such as ancestral beliefs and societal interactions. The Seediq tribe, one of the 16 Indigenous tribes in Taiwan, is renowned for its weaving skills. Women within the Seediq tribe are expected to possess weaving knowledge and skills, as it is considered a sacred duty. Weaving is not only a means of clothing family members but is also influenced by the ancestral teachings referred to as GAYA. According to these teachings, proficient weaving ensures the deceased can reunite with ancestors after death, making weaving a sacred and integral part of a woman's identity (Wang Meixia 2003; Ye Xiuyan 2011; Zeng Lifen 2013; Hwang and Huang 2019).

However, in contemporary times, the traditional practice of weaving is diminishing among Indigenous people. The introduction of ready-made clothing has replaced self-woven fabric due to changes in lifestyle and the diminished necessity for weaving. This decline in traditional weaving skills poses a threat to the cultural ecosystem associated with weaving. In recent years, spurred by the cultural revival movement among Indigenous peoples, tribes have sought to leverage their cultural uniqueness for economic purposes, leading to a renewed appreciation for traditional weaving as a cultural industry.

For instance, Seediq weaving has been designated as a preservation item under Taiwan's Cultural Heritage Preservation Act, with four individuals recognized as skill preservers. Our research team focused on studying the cultural ecosystem of weaving, conducting fieldwork to assess the current state of weaving across various tribes in Nantou. Our findings indicate that despite the diminishing practice of weaving, the Seediq people still consider it a crucial tradition, a symbol of their identity, and women who engage in weaving are respected. Even today, if Indigenous women express a desire to learn weaving, family members generally support the decision, regardless of its economic viability. However, our investigation also revealed that due to the scarcity of individuals practicing traditional backstrap loom weaving and the lack of economic viability, opportunities for learning this traditional skill are limited among Indigenous communities.

This research focuses on ZY Settlement, a Seediq community located in Ren'ai Township, as a case study. The research team has been closely involved with ZY Settlement from 2020 to the present, conducting intensive fieldwork and organizing tribal workshops every six months with university research students. These workshops aim to foster ongoing interaction with the women weavers of the settlement, with themes frequently related to weaving. The study aims to investigate the challenges and break-throughs in the transmission of traditional weaving skills, the survival strategies of social enterprises centered around traditional weaving in ZY Settlement, and the realization process of the dream of a Weaving Craft Village. The specific research objectives are as follows:

1. Examine the difficulties and breakthroughs encountered in the transmission of traditional weaving skills in ZY Settlement.
2. Investigate the survival strategies of social enterprises in ZY Settlement that focus on traditional weaving.
3. Explore the formation of the ideal Weaving Craft Village in ZY Settlement and the supporting systems in place.

1.1 Indigenous People Weaving in Contemporary Context: Skill Inheritance and Micro-industries

In today's changing societal structure, Indigenous people no longer weave for the clothing needs of their families, and the norms set by Gaya have gradually loosened. As a result, traditional weaving skills are facing the threat of extinction. Around the 1990s, Indigenous tribes actively explored cultural industry development, encouraging the establishment of weaving product stores. Seediq Weaving, in particular, experienced prosperity through this model (Wang and Pelin 2012; Hou 2011). However, the emphasis during that period was on product sales, treating cultural tourism as a form of consumption that commercialized Indigenous cultures for the appeal of mainstream audiences (Goss 1999). Scholars expressed concerns about cultural practices like weaving, carving, and dancing being adapted to tourists' preferences, potentially causing harm to tribal cultures (Hu 1993; Hsieh 2004). Approaching crafts as a community industry using consumer theories and economic models can lead to challenges such as market targeting, customer preferences, mass production, price and cost control, difficulties in branding and marketing channels, and the risk of losing cultural significance (Tasi 2018). The same Lai (2020) calls the weaving of the Shanli tribe in Hualien still part of the daily diverse labor of traditional women, calling it an "internally generated weaving habit", while the weaving products and industrialization of weaving products for the external consumer market It is called "externally promoted knitting habit". She also pointed out that excessive response to market demand and so-called innovation may lead to the gradual thinning of relevant social memories.

Indigenous people's traditional weaving faces challenges such as industrialization, the risk of skill loss, and concerns about over-commercialization leading to cultural harm. However, the emphasis on individual differences in neoliberalism and post-modernity provides space for cultural revival and political self-determination among Indigenous people. This has resulted in the development of ethnic tourism, emerging ethnic arts and handicraft markets, repatriation demands for cultural property held in museums or research institutions, and other cultural rights initiatives, offering contemporary Indigenous individuals more opportunities for cultural identity and reflection (Chuang 2019). Yeh and Wu (2014) point out that the economic transformation of traditional weaving not only injects new possibilities into Indigenous people's economy and cultural industries but also allows women to redefine their social roles and identities. Traditional weaving becomes a symbolic code for communication between genders and generates a renewed cultural recognition, serving as an identity and emblem for the community.

In managing folk and local crafts industries, a shift toward experiential operations or electronic channels, decentralizing intermediaries, provides direct communication opportunities between producers and consumers. This facilitates more accessible marketing channels for handmade crafts (Chuang 2019), offering micro-industries increased chances for survival and visibility.

In the current wave of cultural revitalization movements in Taiwan, Indigenous people's weaving is experiencing regeneration through community-driven initiatives and the cultural creative industry (Hwang 2012). Traditional weaving is recognized as cultural heritage, legally protected, and efforts are made to pass down the skills through apprenticeships. Today, crafts have diversified into industrial crafts, cultural and creative crafts, community-driven crafts, and educational crafts. Crafts play a multifaceted role in society, preserving long-lasting traditions through skill inheritance, supporting livelihoods for many craftworkers, and contributing to a small portion of the GDP. Community-driven and educational crafts are rooted in communities and schools, reconnecting people with the essence of local knowledge and instilling a sense of pride and confidence in tradition (Hwang 2021). Government support, through funding initiatives tied to public values such as cultural heritage preservation, rural community development, and local revitalization, provides opportunities for Indigenous communities to develop micro-industries as a response to contemporary threats faced by traditional weaving.

1.2 Endogenous Craft Villages

In the early days of Taiwan, during challenging economic conditions, craft villages were established for the production of handmade products using natural materials, aiming to sell them outside the region. For instance, when the father of the Japanese folk art movement, Yanagi Muneyoshi, visited Guanmiao in Tainan in 1943, he recognized the existence of a bamboo industry craft village where every resident was skilled in bamboo weaving, encompassing aspects such as organization, workplaces, work patterns, product sales networks, and daily usage (Hwang and Lee 2006). While Taiwan has seen a decline in craft villages driven by industrial demands, the concept persists under self-initiated efforts by communities and government policies, as observed in the case of the Zou tribe's Laiji Village in Chiayi County, Taiwan, which envisioned a boar craft village for tribal development (Hou and Liang 2010). Taking the example of the ramie craft village in Showa Village, Fukushima Prefecture, Japan, despite having a population of just over 1,000 people and financial constraints, the local government has invested in recruiting and training "Weaver Girl " since 1994. Over 21 years, they trained 104 individuals, with 30 of them choosing to remain in the village (Kushima 2019). The local government also encourages residents to serve as research volunteers, assisting in the investigation, documentation, and publication of ramie craft culture and various cultural artifacts. The promotion of ramie through exhibitions and sales is integrated with the establishment of a ramie craft museum and Weaver Girl exchange hall, both conveniently located near a rest area along the road for visitors to explore, experience, and shop.

In an ideal scenario for settlement-type crafts, everyone in the community should possess the skills as it becomes an integral part of daily life. Tasi (2018) emphasizes that Indigenous crafts are formed by community culture, environmental context, and historical background. Losing these elements could lead to defeat by external enterprises, and the development of a satisfying community ultimately depends on the community itself.

To shape local characteristics and foster local economic development through craft villages, researchers believe that it relies on local residents' understanding of endogenous development. This involves emphasizing the locality as the primary subject, utilizing existing cultural resources such as human resources, cultural history, industries, land, and landscapes as the foundation. It also involves incorporating external knowledge, technologies, and systems to autonomously create development directions and methods suitable for the inherent natural ecosystem (Hwang and Miyazaki 1996). For example, in the forest-covered town of Mishima in Fukushima Prefecture, Japan, residents have maintained a life craft movement for over 40 years. Their self-established "Emblem of Uchinada" emphasizes the collective formation of residents using local materials, employing inherited techniques from elders, integrating these skills into practical life, and constructing living spaces with their own hands. This approach clearly depicts the residents relying on community culture, prioritizing endogenous development, and viewing tourism development as a natural outcome after building a robust community foundation (Hong 2005).

Therefore, the team emphasizes the importance of placing the locality as the main subject, relying on existing cultural assets, and autonomously creating development directions and methods suitable for the inherent natural ecosystem (Hwang and Miyazaki 1996).

This study also suggests that the operation of craft villages constructed based on tribal characteristics is a feasible direction. It can be achieved through a decentralized neural network, facilitating diverse dialogues on issues and public participation. In the process of "co-production," where mutual needs and empowerment occur, residents in a community work independently for their livelihoods and interests. However, through collaborative efforts on specific topics or activities, they can come together to form areas of knowledge and issue exchange. This organic linking of topics is not constrained by institutional or hierarchical management, and it can strengthen individual capabilities. The dream of a Weaving Craft Village can thus be realized within the manageable scope of the tribal community (Lin 2022).

2 Research Methods and Actions

This research employs a longitudinal approach, utilizing qualitative research methods, including participant observation and interviews, along with elements of action research. In terms of participant observation, the second author of this study has been learning Seediq traditional weaving since 2014. The research team started collaborating with the ZY settlement, the case study for this research, in 2020. One aspect involves team members engaging in long-term visits to the tribal community, establishing friendships, participating in community-led activities, and conducting continuous investigations and interviews for research analysis. On the other hand, the team conducts workshops in the settlement every semester (every six months), involving 10–20 graduate students from the design field each time. These workshops, lasting two days and one night, have been held eight times so far and are ongoing. During the workshop operations, the research team employs action research methods. They assess tribal needs after each workshop, reflect on and improve their actions, and construct action strategies for the next workshop based on these reflections. The team serves as both event planners and participant observers, observing interactions between students and tribal members, reviewing and modifying student submissions, and providing feedback to the tribal community.

3 Analysis and Discussion

3.1 Zhongyuan(ZY) Settlement and the Inheritance of Traditional Weaving Skills

This study takes ZY settlement in Ren'ai Township, Nantou County, Taiwan, as an example. The population of ZY settlement is approximately 800, consisting mainly of Seediq people. Around 1940, due to the construction of a reservoir in their ancestral homeland, they were forced to relocate to the current location at an altitude ranging from approximately 1,200 m in a forested area to 500 m along the riverbank. The livelihood of the community shifted from hunting to agriculture (Ren'ai Township Office)[1]. Initially focused on rice cultivation, in recent years, there has been a growing emphasis on cultivating vegetables and fruits. Plums have become a significant economic crop for the settlement, and efforts have been made to develop tourism. The tribe promotes tours during the blooming season of plums in January and the plum harvest in April, even though the settlement is not located near well-known tourist attractions and is not within the scope of tourism bureau planning. As a result, residents humorously refer to their settlement as the "pass-by, walk-by, easily missed tribe." Despite this, the tribe recognizes the need for industrial transformation and is eager to find distinctive features to highlight and develop. Traditional weaving, with its unique cultural and ethnic characteristics, becomes one of the options for the tribe's development.

In the 1970s, even though factory-produced cloth had replaced handmade weaving in daily clothing, ZY settlement's women continued to be enthusiastic about weaving. At that time, a Catholic priest, observing the widespread skill of weaving among the Seediq people, encouraged women to sell their woven products, marketing them even internationally. To expedite the process, weaving machines were introduced (Wang 2004). Many people in the tribe subsequently engaged in weaving using backstrap looms or weaving machines. However, about a decade later, mass production of fabric in factories rendered handmade weaving economically uncompetitive. Consequently, tribal members gradually found it difficult to subsidize their livelihood through weaving. Despite this, interviews conducted by the research team revealed that, while women in the tribe could no longer use weaving as an economic supplement, they continued to weave as gifts for family and friends, especially for dowries. As a result, visits to tribal households still reveal remnants of fabrics woven by them in the past.

---

[1] The Ren'ai Township Office website: https://www.renai.gov.tw/list/village?model=view& view=1073.

Among the weavers, Seta Iban (1919–2007) was widely recognized as the most skilled. Spending her entire life in ZY settlement, she taught many tribal members the art of weaving. Particularly, the intricate weaving technique known as "puniri," considered the most challenging, is now practiced by only four individuals, three of whom learned it from Seta Iban (Pelin 2014). Therefore, those registered as cultural heritage weavers, as stipulated by the Cultural Heritage Preservation Act, all hail from ZY settlement. For instance, Seta Iban's granddaughter, Seta Bakan (1957--), is registered as a national-level preserver. Similarly, students taught by Seta Iban, namely Lin Ximei (Uma) and Gao Xue Zhu (Robo), are registered as local government-recognized skill preservers[2]. As preservers can apply for government funding to facilitate the inheritance of skills, Uma and Robo, who have been residing in the settlement for a long time, have conducted skill inheritance courses in the community for several years. While Uma conducts her preservation project outside the tribe, she is originally from ZY settlement, and one of the learners in her preservation program is a tribal member who regularly returns to the settlement to collect records of cultural history and to engage in operations related to ramie thread production. The team's interviews in the settlement vaguely conveyed a sense of pride among tribal members, deriving from their roots in Balan Community[3]. There is also a demand for self-ability and expectations for not giving up easily, reflecting a spirit of competition within the traditional society. Weaving, requiring significant endurance, also demands a spirit of self-demand and mutual competition within the ethnic community. This competitive atmosphere within the tribe may serve as a reason for ZY settlement's claim to have more proficient weavers. However, during interviews in the settlement, skill inheritors expressed difficulty in attracting more people, especially young individuals, to participate. The primary reason cited was that traditional weaving involves sitting on the ground, is extremely strenuous, and limits mobility. Moreover, learning traditional weaving may not necessarily lead to favorable employment or entrepreneurial opportunities.

3.2 Micro-industry and Weaver's Home Workshop (WH)

Moreover, within the tribal community, there exists a unique and regularly accessible weaving facility called the Weaver's Home Workshop (WH) (Fig. 2), established in 2016. Its founder, Shuhui, initiated the project by submitting a proposal to the government to establish a studio focusing on weaving, supported by government-funded salaries for tribal members. The workshop covers an area of approximately 400 square

---

[2] Registered as the preserver under the Cultural Heritage Preservation Act, in 2021, Zhang Fengying was nationally recognized as the preserver of the important traditional craft "Seediq Gaya tminun Traditional Weaving." In 2020, Lin Ximei and Gao Xue Zhu were registered by Nantou County as preservers of Seediq Weaving craft. Source: Bureau of Cultural Heritage, Ministry of Culture website https://nchdb.boch.gov.tw/, Accessed on: December 14, 2023.

[3] According to the descriptions provided by the indigenous people, crucial positions within the Seediq community, such as priests involved in ceremonies, are expected to be filled by individuals from the Balan Community. Consequently, these individuals hold higher social status, and their self-expectations include a high level of proficiency in weaving skills, even among women (Hwang, S. H., Huang, H. M., & Chan, T. H. (2024)).

meters, serving as a space for staff to engage in weaving, operate a shop, and facilitate weaving experiences. Over the years, the initiatives undertaken by WH include enabling young and middle-aged women in the tribe, interested in weaving, to revive memories and supplement their livelihoods. This aligns with local employment needs. Product development primarily revolves around creating items such as bags and vests with traditional tribal stories, environmental elements, and tools as design elements. The patterns are developed and tailored to appeal to the general public. Customized designs are also accommodated. However, the project's ultimate goal is to assist tribal members in achieving economic independence. Given the slow pace and limited production capacity of handmade weaving, coupled with its niche appeal, marketing becomes a significant challenge.

WH aspired to sustain the traditional weaving skills and sought to promote weaving culture, even introducing it to primary and secondary schools to cultivate appreciation and interest among students. Despite the commitment to craftsmanship and rooted practices, achieving the required economic value for employment programs proved difficult. Consequently, after six years of implementing the project, WH decided to suspend the application. This led to the need to explore alternative income sources to support personnel livelihoods. The diversified approach adopted by WH includes (1) collaborating with tribal members to develop guided tour programs, (2) partnering with university design departments for weaving pattern development and innovation, (3) re-emphasizing the importance and potential of traditional backstrap looms. For example, translating weaving-related knowledge systems into experiential economies, expanding from offering experiences with weaving machines to allowing visitors to experience the entire process of ramie thread production and weaving tool creation (as shown in Fig. 3), (4) actively participating in markets, encouraging staff to acquire new knowledge and skills (e.g., pattern making for clothing, enriching tribal cultural history knowledge for guiding visitors), and developing new product marketing channels such as online platforms and social media.

Currently, WH's primary financial support comes from government grants related to weaving projects, emphasizing cultural development, rooted craftsmanship, campus promotion, and craft brand development, provided by the Ministry of Culture. In terms of cultural tourism, WH employs a concept of collaborative economics, integrating with other tribal industries such as food and beverage, homestays, specialty agricultural products, and experts in hunting knowledge to develop tribal itineraries. This approach aims to operate content that revolves around cultural and green tourism as a business mechanism (Hwang and Huang 2024). Therefore, this study regards WH as a proponent of cultural preservation and rooted promotion, a connector of tribal cultures, and a type of social enterprise that balances cultural and economic considerations.

3.3 Realizing the Dream of a Weaving Community

Due to the continuous craft transmission by craft preservationists, ZY settlement has embarked on various initiatives through WH, involving skill inheritance, micro-industries, and overall tribal development. Therefore, starting from 2023, the team proposed planning a vision for a Weaving Craft Village, and WH accepted the proposal, applying for the Ministry of Culture's Village Development Project and receiving continuous funding for two years.

The project focuses on connecting tribal members for the joint development of Weaving-related activities and talent cultivation. It employs a strategy based on collaborative economics and is divided into three main components. The core project involves shaping ZY settlement as a Weaving cultural village, including the establishment of the ZY settlement Weaving knowledge system. This encompasses activities such as interviews with elders and investigations into traditional fabrics. Tribal Weaving skill preservationists Uma and Robo are invited to provide traditional backstrap loom Weaving skill courses and workshops on Weaving tools, ramie threads, and tool production for tribal members and youth. The emphasis is not only on skill transmission but also on designing opportunities for tribal youth to document and consolidate knowledge during Weaving skill promotion, extending to teaching Weaving to primary and secondary school students within the tribal community.

The second component focuses on creating a tribal culture with indigenous lifestyle characteristics, including empowering the youth in areas such as tribal history, cultural and historical investigations, design skills, and training for itinerary planning and tour guide personnel.

The third component involves continuous collaboration with universities, leveraging their expertise in cultural and historical investigations, community development planning, and design. Through exchange forums and workshops, universities assist in sharing technical expertise and content development for the Weaving knowledge system, contributing to the creation of innovative products and service offerings. They also collaborate in defining the goals and execution strategies for the Weaving Craft Village vision. The benefits generated include: 1. Offering Weaving courses taught by three tribal Weaving preservationists, enabling tribal members to learn Weaving conveniently and fostering pride among the weavers. 2. Expanding the Weaving experience by offering courses in Weaving tool production, which later became additional tourist experience activities. 3. Identifying other skilled individuals within the tribe, such as engaging a tribal fashion designer to teach clothing pattern design courses, enhancing tribal capabilities, and connecting designers as integral contributors to the Weaving community. 4. Involving tribal youth in interviews with elders, creating opportunities for intergenerational connections and understanding.

3.4 University Collaboration

The university involved in the aforementioned collaboration is the National Yunlin University of Science and Technology (Yuntech), to which the research team belongs. Starting in 2020, before the tribe received funding from the Ministry of Culture, the university initiated collaboration with ZY settlement through research and practical projects supported by the National Science Council. The university conducted design workshops in cooperation with the tribe, and to date, they have organized eight workshops. With a focus on respecting the tribe's autonomy and addressing their needs, the university assisted the tribe in exploring and organizing resources.

Activities included helping tribal members involved in Weaving to compile simple family genealogies, investigating the history of Weaving in the tribe, and conducting surveys on old fabrics for an exhibition simulating the residence of Seta Iban, a spiritual leader in Weaving. The university also encouraged WH to recognize the value of and reuse the Backstrap loom, potentially incorporating it into cultural and economic activities. In addition, the university used its design expertise to innovate patterns, develop a knowledge system for traditional Weaving processes, and create experiential content. They implemented a street corner museum concept to organize the knowledge systems of skilled Weavers in the tribe for external display and explanation.

Leveraging the university's design and web development expertise, they assisted in computer-drawing patterns, designing products, creating websites for showcasing tribal resources, and developing an e-book on indigenous plants.

After years of intensive interaction, the team found that ZY settlement had more skilled Weavers compared to other tribes. Additionally, due to the status of cultural preservationists, they received government subsidies and consistently conducted courses in the tribe. WH, as an actively promoted and regularly open venue, transitioned from primarily selling industrial products to balancing cultural preservation and representation with experiential economics. WH serves as a platform for presenting Weaving culture and skills to external and internal audiences. Therefore, it was assessed that it could evolve into the dream of a Weaving Craft Village.

WH has collaborated with the team for many years, implementing suggestions and innovations. For instance, while the team provided rough sketches, WH was able to weave innovative cultural elements into patterns (see Fig. 4). The team recommended expanding Weaving knowledge into experiential activities such as ramie scraping, and WH extended this to include experiential courses on making Weaving tools. The team designed explanatory signs for various workshops in the tribe, and WH suggested extending this to include guided signs for different areas within the tribe, each with its unique story (Table 1).

Table 1. Analysis of the Realization of ZY Settlement's Weaving Skill Inheritance, Micro-Industries, and Weaving Craft Village Dream

	1. Transmission of Craftsmanship	2. Microenterprise	3. Weaving Craft Village Dream in Balan Community
Distinctive Features	1. Three individuals recognized as cultural heritage weaving skill preservers 2. Ongoing instructional courses 3. Weaving Heritage's elementary and middle school foundational curriculum	1. The only and regularly open Weaving Heritage for external engagement 2. Weaving product development, retail shops, and weaving experiences 3. Cultural tourism itinerary planning	1. Pride of Balan Community in Weaving Mastery 2. Abundance of Skill Preservers and Learners 3. Proactive Advocates - WH 4. Willing Collaborators among the Tribal Members 5. Collaboration with Government and Universities
Objectives	1. Community members can acquire traditional weaving skills 2. Both local schools and outsiders have the opportunity to learn and appreciate 3. Instructors can pass on the techniques and generate income	1. Preservation of traditional craftsmanship 2. Local employment opportunities 3. Collaborative and prosperous economic development within the tribe involving WH and Weaving practitioners	1. Possesses a higher number of skilled Weaving artisans compared to other settlements 2. Weaving Craft emerges as the distinctive feature of Zhongyuan settlement 3. Aspires for people of all ages to have knowledge of and proficiency in Weaving 4. Optimistic assessment of the future development of Weaving Craft 5. Potential for becoming a cultural tourism attraction
Facilitators	1. Skill Preservers 2. Foundation Instructional Training for Weaving Heritage's External Services	Microenterprise Involving WH and Weaving Practitioners	WH and Tribal Members Collaboration
Content and Features	1. Government Funding Provided 2. Offering free or low-cost skill transmission courses within the tribe encourages both internal and external participation 3. Weaving Heritage's Outreach to Nearby Elementary and Middle Schools	1. Educational microenterprise where instructors can generate income 2. Sales of Weaving products 3. Guided tour services 4. Marketing through market stalls 5. Online sales through a website	Content: 1. Organization of Weaving Craft Knowledge System 2. Promotion of Settlement Cultural Development Features: 1. Resident autonomy, minimal involvement from local government 2. Issue-based collaborative relationships 3. Decentralized network connections 4. WH serves as an integrating and intermediary platform

(*continued*)

Table 1. (*continued*)

	1. Transmission of Craftsmanship	2. Microenterprise	3. Weaving Craft Village Dream in Balan Community
University Collaboration	1. Compilation of Weaving Preservers' Stories 2. Organizing stories of weaving preservers and curating exhibitions for Weaver Girl, collaborating with local galleries	1. Creative design of Weaving patterns 2. Planning tribal tours 3. Exploring the translation of experiences into an experiential economy	1. Organization and assistance in constructing the Weaving Craft knowledge system 2. Emphasis on the cultural significance of the Backstrap loom 3. Utilization of computers for website design, innovative Weaving patterns, ethnic plant e-books, etc
Benefits	1. There are more weavers in this tribe compared to others 2. Even if community members do not learn weaving, there is a greater opportunity to become familiar with it 3. Local characteristics are naturally presented	1. Livelihood support 2. Economic unity 3. Learning new skills 4. Fostering innovative thinking	1. Creation of a renewed connection between craft and people 2. Traditional Backstrap loom and cultural ecology reimagined and utilized 3. Expansion of topics and participants 4. Interviews of youth with elders to create generational connections 5. Economic unity as tribal members identify niches and are willing to collaborate 6. Recognition of Weaving as a distinctive tribal feature
Challenges	1. Weaving is laborious and challenging, making it difficult to attract the interest of young people 2. Acquiring weaving skills is also challenging as it is not easily established as a primary source of livelihood	1. Slow handcrafting speed and a limited range of Weaving products, catering to a niche market 2. Difficulty in competing with the capital market for tribal microenterprises 3. The lack of prominent attractions in the vicinity makes it challenging to promote cultural tourism	1. Requires financial support from the government 2. Young adults are busy with livelihoods and cannot fully commit

Fig. 1. Backstrap loom weaving

Fig. 2. WH display space and products for sale

Fig. 3. WH designing a ramie scraping course for visitors to experience

Fig. 4. YunTech students contributing to innovative Weaving pattern design, with WH weaving it and sewing it into a bag

4 Conclusion

The traditional Weaving craft in ZY settlement, like many other Indigenous tribes in Taiwan, faces the challenge of not being essential in daily clothing, prompting the need to consider how to "manage" it to become "contemporary essential." The study explores potential breakthroughs, incorporating elements emphasized by neoliberalism and post-modernity, such as individualized cultural tourism demands. Weaving could thus become a part of the commercial value of cultural tourism. The Indigenous people's pursuit of self-identity and recognition turns Weaving culture into an option, serving as symbolic communication and distinction between tribes. It also allows women to redefine social roles and self-affirmation, gaining financial support from various government departments.

This research addresses the difficulties and breakthroughs encountered in the inheritance of ZY settlement's traditional Weaving skills. It focuses on the survival strategies of social enterprises engaged in cultural preservation and micro-production, the formation of an ideal Weaving Craft Village, and the analysis of support systems. The comprehensive conclusions are as follows:

1. Challenges faced by the inheritance of traditional Weaving skills in ZY settlement include the loss of daily usage opportunities, limited employment or entrepreneurial opportunities for learning traditional Weaving, and the time-intensive nature of mastering traditional Weaving.
2. Breakthroughs in the inheritance of ZY settlement's traditional Weaving skills are attributed to the presence of three cultural heritage preservers, their encouragement of affordable or free courses, and the development of a business model through the sale of textiles, clothing, and experiential learning activities.
3. ZY settlement's WH adopts diverse income streams and services as a strategy for the survival of the social enterprise. This includes the entire process of Weaving production, design, and sales, experiential learning in ramie scraping, tool making, bow weaving, bow weaving tool making, and ribbon weaving. Services also extend to off-site experiential learning, long-term ramie experience and learning services for elementary schools, and the application for various government projects.

4. Yuntech contributes through digital tools by assisting in the design of ZY settlement's website, innovative Weaving pattern design, and the creation of electronic books on ethnic plants.
5. The ideal of ZY settlement's Weaving Craft Village, shaped through preserver registration, recognition as important preservers, skill courses, apprentice transmission, and over four years of investigation by YunTech, is gradually being discussed and understood by the villagers. The main support systems include the social enterprise Weaving Home, the three preservers, the community development association and village office, government project plans, and universities (the research team). This support system is primarily formed intrinsically by the tribal people, uniting through networks related to Weaving and working together practically in economic unity. They apply for government project support, progressively implementing their vision through action.

References

Chuang, C.W.: The trends and prospect of Taiwan's traditional craft industry facing the maker movement. J. Cult. Resour. **12**, 1–55 (2019)

Goss, J.: The Souvenir and Sacrifice in the Tourist Mode of Consumption. Routledge, London and New York (2005)

Hong, D.: Reflections on Sanjiao Town. Newsletter of the Community Development Society of the Republic of China, Issue 39 (2005)

Hou, W.Z.: Weaving Rainbow Dreams: Development of Weaving Craft under the Context of Seediq Culture, Unpublished master's thesis, NYUST Cultural Heritage Conservation Department, Yunlin (2011)

Hou, Y.K., Liang, B.K.: Research on indigenous tourism and local development - a case study of the Zou tribe in Jiubu township. Taiwan Indigenous People Res. **3**(1), 105–148 (2010)

Hsieh, S.C.: Macro Explorations in Ethnic Anthropology: Collection of Papers on Taiwan Indigenous People. National Taiwan University Press (2004)

Hu T.L.: Lan Yu Perspective. Institute of Ethnology, Academia Sinica, Taipei (1993)

Hwang, S.H.: Starting change from the community—opportunities for humanities innovation and social practice. News. Hum. Soc. Sci. **14**(1), 17–20 (2012)

Hwang, S.H.: Six historical stages of Taiwan craft and a roposal for the embryonic form of craft cultural ecosystem. J. Craftology Taiwan (Inaugural Issue) 7–25 (2021)

Hwang, S.H., Huang, H.M., Chan, T.H.: The practice of Sepl based on weaving-derived cultural business mechanisms – a case study of an indigenous settlement in central Taiwan. Maiko Nishi Suneetha M. Subramanian **61** (2024)

Hwang, S.H., Lee, Y.H.: Counteraction against the industrial revolution: the pioneer of arts and crafts-Williams Morris and Yen Shui-Long. In: Lin, D.T. (ed.), Crafts pioneer-Yen Shui-Long, 6–15. Taiwan Crafts, vol. 20, pp. 5–24 (2006)

Hwang, S.H., Miyazaki, K.: Unfolding "Community overall construction" as the regeneration of local culture in Taiwan. Des. Res.**43**(1), 97–106 (1996). (in Japanese)

Hwang, S.H., Huang, H.M.: Cultural ecosystem of the seediq's traditional weaving techniques—a comparison of the learning differences between urban and indigenous communities. Sustainability **11**, 1519 (2019). https://doi.org/10.3390/su11061519

Kushima M.: Life stories observed from the relationship between female immigrants in agricultural mountain villages and nature: starting with the relationship between "Princess" and "Ramie" in Showa Village, Fukushima Prefecture. Jpn. Oral Hist. Res.**15**, 109–124 (2019)

The Inheritance of Traditional Weaving Skills 273

Lai, S.J.: Weaving and memory: daily practices of Seediq Duta group's weaving skills and memory in Zhuoxi township, Hualien county. J. Chin. Ritual Theatre Folklore **209**, 211–274 (2020)

Lin, C.H.: Cultural disadvantage and cultural disadvantage: reflexive perspectives of museums. Technol. Museum **26**(1), 5–28 (2022)

Pelin, I.: Investigation on the traditional weaving skills and cultural asset of Puniri of the Seediq. Cultural Asset Bureau, Ministry of Culture, Taiwan (2014)

Tasi, Z.J.: Design practices for local revitalization. Land Public Governance Q. **6**(2), 68–77 (2018)

Tseng, L.F.: A pilot study on transmission of the Seediq weaving tradition and handicraft Puniri in Nantou county: the three generations of seta Iban as research subject. J. Cult. Heritage Conserv. **24**, 33–57 (2013)

Wang, M.H., Pelin, I.: Activating the Seediq culture: a study of cultural industry in a Seediq community. J. Chin. Ritual, Theatre Folklore **176**, 233 (2012). (in Chinese)

Wang, S.G.: Taiwan Indigenous People's Traditional Weaving. Morning Star Publishing Inc., Taichung (2004)

Yeh, H.Y., Wu, M.: REthnic handicrafts and cultural industry: a case study of female Taroko weaving culture in Xiu-Lin county of Hualien, Taiwan. Taiwan J. Indigenous Stud. **7**(3), 1–37(2014)

Design of Interactive Digital Virtual Display Application for Chinese Heritage Traditional Herbal Medicine Culture

Haoru Li[1], Binlin Feng[1]([✉]), Mingyang Su[2], and Zhuohua Liu[1]

[1] Shenzhen University, Shenzhen, China
fengbinlin2021@email.szu.edu.cn
[2] Tsinghua Shenzhen International Graduate School, Shenzhen, China

Abstract. The project focuses on designing a platform using Unity3D technology to preserve intangible cultural heritage, emphasizing the pharmacological efficacy and processing of herbal treatments in traditional Chinese medicine. Traditional Chinese medicine plays a crucial role in cultural continuity and emotional confront, yet its digitization is confronted with the complexity of its theoretical framework, insufficient public awareness, and the neglect of cultural elements during its propagation.

In response, the research team has engineered an interactive application that transposes the herbal wisdom cataloged in the "Bencao Gangmu" into a digital milieu. This application's distinctiveness lies in its fusion of time-honored medicinal culture with digital innovation. Furthermore, the design posits a new framework for cultural inheritance that effectively simplifies and disseminates the complex theories of Chinese medicine and herbal knowledge through digital means to the general public. The application establishes a conduit that intricately connects traditional Chinese medicinal culture with contemporary society, offering an educational, accessible, and experiential platform, that serves as an innovative exemplar for the digital preservation and inheritance of intangible cultural heritage.

Keywords: Traditional Chinese Herbs · Intangible Cultural Heritage · Unity3D Technology · Digital Conservation · Bencao Gangmu · Interactive Digital Application

1 Introduction

This article exemplifies the therapeutic mechanisms of herbal treatments and the pharmaceutical processing techniques within traditional Chinese medicine, employing Unity3D technology for the design and development of a world heritage platform for the inheritance of intangible cultural heritage, with the aim of promoting the preservation and propagation of the non-tangible cultural heritage of Chinese herbal medicine. In today's materially affluent society, the significance of intangible cultural heritage is paramount for cultural continuity, emotional

M. Rauterberg (Ed.): HCII 2024, LNCS 14717, pp. 274–292, 2024.
https://doi.org/10.1007/978-3-031-61147-6_19

comfort, and the expansion of aesthetic appreciation. However, traditional Chinese medical culture confronts an array of challenges in the digital age, including a complex theoretical system, insufficient public awareness of traditional Chinese medicine, and the neglect of cultural elements during the dissemination process.

To address the aforementioned challenges, this design leverages the Unity3D game engine to create a digital interactive application centered on Chinese herbal culture. It digitizes the traditional herbal information contained within the "Bencao Gangmu" and creates virtual environments with digital human figures. The application primarily encompasses four traditional cultural game modes aimed at disseminating knowledge about pharmacological techniques, art culture, and humanistic history. The development team has conducted research into the "Bencao Gangmu" and analyzed the physical characteristics of actual herbs to produce illustrations of these herbs, which are presented on the platform in an ink-wash painting style.

Utilizing information technology development and an abundance of primary herbal entities along with secondary literature resources, the application provides professional knowledge and healthcare information in the field of traditional Chinese medicine, offering users an immersive cultural experience. The development of this application is intended to support the protection and inheritance of traditional Chinese herbal culture, enhance the dissemination and recognition of Chinese medicine as a global intangible cultural heritage, and deeply explore the roles of Chinese herbs in terms of modern medical value and cultural missions.

2 Current State of TCM Interactive Platforms

Cultural heritage represents the precious assets accumulated by humanity throughout its extensive historical journey, encapsulating information about past lifestyles, thoughts, artistic expression, and technological advances, and epitomizing the history, culture, and value systems of a nation. "Bencao Gangmu," as a comprehensive compendium of traditional Chinese medical science, contains information that has positively influenced subsequent developments in various fields such as medicine, geography, agronomy, meteorology, and natural history [1,2], and has profoundly affected the progression of traditional Chinese medicine and pharmacology [3]. In a diverse and materially prosperous society, intangible cultural heritage plays a significant role in the maintenance of culture, emotional support, and the expansion of aesthetic appreciation [4–6].

Traditional Chinese medicine (TCM), a medical resource endemic to China in the pivotal role of ensuring the health of the populace and is an essential component of the global health system. As the medical paradigm shifts, TCM receives increasing attention on a global scale, encountering novel developmental prospects and an array of challenges concomitantly. Viewed through the lens of cultural transmission, TCM suffers from a deficiency in efficacious mechanisms for its perpetuation and proliferation. The theoretical corpus of TCM traces its roots to the Spring and Autumn and Warring States periods, and over the millennia, it has been subjected to profound study and explication by scholars through successive dynasties. In recent times, TCM practitioners have embarked on extensive research endeavors in an array of fields encompassing foundational theories, medical history and literature, clinical diagnosis and treatment, herbal pharmaceutical preparations, and acupuncture principles, culminating in significant scientific achievements. Nonetheless, much of these research activities have strayed from the intrinsic guiding tenets of the TCM theoretical system. The trend of 'Westernization' in scientific endeavors has stymied the cultural transmission, propagation, and innovative evolution of TCM in contemporary society [7]. Currently, the advancement of TCM is impeded by a dearth of deliberate cultural innovation and construction, a lack of effective avenues for actively engaging the public with TCM culture, a monolithic and excessively specialized nature in cultural communication forms, variable quality, and the absence of enduring promotional mechanisms [8]. These predicaments significantly constrain the societal acknowledgment of TCM's cultural worth and the efficacy of its transmission and heritage.

However, in the current digital era, the dissemination of TCM culture is generally constrained by a dichotomy characterized by "the esoteric nature of the theories and the low TCM literacy among citizens," as well as a dissemination process that focuses more on "knowledge than on cultural context" and one where "activities abound but newsworthy highlights are scarce" [9]. These contradictions present challenges in the areas of heritage and innovation. To achieve creative transformation and innovative development of TCM culture, and to integrate it with modern health concepts, the incorporation of digital technology into the domain of TCM knowledge has emerged as a new trend in contemporary TCM development. Starting from the transformation of traditional cultural resources into digital formats lays a solid foundation for the digital transmission of culture, thereby promoting the orderly and effective dissemination of traditional culture [10].

2.1 The Integration and Development of Intangible Cultural Heritage (ICH) and Digital Technology

The rapid development of digital technology has ushered in a new era of digital media for the protection and transmission of intangible cultural heritage, overcoming the limitations of traditional carriers such as oral transmission, texts, images, and electronic media. This advancement offers a broader range of possibilities for the inheritance and promotion of intangible cultural heritage, allowing its knowledge and value to be conveyed to a wider audience in more diverse and interactive ways. In 1992, UNESCO launched the Memory of the World Programme, initiating the digital construction of intangible heritage through the establishment of digital archives, hosting online exhibitions, and publishing digital publications, thereby promoting its global dissemination. Google's Google Arts & Culture project has digitized collections from museums around the world, breaking through the constraints of time and space and enabling barrier-free access to intangible heritage projects. The European Digital Library, initiated by the European Union, aggregates materials from libraries, museums, and archives from various countries, including a vast array of intangible heritage resources. For instance, the digitalization projects of the Palace Museum in China and the Digital Dunhuang project have enabled the public to appreciate the precious cultural heritage of the Forbidden City at any time and from anywhere through virtual reality technology. In the field of intangible heritage, Tencent's Next Idea innovation competition includes projects such as the use of AR technology to showcase papercutting art and the reenactment of shadow puppetry in animation form, realizing the integrated development of traditional skills and modern technology. Baidu, in cooperation with the Ministry of Culture and Tourism, has launched projects such as intangible heritage cloud exhibitions and cloud performance digital experience scene development, which play an active role in the recording, copyright confirmation, knowledge mapping, and innovative dissemination of intangible heritage. The paper [11] proposes a new type of digital traditional art communication platform based on new media technology, with abundant development space and achievements. The paper [12] presents a system in which users can enhance the act of wrapping the traditional Japanese furoshiki by using image recognition technology and motion image projection technology while engaging with their interest. The paper [13] demonstrates a multimodal 3D capturing platform combined with a motion comparison system, with the focus on preserving traditional sports and games. Although there are many examples of digitalization combined with intangible cultural heritage mentioned above, previous literature mostly discusses the integration of traditional culture and digital media in specific areas and fails to fully consider the diversity and complexity of intangible cultural heritage. These studies, while achieving certain results in specific fields, lack systematic and comprehensive consideration and do not address the fundamental issue of historical facts lacking interest and interactivity, leading to difficulties in mobilizing the public's enthusiasm for understanding and exploration, thereby making widespread promotion challenging. To overcome these challenges, it is necessary to expand the promotion of intangible cultural heritage in a way that is enjoyable and attractive, thereby garnering wider participation.

In the contemporary context of rapidly evolving lifestyles, traditional culture has found itself increasingly distant from modern society and quotidian life, leading to its gradual neglect and oblivion among the younger demographics. In reality, it is not a lack of appreciation for traditional culture among the youth, but rather a dearth of opportunities to engage with and experience it, which hinders their ability to develop a profound understanding. Hence, traditional culture currently encounters a myriad of issues and barriers that must be surmounted through innovative means. For the exhibition and inheritance of intangible cultural heritage, the pressing issue is to discover modernized, innovative methods that resonate with and are favored by the younger generation [14].

2.2 The Application and Challenges of Digital Technology in the Protection of ICH

In recent years, games have garnered increasing attention as vessels for the memory of human civilization and the preservation and transmission of intangible cultural heritage. Stakeholders from various sectors have committed themselves to exploring new avenues that blend 'tradition with modern entertainment' [15,16]. In the confluence of gaming and intangible cultural heritage, two instances stand out. The first is the game "Never Alone" (also known as "Kisima Ingitchuna"), developed by Upper One Games in collaboration with the Inupiat, an Alaska Native people. Grounded in the traditional stories and culture of the Inupiat, the game has players take on the roles of a young girl and a fox, tackling puzzles and embarking on adventures with the aim of imparting the values and cultural heritage of the Inupiat. Another example is the game "Mulaka," developed by Lienzo, which draws inspiration from the traditions and myths of the Tarahumara people of Chihuahua, Mexico. Players assume the role of a Tarahumara shaman, exploring magnificent landscapes, engaging in combat with mythological creatures, and solving puzzles to showcase the culture and traditions of the Tarahumara to the players. Additionally, interactive software centered around traditional herbalism, such as the game "Potion Craft" by niceplay games, serves as a simulation management game where players, acting as potion makers, gather ingredients, learn recipes, brew potions, and trade with customers. This indirectly fosters an understanding and appreciation of traditional culture, historical knowledge, and economic strategies, carrying cultural significance and educational value. The techniques outlined in the paper [17] offer effective strategies for overcoming the bottleneck of TCM, facilitating an enhanced phytochemical diversity, aligning with molecular targets, and elucidating therapeutic mechanisms. In the paper [18], media scene theory is used as the theoretical support, and it is expected that the combination of communication theory and art design practice can provide a reference for the research of digital presentation design of Chinese herbal medicine culture. Although these studies have achieved certain results in specific fields, and the application of digital technology in the field of traditional Chinese herbal medicine is growing, there is a lack of specialized digital presentation platforms for this intangible cultural heritage. Traditional Chinese herbal medicine cannot be presented to the public more intuitively and vividly through virtual reality, interactive displays, and other means, indicating a current deficiency in the digital representation and interaction of this cultural heritage in China. Furthermore, in the construction of global heritage transmission platforms, there is a deficiency in historical authenticity, technological innovation, and preservation of cultural fidelity [19]. The platform has to some extent addressed these technical issues as highlighted.

3   Design Challenges and Solution Strategies

3.1   Enhancing the Appeal of TCM-Themed Applications

In the realm of TCM, when it is utilized as a theme for gaming, the inherent academic nature and specialization often lead to a perception of a lack of appeal among general users. The academic rigor and professional depth inherent in applications themed around TCM can result in content that is complex and esoteric, potentially leading to difficulties in easy comprehension and absorption for the average user, thereby cultivating a general sense of uninterest. This stems from the fact that application players typically seek intuitive entertainment and immediate gratification, whereas the unique terminologies, intricate theories, and detail-oriented practices of TCM can be challenging to seamlessly integrate into a relaxed and enjoyable gaming experience.

To surmount this innate drawback, 'Herbalist's Shop' employs a role-playing application mode in which players assume the identity of a disciple of Li Shizhen, experiencing firsthand the entire process of TCM diagnosis and medication preparation. The application introduces level designs and task assignments aimed at enhancing player engagement and the intriguing nature of the application play experience. At the same time, the incorporation of realistic herbal forms along with original illustrations from 'Compendium of Materia Medica' bolsters the application's educational direction and its entertainment value. Additionally, the utilization of traditional Chinese ink-wash artistic design strives to strike a balance between historical authenticity and artistic appeal, providing an immersive experience environment to attract a broader interest from players.

3.2 Challenges in Accurately Conveying TCM Pharmacological Principles in Gaming Environments

Given the complexity inherent in the pharmacological principles of TCM and the paucity of related scientific explanations, the task of accurately conveying these concepts within a gaming environment, without misleading users, represents a significant challenge [20]. The therapeutic efficacy of TCM formulations is attributed to their multiple chemical constituents, and the interplay and synergistic effects between these constituents, which together form a complex framework of TCM pharmacodynamics. While the clinical effects of these medicines have been widely applied and validated, scientific research into their pharmacological mechanisms and principles of action at the molecular level is still insufficiently developed [21]. Therefore, owing to the lack of research into the specific principles and mechanisms, the design team's research on traditional Chinese herbal medicine has primarily focused on elements such as the appearance, nomenclature, and aliases of the medicinal materials-features that are readily verifiable and widely recognized on a global scale.

During the early stages of developing 'Herbalist's Shop,' the team conducted thorough research into authoritative historical texts such as 'Compendium of Materia Medica,' which served as the foundational basis for the development of application materials, with the aim of ensuring the accuracy and scientific integrity of the application content. The design of the application materials took into full consideration the morphological characteristics of the herbs, enabling players to recognize and understand the true forms of the herbs. Through such methods, the application not only preserves traditional knowledge of TCM but also ensures the accuracy and authority of the popular science information disseminated.

3.3   Integration Strategies for TCM Herbal Dispensing Processes in Application Mechanics

During the application design process, integrating the procedure of TCM herbal dispensing with the gaming mechanism posed a central challenge. To address this issue, the development team identified key elements and potential playability within each step, designing a series of standalone interactive mini-applications specifically. For instance, in the diagnostic phase, the application is modeled after the traditional TCM pulse diagnosis, where players are required to observe and interact with a meridian chart to synthesize the necessary herbal images. In the herb-gathering phase, players are tasked with unlocking the appropriate compartments in a medicine cabinet by deciphering the alternative names of the herbs. In the herb slicing stage, players must slice the herbs fluttering on the screen into the prescribed shapes such as 'blocks,' 'sections,' or 'slices,' according to the specific part of the herb and the desired therapeutic effect. The herb grinding phase is designed as a rhythm application, where players must follow the beat to operate a pestle to grind the herbs.

3.4   Optimization of Guidance and Feedback Mechanisms

In order to enhance user experience and increase the engagement level of this interactive application, timely and effective guidance and feedback mechanisms have been implemented. After extensively consulting with professional educators and analyzing similar interactive applications, the development team accumulated a wealth of design experience. At the initial stage of application development, the team designed a comprehensive tutorial module to ensure that users could quickly familiarize themselves with the application mechanisms and receive real-time feedback during operation. Simultaneously, the dynamic hint functionality of interactive elements within the application was enhanced to guide user interaction. Key operational points were integrated with screen vibration effects to strengthen the sense of feedback from actions. Furthermore, a reputation system and a diary (achievement) system were introduced, aimed at encouraging users to actively learn about herbal medicine and increase their experience points.

4   Development and Realization

4.1   Practical Application Design

The core concept of the application design is to engage users through a role-playing format, allowing them to assume the role of an apprentice to Li Shizhen, the revered Sage of Medicine. This enables users to experience and learn about various aspects of TCM. The process of TCM pharmacology is deconstructed into several modules: "diagnosis, herb gathering, herb slicing, herb grinding, and herb dispensing." Additional gameplay elements such as "herb collecting" and "outpatient visits" have been designed, alongside integrated learning of the knowledge contained within the "Compendium of Materia Medica." To precisely recreate the historical ambiance of the Jiajing period, the design team, with a deep respect for and commitment to cultural heritage, has based their detailed illustrations of various medicinal herbs on the original drawings in the "Compendium of Materia Medica." Building upon this, the team has incorporated the artistic techniques of Song dynasty ink wash paintings to construct the application's visual materials, aiming to faithfully reproduce the artistic aesthetics of that era. The intent of this design is not only to provide a visual feast for users but also to enhance their understanding of the tradition of Chinese medicine through an immersive historical and cultural experience.

Furthermore, within the herbal hut setting of the application's backyard, the design team has created an interactive segment for planting medicinal herbs. This feature not only augments the interactivity of the application but also gives users a more intuitive understanding of the herb cultivation process. By introducing herb collection and outpatient visitation components, the application expands the user's range of activities, thereby enabling exploration beyond the confines of the Eastern Wall Hall. This design is intended not merely to broaden the spatial dimensions of the application but to offer a comprehensive platform for historical and cultural learning, allowing users to gain a more holistic understanding of traditional medical knowledge and cultural experience. Specific details are as follows:

4.1.1 Diagnostic Stage

This application segment is designed as a fast-paced interactive experience that melds the process of TCM diagnosis with knowledge of medicinal herbs. Through gamified learning, the application aims to enhance users' ability to identify medicinal herbs, achieving both educational and entertainment objectives.

At its core, the application conceptualizes around the traditional TCM practice of pulse-taking and inquiry, immersing users in a simulated TCM clinic environment. Throughout the application, users are presented with a series of image-based and text-based challenges. Each level displays various herb images alongside a list of corresponding medicinal herb names. The user's task is to match each image with its correct herb name accurately. Successful matches allow progression to subsequent stages. In addition, the application is capable of gradually increasing its difficulty in accordance with user progression, such as by introducing additional similar herb distractors or reducing the time constraints, thus making the application suitable for users at varying levels of expertise.

4.1.2 Pick-Up Stage

Within the "herb selection stage" of the application design, users engage in a challenging decryption module aimed at reinforcing their memory of the various colloquial names of Chinese herbal medicines and their associations with the physical herbs. By memorizing the herbs and their respective aliases, users are better equipped to retain relevant knowledge about the medicinal herbs. Repetitive interaction with the application aids in consolidating memory, thus enhancing the depth of understanding and retention of knowledge. In contrast to traditional passive learning methods, this interactive application allows users to learn through practice. By actively participating in the decryption module, users gain a more profound learning experience.

4.1.3   Herb Cutting Stage

In the design of this application, the primary objective is to impart knowledge about the different cutting shapes of Chinese medicinal materials—such as "chunks," "sections," and "slices"—through an interactive learning mode, and elucidate how these shapes influence the method of usage and the efficacy of the herbs. This type of interactive learning is intended to enhance users' understanding of the preparation process of Chinese medicinal materials, as well as to increase their interest in this area.

At the onset of the application, users receive a task that specifies the names of the medicinal materials to be prepared, along with the required cutting shapes. Users must use the mouse-controlled virtual knife to accurately slice the herbs into the designated shapes following the guide lines on the screen. For example:

- Cutting into chunks: Users must cut the material into larger chunks, suitable for those herbs that need to be decocted for an extended period to fully release their medicinal properties.
- Cutting into sections: The material needs to be cut into moderate-length sections, a shape commonly used for medicinal stems or roots.
- Cutting into slices: Users are required to cut the material into thin slices, allowing the active components of the herbs to dissolve and release quickly.

The application also incorporates practical knowledge tips that detail the characteristics of the release of medicinal properties for each cutting shape, along with examples of commonly used medicinal materials corresponding to these shapes, helping users to deeply understand and master the practical value of each cutting form.

4.1.4   Herb Pounding Stage

The herb pounding stage is set up as a rhythm-based application. The purpose of this application design is to enable users to thoroughly understand and master the correct cutting shapes and pounding techniques of Chinese medicinal materials, as well as to recognize the importance of these preparation methods in the efficacy of the medicine, through an interactive learning approach. The application aims to enhance users' interest in the preparation processes of Chinese medicinal materials utilizing virtual operations.

Within the application, users take on the role of a traditional Chinese medicine practitioner, where a key task is to use a pestle and mortar to crush the medicinal materials. During the pounding process, users must learn to adjust the pounding force according to the characteristics of different medicinal materials. For example, harder materials such as hawthorn and oyster shells require greater force to ensure that the materials are effectively crushed; while softer materials, such as fresh Rehmannia and fresh aloe, require less force to prevent excessive destruction of active components. Additionally, the frequency of pounding is a critical factor. The application instructs users on how to adjust the speed of pounding according to the specific needs of the material. Rapid pounding can quickly crush the material, but too fast may cause overheating and affect the efficacy of the medicine. To enhance the educational aspect of the application, the actual applications of various crushed medicinal materials will also be demonstrated within the application, such as their use in decoction, making pills, or powder formulations. In this way, users not only learn how to crush medicinal materials but also understand how the crushed materials are further processed and used.

4.2   Software System

In terms of system design, this design focuses on the user experience as the main axis, complemented by the protagonist's journey in medical learning and practice as a secondary axis. By integrating these two axes, a multidimensional application system encompassing prestige, and achievements (diary) has been constructed. The user's application process is not only a journey of personal skill enhancement but also reflects the protagonist's gradual mastery of medical knowledge.

Diary (Achievements) System: This system serves as a recorder of the user's accumulated knowledge, progressively documenting the medicinal herb knowledge learned throughout the application. When all knowledge points concerning a particular herb are activated, the user is considered to have "mastered" that herb (Fig. 1). This process is not merely a representation of skill enhancement within the application but also symbolizes the protagonist's continual illumination of new knowledge on the herbal medicine knowledge tree. The user's control over their character essentially simulates the character's journey of learning medical skills from Li Shizhen.

Fig. 1. Diary (Achievements) System Interface

Prestige System: This system functions as the user's leveling system, where users enhance their prestige by completing tasks. Higher prestige indicates that the user (i.e., the protagonist) has healed more patients, gained more experience, and handled new cases with greater ease. Achieving a certain level of prestige allows for the completion of the application, while a reduction of prestige to zero signifies application failure. The acquisition of prestige and achievements also symbolizes the protagonist's recognition by the people and progress in medical skills (Fig. 2).

Teaching System: Considering the educational purpose of the application, namely to deepen users' understanding and knowledge of traditional Chinese medicine, and because users are bound to initially be unfamiliar with the characteristics and descriptions of herbs, the development team has included the master's teachings as application guidance. Through the master's instructions, users are helped to become familiar with the operations. Additionally, a scene of Li Shizhen's study has been set up as the application's atlas and knowledge base (Fig. 3). Users can access the study at any time for hints and learning, which also symbolizes the protagonist's study of traditional Chinese medicine knowledge from the master. The study's layout carefully features Li Shizhen's manuscripts and herb illustrations, reflecting the historical context and providing content prompts for the application.

4.3 Application Scenarios

In the construction of the application world, the development team referenced authentic historical contexts and artistically enhanced the depiction of historical sites. This was done to display the unique charm of Qizhou and the rich heritage of traditional Chinese medicine within the application. The following detailed elaboration of four critical application scenarios demonstrates the team's pursuit of a balance between realism and artistic representation (Fig. 4).

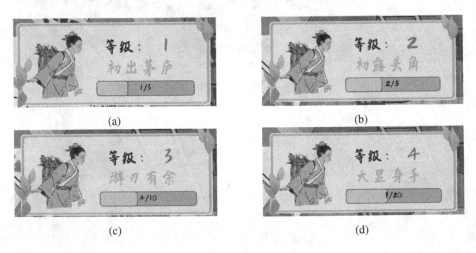

(a)

(b)

(c)

(d)

Fig. 2. Prestige System Interface: Level 1 Interface (a), Level 2 Interface (b), Level 3 Interface (c), Level 4 Interface (d)

Fig. 3. The Application's Atlas and Knowledge Base: Juncus Efusus (a), Perilla Frutescen (b), Sanchi Flower (c), Ginseng (d)

In the domain of digital applications, the precision and creativity in landscape design are pivotal for enriching user experience. This design presents an application world that synergizes reality with imagination, aiming to enhance users' perception and comprehension of Qizhou and the traditional Chinese medicine culture. By simulating the lively streets of Qizhou, the medicinal ambiance of the herbal shop, the scholarly essence of the study, and the natural beauty of the back garden, the work intends to deepen users' understanding and appreciation of Chinese traditional culture.

To authentically recreate the natural and cultural landscapes of Li Shizhen's hometown and to reconstruct the precision of his native place, this design emphasizes the reproduction of micro-details within the scenes. Utilizing up to four

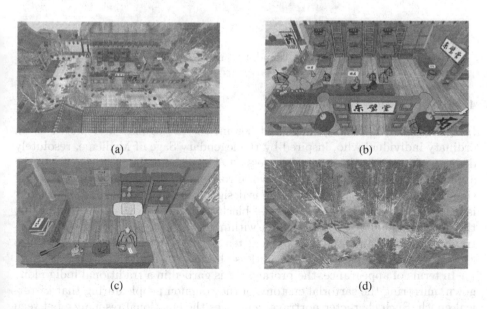

Fig. 4. Main Application Scenarios: Qizhou Street (a), Medicine Shop Environment (b), Study (c), Backyard Natural Landscape (d)

advanced mapping techniques, the design simulates varied ground textures to present the diversity of Qizhou's geographical environment (Fig. 5). The hard stone pavements reflect the historical significance of the ancient city, whereas the soft soil textures reveal the natural scenery of the countryside. The variety of in-ground design not only augments the visual appeal but also fosters an immersive user experience.

Moreover, to enhance the authenticity and depth of the scenes, elements such as slate and wild grass have been meticulously incorporated. The accurate depiction of the texture and pattern of the slate allows users to feel the rich historical connotations of Qizhou's ancient city; while the detailed portrayal and dynamic effects of wild grass enrich the visual and tactile experience. In this design, through the precise crafting of scenes, the goal is to create an environment that reflects reality while blending in elements of imagination, thereby enhancing the user's cognitive engagement with the region of Qizhou and its medicinal culture. Grounded in historical facts, the application deepens the user's understanding and respect for traditional Chinese culture by simulating the vibrant streets of Qizhou, the medical atmosphere of the herbal shop, the academic ambiance of the study, and the natural landscape of the backyard.

Fig. 5. Ground Texture Template

4.4   Application Characters

In the application setting delineated herein, the protagonist is depicted as an ordinary individual who, inspired by the legendary Sage of Medicine, resolutely dedicates himself to the medical profession. Throughout the narrative arc of the application, the character plays a pivotal role, imbuing the story with profound significance. The protagonist's image is designed to reflect the typical characteristics of a person of Chinese descent—black hair and yellow skin—symbolizing the vast community of practitioners within the field of TCM (Fig. 6). In portraying facial features, the development team employed an abstract approach to represent the collective visage of countless physicians within the TCM fraternity.

In terms of appearance, the protagonist is garbed in a traditional indigo long gown, mirroring the sartorial customs of the common people during that historical epoch. Such character portrayal enhances the emotional resonance between the user and the protagonist, allowing the user to empathetically experience the challenges and endeavors faced by an ordinary person pursuing the path of medicine. Through this character design, the aim of the development team is to convey the ethos and core values of TCM practitioners to the user. Despite being an average individual, the protagonist achieves the status of a medical practitioner, supported by a relentless pursuit of medical knowledge and a steadfast will—exemplifying the contribution of TCM to individual accomplishment and societal welfare. As users journey through the application, they accompany the protagonist, sharing in the joys of growth and the rigors of challenge, thereby profoundly appreciating the nobility of medicine and the extensive influence of TCM culture.

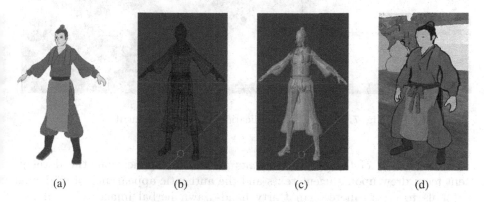

(a)   (b)   (c)   (d)

Fig. 6. Character Design and Implementation Process: Draft Design (a), Modeling Software Modeling (b), Adding Skeletons (c), Game Engine Rendering (d)

4.5 Design of Application's Graphic Elements

In order to better integrate with the theme of traditional Chinese medicine, the development team meticulously designed an application interface imbued with Chinese aesthetic characteristics (Fig. 7). In terms of color coordination, the development team referred to traditional Chinese classical color palettes, primarily utilizing a yellow color scheme with shades such as "Oriole" and "Yellow Seal", coupled with a green color scheme based on "Emerald Green" and "Knotted Green". These two color schemes are not only harmoniously matched and mutually complementary, but they also possess profound cultural significance. The yellow resonates with the solemnity and historical accumulation of ancient texts, while the green represents the therapeutic effects of herbal medicines in traditional Chinese medical science, together conveying messages of health and hope that enhance the application theme. The interface design prioritizes aesthetics while also emphasizing flatness, lightness, and transparency to meet the demands of modern aesthetics and user experience.

Fig. 7. Part of the Application's Graphic Elements

In the design of the herbal elements within the application, the development team drew upon ancient texts and the authentic appearance of medicinal materials to create more than thirty hand-drawn herbal images. To enhance the application's practicality and historical ambiance, the team also designed a series of UI icons inspired by antique objects, such as weights, herb grinders, cutting knives, and medicine gourds (Fig. 8), which are commonly used tools in the preparation of traditional Chinese medicine. These designs are not only aesthetically pleasing but also filled with practical directional significance.

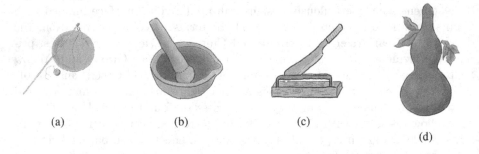

(a)   (b)   (c)

(d)

Fig. 8. UI ICONS for antique objects: Weights (a), Herb grinder (b), Cutting knives (c), Medicine Gourd (d)

4.6   Development and Implementation of the System Based on Unity

Following the completion of the foundational architecture design of the application, the development team proceeded to develop a prototype using the Unity engine. At this stage, the team meticulously outlined and implemented the core framework of the application system, which includes, but is not limited to, the protagonist control system, patient AI state mechanics, medical consultation process, and medication processing workflow as critical functional modules.

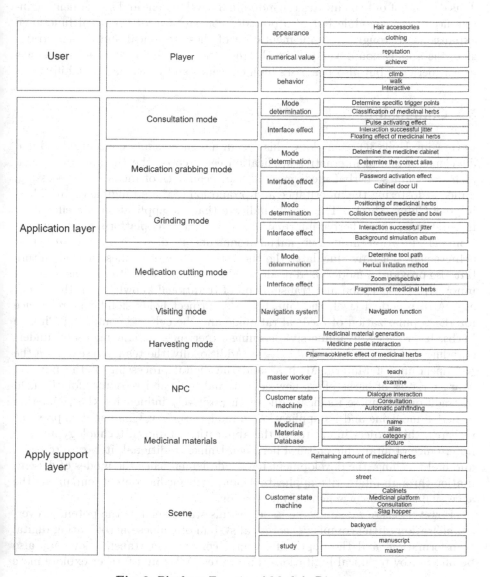

Fig. 9. Platform Functional Module Diagram

Specifically, users can engage in medical consultations and perform a series of medication processing activities such as grabbing, slicing, and grinding herbs through the manipulation of the protagonist. Each component was thoughtfully designed to ensure coherence and realism in the user experience.

Furthermore, to enhance the application's operational efficiency, the development team incorporated object-pooling techniques to optimize algorithm performance. Concurrently, the team modularized the entire application framework (Fig. 9), decoupling key modules such as consultation, medication dispensing, slicing, and grinding to delineate each module's function and responsibilities. This design not only facilitates the individual development and subsequent maintenance of each module but also provides convenience for potential functional expansions. Through the implementation of these technical and design strategies, the application developed by the team not only guarantees an immersive user experience but also possesses high efficiency and good maintainability.

5   Conclusion

Leveraging Unity3D technology, this design has successfully conceptualized and developed a digital interactive application centered on the therapeutic mechanisms of Chinese herbal medicine and the techniques of medicinal processing, aimed at fostering the inheritance and promotion of the intangible cultural heritage of Chinese herbs. The results indicate that the application can effectively integrate traditional herbal information, creating a novel platform for dissemination and education through virtual environments and digital human figures. This achievement not only elucidates the theoretical value of Chinese herbal culture but also provides a modernized mode of education and inheritance, ensuring the innovative preservation and transmission of traditional knowledge in the digital age. At a practical level, the launch of this project holds significant relevance for the popularization of medical rationale and the cultural context of Chinese herbs. It provides an immersive learning experience, enhancing users' understanding and interest in herbal culture. Additionally, the team's research on the "Compendium of Materia Medica" and the digital processing of the physical characteristics of herbs offers new educational tools and resources for the field of traditional Chinese medical education, positively influencing the promotion of herbal medicine and its application in modern society. Compared to previous research, this project innovates in the application of digital technology and the inheritance of intangible cultural heritage. Unlike traditional literature research and oral teaching, the development team's design enriches the modes of dissemination through interactive applications and multimedia content, enhancing the accessibility and engagement of information.

However, there remain some issues in this study, such as the potential oversimplification of the complex theoretical system of Chinese herbs during digital transformation, and the depth of cultural connotation transmission may also be affected by technical limitations. Future research could further explore more advanced virtual reality technologies to more comprehensively represent the multidimensional characteristics of Chinese herbal culture, considering the personalization of user interaction experiences to meet the needs of diverse user groups. Moreover, future work could also aim to promote this platform on a global scale, making it a significant portal for international audiences to recognize and learn about traditional Chinese medicine and culture.

References

1. Lihong, L.: Classical Chinese Medicine. The Chinese University of Hong Kong Press, China (2019)
2. Fitzgerald, M., Heinrich, M., Booker, A.: Medicinal plant analysis: a historical and regional discussion of emergent complex techniques. Front. Pharmacol. **10**, 1480 (2020)
3. Silverman, H., Ruggles, D.F.: Cultural heritage and human rights. Cultural heritage and human rights, p. 27 (2007)
4. Giglitto, D., Ciolfi, L., Bosswick, W.: Building a bridge: opportunities and challenges for intangible cultural heritage at the intersection of institutions, civic society, and migrant communities. Int. J. Herit. Stud. **28**(1), 74–91 (2022)
5. Li, M.: Traditional music as intangible cultural heritage in the postmodern world (2013)
6. Croizier, R.C.: Traditional Medicine in Modern China: Science, Nationalism, and the Tensions of Cultural Change. Harvard University Press, Cambridge (1968)
7. Karchmer, E.I.: Orientalizing the Body: Postcolonial Transformations in Chinese Medicine. The University of North Carolina at Chapel Hill, Chapel Hill (2005)
8. Research on the development of intangible cultural heritage traditional handicraft education inheritance and socialization inheritance. Int. J. Front. Sociol. 4(5) (2022)
9. Lin, A.X., Chan, G., Hu, Y., et al.: Internationalization of traditional Chinese medicine: current international market, internationalization challenges and prospective suggestions. Chin. Med. **13**, Article number: 9 (2018). https://doi.org/10.1186/s13020-018-0167-z
10. Zhang, Y., Yousaf, M., Xu, Y.: Chinese traditional culture and Art communication in digital era: strategics, issues, and prospects. J. Med. Stud. **32**(1) (2019)
11. Xia, Z.: Communication platform of digital traditional art based on new media technology. In: 2021 4th International Conference on Information Systems and Computer Aided Education (ICISCAE 2021). Association for Computing Machinery, New York, NY, USA, pp. 2658–2661 (2021). https://doi.org/10.1145/3482632.3487490
12. Kobayashi, K., Nagata, K., Masuko, S., Hoshino, J.: FUROSHIKI: augmented reality media that conveys Japanese traditional culture. In: Proceedings of the 17th International Conference on Virtual-Reality Continuum and its Applications in Industry (VRCAI '19). Association for Computing Machinery, New York, NY, USA, Article 27, pp. 1–5 (2019). https://doi.org/10.1145/3359997.3365716
13. Destelle, F., et al.: A Multi-modal 3D capturing platform for learning and preservation of traditional sports and games. In: Proceedings of the 23rd ACM international conference on Multimedia (MM '15). Association for Computing Machinery, New York, NY, USA, pp. 747–748 (2015). https://doi.org/10.1145/2733373.2807975

14. Ma, Z., Guo, Y.: Leveraging intangible cultural heritage resources for advancing China's knowledge-based economy. J. Knowl. Econ. 1–33 (2023)
15. Hill, J., Bithell, C.: An Introduction to Music Revival as Concept, Cultural Process, and Medium of Change, p. 29. The Oxford Handbook of Music Revival, Oxford (2014)
16. Mulhern, F.: Integrated marketing communications: from media channels to digital connectivity. In: The Evolution of Integrated Marketing Communications, pp. 11–27. Routledge, London (2013)
17. Wong, V.K.W., Law, B.Y.K., Yao, X.J., et al.: Advanced research technology for discovery of new effective compounds from Chinese herbal medicine and their molecular targets. Pharmacol. Res. 111, 546–555 (2016)
18. Yang, Y.: Research on digital presentation design of Chinese herbal medicine culture under the construction of media scene theory-Taking Atractylodes macrocephala as an example. Zhejiang A&F University (2023). https://doi.org/10.27756/d.cnki.gzjlx.2022.000157.
19. The Current Status, Problems and Integration of the Protection and Inheritance of China's World Cultural Heritage in the Context of Digitalization
20. Liu, Y.: Investigating the translation of metaphors used in diagnosis and treatment in Chinese medicine classics Neijing and Shanghan Lun (2022)
21. Zhao, J., Jiang, P., Zhang, W.: Molecular networks for the study of TCM pharmacology. Brief. Bioinform. 11(4), 417–430 (2010)

AI Tools to Enhance Cultural Identity in Traditional Visual Communication: A Case Study of Milan Chinatown

Xinxi Liu[1] and Yuan Liu[2]([✉])

[1] Politecnico di Milano, Campus Bovisa Durando, Via Giuseppe Candiani, 72, 20158 Milan,
Italy
xinxi.liu@mail.polimi.it
[2] Beijing Institute of Fashion Technology, Beijing 100029, China
yuan.liu@polimi.it

Abstract. At present, Milan's Chinatown is becoming "featureless" - a zone filled with "European-style" buildings and urban storefronts with a lack of Chinese character. The current language of visual media does not express the local cultural identity properly. Our approach is to understand the reasons for the blurring of cultural identity. The research methodology relies on field research, questionnaires, and secondary research. We also talk about the value of AI-generated tool-based language to extract the expression of cultural identity. It also generates reflections for potential future educational transformations. As an output, we generated a theoretical framework that combines both visual communication elements and cultural identity. The framework consists of a knowledge system that allows designers to develop communication design based on this approach and combined with AI tools, which can help Chinese styles to be better integrated into Western aesthetics and re-invent centuries-old concepts into modern visual directions.

Keywords: Culture identity · Visual communication · AI tool · Chinatown

1 Introduction: Cultural Identity Within Traditional Visual Communication

The crucial areas that Erikson (1968) emphasized: "as cultural identity, contains ideology (beliefs and values), love (personal relationships), and work, which as central to the formation of an adolescent's identity". Kidd (2012) defines culture as the way of life, in which a place or a community reflects a specific cultural identity, also related to the culture of the individual and the society. In these communities, virtual communication design is utilized to demonstrate to the viewer about the cultural values. Communication can be presented in our lives in a variety of ways to enhance the sense of cultural identity, it can be expressed through verbal ways such as words, pictures, texts, and symbols. Non-verbal ways also exist such as facial expressions and body movements. Lull (2000) thinks communication is concerned with making meanings, and this kind

© The Author(s), under exclusive license to Springer Nature Switzerland AG 2024
M. Rauterberg (Ed.): HCII 2024, LNCS 14717, pp. 293–308, 2024.
https://doi.org/10.1007/978-3-031-61147-6_20

of meaning depends very much on the specific cultural contexts and literacies involved. We consider that communication transmission has a lot of connection with culture, as someone attempts to understand the concepts involved through a specific object or place, indeed communication is created.

At present, Milan's Chinatown is becoming "featureless" - a zone filled with "European-style" buildings and urban storefronts with a lack of Chinese character. The long and fruitful history of Chinese culture is gradually excluded from the spatial representation of the area. In a sense, the current language of visual media does not always consider the pros and cons which is represented by cultural identity. Relph (1976) claims that the identity of a place comprises three interrelated components, which are physical features and appearances, activities, and meaning and symbols. Chinatown's cultural identity is facing great challenges, and it becomes especially important to maintain an independent visual tone for places such as Chinatown.

This research aims to explore the cultural factors that already exist within China-town's visual appearance and the reasons behind the blurring of cultural identity. The research methods rely on field research, questionnaires, and secondary research. We also made the AI language of generating tools as a creative idea to refine the cultural identity related to Chinese culture, since it has a large representative sample, also it can be understood as an approach that helps to broaden the ideas and generate thoughts for possible future educational transformations.

2 Plight of Chinatown: Chaos of Culture Identity

Many researchers have concluded that Japanese immigrants quickly "lost" their national architectural traditions after arriving in the United States and immediately adopted local architectural habits (Dubrow, 2002; Low et al., 2002; Pader, 2002). Loukaitou-Sideris (2002) described the streets in metropolitan Los Angeles have been transformed by new immigrant groups over the past two decades, and how they are faced with adapting or changing the built environment to reflect national cultural identity. The development of Milan Chinatown is based on the urgent need for Italian identity to be integrated into the morphology of the local urban area. The identity of a place, which is closely linked to the personal and social identity of inhabitants, is recorded, and embodied in the traditionally built forms and reflects the choices of a specific culture (Watson & Bentley, 2007). Although Milan's Chinatown is rooted in the local culture, its own cultural identity is gradually weakening. Take Milan Chinatown as an example, we refer mainly to Relph's (1976) study to explore the synthesis embodiment of cultural identity.

2.1 Physical Features and Appearances

China town includes a wide range of racial identities in places that may seem unnoticeable. Specific cultural meanings are expressed in the very definition of their entrances, which are conventionally marked by Chinese-language street signs and symbolic gates (Chaskin, 1996; Lai, 1997). On specific occasions, Chinatown is decorated for traditional national holidays such as the Chinese New Year, the streets are decorated with lanterns, dragons, and lights in the form of Chinese architecture (see Fig. 1). Mazumdar (2000) points out that buildings and artifacts can convey identity. But people's identity-based social constructions interact with these places to give the environment meaning (Manzo, 2003). Nevertheless, lanterns or Chinese architectural ornamentation can express cultural identity to some extent, but these purely verbal means of communication are not common. Seattle's Chinatown International District comprises a variety of Asian ethnic identities, including Chinese, Filipino, Japanese, Korean, Vietnamese, etc. Regardless of how adamant some of the Chinese representatives were about retaining the name "Chinatown", they did not express opposition to having a "Japantown" or "Little Saigon" (Abramson, Manzo & Hou, 2006). One of the problems that arises in Milan's Chinatown is that if there are no special holidays, the stores in Chinatown are not distinguished from the local streets, except for the stores with Chinese characters on their storefront, which can help people determine the nation of stores. In fact, the whole street is not so different from the local streets (see Fig. 2).

Fig. 1. Holidays and festivals in Chinatown (sourced from Google Maps).

Fig. 2. Normal times in Chinatown (photos taken by the author)

2.2 Activities

Helen Chung, a Tasmanian of Chinese descent, made the following comment in a news article published in May 1987: "Seventeen years ago," she said, "there was no multicultural policy in Australia. Now things are different, and Chinatown attracts tourists and status - there are stores, restaurants, dragon festivals, and parades" (Anderson, 1990). According to the head of the URA's Environmental Protection Department, this is part of the government's overall vision to revitalize Chinatown by developing a pedestrian-friendly environment with better stores and facilities for people, thereby encouraging a more active street life (Lee, 1997). The National Arts Council has purchased a number of units at highly subsidized rents under its arts housing program for a variety of literary and performing arts groups, including Peking Opera, Classical Chinese music, and Mandarin or bilingual theatre groups (Henderson, 2000). Such artistic street activities with their national culture can create a cultural identity to a certain extent. An Events Sub-Committee was formed to organize the Lunar New Year, the August Lantern Festival, and the Dragon Boat Festival. We conclude that this type of event occupies an important place in Chinatown. The government and other sponsors value these events. In the Chinatown area, there are occasional performances by artists wearing traditional Chinese costumes and playing traditional Chinese instruments such as the erhu, guzheng, pipa, etc. (see Fig. 3). This form of music attracts people from both local and non-local cultures to stop in their tracks for a moment of enjoyment.

Fig. 3. Artists wearing traditional Chinese costumes and playing traditional Chinese musical instruments (photos taken by the author).

2.3 Meaning and Symbols

The Chinese character has become essential to recognize the Chinese stores in Milan. The main purpose of foreign language learning can be understood as psychologically transforming a student into having the so-called "secondary culture identity" (Karaulov, 1987; Khaleeva, 1989; Gal'skova, 2000; Nechaev, 2014). Language does not exist on its own, the connection between language and culture is very intimate. Chinatown relies heavily on its own cultural identity in order to stand out from the rest of the city landscape. This small neighborhood is filled with objects, languages characters, patterns, and colors that represent the identity of the ethnic group. The aim of all is to create a unique ethnic atmosphere.

In the case of Brisbane's Chinatown Mall, for instance, across the two entrances are the typical bright red, albeit very stereotypical, Chinese arches, each guarded by a pair of stone lions presented by the Overseas Chinese Affairs Department of the People's Republic of China. The Chinese pavilions scattered along the shopping center are similarly ornamented with golden roofs adorned with golden dragons, as well as red and green pillars, giving the area an immediate Chinese character. In addition, the surrounding streetlights are decorated with Chinese motifs and the street signs have both English and Chinese characters (David, 2005). A Guide to Brisbane's Chinatown illustrated with photographs of elaborately tailored models in Chinese opera costumes, a pagoda featuring a Chinese garden, red lanterns, lion dances, and bamboo steamer snacks - as well as explanations of the Chinese astrological signs and feng shui (David, 2005). Many widely recognized Chinese elements appear here: "Lanterns, spring couplets, porcelain, Chinese paintings, Cheongsams, Chinese dresses, Fans, Calligraphy (ink), Chinese knots, Chinese embroidery, Dragons, Gourds, Types of facial make-up in Beijing opera, Tiger shoes, etc." (see Fig. 4). However, these verbal communication mediums are only utilized in a limited number of stores in Chinatown. These classic stores are more likely to sell products related to the culture of the Asian region. These types of Chinese stores are not properly utilizing these verbal communication mediums to display their merchandise. As a consequence, this may cause cultural identity confusion under the visual media communication of these kinds of stores.

Fig. 4. Some verbal communication media in Milan's Chinatown (photos taken by the author).

3 Methodology

The first framework we refer to is from visual communication, the variables include position, color, size, shape, and orientation (Clarkson, 2015). Graphic elements are units of information that can be used in the production of an image, slide show, or poster. The visual communication image element variables in this study were selected mainly for "position", "color" and "size" to be used, "shape" and "orientation" are not applicable in this analysis, as they do not figure in the storefront design of this research.

The second framework is about cultural identity (Relph, 1976) which comprises three interrelated includes physical features and appearances, meaning and symbols, and activities. The frame of reference for the cultural identity in this study is based on an analysis summarizing the cultural identity of Milan's Chinatown according to the three components mentioned above. Based on these two frameworks, a frame for bridging visual communication and cultural identity was generated.

First, the author went to the field to research and photograph the storefronts of restaurants in Milan's Chinatown and local restaurants. The authors analyzed which characteristic elements are used in the visual communication design of the storefronts of the respective restaurants. Food and cooking can be an avenue toward understanding complex issues of culture change and transnational cultural flow (Wilk, 1999). The reasons for choosing Milan Chinatown restaurants and local restaurants as the starting point of the cultural research is that the authors find that most of the groups who do not belong to the Chinese culture go to Chinatown more often and choose to eat Chinese food. Moreover, the food culture also reflects some traditional Chinese culture to a certain extent. Therefore, the authors chose Chinese and Italian restaurants as the objects of investigation in this research. The research restaurants involved in this survey were selected based on the standards of:

1. Recommendations from Italian people who are locals.
2. Highly popular and highly rated rankings of Italian and Chinatown restaurants by TripAdvisor and Google Maps.
3. Representative travel attractions in Milan, Italy.

Afterward, based on the analysis conclusions drawn from the visual communication design of Milan's Chinatown and local restaurant storefronts. We used AI tools to create a series of visual communication design proposals and artificially selected several sets of the best visual design solutions. Finally, the experiment in the form of a questionnaire survey was conducted to summarize and analyze which visual elements and visual communication scenarios were considered by people of non-native cultures to be the most reflective of Chinese culture and aesthetics. The results of the research will provide a conceptual basis for Milan's Chinatown to clarify its own cultural identity and to make the Chinese style better integrated into Western aesthetics. A centuries-old concept will be re-injected into a modern visual direction. It will also help designers to better understand the principles of Chinese cultural identity and apply them to communication design, thus helping Chinatown clarify its own cultural identity.

4 Discussion: Visual Identity under the Cultural Context

The approaches used to enhance the cultural identity of a specific culture are summarized and analyzed. The results are also presented in the form of a matrix (Table 1). The table further summarizes the cultural identity indicators in visual communication (Table 2) and presents the conclusions based on this scale.

According to the above framework of combining visual communication elements and cultural Identity, the importance of "semiotic symbolism" and the "symbolism of color" approach is derived from the commonality of Italian restaurant storefront design. For example, among a group of Italian restaurant storefront designs for text combination images, many Italian national and cultural symbols are involved, such as pizza, pasta, cafè, Italian, and so on. Afterward, the method of enhancing cultural identity is derived from the Italian restaurant storefront design and applied to enhance the cultural identity design of Chinese restaurant storefronts.

Table 1. Visual communication factors that can be used to enhance the Cultural Identity of a particular community

Method of Analysis	Visual communicati on factors	Reference	Target of use	Appearance of effect	Methods of effect
Visual communica tion elements	Color	Ip, D. (2005). Loukaitou-Sideris, A. (2002). Clarkson, M. (2015).	Visual communication and architecture	- Red Chinese arches were chosen to be used at one of the entrances to the Brisbane Chinatown shopping center. - Golden roofs decorated with golden dragons. - Red and green pillars. - Decoration of buildings with Mexican stylistic features with Aztec motifs on the roofs.	- The decorative properties of the representative colors of the national culture. - Decorative properties of ethnic motifs.
	Size	Ip, D. (2005).	Visual communication and streetlights, street boards	- The surrounding streetlights are decorated with Chinese motifs. - Road boards have both Chinese and English text.	- Identification of text. - Text as ornamentation of the pattern.
	Position	Loukaitou-Sideris, A.(2002). Liu, J. (2016)	Visual communication and store signage	- Large red Chinese characters on a white or yellow background provide Chinese customers with information about the agency's products and services. - Signage is important for identifying locations.	- Functionality of text. - Functionality of colors.
Culture identity elements Relph, E. (1976). Plac e and placelessne ss (Vol. 67). London: Pion.	Physical features and appearances	Loukaitou-Sideris, A.(2002). (Bentley 1985) Liu, J. (2016)	Visual communication and architecture	- The roof above the entrance to Cathay Bank, the pagoda-shaped top on the signboard of the minimal. - Vertical and horizontal rhythms. - Materials and colors are part of the visible details of the alley space and part of the visual image one captures. - Rhythm: Visual stimulation is also important to make a space more interesting.	- Ethnicity of materials. - Ethnicity of colors. - Architectural forms in ethnic motifs. - The chronology of decoration in space. - Rhythm of visual symbols.
	Activities	James, R. (1993).	Visual communication and community environment	- Social activity on the streets creates a "performative" environment, a landscape of voices and music that, more than any architectural form, constitutes the "Mexican character" of this national region.	- Ethnicity of auditory elements. - Ethnicity of performance forms.
	Meaning and symbols	Loukaitou-Sideris, A. (2002). Ip, D. (2005). Liu, J. (2016)	Visual communication and environment	- Bamboo decoration on the front of the dining room. - Road signage is available in both bilingual texts. - Artwork: Hutong walls are great places for artwork and installations, providing the community with an opportunity to express its values and concerns.	- Symbolism - Art Symbolism

Table 2. Cultural Identity indicators in visual communication

Visual Communication Elements	Visual Communication Factors	The Culture Identity Indicators in Visual Communication	Connotation interpretation
Color	Decoration color	Architectural forms in ethnic patterns	The architectural shapes with local characteristics are applied to the pattern through certain design methods so that it has a certain ornamental character and at the same time has the local cultural identity.
	Decorative pattern	The chronology of interior decoration	Materials and colors as well as other elements of the decoration reflect to some extent the different ethnic periods represented in the whole space.
		Symbolism of material	Specific materials to a certain extent reflect the cultural identity of a specific regional ethnic group, for example, the use of bamboo patterns can emphasize the texture and pattern of the material itself.
	Function of color	Symbolism of color	The use of specific colors reflects to some extent the cultural identity of ethnic groups in a particular community.
Size	Identity of the text	Semiotic symbolism	Characteristic graphic symbols represent to some certain extent specific ethnic groups.
	The decorative properties of text as pattern	Patterned symbols	The characteristic ethnic symbols are made into decorative motifs through certain design approaches.
	Functionality of text	Symbolic art symbolism	In addition to directly conveying language-related information, distinctive ethnic symbols have a certain artistic quality. They can indirectly convey the cultural identity of a particular ethnic group, for example, the use of symbols on signage and public artwork is a visual display of identity and value.
Position	Visual ornamentation of patterns	Rhythm of visual symbols	It is important to note the way elements are used which affect visual appropriateness, for instance parallel lines make the space deeper.

5 Field Research Identity of Visual Communication in Both Restaurants and Chinatown

To record and classify the names and categories of stores that currently exist in Milan's Chinatown, we organize a field study engaging eating establishments, clothing & goods retail, consumable retail, offices & institutions, and services (see Fig. 5). The different categories of stores were visually marked with different colors on a map of the Milan Chinatown area (see Fig. 6).

Fig. 5. The names and categories of stores that currently exist in Milan's Chinatown.

The storefronts of Milan Chinatown restaurants and local restaurants were each divided into two groups, one with text-combined images and the other with text-only, 4 groups in total. According to the first framework of visual communication, this analysis summarizes the storefront designs of Milan Chinatown and local restaurants by combining position, color, and size in the variables of image elements. We analyze the position and color of text and images by pixel counting since it can express the proportion of vision very accurately. In addition, the second framework of cultural identity is used to analyze and summarize which elements, symbols, or images in the storefronts of restaurants can reflect Chinese or Italian cultural factors. The following are the conclusions based on the research framework of this dissertation:

Milan Chinatown-text combination image of a total of 32 restaurants (see Fig. 7). Color and size (%):

Fig. 6. The different categories of stores were visually marked with different colors on a map of the Milan Chinatown area.

- Background color: black 28% (9), white 25% (8), green 16% (5), red 16% (5), brown 13% (4), yellow 2% (1);
- Font colors: white 59% (19), black 19% (6), yellow 16% (5), red 6% (2);

Cultural factors:

- Chinese characteristic patterns - Ruyi pattern, Chinese knot style pattern;
- Animals - deer, panda, bear (in chef's clothes), chicken, cat, duck;
- Characters - traditional Chinese chef image (white suit), cartoon version of chef image (chef's hat), cartoon version of kuafu;
- Food - buns, hot pot, barbecue, noodles (bowl), red beans, milk tea;
- Tools and others - chopsticks, fire, wheat, landscape (ink style);

Milan Chinatown- Text-only group image of a total of 28 restaurants (see Fig. 8). Color and size (%):

- Background color: black 36% (10), white 7% (2), green 22% (6), red 22% (6), brown 7% (2), yellow 3% (1), pink 3% (1);
- Font colors: white 43% (12), black 11% (3), yellow 25% (7), red 14% (4), blue 7% (2);

Cultural factors:

- Typeface morphology - Chinese brush lettering;

Italian restaurant - Text combination images for a total of 24 restaurants (see Fig. 9). Color and size (%):

- Background color: black 33% (8), white 13% (3), red 17% (4), brown 17% (4), yellow 3.5% (1), blue 3.5% (1), green 13% (3);
- Font colors: white 38% (9), black 16% (4), yellow 8% (2), red 33% (8), orange 5% (1);

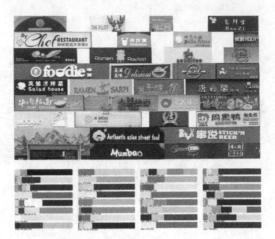

Fig. 7. Milan Chinatown - Text combination images

Fig. 8. Milan Chinatown - Text only group images

Cultural factors:

- Patterns - scrollwork, geometric lines (arcs, diamonds);
- Animals - cows, lions, cats;
- Characters – a cartoon version of a chef (holding a pizza);
- Food - pizza, ham sausage, pasta, cafè, gelato;
- Tools and others - dough roll cookware, duomo silhouette, crowns;

Italian restaurant - Text-only group of images for a total of 36 restaurants (see Fig. 10). Color and size (%):

- Background color: black 39% (14), white 14% (5), red 14% (5), brown 22% (8), yellow 3% (1), blue 5% (2), pink 3% (1);

Fig. 9. Italian Restaurant - Text combination images

- Font colors: white 50% (18), black 8% (3), yellow 22% (8), red 16% (6), orange 4% (1);

Cultural factors:

- The name includes the local specialty "piazza\cafè";

Fig. 10. Italian Restaurants - Text only group images

6   AI Tools to Engage Visual Communication Design

In terms of improving storefronts to enhance cultural identity, the researcher selects 5 storefronts from the restaurants in Milan's Chinatown. According to the geographical characteristics of the restaurants and combined with Chinese characteristic cultural symbols. The method of "Culture identity indicators in visual communication" analyzed in Table 2 is applied to design thinking. After that AI tools are involved in designing and generating new restaurant storefronts. The AI generation logic and design methodology are presented in table form (Table 3).

Table 3. A new method of storefronts design for five restaurants

Name of Restaurant (English)	Name of Restaurant (Chinese)	Introduction to the restaurant and geographic characteristics	AI Design Generation Logic	Indicators of cultural identity
Chabaidao	茶百道	Local tea drink chain brand in Chengdu, Sichuan Province, China. Chengdu's characteristic cultural symbols such as the panda, Sichuan opera face painting, bamboo, etc..	- Create a banner for my food supplements store named "Chabaidao" with all kinds of Chinese tea, panda, and bamboo supplements. - Create a banner for my food supplements store named "Chabaidao" with all kinds of panda drinking bubble tea, and bamboo supplements.	Semiotic symbolism: panda, bamboo Symbolism of color: green
Mao hotpot	毛灶	Hot pot, mandarin duck hot pot, Manfrotto	- Hotpot logo design vector silhouette of yuanyang hotpot template illustration, illustration. - Hotpot logo design vector silhouette of yuanyang hotpot, Chopstick template illustration, illustration.	Semiotic symbolism: chopstick Symbolism of color: red, gold
Mo	凉皮肉夹馍	Tang Dynasty Chang a (now Xi'an) City, Terracotta warriors and Horses of Qin Shi Huang's Mausoleum, and the art of paper cutting.	- A paper artwork of the terracotta warriors and horses eat cold skin and roujiamo, In the style of vibrant illustrations, typography, illustration, poster, ink wash painting. - Cold skin and roujiamo, lantern, in the style of vibrant illustrations, typography, illustration, poster, ink wash painting. - Roujiamo on the plate, Chopstick, lantern, in the style of vibrant illustrations, typography, illustration, poster, black and white ink painting.	Semiotic symbolism: Xi'an architecture, bowls, chopsticks Symbolism of color: red, yellow, blue, green
Tang Gourmet	小唐汤包	Jiangnan Snacks, Jiangnan Water, "Venice" of the East. Water Alley. Water on the bottle boat, The lotus pond, The moonlight, Jiangnan gardens.	- Vector art, logo, Simple and clean line art of nature with pond. And There are buns and chopsticks on the plate, illustration. - The word "white steamed stuffed bun" shaped like a white steamed stuffed bun, typography. - The word "white steamed stuffed bun" shaped like a Steamed Savory Buns, typography.	Semiotic symbolism: baozi, Jiangnan Garden architecture, lanterns Symbolism of color: red, yellow, blue, green
Anatra Pechinese	北京烤鸭	Roast Duck, Quanjude (is the old cultural symbol of Beijing). Quanjude Roast Duck is one of the city famous signs of Beijing.	- Create a logo with the pattern Duck render, painting. - Create a logo with the pattern Yellow Duck render, painting. - Create a logo with the pattern Yellow Duck and Chinese knot render, painting.	Semiotic symbolism: Chinese knots, abstract patterns Symbolism of color: red, yellow, blue, green

7   Case Study and Discussion: A Questionnaire for Cultural Identity

7.1   Subject

To achieve effective results, 43 native Italians were invited to participate in this evaluation experiment. All participants had normal or corrected eyesight of 1.0., and participants were invited to fill out an evaluation questionnaire.

According to the questionnaire process, the evaluation questionnaire has 5 groups of Milan Chinatown restaurant storefront comparison groups (see Fig. 11). Respondents were invited to choose the restaurant storefront design that is more representative of China from each comparison group (old storefront, new storefront) and to explain the reasons for their choices. At the end of the experiment, the response data collected from the participants were further statistically analysed.

Fig. 11. Old storefront vs. New storefront

7.2 Discussion

A number of 43 questionnaires were received in the five comparison groups of storefronts. The respondents were invited to choose which of the old and new storefronts was more representative of Chinese culture. The proportions of the five questions were 55.8%: 44.2%; 53.5%: 46.5%; 65.1%: 34.9%; 23.3%: 76.7%; and 32.6%: 67.4%, respectively. Questions 1, 2 and 3 indicated that the AI method enhanced cultural identity to some significant extent. Questions 4 and 5 demonstrated that the AI method does not work as assumed.

There are six factors that can be derived from the analysis to influence the awareness of cultural identity:

1. National representative colors;

In the questionnaire, the author synthesized the answers "yellow color is a very important one in Chinese culture", "the colors red and yellow", "red, black, and gold are the main colors"., and "red, black, and gold are the main colors". The use of specific colors to a certain extent reflects the cultural identity of specific regional ethnic groups, as Chiang (2015) explained why Chinese people like red color and firecrackers for the spring festival. Most Italians consider red to be the color of China's cultural identity, and it can be normally addressed from firecrackers, spring couplets, lanterns, red envelopes, Chinese knots, the walls of the Forbidden City, the Chinese flag, etc.

2. Ethnic symbols;

In the questionnaire, the author integrated "panda", "mountain patterns", "bamboo, rice bowl, cute mascot", "lanterns, dragons, typical culture and food", "traditional Chinese paintings", "the flag", "Great wall of China, Yin and yang", "The typical clothes, the circle", "clothes, the circle", as characteristic pattern symbols represent specific ethnic groups.

"A Russian student described her affection for Chinese New Year's Eve as follows: When I reached the destination, I saw a red city decorated with paper lanterns, scrolls, and an upside-down '福' (which sounds the same as 'happiness has arrived') on every door. There were many houses with the paintings of the Door God (门神) on the front doors" (Chiang, 2015).

3. The combination of national colors and characteristic pattern symbols;

In the questionnaire, the author summed up "colors and representation of the food", "simplicity of the image and the presence of red color", "black, red, and gold together with a simple pattern design", "red and yellow patterns with traditional objects". The combination of factor 1 and factor 2 can better represent the cultural identity of a specific ethnic group.

4. Texts as distinctive national symbols;

In the questionnaire, the author summarizes the main answers of "enormous Chinese characters", "simple bilingual title with Han characters", "the Chinese letter", and "the Chinese letter". Characters as characteristic national symbols become decorative patterns through certain design approaches and reflect the cultural identity of a particular nationality. Of all the things valued by these participants, the Chinese language is viewed as the most important component of Chinese culture (Chiang, 2015).

5. The use of national colors in fonts;

In the questionnaire, the author has combined "the use of characters sided seals", "the combination of colors and the font used", "the presence of Chinese words and the gold and red color", "the Hanzi (red writing)", "the combination of colors and the font used". The analysis concludes that the use of factor 1 and factor 3 in combination can to some extent better reflect the cultural identity of a particular ethnic group.

6. The architectural forms in ethnic symbols;

In the questionnaire, the author combined the answers as "traditional Chinese architecture", "siheyuan architecture and hutong", "the geometry of the Chinese roofs", and "The geometry of the Chinese roofs". Architectural forms with local characteristics are applied to the patterns through certain design methods. To make them have certain decorative features and carry the local cultural identity.

Some participants suggested that "from a tourist's point of view, it is nice if you can understand from the restaurant's appearance what kind of food is served there. I think it would also be interesting if the name of the restaurant would be translated also into English. It would be easier for tourists to remember the restaurant better and it may teach a little bit of Chinese and about its culture to people from overseas". A portion of the respondents indicated that the reason not to choose the AI-generated storefronts was that some preferred a minimalist storefront design without too much decoration. One of the participants mentioned, "When I feel the less is more vibe, I feel like I'm in an authentic place. Less is more". But they also admitted that the new design did enhance their understanding of the type of products sold within this restaurant. Therefore, in subsequent designs, when designers use AI, they have to control the number of cultural elements in the products they design based on aesthetic reasons.

8 Conclusion

The approach of cultural identity indicators is a valid area for today's needs of visual communication. Designers can reasonably consider the cultural identity of a specific ethnic group in their products by considering these factors, especially by using the combination of ethnic colors and text characters. The experiment involves the multiple use number of cultural elements in the design of two groups of these new storefronts, which should be rethought and redesigned to be more in harmony with the consumers' aesthetics. This research uses an AI generation tool to refine the cultural identity related to Chinese culture. The AI tool has a large number of representative samples of visual communication, which can be used to explore the creativity of AI tools. It helps to extend the scope of this research and to generate ideas for the possible future transformation of creative education. The results will provide a reference source for the conceptual basis of cultural identity design, and designers can base on this principle and combine it with AI tools to carry out communication design, which will help the Chinese style to better integrate with Western aesthetics and re-invent the centuries-old concepts into a modern visual direction.

Acknowledgments. This research is supported by 11000024T000003073871, Classified Development of Municipal Colleges and Universities - the Project of Constructing the Emerging Interdisciplinary Platform Based on "Clothing Science" of Beijing Institute of Fashion Technology.

References

1. Anderson, K.: 'Chinatown re-oriented': a critical analysis of recent redevelopment schemes in a Melbourne and Sydney enclave. Aust. Geogr. Stud. **28**(2), 137–154 (1990)
2. Bentley, I.: Responsive Environments: A Manual for Designers. Routledge, London (1985)
3. Butina-Watson, G., Bentley, I.: Identity by Design. Routledge, London (2007)
4. Chaskin, R.J.: Urban Enclaves: Identity and Place in America (1996)
5. Clarkson, M.: Elements of Visual Communication. Retrieved from IEEE (2015)
6. Chiang, S.Y.: Cultural adaptation as a sense-making experience: international students in China. J. Int. Migr. Integr. **16**, 397–413 (2015)
7. Erikson, E.H.: Identity: Youth and Crisis. Norton, New York (1968)
8. Gal'skova, N.D.: Sovremennaya metodika obucheniya inostrannym yazykam [Modern methods of teaching foreign languages]: Moscow: Glossa (2000)
9. Henderson, J.: Attracting tourists to Singapore's Chinatown: a case study in conservation and promotion. Tour. Manag. **21**(5), 525–534 (2000)
10. Ip, D.F.: Network as capital: PRC immigrant entrepreneurs in Brisbane. In: Tseng Y.-F. (ed.), Asian Migration: Pacific Rim Dynamics, pp. 149–164. Interdisciplinary Group for Australian Studies, National Taiwan University, Taipei (1999)
11. Ip, D.: Contesting Chinatown: place-making and the emergence of 'ethnoburbia' in Brisbane, Australia. GeoJournal **64**, 63–74 (2005)

12. James, R.: The Enacted Environment of East Los Angeles (1993)
13. Kidd, W., Teagle, A.: Culture and Identity. Bloomsbury Publishing, London (2012)
14. Karaulov, Y.N., Shmelev, D.N.: Russkii yazyk i yazykovaia lichnost [The Russian language and a linguistic identity] (1987)
15. Khaleeva, I.I.: Fundamentals of the theory of teaching foreign speech understanding (preparation of an interpreter). M.: High School. (Haleeva II, Vysshaja shkola) (1981)
16. Lull, J.: Media, Communication, Culture: A Global Approach. Columbia University Press, New York (2000)
17. Loukaitou-Sideris, A.: Regeneration of urban commercial strips: ethnicity and space in three Los Angeles neighborhoods. J. Archit. Plan. Res. 334–350 (2002)
18. Lai, D.C.: The visual character of Chinatowns. Understanding ordinary landscapes, p. 81 (1997)
19. Lee, J.: Facelift for Chinatown parks. The Straits Times, 20 August 1997
20. Liu, J.:Redefining urban alleywalls: Urban design for active public space in Maynard Alley, Chinatown-International District, Seattle (Doctoral dissertation) (2016)
21. Mazumdar, S., Mazumdar, S., Docuyanan, F., McLaughlin, C.M.: Creating a sense of place: the Vietnamese-Americans and Little Saigon. J. Environ. Psychol. 20(4), 319–333 (2000)
22. Manzo, L.C.: Beyond house and haven: toward a revisioning of emotional relationships with places. J. Environ. Psychol. 23(1), 47–61 (2003)
23. Nechayev, N.N.: Psychological patterns of development of students' secondary language personality. Procedia Soc. Behav. Sci. 154, 14–22 (2014)
24. Relph, E.: Place and Placelessness, vol. 67. Pion, London (1976)
25. Wilk, R.R.: Real Belizean food: building local identity in the transnational Caribbean. Am. Anthropol. 101(2), 244–255 (1999)

A Preliminary Study on the New Southbound International Co-creation and Design Empowerment of Ethnic Studies - A.R. Application of the Taivoan Tribe

Li-Hsun Peng[1]([⊠]) [iD], Chi-Yu Pan[1], Indarti[2] [iD], and Mohammad Adam Jerusalem[3] [iD]

[1] National Yunlin University of Science and Technology, Yunlin 64002, Taiwan
penglh@gemail.yuntech.edu.tw
[2] Universitas Negeri Surabaya, Surabaya 60213, Indonesia
[3] Universitas Negeri Yogyakarta, Yogyakarta 55281, Indonesia

Abstract. As the hometown and origin of the Austronesian language family, Taiwan should have sufficient heights to carry out closer academic exchanges and cooperation with neighboring countries substantially and efficiently. Therefore, this study expects to use sustainable design through southbound inter-school discussions. Discuss the sustainable environment and design issues of Taiwan's Pingpu ethnic group and remote rural community residents with partners from Vietnam, Indonesia, and other schools. In today's post-epidemic era, we break through the difficulties of various research and course exchanges and conduct efficient, substantive, and in-depth discussions and long-term talks on specific topics. The Plains indigenous peoples' cultural revival movement and its proof have attracted attention from all walks of life in recent years. The public's stereotypes and misperceptions of the Plains indigenous peoples have made ethnic consciousness more awakened, which will help the continuation and inheritance of culture and make Taiwan's native culture more diverse. The revival of ceremonies and ceremonies of contemporary Taiwan Plains indigenous peoples, how to promote the creation of tribes, how to combine the cultural creativity of Plains indigenous peoples with current popular culture, and promote the development of local cultural and creative industries reconstruction of tribal organizations. Give Plains indigenous peoples more opportunities to regain their charm and uniqueness.

This project hopes to promote the cultural heritage of the Plains indigenous peoples through global localization and globalization on the earth in the future form of the artistic and creative industry. Using AR to promote and integrate them into digital and design applications. Explores how to give young people a better understanding and interest in the culture of the Plains indigenous peoples so that the culture can continue and pass on. The hope is to continue expanding the international research exchanges between the five universities in Indonesia and Vietnam. As well as co- creating curriculum design and proposing how ethnic groups can carry out international Observation, interaction, and study in southbound countries to implement sustainable agricultural and creative practices, expand international cooperation, and sustainable development. Establishing design and innovation

© The Author(s), under exclusive license to Springer Nature Switzerland AG 2024
M. Rauterberg (Ed.): HCII 2024, LNCS 14717, pp. 309–324, 2024.
https://doi.org/10.1007/978-3-031-61147-6_21

topic practice models further deepens the brand of sustainable agricultural innovation and promotes local sightseeing and brand building of agricultural innovation in the form of a digital sustainable agricultural innovation brand.

Keywords: Taivoan ethnic group · Plains indigenous peoples · Design empowerment

1 Introduction

Through years of cultural accumulation, Taiwan's aboriginal groups have demonstrated a unique history and beautiful culture in a modern society that is gradually opening up and respecting diverse ethnic groups; the contents on display are not limited to daily necessities, clothing decorations, and sacrificial cultural relics. Or hunting tools, etc. When the cosmology and aesthetics of each ethnic group are preserved by the tribe members or unearthed by the world, they become Taiwan's precious tangible or intangible cultural heritage and should be preserved and preserved. However, the diversity of ethnic groups and the development of indigenous culture have been hampered by the urgent dilemmas faced by the Pingpu ethnic group in Taiwan today, such as the widening resource gap between urban and rural areas, causing young people to move to cities; the remaining workforce is limited, and cultural transmission is decreasing year by year; coupled with the problem of population aging, for example, the report of the National Development Council (2020) mentioned: "Our country has become an aging society in 1993, and transformed into an aging society in 2018... In 2021, the super-elderly (85 population above 10 years old accounts for 10.5% of the elderly population, which will increase to 27.4% in 2070." When the tribal youth returned to the tribe and wanted to restart the construction work, even with school support and government subsidies, it was still lower than the maintenance level of ordinary families. Even though the tribal villagers and elders wanted to work together and share the difficulties, they were forced to. The reality of survival is helpless. No matter how much we want to preserve traditional culture, we must bow to survival.

During the Qing Dynasty, it was found that the Qing Empire recorded them as "raw fan, Hua fan, cooked fan" (Hsu, 2009); during the Japanese colonial period, to manage the tribal people, the government divided them into "Gaoshan ethnic group" and "Pingpu ethnic group." After the Republic of China took over Taiwan, the aborigines were divided into "mountain aborigines" and "flatland aborigines" (Taichung Education University, 2008). During the population census process of the National Government, some Pingpu ethnic groups were forcibly deprived of their Pingpu ethnic identity due to the cultural gap between the two parties. In recent years, the Pingpu ethnic group has been on the boundary between culture and identity, and must correct its name. Even if the future is full of difficulties, we must find new ways out and the possibility of positive development in desperate situations.

Therefore, this project uses design empowerment to co-create and cooperate with tribes to rebuild the context of local industries and explore ethnic culture and identity. Empowerment Design (Barab, 2015), helping tribes solve their current difficulties, can also cultivate local youth's design and marketing capabilities and assist research subjects in achieving the goals of local industrial upgrading, circular economy, and sustainable development. The research subjects of this project are mainly the Liuchong Creek tribe of the Taivoan tribe. Through design expertise and research, we explore the cultural characteristics of these two tribes and work with community development to solve the multiple difficulties encountered. Through personal experience, the process and discussion of efforts to solve tribal needs will help students and graduate students understand social needs through practice, gain a deep understanding of Aboriginal ethnic culture, and identify development issues with cultural depth., these processes have allowed the Pingpu ethnic culture to be based in Taiwan and look at new opportunities in Southeast Asia and even the world.

During the actual implementation, we stand with the Pingpu ethnic group from the same and equal perspective and on the premise of respecting the traditions of the Pingpu ethnic group, connecting the intangible tribal culture and tangible creative output, and making good use of digital technology to Graphic teaching materials, video teaching materials, cultural and creative products, food and agriculture education, artistic creation, public art, digital tours and many other aspects are expected to enable students and tourists to have more interactive experiences through this project to enhance learning. Effect: Through various forms of educational resources and cultural creations, multicultural awareness is established; educational resources and cultural creations have a common platform to display, and community cultural exchanges are strengthened; when all the above benefits are integrated, it can effectively enhance the cultural and creative industry Development, each tribe builds and learns from each other, observes and emulates, and achieves a model of practical design empowerment.

2 Research Purposes and Background

This project team hopes to combine cross-field expertise and the encouragement and co-creation of participatory design to work with the Pingpu ethnic group to respond to the development of Pingpu ethnic culture and promote various issues, "standing on the side of the colonized." The stance is to use the magnanimity of forgiveness and reconciliation; to use positive thinking to transform the unfortunate past and the experience of persecution, and become the driving force for cultural transformation and growth" (Peng, Luo, & Duan, 2008). It is hoped that through research and practice, the cultural characteristics and values of various tribes can be enhanced, the tangible tribal assets, intangible cultural creativity, and the aesthetics and spirit of Taiwan's local Pingpu ethnic culture can be demonstrated, as well as both soft and hard power. Tool design practice.

Some scholars believe this space between the two is the third space. It neither belongs to the former nor the latter; instead, it is formed by blending the two cultures. This hybrid state also forms the theme of post-colonialism. Hybridity is the willingness to learn and absorb alternative cultures., which also implies the meaning of innovation from another perspective (Hayward, 2017; Jiang, 2003). Therefore, our third space is based on the Austronesian culture, combined with the team's design expertise and industry experts to create through field surveys and interviews in line with the needs of the tribes so that students can understand Taiwan's role in the Austronesian language group position. This project serves as an intermediary between Aboriginal tribes and students. Based on the foundation laid by the Aboriginal design team of Yunnan University of Science and Technology in the tribes over the years, this project applies the professional capabilities of design to understand the importance of Austronesian culture and identify cultural characteristics. Through professional research, in-depth exploration, and working with Taiwan's aboriginal communities to solve the multiple difficulties encountered in community development. Such personal experience and discussion of the efforts to solve tribal needs will help students understand the needs of society at an early stage. Through an in-depth understanding of aboriginal culture, we use the tribes and cultures of aboriginal peoples and cooperate with Taiwan's new technology and innovation, from graphic teaching materials, video teaching materials, cultural and creative products, food and agriculture education, artistic creation, public art, Digital tours, and other aspects will explore emerging industries, build a new industry atmosphere for indigenous groups, and identify more new opportunities for industry development (Fig. 1).

Fig. 1. The project team went to the tribe to participate in local guided tours and courses (photographed from this study)

2.1 Research Targets

Since this study is connected to Taiwan's indigenes issues and survey, thus this research has been submitted to the review process of the Cheng Kung University's Ethics Review Committee and is undergoing standard review procedures and controls. The case will be closed before the completion of the research. The current case number is 112–267.

The object of this study is the long-term collaborator of our research team, the Liuchong Creek Tribe in Baihe District, Tainan City (originally a mixed settlement of the Qieba Society of the Taivoan Tribe and the Duojie Society of the Llor Tribe). The tribe's early administrative and policy deficiencies resulted in the tribe's loss of aboriginal identity. In recent years, it has gradually improved through the joint efforts of local tribe members and surrounding forces, academic research, international exchanges, and design support. Through a three-year long-term plan, the laboratory can intervene with more in-depth design training than previous cultural and creative outputs to support local industries and community groups. Regarding the location and status of tribes, this study will be detailed in Sect. 2.

2.2 Research Goals

1. International competition and cooperation integration courses and research: According-ing to the 2019 Global Competitiveness Report provided by the World Economic Forum and the 2022 World Competitiveness Annual Report by the Lausanne School of Management in Switzerland. According to the report, Taiwan ranks 12th and 7th in the world, respectively (National Development Council, 2022), significantly impacting the total population.

This achievement is worthy of high praise for Taiwan, which has a base of only 23 million people. However, despite its enormous economic foundation, Taiwan's diplo-matic exchanges still suffer from diplomatic suppression, and the space for Taiwan to participate in international competition and cooperation is marginalized. As Taiwan gradually moves towards a declining birthrate and an aging population, problems arise in local sustainable industries, and a consensus between the government and the opposition is gradually formed. As far as the New Southbound Policy is concerned with education, it has gone beyond Taiwan and into Southeast Asia and extensively exchanged opinions with foreign institutions, which has significantly changed the current educational struc-ture. Therefore, expanding international academic exchanges, striving for cross-border cooperation, and learning from the experiences of others may be our research goals and solutions.

2. Sustainable agricultural innovation and empowerment: When promoting the culture and cultural identity of indigenous tribes, this plan proposes the need to introduce

The concept of "sustainable agricultural entrepreneurship" is designed and empow-ered by this Empowerment Design research team (Barab, 2015). In addition to helping tribes solve their current agricultural difficulties, it can cultivate local youth's design and marketing capabilities, improve the competitiveness of tribes' primary industries through agricultural innovation and creativity, and assist in research. The objective is to achieve local industrial upgrading, circular economy, and sustainable development goals. During this process, the team connected with foreign teams and shared their experiences implementing local community development processes with cooperating national universities. They tried different peer models and methods to find the devel-opment of indigenous tribes suitable for this research field. During the progress of this project, our team can also cultivate the design and event planning abilities of our school students in the process of research and activity participation to enhance the learning of relevant knowledge so that team members can have sustainable agricultural inno-vation implementation experience in the future, and establish sustainable agricultural innovation. Continue the operation mode of Agricultural innovation.

3. Mixed reality is integrated into community revitalization: The low birthrate and aging population severely impact local labor-intensive industries. The current operating model of tribes for tourists is more inclined to go into the natural environment than static exhibitions. Experience the difference compared to the city. These include local hiking guides that visit tribes, professional handicraft teaching, local-style meals, etc. No matter where in Taiwan, the only available human resources are already exhausted. Therefore, this research team cooperates with tribes and communities that cooperate

with design training, conducts field surveys to deeply explore communities and tribal culture, digitally archives local cultural assets, and uses mixed-reality digital media to explore tribal cultural preservation and tourism aspects. Establish a new operating model to liberate the tribal workforce with technology and drive the local economy with culture. The research team also conducts A.R. culture and sightseeing tour guides for tribes and communities empowered by design and establishes sustainable business models.

3 Literature Reviews

3.1 The Development of Taiwan's Austronesian Cultural Advantages

As early as 1963, Yale University anthropologist Isidore Dyen had proposed that Taiwan may be the birthplace of Austronesian languages (Dyen, 1963). Then, in 1979, archaeologist and anthropologist Peter of the Australian National University Bellwood even defined Taiwan as "Taiwan as Austronesian Homeland" (Bellwood, 1979, 1991); in 1984, Robert Andrew Blust, a scholar at the University of Hawaii, also analyzed linguistics. They proposed the "Out of Taiwan Hypothesis" (1984, Blust). As early as 2008, scholar Zhang Zhishan proposed "using the spread of paper mulberry to test the possibility of Austronesian language migration hypothesis." Subsequently, National Taiwan University biodiversity researcher Zhong Guofang (2015) studied and examined the distribution of Austronesian language families. The region and the DNA composition of the paper mulberry plant are shown in Fig. 2. Root analysis was conducted. The research results support their proposal and show Taiwan's importance in forming the Austronesian language and culture. Paper mulberry is a widely distributed and representative plant in Austronesian culture. It is also often made into bark clothing and daily necessities by aboriginal people across Taiwan. The dispersal route of paper mulberry makes it possible to understand the migration footprint from Taiwan to the South Island (Seelenfreund et al., 2011). Research evidence shows that these paper mulberry trees are not native species and were introduced through artificial propagation. They also point out that the origin of the introduction of paper mulberry trees is most likely from Taiwan. These research results also show "out of Taiwan" (Chang et al., 2015; González-Lorca et al., 2015) (Fig. 3).

3.2 The Laboratory's Primary Design Empowerment Experience

In recent years, our laboratory has participated in or led continuous academic exchanges with Yunlin University of Science and Technology and partner schools such as National Chung Hsing University, Kaohsiung University of Science and Technology, and Donghua University; for example, teachers and students of the founding department of Yunlin University of Science and Technology, and Kaohsiung Huang-yao, LIN, director of the Department of Cultural and Creative Industries of HKUST, has been participating in the USR social practice program of the Ministry of Education chaired by Associate Professor Dr. Hsun-Long LIN of the Department of Veterinary Medicine of National Chung Hsing University since the beginning of 2018. In the past five years, he has used design training to engage in "LangLangLeHuo-Stray animal reduction."

Fig. 2. "Out of Taiwan," Austronesian Roots (Zhang, 2015).

Fig. 3. Diagram of the significant Austronesian clades (from Encyclopedia Britannica, 1998).

"Practice of Reduction and Welfare of Stray Animals," and was upgraded to the second phase (2020–2022) of the Ministry of Education's USR Project - University Characteristic In-depth Development Plan: "Walk with Love - Stray Animal Reduction and Welfare Practice" (LangLangLeHuo-Stray animal reduction, 2019), gradually solving the social problems caused by stray animals, is an excellent example of cross-school cooperation. At the School of Design of Yunlin University of Science and Technology, Director Shyh-Huei HWANG leads the USR social practice program of the Ministry of Education, with the "Social Practice Program of the Laiji Tribe of the Tsou Tribe: Bringing into full play the inherent cultural talents and Lishan spirit of the Tsou Tribe" (TCSA Taiwan Corporate Sustainability Award, 2021). The School of Design has also co-created teaching with partner schools in various countries in recent years. Students on campus from Vietnam, Malaysia, Indonesia, and other countries have accumulated experience in ethnic studies through teaching and research cooperation.

3.3 Liuchong Creek Tribe and Its Literatures

This research team has been participating in and assisting the Yuan Zhu tribe and the Pingpu ethnic tribe for a long time since 2012. In the past ten years, it has worked with the Dongpu Yi-Lin of the Bunun people, the Shuanglong tribe of the Bunun people, the Wangxiang tribe of the Bunun people, and the Seediq Qingliu Tribe of the Pingpu Tribe, the Jibeishuo Tribe of Tainan Dongshan, the Liuchong Creek Tribe of Tainan Baihe, and the Niu Mian Tribe of the Kaxabu Tribe in Puli, Nantou, etc., to jointly create an experience of design empowerment and ethnic cultural development. Since the loss of young adults in the tribe is quite severe, the planning team and tribal organizations hope to cooperate with the local social organization Tainan Liuchong Creek Pingpu Association and the local elementary school Hedong Elementary School Liuxi branch to apply it in the local area. The cultural knowledge and experiences of tribal elders are used to teach the next generation still in the tribe to understand their own tribal stories, thereby planting the seeds of cultural inheritance. Therefore, since 2015, the team has been working with the tribe to organize and co-create educational activities through local associations and primary schools, leading students from Liuxi Elementary School to understand their hometown and further allowing the children to increase their understanding of their ethnic group. As for the records of the cultural work camp (pictured), it is hoped that the tribe's power can be used to enhance the cultural identity of the next generation towards their own tribe. This research team believes that the tribe has experienced a period of cultural rupture in the past, and it will take a long time to reconnect with the ancestors and establish cultural identity through the introduction of design training. The creation, aesthetics, and design power of the tribe will be cultivated. Help the tribe members fully understand the tribal culture; one day, we can confidently tell our stories (Fig. 4).

Fig. 4. The project team has held summer tribal cultural design camps at the Liuxi Branch of Donghe Elementary School for many years since 2015. (Photographed from this project)

To perpetuate tribal culture and legends, the research team has collaborated with tribal schoolchildren through a design training camp to work together to materialize past tribal legends; through mosaic collages of schoolchildren's paintings, the research team has collaborated with tribal schoolchildren, The tribe members work together to create a tribal story wall. This research team believes that the tribe has experienced a period of cultural rupture in the past, and it will take a long time to reconnect with the ancestors and establish cultural identity through the introduction of design training, the creation, aesthetics, and design power of the tribe will be cultivated. Help the tribe members fully understand the tribal culture; one day, we can confidently tell our stories.

4   Methodology

This project uses the SDGs and the United Nations Sustainable Development Goals as the basis for action, interacts with local organizations and farmers who hope to improve their cultural and commercial values and investigates local areas using Long-Term Observations and Participant Observation. After identifying the characteristic industries, such as culture and commerce of the group that can serve as the foundation, we conduct Action Research and use A.R. digital media to do a certain degree of Design Empowerment for the local area and analyze several domestic and foreign research objectives to achieve From the perspective of qualitative research, a sustainable design development model based on design empowerment is derived; during the implementation process of this project, through cooperation and discussion with local groups, it is used to construct a 2024 new design empowerment that can be applied by local groups.

4.1   Long-Term Observation and Participation in Local Networks

If you want to comprehensively understand the target culture and the reason for its existence, Jorgensen (1989) believes that the participant observation method is most suitable for studying human existence. The method of participation and Observation in local activities is particularly suitable for academic questions, especially when local understanding is less mature. Whether you are an outsider or in the midst of it, as long as it is an observable phenomenon, it is worth recording. Different living environments or situations can give rise to entirely different development models, which can be obtained through interaction with the team. More information is also an unstructured observation method.

In the past, the design industry preferred experts to lead design teams when it came to local groups, with locals having no say, or experts and scholars only explored humanities and history but ignored subsequent commercial output. This research team's entry is from the cultural and design aspects, using design empowerment methods to work with local residents through participating in local networks to break the traditional model of the past. Through regional and field integration and the addition of innovative digital tools, a unique social innovation network can be created from a professional and collective perspective (Easterday et al., 2018).

Since the development field has been cultivated in the local area for a long time, each region has different action modes. The business development process is expanded in line with the development goals of the SDGs so that local groups can have sustainable development space; all stakeholders and relevant parties should deliberate efforts to promote multi-directional technology transfer to achieve the Sustainable Development Goals (United Nations, 2019). The National Commission for Sustainable Development of the Executive Yuan hopes to rationally develop various models and management models of sustainable development from the perspectives of natural sciences, ecology, economics, and sociology (National Commission for Sustainable Development of the Executive Yuan, 2009). Therefore, in cooperation with local groups to build independent management models and models, local capabilities should be continuously explored during the implementation process, and action research should be used to strengthen capabilities that are outstanding and consistent with the SDGs. The connotation of action research lies in improving participants while actively participating in the research process (Kemmis, McTaggart, Nixon, 1998). To lead the Taiwanese team to face the world and establish international design experience; therefore, in action research, by constantly trying new ideas in practical experience as a new method to improve the team's current situation and enhance knowledge, it is a more beneficial choice for those who stick to the rules. In addition, it can also implement design training for tribes more effectively. Progress can only be made through the three stages of exposing problems, taking action, and introspecting and introspecting (Pan, 2004). Only participatory research can create a completely new benefit model for beneficiaries that is entirely different from the past.

4.2 Integrated Application of Mixed Reality Technology

Due to its digital characteristics, mixed reality can be displayed in any field; as long as the equipment is suitable, it can be used in various fields (Zhan, 2013; An, 2020). Therefore, it is very suitable for this research operating model of tribal and rural community fields at home and abroad. Depending on the local situation, V.R. can be used as the basis for purchasing equipment, or the equipment carried by tourists can be used to design a Mixed-reality system for tribes and communities. For example, at the Liuchong Creek tribe's public house, tourists use their mobile phones as a control platform to operate and create the tribe's navigation system through LBAR (Location-Based Augmented Reality) technology. In addition, the system construction of mixed reality will require many digital cultural assets; these materials can also become critical for historical comparison and tribal cultural and historical reference (Key Commentary Online Media Group, 2019). Combining augmented reality technology with appropriate software interface design can demonstrate unique local characteristics from multiple aspects, such as the operation surface, system surface, and digital model surface.

After the augmented reality system is established, it is verified using the TAM Technology Acceptance Model. This model quantitatively profiles people's acceptance of new technologies (Kaur, Goh, and Kng, 2018). It has many applications and can be used as a standard testing environment for developing new systems. Based on this architecture, Hammady et al. proposed an improved version of the TAM model, specifically for acceptance testing of augmented reality (Hammady, Ma, AL-Kalha, and Strathearn, 2020). This model clearly points out the characteristics of each property. The interactive influence is shown below. This model starts from the acceptance of new things (P.I.) and explores the impact of ease of use (EOU), enjoyment (ENJ), and usefulness (USF) on future use intention (WFU). Subsequently, the system publishes questionnaires. And perform statistical analysis to investigate whether local groups' augmented reality innovations can increase tourists' willingness to use them (Fig. 5).

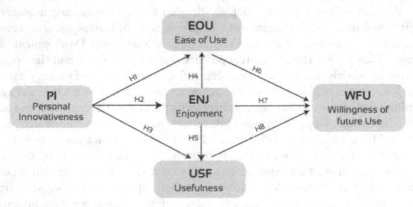

Fig. 5. New TAM model, taken from Hammady R, Ma Ma, Strathearn C, 2020

5 Analysis

5.1 Preliminary Research Outcomes

This project aims to build a social innovation network through design empowerment, international sustainable development models, and the practical concept of university social responsibility. It focuses on the cultural identity of the tribe and combines branding, mobile tours, and southbound International exchanges and links to create opportunities for the sustainable development of the Liuchong Creek tribe of the Taivoan tribe in China. Through this project, the university and the tribes and ethnic groups jointly created the project, using a design and empowerment method to work with the indigenous groups to cultivate the ethnic groups. Then we connected with Teacher Indarti from the Fashion Design Department of Surabaya State University (UNESA) in Indonesia; Dr. Trang le Khanh from the School of Textiles, Leather and Clothing at Hanoi University of Science and Technology (HUST) in Vietnam, and Teacher Hoang Thi Ai Nhan from Ho Chi Minh University of Economics in Vietnam to expand Indonesia and international research exchanges between schools in Vietnam, as well as curriculum design co-creation, and proposes how ethnic groups can conduct international Observation and exchange learning in southbound countries, expand international cooperation, sustainable design, and innovation in the sustainable practice of agricultural cultural creation Establishment of issue practice model.

Comparing the results of research analysis with the Research Goals as follows:

5.2 Two Years' Preliminary Results

1. International competition and cooperation integration courses and research:

First-year project - Integrate tribal design studios to create a sustainable agricultural brand. In the first year of this project, the university, tribes, and rural communities will integrate tribal design studios based on the needs of sustainable agricultural innovation and design empowerment methods, taking inventory of the tribe's agricultural specialties, working with the aboriginal groups to deeply cultivate the ethnic groups, and developing packaging and visual design systems that can be sold sustainably. Through the international links of Yunnan University of Science and Technology, the pipeline established this year will continue to develop, and the research and cooperation relationships with Indonesia's Surabaya State University (UNESA) and Vietnam's Hanoi University of Science and Technology (HUST) will expand international connections between schools in Indonesia and Vietnam. Research and exchange, lead masters and doctoral students to participate in the ICCIE International Technical and Vocational Education Symposium (Scopus Indexed) hosted by Yogyakarta State University (UNY) every October. And continue to work with the Liuchong Creek tribe to jointly shape the local agricultural entrepreneurship brand, and through grounded theory and cultural identity scale, we conduct research and evaluation on ethnic cultural identity.

Taking the Liuchong Creek tribe as an example, the team used in-depth interview methods to conduct grounded theory discussions, interviews, and analysis, combined with integrated design workshops, to jointly shape the local agricultural brand image, establish a production and marketing model, and communicate through Deepen the sense of mission of its local cultural brand through design training. For the Liuchong Creek tribe of the Taivoan ethnic group, we continue to promote the multicultural and local dynamic design workshop operation model every semester and invest in The development of the Taivoan's Liuchong Creek Tribe hopes to discover the local characteristics of the tribe, discuss with local residents, and create a sustainable agricultural brand with local characteristics through sustainable design and co-creation. Since agribusiness branding is not a separate industry shaping and marketing issue, it often involves more complex interest relationships. This project uses the Social Innovation Networks model proposed by Easterday, Gerber, and Rees Lewis (2018) through university and graduate school courses to train students from universities and graduate schools and jointly organize studios., work with locals to build agricultural brands, and use the agricultural brand method to lower the financial threshold for industrial start-ups. Not only does this project team co-create brands with tribes, but it is also expected that this project can actually improve the quality of co-creation with tribal's brand value.

Second-year plan - Promote tribal brands with digital agricultural innovation concepts. The second-year plan continues the first year to shape the physical sustainable agricultural innovation brand, introduce the development of digital content systems, deepen the sustainable agricultural innovation brand, and use the digital sustainable agricultural branding approach to promote local tourism and agricultural branding. By integrating the design studio network, visitors from the Liuchong Creek tribe are invited to experience the system and fill in the cultural identity scale. Lead graduate students to attend international seminars and invite teams from southbound exchange countries to communicate and exhibit with each other. Expand international cooperation, learn from each other, observe the content of sustainable management, and compile the results together.

2. Sustainable agricultural innovation and empowerment:Taking stock of the preliminary results: 1. Cultivate participating students. Through members from across departments and fields, they collaborate and design in a studio manner. Workshops and camps are held occasionally to enable participants to improve their organizational, planning, and management capabilities. 2. Through the grounded theory and cultural identity research of the Liuchong Creek Tribe, graduate students will be allowed to step into the field, apply qualitative and quantitative data collection methods, and conduct qualitative coding and quantitative statistical analysis to cultivate comprehensive research and analysis capabilities. 3. Use integrated design to carry out the branding process and cultivate the participants' ability to analyze, summarize, and extract literature on brands, industries, and objects. 4. The fund-raising process of agricultural brand creation, training participants' abilities in brand discussion, marketing, and entrepreneurial management.

5.3 Summary

3. Mixed reality is integrated into community revitalization:The Liuchong Creek Tribe is an aboriginal tribe in southern Taiwan. Through long-term design training cooperation with researchers, the teachers and students of the department have developed agricultural design products for the Liuchong Creek tribe. Its agricultural products carry out visual marketing design, pilot agricultural entrepreneurship tours, summer internships and other methods, including corporate identification system and packaging design, so that the products can be combined with the image of the Liuchong Creek tribe, allowing farmers and localities to jointly enhance their visibility, and hope to enable Causes spillover effects, allowing other farmers in the tribe to integrate marketing together (Fig. 6).

Fig. 6. Constructing software interface on Unity (designed by this research team)

The research team used Location-Based Augmented Reality technology to build an A.R. system on mobile phone software to provide tourists with two different navigation methods: the first is without a tour guide., you can freely visit the tribe through your mobile phone; the second is that with the help of a tour guide, you can also guide the tribe through text descriptions and 3D models. With the help of the new system, tourists can better understand the local customs and customs. In this system, tourists can visit the tribe on the spot and click on the 3D model to view the tribal story. This method is playful and allows tourists to gain an in-depth understanding of tribal history and culture during the visit. The development team chose the Unity engine as the infrastructure for the mobile program. To present the map in the virtual environment, we chose Unity's Online Maps plug-in, combined with the 3D model drawn by team members, to display the complete system in the application.

Yu-Ting YAN was a master's degree graduate from the researcher's laboratory. Her Master's thesis under first author's guidance entitled "Research on Using Augmented Reality Combined with Liuzhong Creek's Tribal Guide" (Sources: https://hdl.handle.net/11296/x74t3e) research on the form of A.R. tour in Liuchong Creek, on the unique culture of the tribe is integrated into the APP, breaking away from the original oral-based tour mode of the tribe and using expanded Mainly based on augmented reality software; integrate knowledge points into the system and games, and use simple voice instructions to attract young users, concerned about tribal culture (Fig. 7).

Fig. 7. The operation screen of the Liuchong Creek AR tester is taken together with the local attractions - the suspension bridge ruins and the longan stove (designed by this research team)

6 Conclusion

Taiwan's various international competitions in recent years have continuously demonstrated the country's soft power, and its national strength has been thoroughly improved under the fierce global competition and international competition; the National Development Council also pointed out that Taiwan's response to the COVID-19 epidemic Despite the severe test, it was still able to achieve this good result: "In the 2022 IMD World Competitiveness Annual Report, Taiwan ranked 7th among the 63 rated countries. The overall ranking improved for the fourth consecutive year and achieved its best performance since 2013" (Central News Agency, 2022/06/15). Taiwan also ranked 26th among countries in this year's World Happiness Report, ranking first in Asia (New News, 2022/05/19). Taiwan's per capita GDP in 2022 is estimated to reach US$35,000, ranking 21st globally (Business Today, 2022). Taiwanese people should have greater self-confidence and responsibility as global citizens, mediate Taiwan's culture to the world stage, and use team strength to fully demonstrate the beauty of Taiwan's aboriginal culture. Given this, this project and its team hope to serve as a pathfinder for Austronesian culture, standing on the university side, first connecting with the primary partner tribes and communities in Taiwan and then connecting with partner schools and teachers in Indonesia and Vietnam, bringing their majors to ours Conduct in-depth research and teaching connections with the courses; during the three-year research period, conduct international links in line with the SDGs sustainable innovation design issue orientation; when connecting the design profession with indigenous culture, we can Think about the keywords of design anthropology, and use an anthropological perspective to examine how design behavior is formed? How to connect communities for co-creation cooperation (Akama, Pink, & Sumartoji, 2018)? And establish a reference model of operation based on these principles.

In cross-border cooperation, this project can also use this to exchange new knowledge on design, fashion, research theories, and other countries from various countries and continuously update the pulse of world design research among the foreign institutions that have agreed to participate in this project, Indonesia's Yogyakarta State University is renowned for its design Empowerment methods are used to create clothing designs using traditional ethnic groups' pictures and texts to assist local families of disadvantaged ethnic groups. Indonesia's Surabaya State University and two schools in Vietnam (Hanoi University of Science and Technology and the Ho Chi Minh University of Economics) have cooperated with our team in the past to use marine Waste materials or leftover materials from the garment industry can be redesigned and used to achieve environmental sustainability and promote industrial innovation. Through the integration of this project, in cooperation with international universities, the theme of sustainable design will continue to be expanded as a future research direction; during the execution of the project, it will also be possible to share the sustainable design of universities in various countries and the development of design training. Development experience, this cooperation opportunity will be used to analyze cases in various countries, and a development framework for design intervention in environmental sustainability and promotion of local community well-being will be summarized. Then, the process model of sustainable design will be obtained.

Acknowledgments. This study was funded by the Ministry of Science and Technology, Taiwan (Research grant number MST109-2420-H-224 -002 -MY3).

Disclosure of Interests. The authors have no competing interests to declare relevant to this article's content.

References

Akama, Y., Pink, S., Sumartojo, S.: Uncertainty & Possibility New Approaches to Future Making in Design Anthropology, Bloomsbury Academic, NY, USA (2018)

An, B.H.: Research on applying augmented reality technology in cultural asset preservation and sightseeing guidance. Department of Industrial Design, National Kaohsiung Normal University. Kaohsiung City (2020)

Barab, S., Thomas, M.K., et al.: Empowerment Design Work: Building Participant Structures that Transform, sashabarab.org (2015). https://sashabarab.org/wp-content/uploads/2015/03/icls_2 002.pdf

Bellwood, P.: Man's Conquest of the Pacific. Oxford Press, New York (1979)

Bellwood, P.: The austronesian dispersal and the origin of languages. Sci. Am. **265**, 88–93 (1991)

Blust, R.: The austronesian homeland: a linguistic perspective. Asian Perspect. **26**(1), 45–67 (1984)

Business today, Surpassed Switzerland and moved up to one place. Taiwan's GDP last year ranked 21st in the world! (2022). https://www.businesstoday.com.tw/article/category/183025/post/202304120061

Central News Agency., IMD World Competitiveness Rating: Taiwan has progressed for four consecutive years, ranking 7th globally. https://www.cna.com.tw/news/afe/202206150014.aspx. Accessed 15 June 2022

Chang, C.S., Liu, H.L., et al.: A holistic picture of Austronesian migrations revealed by phylogeographer of pacific paper mulberry. Proc. Natl. Acad. Sci. **112**(44), 13537–13542 (2015)

Chong, G.F.: What is the "Taiwan theory" told by folk plants? Taiwan is the homeland of pacific paper mulberry. PanSci. (2015). https://pansci.asia/archives/86574

Dyen, I.: The position of the Malayopolynesian languages of Formosa. Asian Perspect. **7**(1/2), 261–271 (1963)

Easterday, M.W., Gerber, E.M., Rees Lewis, D.G.: Social innovation networks: a new approach to social design education and impact. Des. Issues **34**(2), 64–76 (2018)

González-Lorca, J., Rivera-Hutinel, A., et al.: Ancient and modern introduction of Broussonetia papyrifera ([L.] Vent. Moraceae) into the Pacific: genetic, geographical and historical evidence. N. Z. J. Bot. **53**(2), 75–89 (2015)

Hayward, S.: Cinema Studies The Key Concepts. Routledge, Lodon (2017)

Hsu, C.M.: Fan School and Fan Tong Educational Institute, Encyclopedia of Taiwan, Ministry of Culture (2009). https://nrch.culture.tw/twpedia.aspx?id=11157

Jorgensen, D.L.: Participant Observation: A Methodology for Human Studies, p. 12. Sage Publications, Inc., Thousand Oaks (1989)

Kemmis, S., McTaggart, R., Nixon, R.: The Changing Field of Action Research. The Action Research Planner, p. 4. Springer, Singapore (2014). https://doi.org/10.1007/978-981-4560-67-2

LangLangLeHuo-Stray Animal Reduction Plan to Deepen the Cultivation of National Chung Hsing University (2019). https://usr.nchu.edu.tw/教育部usr-浪愛齊步走計畫

National Council for Sustainable Development, Executive Yuan. Sustainable develop-
    ment policy framework. National Council for Sustainable Development, Executive
    Yuan (2009). https://ncsd.ndc.gov.tw/Fore/nsdn/archives/meet3/detail?id=13c48ab2-e655-
    4f2b-a317-d7abab9e01f9
National Development Council. IMD World Competitiveness. National Development Council of
    the Republic of China (2022). https://www.ndc.gov.tw/cp.aspx?n=5DE406C89FFD8BCF&s=
    65A3A67E1278FD73
New news. The 2022 World Happiness Report is out! Taiwan beats Japan and South Korea to
    retain the first place in East Asia. https://www.storm.mg/lifestyle/4339326. Accessed 19 May
    2022
Pan, S.Z.: Basic requirements for action research. Natl. Educ. Res. Collect. (12), 163–177 (2004)
Peng, L.H., Luo, J.J., Duan, D.L.: Use third space theory to interpret the contemporary significance
    of Sonia Delaunay's creations and the inspiration it brings to us in implementing Taiwan's
    localization perspective. Int. J. Art Educ. 6(1), 158–172 (2008)
Seelenfreund, D., Clarke, A., et al.: Paper mulberry (Broussonetia papyrifera) as a commensal
    model for human mobility in Oceania: anthropological, botanical and genetic considerations.
    NZ J. Bot. 48(3–4), 231–247 (2011)
Taichung University of Education (2008) Understanding Taiwan's Aboriginal Culture. http://www.
    ntcu.edu.tw/AEC095182/final/c.html
TCSA Taiwan Business Sustainability Award 2021 University Impact 100% (USR Impact 100)
    Pp.39, 41. (2021). https://tcsaward.org.tw/tw/about/publication/376
United Nations. Executive Summary. The future is now: science for sustainable develop-
    ment. United Nations (2019). https://sdgs.un.org/zh/kanwu/quanqiukechixu-fazhanbaogao-
    2019-24576
Zhan, Y.J.: Apply augmented reality to campus mobile tours. Institute of Information Education,
    National Taiwan Normal University. Taipei City (2013)

Digital Storytelling of Intangible Cultural Heritage: A Multimodal Interactive Serious Game for Teaching Folk Dance

Yun Xie⬤, Mingyang Su⬤, Xiaomei Nie(✉)⬤, and Xiu Li⬤

Tsinghua Shenzhen International Graduate School, ShenZhen 518055, China
nie.xiaomei@sz.tsinghua.edu.cn

Abstract. As part of the intangible cultural heritage, folk dance is of great significance to the cultural identity of society. Digital technology is widely used to display tangible and intangible cultural heritage. Interactive digital storytelling become a normal way of museum exhibitions and virtual and augmented reality applications. This form has a good effect on digital assets of dance, to display background information, related events, and characters of cultural heritage objects. In this research, we design a folk dance teaching serious game based on multi-modal interaction. Through digital interactive narrative, players can learn folk dance movements and understand the cultural connotations behind the dance movements at the same time, to help folk dance get a better inheritance.

Keywords: Folk dance · Intangible Cultural Heritage · Serious Game

1 Introduction

As an important expression of national culture, folk dance carries profound social significance. To better protect this intangible cultural heritage (ICH), dance can be "digitized". Digitization can include semantic descriptions of dance, audio and video recordings, or computer animations, such as dance movements of real-world human performers captured through motion capture technology.

However, digitization is not enough to effectively inherit folk dance. Folk dance is a people-centered living inheritance. It is a living record of people's behavior, thoughts emotions, and other spiritual levels [1]. Digitalization preserves the physical form of folk dance recording but lacks the inheritance of its intangible elements including emotion, perception, motivation, and culture. The participants' practical experience of folk dance is an essential part of the inheritance.

Serious games have the potential to digitally inherit these valuable cultural resources [2]. Combining digital folk dance with serious games, through the addition of digital interactive storytelling and the design of interactive functions, brings users a better dance learning experience, allowing people to experience and learn this intangible cultural heritage in an unprecedented way.

This research mainly studies the development of interactive serious games for digital folk dance visualization. Our goal is to learn dance movements in

M. Rauterberg (Ed.): HCII 2024, LNCS 14717, pp. 325–335, 2024.
https://doi.org/10.1007/978-3-031-61147-6_22

a way that players are willing to accept learning and understand the cultural meaning behind the dance. After playing the game, in addition to learning the dance movements, players can also have a deeper understanding of the story background and cultural origins of folk dances, thereby achieving better dissemination of intangible culture.

2 Related Work

2.1 Folk Dance

Early research on folk dance mainly focused on the recording and digital presentation of dance movements, usually converting these movements into single-dimensional digital expressions, such as image-based dance videos or digital presentations with motion capture as the core. At the same time, research represented by digital dance ethnography focuses on deepening the cultural experience of dance, trying to improve the effect of cultural communication by semantically organizing relevant cultural data or displaying digital dance performances on multiple interfaces.

In terms of recording dance movements, motion capture is the most common application technology [3]. It uses mechanical, magnetic, and optical capture to achieve precise motion data capture and detailed recording of physical characteristics using systems based on cameras, sensors, or a mixture of both, parameters of position, rotation, joint angles, and kinematic indicators [1].

Matus [8] used motion capture technology to 3d visualize slovak folk dance movements and developed a three-dimensional folk dance visualization application for demonstration and teaching of folk dance. They digitized dances from different regions of Slovakia, and users can view and learn these dances at any time.

The EU Intangible Cultural Heritage i-Treasures project [4] is committed to protecting intangible cultural heritage. They built the first multi-modal dataset of intangible cultural heritage, which contains video, audio, depth, motion capture data, and other modalities such as electroencephalography or ultrasound data. Increase public access to inventory and participation in the inventory process through multi-modal intangible cultural heritage datasets and digital platforms to manage a wide range of multimedia digital content, including folk dances.

The digital research on Cyprus folk dance records the dance movement data related to its cultural aspects [9], uses the relational database model to construct dance data and metadata information, and reproduces the current situation of Cyprus folk dance. They proposed a framework based on the principles of Laban movement analysis, implemented a virtual reality simulator for folk dance teaching, and tested it on Cypriot folk dance. A dance sequence performed by a 3D avatar is presented to the user. Data were collected using PhaseSpace's Impulse X2 optical motion capture system with active markers.

However, countless examples show that although the content and form of dance have been successfully recorded by physical things, the dissemination of non-material cultural dissemination of dance is limited. Therefore, the core of the current dance digital research field is gradually transformed into a dynamic content presentation method using "people" as the carrier.

2.2 Serious Games

Serious game design framework and related theoretical research for cultural heritage are relatively systematic [6], which mainly includes research on the macro design, development, and evaluation framework of serious games for cultural heritage and the design methods of serious game content. As for serious games in the field of intangible cultural heritage, although innovative paradigms such as heritage dynamic aesthetics [12], cultural user experience [10], and interactive narrative [5] have emerged, they are still in the development stage and have not yet been systematically studied theoretically.

Iris Kico et al. [14] developed a visual folk dance teaching game based on different interactive motion capture technologies. The motion capture system records the folk dance movement performances of teachers and users. The teacher's dance performance is pre-recorded offline, and the user's performance is recorded and streamed to the app in real-time, and users can learn the dance by comparing the movement data.

The Elmedin team [12] conducted a case study on the intangible cultural heritage technique of Old Bridge Diving in Mostar and integrated local and remote interaction mechanisms into the simulation game to explore the value of combining virtual reality technology and web technology to enhance user immersion and presence.

Efthymios Ziagkas' terpsichore project [11] combines experiential learning theory to build a VR game learning environment for Greek traditional dance. The game simulates a dance learning situation guided by a teacher and enables learners to imitate movements independently through task settings. By capturing and capturing learner movement data, the terpsichore project Comparison with expert action data gives learners feedback. They used motion capture technology and the Vicon 3D recording system to capture and digitally record six dances from different regions of Greece. They digitized, modeled, archived, electronically preserved, and presented intangible cultural heritage content related to traditional dances at a low cost to a wide range of users.

In terms of folk dance inheritance, current research only focuses on the reenactment of folk dance movements or related semantic information as database supplements but lacks an explanation of the folk dance culture itself. Serious games provide a good solution to this problem. Through the role-playing form of game narrative and interactive mechanism settings, it can bring players a cultural experience with a stronger sense of immersion and participation, thereby improving the learning of folk dances-and communication effects.

3   Concept

We built a folk dance teaching game based on multi-modal interaction, aiming to establish the connection between folk dance movement teaching and folk dance cultural experience so that players can obtain accurate dance movement guidance and good cultural experience, and help folk dance get better inheritance and protection (Figs. 1 and 2).

Fig. 1. Folk Dance Teaching Serious Game System Overview

Taking the Chinese Hmong dance as an example, we built a folk dance teaching game based on multi-modal interaction to help players learn Hmong dance movements and understand Hmong dance culture. Inspired by field theory, we provide a three-dimensional virtual environment that can enhance players' cultural awareness and players experience by constructing a virtual three-dimensional teaching environment and narrative background for digital dance. In this virtual environment, players can learn and experience the movements and cultural connotations of Hmong dance by controlling virtual avatars and digital characters for intelligent dialogue and interaction. Through the guided teaching and timely feedback of digital characters, players can more easily immerse themselves in the context of Hmong dance culture. Our game uses the Unreal 5.1 development platform for game construction and development.

3.1   Motion Data Capturing and Editing

Dance involves a large number of complex movements,and a high degree of precision must be maintained. Therefore, we used the optical motion capture method with passive markers to objectively record the movement data of the Hmong dance. Optical systems with movable markers use equipment to capture data on skeletal points of dancers' dance dynamics, which can minimize marker exchange

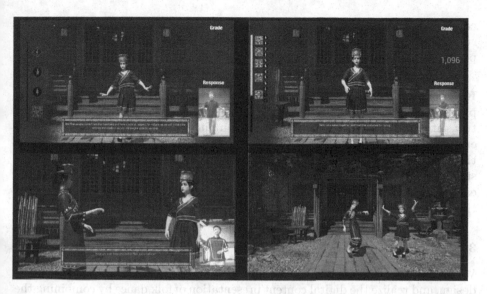

Fig. 2. Folk Dance Teaching System in Game

and identification. Although each marker may not be uniquely identified, it can provide the greatest possible accurate data.

After collecting the data, we used Motion Builder to process the data to present the dance more realistically. For example, errors and redundant movements in dancers' performances are deleted, and unnatural limb positions and twisted joints in the data are repaired.

Finally, we imported the motion capture data into UE and redirected it to the 3D virtual character we made, so that the virtual character could show the corresponding dance movements.

3.2   Game System Design

The game system framework of this research is divided into three modules: situational awareness, mechanism structure, and kinesthetic interaction. Each module is specifically designed from the perspective of content design and interaction design based on the folk dance teaching model.

Situation Awareness Module: Construct a game situation based on the learning content. Through the design of the four elements of audio-visual, narrative, character, and plot, it gives players a basic aesthetic experience and sensory experience and initially forms an understanding of the game learning situation.

Mechanism Structure Module: Mechanically transform the learning content, set game learning challenges, and form different types of game learning core cycles through the design of four game form elements: goals, procedures, rules, and resources, so that learners can complete the game challenges in the process and acquire knowledge.

Kinesthetic Interaction Module: Sets the embodied interactive behavior of player game learning, including the three links of player behavior input, behavior translation, and game system feedback. Combined with the game loop model of embodied experiential learning, players can interact with the game environment through the body and actively accumulate kinesthetic experience, further construct knowledge concepts, and deepen memory. In the folk dance serious game, each link of the kinesthetic interaction module needs to be designed based on the content characteristics of the learning object.

3.3   Game Content Design

We regard the cultural elements of folk dance as the core of the game content design, and realize the digital content presentation of folk dance by combining the cultural elements of folk dance with the system structural elements of the game [7]. Combined with field theory, this research summarizes the content design goals of folk dance into three directions: performance environment, performance content, and performance culture, which correspond to each module of the game system.

Performance Environment: Specifically refers to the performers of folk dances, the props used, performance time and venue settings, etc. This part of the content corresponds to the situational awareness module of the game. By digitizing folk dances, the visual content of the game is constructed. The dance performance environment is mainly based on the national characteristics of the characters, the props they hold, and the virtual environment they are in, so as to facilitate users to understand the Hmong groups. There is a clear understanding of the visual characteristics of dance.

Performance Content: Specifically refers to the body dance movements of folk dance, including dance postures, dance rhythm, etc. This part of the content is realized through the game mechanism structure module and the kinesthetic interaction module. Various game mechanisms are used to match the process characteristics of folk dance to form game-learning challenges. Players can have a game learning experience of folk dance in an embodied and interactive way, forming a Kinesthetic experience and memory for knowledge of folk dance characteristics.

Performance Culture: Specifically refers to the cultural context and cultural implications of the application of folk dance. This part of the content is presented through the combination of the situation awareness module and the mechanism structure module. It mainly explains the in-depth cultural origins and background of national dance and creates an in-person national experience for players from a macro perspective through the narrative, plot, and role elements of the game. Dance game learning context.

In terms of game-level design, we combined it with the teaching process of folk dance. We divided Hmong dance learning into three stages, including static movements, dynamic rhythm, and complete dance teaching. In each teaching stage, there will be a corresponding virtual character explaining the culture behind the dance movement. Regarding the accuracy of dance movements, we use action recognition technology to capture the player's joint information in the 3D space, calculate the angle between the player's bone vector and the virtual character's bone vector, accurately evaluate the player's movement form, and then give positive feedback to encourage the user to continue learning to ensure players receive high-quality movement guidance and form training. In terms of the experience of dance culture, we combine intelligent dialogue and game narrative design to allow players to gain an in-depth understanding of the national cultural background carried by each dance movement by interacting with virtual characters. The art design carefully creates an immersive experience, allowing players to personally experience the presentation of visual elements such as Hmong costumes, scenes, and regions.

3.4   Intelligent Conversation and Storytelling

In terms of interaction, we use action recognition and speech recognition as the main interaction methods. Players can interact with virtual digital entities through body movements and conversations, thereby experiencing dance movements and cultural connotations. Through monocular motion capture technology, we have achieved accurate capture and analysis of players' dance movements. Motion interaction allows players to capture their dance movements through a camera and present them digitally on the screen. We use voice-intelligent dialogue technology to simulate real dialogue scenarios, allowing players to ask questions, seek guidance, and even have in-depth cultural exchanges. The virtual digital character guide uses ChatGPT technology to understand the player's questions and provide corresponding answers and suggestions. Our intelligent conversation technology is jointly implemented by Azure and ChatGPT (Fig. 3).

To help players better understand the Hmong dance culture, we set up a narrative background of the game for users. The player will play the role of a tourist from a foreign country who strays into a Hmong village in the mountains. In Hmong culture, "dance" is a "ritual" that can pray to gods to gain strength. Therefore, in the game setting, the player needs to learn the Hmong dance to gain the power of the gods and help the Hmong people solve their problems, obtain their help, and leave the Hmong village.

To enhance the fun of learning, we have adopted the form of interactive narrative. Players can learn about the daily life of the Hmong people and the culture behind the dance through free dialogue with the virtual characters in the game. When players are learning dance, the virtual character will explain to

Fig. 3. Interaction System in Game

them the origin of these movements: For example, the characteristic rhythm of the Hmong people and the duck step dance rhythm are derived from the Hmong people's love for ducks, and therefore the imitated movements. We provide players with some dialogue options and set the basic content for the background and personality of the virtual character through chatGPT. Players can choose the direction of the conversation according to their preferences, and the virtual character will automatically generate conversation content through chatGPT, and realize natural dialogue and communication with players through the Azure application.

4   Pilot Study

We conducted a pilot study to test the learning effects of dance movements and cultural awareness from the game as well as to test the overall usability of the game. Assuming that the game is more useful for teaching dance movement and cultural understanding than simply teaching dance, we also expect the game's overall usability and appeal to be at least satisfactory.

To test the effectiveness of this multimodal interactive narrative serious game in dance education and cultural experience, we recruited 12 participants. To maintain gender balance, we recruited 6 males and 6 females, with an average age of 21.5, the variance is 1.49. Our game focused on a broader extra-cultural audience, and none of the participants fully understood Hmong dance culture. Among them, 6 have experience playing dance games or have basic knowledge of dance, and 6 have no basic knowledge of dance.

For the experiment to proceed smoothly, we will provide players with a set of experimental devices including experimental venues, game platforms, interactive equipment, and evaluation questionnaires. The experimental space is about 2×2 square meters. We will provide participants with a multi-modal interactive folk dance serious game. The interactive equipment consists of a high-definition color camera and a 72-inch TV that supports voice recognition to ensure that participants can obtain a high-quality interaction experience. With these experimental setups, we can collect comprehensive data to validate our experimental hypotheses and draw meaningful conclusions.

We first asked participants to fill out a cognitive consent form and complete a demographic survey, then introduced them to the background and goals of the research, and conducted interviews to communicate during this process while ensuring they understood the purpose of our research. Subsequently, we explained the experimental tasks and game content in detail, elaborating on the three stages of the task and the required technical details. We then guide participants to the display and begin acclimating to our device so they can become familiar with the system's interactions, during which we walk them through step-by-step instructions and answer their questions. After the adaptation phase, each participant experienced the dance game under different conditions with different ways of participating. Evaluation questionnaires will be distributed after the experience of each condition to collect subjective feedback from participants. After players fill out the questionnaire, we will conduct interviews based on the results to obtain more in-depth feedback and insights.

Participants were randomly divided into two groups. One group of members learned the dance through the game, while the other group used the offline teacher's narration method to teach. Members of each group were taken to different spaces, where corresponding dance learning methods were prepared. For this application, a quick explanation of its functions and controls is given. Participants have thirty minutes to learn the dance.

5   Results

The preliminary experimental results are shown in Fig. 4. In particular, the results showed that serious games were slightly better at learning dance compared to offline instruction. Participants who used serious games had an average score of 4040 points, while those who used videos had an average score of 3578 points, but generalizations cannot be made because the difference was not significant. In terms of cultural experience, there is a very obvious gap between the two. The cultural experience effect of games is obviously better than offline teaching. The results of the questionnaire survey are shown in Fig. 5, which are also positive, but again not significant. All the different parts of the program, the possibility of learning dance using serious games, and the overall experience were reviewed positively.

Method		Dancers score						Average
Teaching Game	Dance Movement Learning	4032	4458	5210	3680	2580	4280	4040
	Cultural Experience	8	9	8	7	8	9	8.166666667
Offline Teaching	Dance Movement Learning	2870	3780	4130	5180	2450	3060	3578.333333
	Cultural Experience	3	2	5	5	4	3	3.666666667

Fig. 4. Hmong Dance Movement Learning and Cultural Experience Results

Question	Users answer						Average
How do you rate the ability to learn the dance using the serious game?	8	9	7	8	9	8	8.166666667
How do you rate the overall experience with the serious game?	9	10	7	9	8	10	8.833333333
How do you rate the user interface?	9	10	8	9	8	9	8.833333333
How do you rate the ability of interaction with the displayed dance?	8	10	8	9	8	10	8.833333333
How do you rate the quality of the Hmong dance visualization?	10	9	9	9	7	9	8.833333333
How do you rate the overall experience with the virtual environment?	10	10	8	8	9	9	9
How do you rate the overall experience with the virtual characters?	9	10	8	9	9	10	9.166666667
How do you rate the overall experience with the Hmong culture?	8	9	7	9	9	9	8.5

Fig. 5. Interaction System in Game

6   Conclusion

In this research, we delve into the possibilities of enhancing cultural experiences during the digitization of folk dances. Through a comprehensive analysis of the multimodal performance of folk dance and the interactive narrative game framework, we propose a digital serious game framework for folk dance aimed at improving players' cultural understanding and experience.

We aim to effectively utilize intelligent technology, and combine it with digital dance performance and player experience methods, to effectively enhance the experience of national dance cultural heritage and transform it into rich cultural resources. At the same time, we are also committed to cultivating participants' respect and understanding of cultural diversity and promoting cross-cultural communication and sharing.

Through comparative experiments, we verified the importance of multi-modal content representation and intelligent interaction in enhancing cultural experience. We confirm that the construction of a virtual environment related to national culture plays a key role in the inheritance of national dance and greatly enhances players' sense of immersion. At the same time, players can deeply experience the cultural stories and emotions behind the dance through interactive narrative game participation. This in-depth participation not only makes the learning process more attractive but also enhances players' understanding and emotional investment in national dance culture.

This research aims to promote the development of digital national heritage and provide players with a deeper, more interesting, and more engaging cultural experience while protecting and inheriting precious national dance cultural heritage. Through this research, we expect to provide valuable guidance and support for enhancing and innovating digital cultural heritage projects.

Acknowledgements. This work was supported by a research grant from Shenzhen Key Laboratory of Next Generation Interactive Media Innovative Technology (Funding No: ZDSYS20210623092001004), and the Center for Social Governance and Innovation at Tsinghua University.

References

1. Hou, Y., Kenderdine, S., Picca, D., Egloff, M., Adamou, A.: Digitizing intangible cultural heritage embodied: state of the art. J. Comput. Cult. Herit. **15** (2022). https://doi.org/10.1145/3494837
2. Margounakis, D., Karalis, T., Iliou, T.: Interactive Serious Games for Cultural Heritage. Internet Of Things, Infrastructures And Mobile Applications, pp. 606–617 (2021)
3. Muangmoon, O., Sureephong, P., Tabia, K.: Dance training tool using kinect-based skeleton tracking and evaluating dancer's performance. Adv. Artif. Intell. From Theory Pract. 27–32 (2017)
4. Dimitropoulos, K., et al.: Capturing the intangible an introduction to the i-Treasures project. In: 2014 International Conference On Computer Vision Theory and Applications (VISAPP), vol. 2, pp. 773–781 (2014)
5. Nikolakopoulou, V., et al.: Conveying intangible cultural heritage in museums with interactive storytelling and projection mapping: the case of the mastic villages. Heritage **5**, 1024–1049 (2022). https://www.mdpi.com/2571-9408/5/2/56
6. Bellotti, F., Berta, R., De Gloria, A., D'ursi, A., Fiore, V.: A serious game model for cultural heritage. J. Comput. Cult. Herit. **5** (2013). https://doi.org/10.1145/2399180.2399185
7. Quaggiotto, M., Tresso, T.: Digital storytelling formats for the communication of intangible cultural heritage in rural and marginal territories: the case of the Quattro Province area. AMPS Proc. Ser. **1**, 450–458 (2023)
8. Hajdin, M., Kico, I., Dolezal, M., Chmelik, J., Doulamis, A., Liarokapis, F.: Digitization and visualization of movements of Slovak Folk dances. In: Auer, M., Tsiatsos, T. (eds.) The Challenges of the Digital Transformation in Education. ICL 2018. AISC, vol. 917, pp. 245–256. Springer, Cham (2019). https://doi.org/10.1007/978-3-030-11935-5_24
9. Stavrakis, E., Aristidou, A., Savva, M., Himona, S.L., Chrysanthou, Y.: Digitization of Cypriot Folk dances. In: Ioannides, M., Fritsch, D., Leissner, J., Davies, R., Remondino, F., Caffo, R. (eds.) EuroMed 2012. LNCS, vol. 7616, pp. 404–413. Springer, Heidelberg (2012). https://doi.org/10.1007/978-3-642-34234-9_41
10. Lameras, P., Philippe, S., Oertel, L.: A Serious Game for Amplifying Awareness on Multimodal Teaching: Game Design and Usability Study. Internet Of Things, Infrastructures And Mobile Applications, pp. 559–570(2021)
11. Ziagkas, E., et al.: Greek traditional dances 3D motion capturing and a proposed method for identification through rhythm pattern analyses (Terpsichore Project). In: Kavoura, A., Kefallonitis, E., Theodoridis, P. (eds.) Strategic Innovative Marketing and Tourism. SPBE, pp. 657–665. Springer, Cham (2020). https://doi.org/10.1007/978-3-030-36126-6_73
12. Selmanović, E., et al.: Improving accessibility to intangible cultural heritage preservation using virtual reality. J. Comput. Cult. Herit. **13** (2020). https://doi.org/10.1145/3377143
13. Marques, C., Pedro, J., Araújo, I.: A systematic literature review of gamification in/for cultural heritage: leveling up, going beyond. Heritage **6**, 5935–5951 (2023). https://www.mdpi.com/2571-9408/6/8/312
14. Kico, I., Dolezal, M., Grammalidis, N., Liarokapis, F.: Visualization of Folk-Dances in virtual reality environments. In: Kavoura, A., Kefallonitis, E., Theodoridis, P. (eds.) Strategic Innovative Marketing and Tourism. SPBE, pp. 51–59. Springer, Cham (2020). https://doi.org/10.1007/978-3-030-36126-6_7

Biemodernism and Cultural Computing

Bie-Modernism Cultural Computing of Literary Works of "Three Musketeers of Tie Xi" Based on the Pre-trained Dialogue Models ChatGLM3

Jiafeng Lin[(✉)] [iD] and Zhaoyang Sui [iD]

Shanghai Normal University, Shanghai 200040, People's Republic of China
545773081@qq.com

Abstract. Contemporary China has accelerated its embrace of capitalism and modernization following its Reform and Opening Up. This process has given Chinese society a unique Bie-modern Condition, i.e., a mixed social system of premodernity, modernity, and post-modernity. Bie-modernism is a systematic theory based on this. The theory is constructed with the aim of helping the social subject to accomplish the transcendence of Bie-modernity in order to enable full-fledged modernity. Bie-modernism Cultural Computing is an emerging intersectional theory that refers to Bie-modernism theory's use of computer science, artificial intelligence, and other scientific tools to enter into the study of the cultural field in the hope of reaching its theoretical goals through the methods of cultural computing. In this paper, a total of 46 fiction texts by well-known young Chinese writers Shuang Xuetao, Ban Yu, and Zheng Zhi are taken as the objects of study. In the mid-to-late 1990s, an unprecedented and far-reaching wave of layoffs occurred in Northeast China, resulting in dramatic changes in the lives of nearly 10 million people. These three writers not only grew up in this environment, but also turned their pens to it when they became writers: they quickly gained fame for their brilliant depictions of the experiences and emotions of the people who lived in it. They were named the "Tiexi Three Musketeers" and were regarded by the media as a sign of the "Northeast Renaissance". At the same time, they were also recognized by many critics as the rising "New Northeast Writers Group". In the view of Bie-modernism, because of its significant Bie-modernity, this particular period and the social environment it created can actually be described as a Bie-modern Condition. In the theoretical hypothesis of Bie-modernism, then, the literary works of these three authors would reflect the Bie-modern Condition to some extent. Based on the method of Bie-modernism cultural calculation, this thesis will use the pre-trained dialogue models ChatGLM3 to calculate the percentage of pre-modernity, modernity and post-modernity in the research subjects. This project can be considered as a text classification task for pre-modernity, modernity and post-modernity. And it specifically uses P-Tuning v2 for Prompt Tuning of ChatGLM3-6B. Finally, the model is made to understand the difference between the three feature values and output the classification results in a canonical format.This paper will further find the common features of Shuang Xuetao's, Ban Yu's, and Zheng Zhi's works through percentage analysis, verify the accuracy of the above hypothesis, and make literary criticism. In addition, in the course of the implementation of the study, the theoretical content, the horizons involved and the

M. Rauterberg (Ed.): HCII 2024, LNCS 14717, pp. 339–360, 2024.
https://doi.org/10.1007/978-3-031-61147-6_23

specific methodology of the Bie-modernism Cultural Computing will be further updated.

Keywords: Bie-modern · Bie-modernism Cultural Computing · Large Language Models · ChatGLM3 · P-Tuning v2 · Text Classification

1   The Research Objects, Research Hypothesis, and Goals of This Project

1.1   The Research Objects

The research objects of this project are the well-known literary works of three emerging Chinese writers: Shuang Xuetao, Ban Yu, and Zheng Zhi. After 2015, Shuang Xuetao, Ban Yu, and Zheng Zhi, three Shenyang-born writers who quickly gained fame for writing about the experiences and emotions of workers and their sons and daughters in northeastern China since the economic reforms of the 1990s, came to prominence. They were named the "Three Musketeers of Tiexi" (Tiexi District, part of Shenyang City, Liaoning Province, is one of the central districts of Shenyang City, an old industrial area in China.), and were regarded by the media as a sign of the "Northeast Renaissance". At the same time, they were also recognized by many critics as the rising "New Northeast Writers Group".

It is generally agreed that the main feature of the excellent works of these three writers is that they present, to varying degrees, the modernization process of Northeast China after the Reform and Opening Up. In particular, it depicts people struggling to survive the phenomenon of "wave of layoffs" under the impact of the market economy in the northeastern region, which is an old industrial base. It can be said that this process of modernization gives the people living in it a Chinese Modernity Experience. This particular Modernity Experience has been appropriately categorized and studied by the Bie-modern theory proposed by Chinese scholar Wang Jianjiang. Bie-modern theory suggests that contemporary China entered a temporal state in which pre-modern, modern and post-modern coexisted after the beginning of Reform and Opening up. In this theoretical vision, this particular Modern Experience is referred to as the Bie-modernity Experience. Huang Ping, a professor of Chinese at East China Normal University, describes this experience as "a universal working-class nostalgia hidden in local nostalgia" [1]. The wording of this description is already full of Bie-modern characteristics, and in describing the reasons for the emergence of this group of writers, he aptly says: "The modern dilemma of industrial civilization has made this group of Liaoning writers" [1].

Specifically, this study focuses on a total of 46 selected novels by Shuang Xuetao, Ban Yu, and Zheng Zhi. Among them, 25 of them include Shuang Xuetao's works. 14 works by Ban Yu. Zheng Zhi's works are 7. This number depends on the total amount of works published by the three writers and the specific time of publication, and the selected works are the more representative works among their works [2].

1.2 The Research Hypothesis

Based on the theoretical concept of Bie-modernism, this study argues that the contemporary Chinese society is a Bie-modern society, presenting a Bie-modern Condition, and that Shuang Xuetao, Ban Yu, and Zheng Zhi, as excellent writers of contemporary literature, are able to accurately embody the main features of Bie-modern society in their works: The hybridization of pre-modern, modern and post-modern.

1.3 The Goals of This Project

Based on the Bie-modernism Cultural Computing approach, the pre-trained Large Language Models GLM was applied to compute the percentage of pre-modernity, modernity and post-modernity in the research objects. In this project, the analysis of the percentage of pre-modernity, modernity, and post-modernity can be shortened to an analysis of the percentage of Bie-modernity.

This project will further find the common features of Shuang Xuetao's, Ban Yu's, and Zheng Zhi's works through percentage analysis, verify the accuracy of the above hypothesis, and make literary criticism.

In addition, in the course of the implementation of the study, the theoretical content, the horizons involved and the specific methodology of the Bie-modernism Cultural Computing will be further updated.

2 Introduction to Bie-Modernism Theory and Bie-Modernism Cultural Computing

2.1 The Concept of Bie-Modernity and Social Formation, Characteristics

The concept of "Bie-modern" was proposed by Prof. Wang Jianjiang, a well-known Chinese scholar, in 2014. This academic concept has been used to summarize the state of Chinese society since the Reform and Opening Up. Contemporary China has embraced capitalism and modernization at an accelerated pace following the Reform and Opening Up process. This process has led to a unique spatial and temporal phenomenon in Chinese society. Originally, in the developed countries of the West, epochs were characterized in a linear direction: pre-modern, modern, and post-modern. In China, they exist simultaneously and are characterized by distinctive features. As a result, Prof. Wang Jianjiang creatively used the term "Bie-modern" to summarize this social situation of mixed epochal characteristics, and constructed the theoretical system of Bie-modernism based on this concept.

Specifically, "Bie-modern" refers to the mixed social phenomenon of pre-modernity, modernity and post-modernity that exists in China. The reason for this phenomenon is mainly due to the fact that the process of modernization in China has been distorted by the intervention of many factors. First of all, pre-modernity is still prevalent in Chinese society in social, economic and cultural aspects, and under the feudal system since the Zhou Dynasty, it has been integrated into the social operation mechanism and is difficult to be eradicated. Secondly, China was once in danger of extinction, and after a long period of democratic revolution and wars of unification, it missed the best opportunity to enter the phase of modernization. This led to the fact that China's modernity development was inadequate from the very beginning. Thirdly, when China began the process of modernization with the Reform and Opening up, the elements of modernity introduced from the West were actually already full of post-modernity features, that is, the real sense of China's modernization process was mixed with post-modernity.

The fundamental characteristic of Bie-modern society is the characteristic of "Spatialization of Time". This refers to the co-temporal character of pre-modern, modern and post-modern features existing at the same stage in time. This feature has a distinctive temporal hybridity. Bie-modern society is full of pre-modern elements, such as patriarchy, superstition, blood ties, revenge, corruption, dictatorship, etc. At the same time, it also possesses certain characteristics of a modern society, such as modernized production methods, capital markets, transnational trade, modern science and technology, and the enactment of modern laws. At the same time, this society is also full of post-modernity characteristics, such as people's rebellion against rationality, the use of collage and other post-modern art techniques, and so on. In fact, Bie-modern society is a double-sided interpretation of "unfinished modernity" in Chinese society. Based on the perspective of "modernity", it has not achieved sufficient modernity. Based on the perspective of "post-modernity", it is a state of insufficient modernity that is both "incomplete" and "transcendent".

On the basis of the basic characteristic of "Spatialization of Time", the Bie-modern society has the complexity and variability of "Harmonious Complicity" as its main developmental dynamic structure. "Harmonious Complicity" refers to the blurring of the boundaries and mixing of pre-modern, modern and post-modern elements in Bie-modern society due to the specificity of their localization. This has given rise to characteristics that cannot simply be characterized as pre-modern, modern or post-modern. When China began to embrace capitalist modernity in the 1980s, this collection of rationality, rule of law, democracy, and republican spirit has actually entered the Chinese society, where pre-modernity is deeply rooted, wrapped in the "hidden worries of modernity" and post-modernity. After entering, due to the special social, institutional and conceptual environments, modernity, as an imported product, presents unique local qualities. Failing to purge pre-modernity, this kind of modernity harmonizes with pre-modernity for the sake of survival, completely abandoning its subversive power over pre-modern factors.

As mentioned in Prof. Wang Jianjiang's study: The scomplicity's of the Bie-modern era includes the adaptation and harmonious coexistence of the modern, post-modern and pre-modern in the same society; the non-compliance with the law, the abandonment of principles, the compromise, the mutual deal, the peace and the win-win; the constant change of rules and the practice of subterfuge; the selective forgetting and obscuring of history; the community of interests is knowingly breaking the law. The pre-modern way of thinking and acting is expressed by the absence of modern institutions and the post-modern way of crossing borders, deconstructing centres and dissolving policies and regulations, creating a chaotic harmony" [3].

2.2 Bie-Modernism's Theoretical Purpose and Theoretical Composition

Bie-modernism is a comprehensive theory based on the situation of Bie-modern society. The purpose of this theory is to refine, analyze and study the situation of Bie-modern society with a complete theoretical system, and ultimately to help the social subject to transcend Bie-modernity, so as to contribute to the fullness of modernity. The theory holds that Bie-modern society is a society that has not yet completed the construction of full modernity. Bie-modernism should criticize the many Bie-modern phenomena existing in Bie-modern society under the guidance of the goal of constructing full modernity, and put forward the goal and direction in which Bie-modern society should develop.

Based on the foundation that "Bie-modern is a distillation of the current social situation in China", the theory of Bie-modernism is first and foremost a social theory. That is to say, it not only focuses on social phenomena, but also applies sociological theories to analyze and study Bie-modern society.

Second, the theory of Bie-modernism is a philosophical theory. The theory is named after a philosophical proposition from China: Bie. In the history of Chinese philosophy, it is well connected with the mainstream ideas of Laozi, Zhuangzi, Confucius and later on, Buddhism, Taoism and Confucianism. It fully reflects the generalization of particularity, hybridity, and reflexivity in Chinese philosophy. In addition, Bie-modernism as a philosophical theory pays attention to the individual subjects in the Bie-modern Condition as both the source of the Bie-modern Condition's emergence and the audience that the Bie-modern Condition most deeply affects. The goals of Bie-modernism include the defense of the right to life of individuals in the Bie-modern Condition, which led to the development of the theory of Life Equity.

Thirdly, the main manifestation of Bie-modern society is most noticeable in culture. It is mainly shown in literary and artistic works. Writers and artists living in Bie-modern society are the subjects of Bie-modern Condition. Therefore, the literary works or art works created by them always consciously or unconsciously embody the Bie-modern characteristics of the times. Among them, they can be divided into Bie-modern art and Bie-modernism art. Bie-modern art is to use post-modern art techniques as the main creative techniques, and to create art works whose contents fit the characteristics of Bie-modern, and whose main qualities are hybridization, collage, and chaos. Bie-modernism art is a work of art that expresses criticism, reflection and transcendence of the Bie-modern Condition due to the creator's knowledge of the Bie-modern Condition. Therefore, the theory of Bie-modernism also has the horizons of literary, artistic and aesthetic theories.

Bie-modernism theory does not only include the three main theoretical horizons mentioned above. It also encompasses the theoretical horizons of legal theory, political theory, economic theory, publishing and editing theory, computer science and so on. Therefore, Bie-modernism theory is a systematic theory covering a wide range of cross-industry, interdisciplinary and inter-professional. Currently, there are 27 subcategories in this theoretical system to explain and study Bie-modern Condition, such as "Spatialization of Time" and "Harmonious Complicity" mentioned earlier. This study adopts the part of the Bie-modernism theoretical system that intersects with computer science, i.e., Bie-modernism Cultural Computing.

2.3 The Relationship Between the Research Objects of This Project and Bie-Modernism

In 1997, Li Mo graduated from elementary school. He began to experience a special period of his life: his peers gradually disappeared, the girl he had a crush on suddenly stabbed his teacher with a pen, and his parents spent the whole day worrying about sending cigarettes and alcohol to their leaders. At that time, Li Mo did not know the specific meaning of 'retain the job but suspend the salary' in his parents' mouth. Nor did he know that the word 'layoff' (in this case, the wave of layoffs in northeastern China in the 1990s) would sweep across the northeastern plains and beyond [4].

This is the story of Li Mo, one of the research objects of this study, a character depicted by the writer Shuang Xuetao in his novel Long Ya Shi Dai (The Age of Deafness), and a story that the writer himself experienced. In fact, this is a story that took place in countless ordinary northeastern working families of that era.

After the founding of the People's Republic of China, the implementation of the planned economy system enabled workers in this country to hold the State's "golden rice bowl". Workers are assigned jobs by the State, and the State takes care of all their affairs "from cradle to grave". Due to the special nature of the jobs and the underdeveloped science and technology and legal system in China at that time, this "golden rice bowl" could even be replaced by the heirs of the workers after their retirement, thus giving birth to the saying that this was the golden age of the workers. As China's industrial base, the Northeast had the largest number of factories and workers in the country.

In 1978, the Reform and Opening Up, which actively embraced capitalist modernity, was proposed, and the process of China's real modernization began. The market economy greatly impacted the original planned economic system. As an old industrial base, the Northeast region naturally bore the brunt of the impact. A large number of factories could not compete with the new industries. Under the circumstance of downward economic returns, the collective layoff of workers became inevitable. In February 1983, the National Labor and Personnel Department issued a notice on the trial implementation of the labor contract system, and in 1986, the labor contract system was officially implemented. This move changed the original life-long contractual relationship between the state and the worker.

As China entered the 1990s, it faced the critical moment of joining the globalized market. Since the decision on reform was made, millions of state-owned enterprise workers have been laid off in just a few months, and the intensity of the implementation was beyond expectation - between 1998 and 2000, 7 to 9 million workers were laid off almost every year, and as of 2003, the cumulative total of laid-off workers in state-owned enterprises amounted to 28.18 million. After that, China's accession to the WTO ushered in a rapid economic progress, and the process of modernization was greatly accelerated.

The historical narrative is calm, but the individuals laid off from work are full of surprise and pain. The former "Eldest Sons of the Republic" have fallen into disrepair in the process of modernization. In the process of modernization, more complex and varied patterns are being nurtured. As northeasterners who grew up during this period, Shuang Xuetao, Ban Yu, and Zheng Zhi undoubtedly have rich personal feelings. As writers, their keen capture of these personal experiences and their skillful use of words clearly enable us to see in their literary works the progress of this era, as well as the sorrow and pain of individuals submerged in this historical trend.

After the theory of Bie-modernism was put forward, we have a theoretical tool to analyze these literary works, social phenomena and even historical stages more appropriately and accurately, as well as a theoretical tool that can explain this subject's life experience. In this theoretical field of vision, we can clearly recognize that the life of this new wave can be summarized by "Bie-modern" and can be analyzed by the various categories derived from it.

The literary works of Shuang Xuetao, Ban Yu, and Zheng Zhi are categorized as "New Northeast Literature", and their common feature is that they describe the lives of people who were laid off in the 1990s in Northeast China. In fact, this characteristic is typical and distinctive of Bie-modernity in the vision of Bie-modernism theory. First of all, the wave of layoffs is generated by the impact of the market economy in the process of modernization, which impacts on the economic system that is very rich in pre-modernity. Secondly, in this trend, all kinds of pre-modernity factors conspire with modernity factors, so that the people living in it get the experience of Bie-modernity, witnessing the fresh color when society encounters modernity, and at the same time stimulating the maladjustment arising from its original pre-modern qualities. Furthermore, the rise of modernity has made emotional subjects, including writers, more concerned with the individual rather than the collective, and as a result, the sense of individual rights has been more emphasized. However, as this modernity is mixed with post-modernity, this so-called individual awakening is also rich in the meaning of no subject, and separation, loneliness, and wandering become the recurring textual keywords.

This project attempts to use the methodology of Bie-modernism Cultural Computing to calculate the percentage of pre-modernity, modernity and post-modernity in the texts of the research objects. This will be done in order to verify that Bie-modernity is indeed present in the research object texts and to focus on the level of its significance. Finally, the results will be used as a basis for textual analysis and criticism.

2.4 Bie-Modernism Cultural Computing

Bie-modernism Cultural Computing is an emerging cross-cutting theory that refers to the theory of Bie-modernism as a doctrine of social analysis, utilizing scientific tools such as computer science and artificial intelligence into the study of the cultural field. In the post-truth era, Bie-modernism Cultural Computing is concerned with the difference between real modernity and pseudo-modernity, the real world and the false world. Its fundamental purpose is to eliminate pseudo-modernity with the help of computational means and touch the real modernity and the real world [5].

Currently, Bie-modernism Cultural Computing is mainly applied to Bie-human research, artificial intelligence writing analysis and the proportion of modernity elements in literary works. Combined with the existing research results, it can be seen that this theory not only updates the scope of application of computer theory tools, but also greatly broadens the research space in the field of culture, provides a new possibility for the production of knowledge, and enriches the theoretical content of cross-disciplines.

Previously, Prof. Wang Jianjiang and other scholars studied the percentage of modernity in world literary masterpieces through Bie-modernism Cultural Computing [3] Their project used nearly 500 feature labels and another nearly 100 feature labels to generate sentence vectors after splitting the dataset using Bert-Base-Chinese for pre-training, and the processed data was fed into a model built by Transformer and MLP neural networks for training. After validation, the predicted text was first divided into sentences by using a full stop as a separator, and then these sentences were fed to the training model for prediction, and the prediction results were written into a table to obtain the number of pre-modernity, modernity and post-modernity in it, and their percentage of the total text. Their project successfully analyzed the content of modernity in the world's literary masterpieces and with its experimental results successfully verified the key to the success of the novels of Nobel Prize winner Mo Yan.

The methodology of Bie-modernism Cultural Computing can be divided into Bie-modernism Cultural Computing Method, Bie-modernism Percentage Analysis Method. The cultural calculation method is actually a method of taking cultural products as research objects and calculating and analyzing them through computer science. Specific methods include word frequency statistics, sentiment analysis, and so on. With the introduction of pre-trained Large Language Models, the methods of cultural computation are even richer, for example, the method used in this study is to fine-tune and train the existing Large Language Modeling tool GLM to recognize the context indicated by a specific text, and to further identify the categories of modernity indicated by the text in order to compute the proportionate content of modernityty in the study text.

The Bie-modernism percentage analysis method, on the other hand, uses Bie-modernism as a guiding theory to analyze epochs in social formations across borders using gold identification (i.e., percentage of gold content) in order to characterize the specific attributes of the epoch. This analytical approach is simultaneously able to be introduced into the theory of social computing for development.

Inspired by the research of Prof. Wang Jianjiang and others, we intend to use another specific cultural computing approach to study the literary text analysis of our research object. This approach is unfolded under the open-source pre-training framework GLM developed based on the deep learning model Transformer, and the open-source Chinese-English bilingual dialog model chatGLM3-6B developed based on this framework is utilized for model training. And through the self-built dataset for Prompt Tuning, the text generation by chatGLM3 is used as the representation of text classification, and the final calculation results.

2.5 Considerations for This Project

In addition to the following elements, complex feature intermixing should also be considered. Therefore, during the acquisition of the dataset used for pre-training, this study will prioritize the percentage of various modernity in the selected data (sentences, paragraphs) and select the one with the largest percentage as the most salient feature for that data.

A. Pre-modernity, modernity, and post-modernity elements in the study of the material and environmental aspects of the text.
B. Pre-modernity, modernity, and post-modernity elements in the study of the institutional and legal aspects of the text.

C. Pre-modernity, modernity, and post-modernity elements in the study of the thoughts and ideas aspects of the text.

D. The author's critical, transcendental portrayal of the Bie-modern Condition as reflected in the research text.

3 Pre-trained Large Language Models GLM and Experimental Methodology

3.1 Natural Language Processing and Large Language Models

The concept of Natural Language Processing (NLP) began to take shape roughly in the 1950s, with the rise of computer science and early explorations of artificial intelligence, which led to attempts to use computers to process and understand human language. Since then, Natural Language Processing has gone through several stages of development, from the initial rule-based approaches to statistical methods to today's deep learning-based approaches. Currently, the industry mainly uses language modeling approaches to solve natural language processing problems. And language modeling can be divided into four main development stages: Statistical Language Models (SLMs), Neural Language Models (NLMs), Pre-training Models (PLMs) and Large Language Models (LLMs).

Typically, LLMs refers to Transformer Language Models that contain tens or even hundreds of billions. These models are trained on large-scale textual data, such as GPT-3, PaLM, Galactica, and LLaMA. In the field of natural language processing, especially pre-trained Large Language Models, LLMs have demonstrated a strong ability to understand natural language and solve complex tasks (through text generation), and can be applied to a wide range of natural language processing tasks [6]. The main applications include: text classification, text generation, knowledge acquisition, question and answer systems, natural language reasoning, and code generation.

3.2 Reasons for Choosing LLMs for This Project

There are many Chinese Large Language Models in the industry, but there are fewer studies combining LLMs with Chinese-related academic theories, for example, the latest papers related to Bie-modernism Cultural Computing only use Transformer and MLP-based implementations [3], i.e., based on the Neural Linguistic Models and pre-training models, which are typical of small language models.

LLMs' Emergent Abilities are defined as "capabilities that do not exist in a small model but arise in a large model" [7]. This is one of the most significant features that distinguish LLMs from previously pre-trained models. These include in-context learning (ICL), which generates the expected output for a test instance by completing the input text in a sequence of words without additional training or gradient updating, as well as instruction following and step-by-step reasoning [8] These features allow LLMs to handle complex text classification tasks better than small pre-trained models.

Bie-modernism is more abstract as a humanistic theory. We need to hypothesize the components of pre-modernity, modernity, and post-modernity respectively in the context of the text. This task is required to analyze the data of Chinese novel corpora and derive specific calculation results. So we need to use the LLMs tuning with the processing of large amount of text, and the ability of basic reasoning. Therefore, both in terms of innovation in the application of Bie-modernism Cultural Computing and in terms of considering the contextual reasoning capabilities required for this complex and huge text classification task, we chose to use LLMs and tune it to solve the text classification problem about Bie-modern Condition.

3.3 Training and Tuning of LLMs

The formation of an LLMs consists of several stages. In the field of natural language processing, the first step is to produce a corpus. In order to pre-train the LLMs, a mixture of different data sources is required instead of a single corpus. After that, data preprocessing is performed, which generally includes steps such as: quality filtering, de-emphasis, privacy reduction and tokenization.

The second stage is the architecture design of LLMs, which is commonly used by LLMs as Transformer. Different LLMs choose different architectures, which are roughly categorized into three types, i.e., encoder-decoder architecture, causal decoder architecture, and prefix decoder architecture. In addition, the respective configurations of the four main components of the Transformer, including normalization, position embeddings, activation functions, and attention and bias, are crucial for LLMs. Their differences play a significant role in the performance of LLMs.

The next step is to perform pre-training, through pre-training on large-scale corpora, LLMs can acquire fundamental language understanding and generation capabilities, playing a crucial role in encoding general knowledge into the extensive model parameters. For training LLMs, there are two commonly used pre-training tasks, i.e., language modeling and denoising autoencoding. There are also many optimization methods, and these are also useful for training LLMs, such as batch training and adjusting the learning rate. At this point, the pre-training of LLMs has been basically completed, and some basic Q&A and text processing based on the initial corpora can be performed.

After pre-training, LLMs can acquire generalized capabilities to solve various tasks. However, a growing body of research suggests that LLMs' capabilities can be further adapting to specific goals. The original corpora did not have enough texts related to Bie-modern theory. The Bie-modernism-related text processing carried out in this research requires tuning based on the pre-trained LLMs: we input the Bie-modern-related texts we collected and trained them. There are many ways of tuning, such as Prompt Tuning and Fine-tuning. Fine-tuning, which is currently commonly used in the industry, usually involves updating the model's task-specific parameters, which may include some or all of the model's parameters, and it allows the model to learn based on task-specific data, thus improving its performance on that task.

This time we will choose Prompt Tuning. Therefore, focus on Prompt Tuning and explain why it was chosen. Prompt Tuning is a simple and effective mechanism used to learn "soft prompts" to conditionally fine-tune pretrained language models for specific downstream tasks. This approach, learned through backpropagation, allows adjustments to include signals from any number of token examples. Unlike the discrete text prompts used in GPT-3, Prompt Tuning employs end-to-end learning, enabling tuning to include signals from any number of token examples [9] Specifically, Prompt Tuning adds trainable successive prompt vectors to the input sequence, e.g., in a text classification task, where the input text is combined with the prompt vectors, and then predicts the mask tokens that follow the prompt vectors. Only the prompt vectors are updated during the training process, while the other parameters of the pre-trained language models remain fixed. Compared with fully fine-tuning the pre-trained language models, Prompt Tuning requires only few parameters to be adjusted, which can reduce training time and storage cost. At the same time, it can avoid storing a copy of the models for each task, simplifying the deployment process.

Prompt Tuning typically requires fewer computational resources since it only updates a small number of parameters, making it a more efficient training option, especially when resources are limited. Also, Prompt Tuning maintains the generalization ability of the model to a certain extent since it does not involve a full tuning of the model backbone, making it better able to migrate to new and unseen tasks. So Prompt Tuning is suitable for those cases where there is less task-specific data or the model cannot be completely retrained. At the end of the tuning, based on the task definition, we can then evaluate the model and test the generated results against the specific task.

3.4 Introduction to General Language Model and ChatGLM3-6B

GLM (General Language Model) is a pre-training framework for generalized language models based on autoregressive blank infilling [10]. Its main features are reflected in the pre-training objective, where the model is asked to generate missing words by autoregressive blank infilling by randomly masking consecutive word fragments in the input text. This blank-filling pre-training approach combines the advantages of self-encoder and auto-regressive language models; in terms of model architecture, GLM possesses the use of a single Transformer encoder, which normalizes the order and residual connectivity by rearranging the layers; 2D positional encodings; parameter sharing; and support for multi-task learning, which allows for the simultaneous optimization of multiple pre-training objectives, among others.

ChatGLM3-6B is an open-source dialog bot developed based on the GLM-130B model with 61 billion parameters, which is a 10% scale version of GLM-130B for both English and Chinese, mainly used for Chinese Q&A. It uses the GLM algorithm as the model architecture with the bidirectional attention mechanism [11].

The most beneficial feature of the GLM model that we support in this research is the 2D positional encodings. The GLM uses the novel 2D positional encodings to represent the relative positional information within the word fragments, which allows the model to process multiple word answers without changing the number of [MASK] tokens, which is very important to support the autoregressive generation as well as the analysis of long texts. Our current Bie-modernist text classification and analysis task is to classify long text. And GLM achieves state-of-the-art results in both natural language understanding and text generation tasks, which demonstrates its advantages in general-purpose language modeling. Specifically, GLM's average F1 score on the SuperGLUE benchmark test set is 4.6%-5.0% higher than that of BERT [10].

The task of this project is essentially a text classification task, so the next section focuses on the process by which the GLM categorizes text by converting the text classification task into a cloze generating task, which in turn categorizes the text. Typically, for downstream Natural Language Understanding (NLU) tasks, a linear classifier accepts as input a representation of sequences or tokens generated by a pre-trained model and predicts the correct label. These practices differ from generative pre-training tasks and lead to inconsistencies between pre-training and fine-tuning. Instead, GLM reconceptualizes the NLU classification task as a cloze generative task, following the approach of PET (Schick and Schütze, 2020a) [12]. Specifically, given a labeled example (x, y), the input text x is converted to a close question c(x) by a pattern containing a single mask token. For example, in a sentiment classification task, a candidate label y ∈ Y is mapped to a close answer, called verbalizer v(y), e.g., converting "positive" to "good" [10]. Each label y corresponds to verbalizer v(y), so $p(v(y)|c(x))$ denotes the probability of predicting label y given a cloze question. The final probability distribution p(y|x) is obtained by normalization. The model is trained by maximizing p(y|x) so that the model can predict the correct sentiment classification label y based on the input text x.

(1) is the specific equation:

$$p(y|x) = \frac{p(v(y)|c(x))}{\sum_{y' \in Y} p(v(y')|c(x))} \tag{1}$$

As a result, with this transformation, GLM is able to achieve better performance on text classification tasks. The reason for choosing ChatGLM3-6B is that it is the better of the current open-source pre-trained large models in the Chinese task of low data volume fine-tuning training. In order to get the low data volume fine-tuning training, the output obtained from long text input is as accurate as possible.

3.5 Specific Experimental Methods for This Project

Specifically, the main steps in this study are preprocessing data, model tuning training, and output result validation.

A. The manually labeled raw data is preprocessed using Python so that it outputs a JSONL file. The dataset structure is divided into Prompt, Response. Prompt is used as a command to request the model output format, and the textual content (words or sentences) that characterize modernity, pre-modernity, and post-modernity. Output is the result of the attribution of modernity, pre-modernity, and post-modernity facets.
B. We utilize the ChatGLM3 source code with the ChatGLM3-6B model in conjunction with our own dataset for model tuning, and use the P-Tuning v2 method to achieve fine-tuning, which is efficiently fine-tuned by introducing consecutive Prompts at each layer of the pre-training models, as well as adjusting a very small percentage of the parameters. Checkpoint is then obtained to save the parameters of the model, i.e., weights and biases as well as the performance metrics achieved when trained to that point in time.
C. After training, the text content of the research object is inputted, and the model is asked to output the weight of pre-modernity, modernity and post-modernity in the research object, in order to analyze and verify the significance of Bie-modernity in the research object.

4 Specific Course of the Experiment

4.1 Experimental Environment

ChatGLM3-6B development team's hardware requirements based on practice are memory >= 8 GB, video memory: >= 5 GB (1060 6 GB, 2060 6 GB). In addition, Python version 3.10.12 is recommended, Transformer's library version 4.30.2 is recommended, and Torch version 2.0 and above is recommended for the best inference performance.

Our environmental information as shown in Table 1 is compliant.

Table 1. Experimental environment.

Environment Information	Version/ Configuration
OS	ubuntu22.04
Python	Python 3.10
pyTorch	2.1.0
transformers	4.30.2
Cuda	12.1
CPU	16vCPU Intel(R) Xeon(R) Platinum 8352V CPU @ 2.10 GHz
GPU	RTX 4090 (24 GB) * 1

4.2 Data Preparation

We prepare a collection of examples for pre-modernity, modernity and post-modernity text collection, first of all, extract the sentences in the book in the EXCEL file and mark in front of each sentence whether it is pre-modernity, modernity or post-modernity. Then use Python's pandas and json libraries to transform the file into a JSONL file and transform each piece of data into a {"prompt": "<prompt text>", "response": "<response text>"} format.

For example:

{"prompt": "请识别以下文本, 判断它属于前现代性, 现代性, 还是后现代性: 小姑抓着一把毛嗑儿, 侧身斜卧在炕上, 跟我奶摆扑克, 上下两横排, 各六张打头的, 这叫十二月, 算命用的, 能看出来今年哪个月顺当, 哪个月里有坎坷。", "response": "前现代性"}.

The text of the study is in Chinese, so the examples are also in Chinese. The content of the paradigm can be translated as "{"prompt": "Identify the following text and determine whether it is pre-modernity, modernity, or post-modernity: Auntie grabbed a handful of sunflower seeds, reclined on her side on the bed, and set up a poker game with my mother: two horizontal rows of six heads up and six down. This is called December. It's for fortune-telling, so you can tell which month is going to be good this year, and which one is going to be rough.", "response": "pre-modernity"}". This sample text taken from 《盘锦豹子》 (Leopard of Panjin) by author Ban Yu.

4.3 Model Tuning

After importing the data into the model, fine-tuning can begin. The method we have chosen falls under the category of prompt tuning, specifically the P-Tuning v2 method, which is a proprietary fine-tuning technique for the ChatGLM model. Previous prompt tuning methods do not perform well on small to medium sized LLMs, especially for difficult sequence labeling tasks. In contrast, the P-tuning v2 used in this work increases the tuning capability by adding successive prompt vectors to each layer of the pre-trained models, matching or even exceeding the performance of fine-tuning and requiring very little parameter tuning.

The key features of P-Tuning v2 are the extension of the P-tuning and Prefix-tuning methods and the enhancement of model performance by integrating Deep Prompt Encoding and Multi-task Learning strategies [13].

Here is a brief description of both strategies:

Deep Prompt Encoding: Instead of just introducing prompts at the input layer of the model, P-Tuning v2 embeds learnable continuous prompt vectors in each attention layer of the Transformer models. These prompt vectors participate in the attention computation as additional key and value vectors, thus directing the model to focus on task-relevant input features. This approach not only significantly increases the proportion of learnable parameters in the model, but also ensures efficient parameterization.

Multi-task Learning: P-Tuning v2 utilizes a multi-task learning strategy to pre-train continuous prompt vectors based on datasets from multiple tasks, and then migrates this learned knowledge to downstream tasks. Since the initialization of continuous prompt vectors is usually random, which may lead to optimization difficulties, P-Tuning v2 achieves multi-task pre-training by training multiple datasets simultaneously and sharing the parameters of continuous prompt vectors to provide a more optimal initialization for the prompt vectors.

In terms of implementation, P-Tuning v2 fuses these vectors by introducing successive prompt vectors in each attentional layer of the model and utilizing the path of the pastkeyvalues parameter. This approach enables parameter-efficient fine-tuning of large models on resource-limited hardware.

In summary, P-Tuning v2 effectively improves the performance and generalization of the model, enabling it to adapt to various downstream tasks while maintaining efficient parameter utilization.

In general, the larger the data volume, the lower the total number of epoch. The larger the data volume, the larger the batchsize is recommended to design. And the product of batchsize and steps is the total data volume. Because we have less data volume this time, so we will adjust the batchsize smaller. Empirically, the relationship between the total data volume X and the above parameters can be viewed as Eq. (2).

$$X = \text{MAX\_STEP} \times \text{BATCHSIZE} \times \text{gradient\_accumulation\_steps} \qquad (2)$$

Therefore, the main parameter to be tuned is: LR (Learning Rate), which indicates how fast the parameters are updated when fine-tuning the model. Generally, a smaller learning rate results in a more stable training process, but may take more time to converge. This value is used as 2e−2.

MAX_SOURCE_LEN and MAX_TARGET_LEN: These two parameters control the maximum length of the input and output sequences. They are set to 1024 and 128, respectively.

DEV_BATCH_SIZE: This is the size of each batch, i.e. the number of examples used in each optimization step. Adjusting this to 1 will cause the model to use very few samples for each update.

GRAD_ACCUMULARION_STEPS: This is the number of steps of gradient accumulation before a single parameter update is performed. It is set to 16. This means that the model will perform 16 forward and backward propagations before performing a single parameter update.

MAX_STEP: Maximum number of steps for training. Set to: 100.

SAVE_INTERVAL: The number of steps between model saves. Set to: 500.

Finally, the script is run and the tuned model can be run after successful training.

4.4 Model Training and Test

Figure 1 is a plot of the loss curve we drew based on the train.log using the Matplotlib library in python. Because of the small amount of data in this project, and the text classification task is relatively simple compared to the complex text generation task, the loss decreases faster, and it has converged when the step is nearly 10. This shows that the model training effect is good.

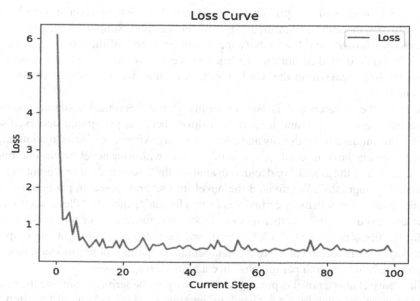

Fig. 1. Loss curve

The ratio of the training set to the test set for this training model was approximately 9:1, with 1344 data in the training set coming from a portion of the study text, and 198 data in the test set sampled from text outside of that portion of the text. Both sets were collected during the same time period and completed by the same person.

The model training method is a the model tuning, so the validation method is different from the traditional deep learning method, more simple. The test approach is to add the specified text "Please identify the following text and determine whether it belongs to pre-modernity, modernity, or post-modernity:" from training the model in front of each piece of data, integrate it into TXT format, and input it into the model to cycle the input and output to get the text classification results for each piece of data, i.e., pre-modernity, modernity, and post-modernity. The model accuracy is derived by comparing it with the previous manual classification results. Equation (3) is the calculation of the accuracy.

$$\text{Accuracy} = \frac{\text{Number of Correct Predictions}}{\text{Total Number of Predictions}} \tag{3}$$

The output of this project was measured to be 73.74% correct. Considering the complexity of the Bie-modern Condition, the confusing nature of pre-modernity, modernity, and post-modernity texts, the unknown nature of the original LLMs corpora, and the small amount of data, we believe that the training task worked well.

4.5 Data Input

The research object s of this project are the 46 novels of Shuang Xuetao, Ban Yu and Zhneg Zhi. So, the sample identified is one novel at a time. Simply entering the entire novel in TXT format would not satisfy the maximum length of the input sequence. So we use Python's os and re libraries to batch process novel files in TXT format. First remove the line breaks from the whole novel. After that, we use "!。?" as the basis to split sentences.

Because the research text is Bie-modernity in the theoretical assumptions, each chapter may have multiple and frequent transitions between paragraphs and even sentences of pre-modernity, modernity and post-modernity. After several tests, reading experience, balancing the contextual variations of passages within the novel and the maximum input sequence of the model, we decided to analyze three sentences as one input to form a "research paragraphs". We divided the novel into several "research paragraphs" and preceded each string with the specified text format for tuning models: "Please identify the below text and determine whether it is pre-modernity, modernity, or post-modernity:". Finally, the file is composed of TXT format, and the batch cycle of input and output is performed in the model to calculate the number and proportion of pre-modern, modern, and post-modern "research paragraphs" in each novel, respectively.

The above is how a novel is processed. Next we edit the script to combine the novels to be processed into one folder for batch processing, combine the output files into one folder as well, and finally process the counting files to output the overall scale graph through Python's matplotlib library.

4.6 Data Output

Run the script, because this training standardizes the output format of the model, so this task can be regarded as a text classification task. That is, in the target folder batch output of each novel text "research paragraphs" features pre-modernity, modernity and post-modernity number and percentage.

Table 2 shows the specific identification data of the research object s (46 novels) of this project. The data in the pre-modernity, modernity, and post-modernity columns are the corresponding percentages of "research paragraphs" in the novels, and the total value of the three items is one.

4.7 Deficiencies of the Experiment

This experiment still has some deficiencies. The first is the small amount of training dataset. Although the text classification task of categorizing "three-sentence paragraphs" into three types of features used in this study is relatively simple for ChatGLM3-6B, the composition of the Bie-modern Condition is more complex. The initial corpora do not have comprehensive knowledge accumulation in this area and cannot accurately perform inferences after fine-tuning with a small amount of training dataset, so we may increase the data volume by 1–2 orders of magnitude in the future to continue the experiment.

The second thing is that the models chosen for this project are the base models of the GLM series, not only the more powerful and longer text-supporting models such as ChatGLM3-6B-Base and ChatGLM3-6B-32K, as well as other excellent models. As of the time of submission, the more advanced GLM4 is available. We will continue to model fine-tune the training and comparative analysis in the future.

Thirdly, the initial corpora of LLMs used in this experiment is not accurate enough for Bie-modern content recognition, which can lead to difficulties in pre-training and computation and increase the difficulty of fine-tuning. This ends up having an impact on the results of the calculations. The Bie-modern Condition is a more complex social system, so the methods and ideas for its study still need to be improved and innovated.

5 Results of This Project and Critical Analysis

5.1 Results of This Project

According to the experimental output, pre-modernity, modernity and post-modernity proportions account for 38.83%, 40.45%, and 20.72% of the study text as a whole, as shown in Fig. 2. This result illustrates that the theory of Bie-modernism is correct in its assumption of the existence of a Bie-modern Condition in the study text, accomplishing the goals of this project.

Specifically, among the three writers, the percentage of Bie-modernity in the works of Shuang Xuetao and Ban Yu is very close, while the data of Zheng Zhi's works are more unique, as shown in Table 2.

Table 2. Data on the percentage of pre-modernity, modernity and post-modernity in the research texts [14].

Writers	Name of the novel and date of publication	Pre-modernity	Modernity	Post-modernity
Shuang Xuetao	翅鬼 (Winged Ghost) 2012	48.29%	17.89%	33.72%
	我的朋友安德烈 (My Friend Andreas) 2013	39.69%	39.69%	20.62%
	无赖 (Rogue) 2013	50.89%	33.93%	15.18%
	冷枪 (Sniper's Shot) 2014	44%	38%	18%
	大路 (Main Road) 2014	16.67%	46.15%	37.18%
	跛人 (Lame Man) 2014	22.22%	44.44%	33.33%
	长眠 (Long Sleep) 2014	37.98%	37.24%	24.81%
	大师 (Great Master) 2014	52.80%	41.60%	5.60%
	自由落体 (Free Fall) 2015	31.47%	49.65%	18.88%
	终点 (Endpoint) 2015	22.22%	72.22%	5.56%
	平原上的摩西 (Moses On The Plain) 2015	42.45%	46.51%	12.05%
	走出格勒 (Step Out of Geller) 2015	38.32%	42.99%	18.69%
	跷跷板 (See-saw) 2016	35.00%	45.83%	19.17%
	光明堂 (Hall of Light) 2016	56.94%	25.47%	17.60%
	天吾手记 (Tian Wu's Notes) 2016	23.13%	48.82%	28.05%
	聋哑时代 (Age of Deafness) 2016	34.96%	38.24%	26.80%
	宽吻 (Bottle-nose) 2017	18.62%	55.86%	25.52%
	北方化为乌有 (The North Has Been Reduced to Nothing) 2017	40.41%	40.41%	19.18%
	飞行家 (Aviator) 2017	42.05%	40.73%	17.22%
	间距 (Interval) 2017	26.71%	41.61%	31.68%
	起夜 (Wake Up at Night) 2019	41.44%	34.23%	24.32%
	剧场 (Theatre) 2019	32.41%	43.52%	24.07%
	猎人 (Hunter) 2019	32.43%	25.68%	41.89%
	心脏 (Heart) 2019	30.68%	50.00%	19.32%
	杨广义 (Yang Guangyi) 2019	66.67%	28.79%	4.55%

(continued)

Table 2. (*continued*)

Writers	Name of the novel and date of publication	Pre-modernity	Modernity	Post-modernity
	Summary of data	21.71%	41.16%	37.12%
Ban Yu	工人村 (Workers' Village) 2016	51.64%	31.34%	17.01%
	盘锦豹子 (Leopard in Panjin) 2017	53.62%	34.78%	11.59%
	渠潮 (Tide in Canal) 2017	38.60%	39.30%	22.10%
	山脉 (Mountains) 2018	22.54%	50.87%	26.59%
	逍遥游 (Xiao Yao You) 2018	41.87%	35.96%	22.17%
	冬泳 (Winter Swimming) 2018	43.75%	42.61%	13.64%
	肃杀 (Chill) 2018	40.85%	40.85%	18.31%
	空中道路 (Pathways in the Air) 2018	25.26%	51.58%	23.16%
	枪墓 (Gun Grave) 2018	37.13%	47.52%	15.35%
	双河 (Two Rivers) 2019	32.32%	50.00%	17.68%
	蚁人 (Ant Man) 2019	25%	40.62%	34.38%
	夜莺湖 (Lake Nightingale) 2020	44.76%	26.57%	28.67%
	梯形夕阳 (Trapezoidal Sunset) 2020	35.42%	43.75%	20.83%
	安妮 (Annie) 2020	13.95%	51.16%	34.88%
	Summary of data	21.83%	42.07%	36.10%
Zheng Zhi	生吞 (Swallow Raw) 2017	52.89%	31.86%	15.25%
	仙症 (Immortal's Disease) 2018	65.86%	23.69%	10.44%
	蒙卡地罗食人记 (Cannibalism at Moncadillo's) 2019	49.47%	36.17%	14.36%
	他心通 (Telepathy) 2019	58.44%	33.12%	08.44%
	森中有林 (Forest within Forest) 2019	51.65%	38.05%	10.29%
	凯旋门 (Triumphal Arch) 2020	49.07%	41.61%	09.32%
	霹雳 (Thunderbolt) 2020年	25.40%	38.09%	36.51%
	Summary of data	50.40%	34.66%	14.94%

In Shuang Xuetao's works, pre-modernity accounts for 21.71%, modernity accounts for 41.16%, and post-modernity accounts for 37.12%.

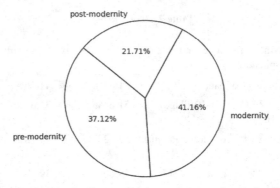

Fig. 2. Percentage of premodernity, modernity, and postmodernity in all research texts.

In Ban Yu's work, pre-modernity accounts for 21.83%, modernity accounts for 42.07%, and post-modernity accounts for 36.10%.

In Zheng Zhi's works, pre-modernity accounts for 50.40%, modernity accounts for 34.66%, and post-modernity accounts for 14.94%.

5.2 Critical Analysis

In the experimental results, we conclude that Shuang Xuetao's works are very similar to Ban Yu's works in terms of data. This also verifies the reading experience of most readers: in the evaluation of "Three Musketeers of Tiexi", Shuang Xuetao and Ban Yu are always mentioned together, and they are always the two most frequently mentioned. Obviously, whether from the readers' reading or according to our experiments, the styles of the works of these two authors are relatively close to each other. Of course, the two also have considerable differences, but this would require a separate study to explore more deeply.

This is certainly not meant to be a comparison of the merits of the three authors' works. Compared to Shuang Xuetao and Ban Yu, Zheng Zhi became famous later, although he started writing earlier.Zheng Zhi's initial writing focused on young adult stories that were generally considered less readable by readers, while the masterpiece that made him famous, Swallowed Raw, was critically acclaimed. This leads us to notice another remarkable data in the experimental results, the percentage of pre-modernity in Zheng Zhi's works is much higher than that of post-modernity and modernity.This data shows that more pre-modernity factors are reflected in his fictional texts, which is also in line with the readers' experiential feelings. In fact, we can also find this feature in the naming of his novels. At the same time, we can also find the gradual change of his writing style from the change of the percentage of post-modernity in his works. Interestingly, for his literary works, researchers often consider using Lacan's psychoanalytic doctrine for their studies [1]. This can also be considered as a complex expression of the Bie-modern Condition.

The results of this project show that there is indeed a "Bie-modern" character in the fictional texts of the emerging group of Chinese writers, the "New Northeast Writers Group". Based on the reading experience, readers tend to classify the works of these three authors into the scope of realist literature. This classification can show that Bie-modern Condition exists not only in literary works but also in the real world. On the one hand, this condition enters the literary work in the writer's capture of it; on the other hand, the reader reads these literary works, gains a reading experience of the Bie-modern Condition, and in turn empathizes with them by the extent to which this experience is relevant to his or her own life experience, and favors these literary works.

In conclusion, the results of this project are accurate and credible, and the research methods used in this project are worthy of continued exploration and improvement, and are useful for updating Bie-modernism Cultural Computing.

References

1. 黄平.: 出东北记. 上海文艺出版社, 上海 (2021). (in Chinese)
2. These are selected from their published novels and novellas. Separately: 双雪涛.: 平原上的摩西. 百花文艺出版社, 天津 (2016); 双雪涛.: 飞行家. 广西师范大学出版社, 桂林 (2017); 双雪涛.: 翅鬼. 广西师范大学出版社, 桂林 (2019); 双雪涛.: 猎人. 北京日报出版社, 北京 (2019); 双雪涛.: 聋哑时代. 广西师范大学出版社, 桂林 (2020); 双雪涛.: 天吾手记. 北京日报出版社, 北京 (2022); 班宇.: 冬泳. 上海三联书店, 上海 (2018); 班宇.: 逍遥游. 春风文艺出版社, 沈阳 (2020); 郑执.: 生吞. 浙江文艺出版社, 杭州 (2017); 郑执.: 仙症. 北京日报出版社, 北京 (2020). (in Chinese)
3. Wang, J., Chen, H., Ma, T., Qi, Z., Yang, Z., Zhang, S.: A cultural computing of the share of modernity in world literary masterpieces by bie-modernism. In: Rauterberg, M. (ed.) HCII 2023. LNCS, vol. 14035, pp. 603–617. Springer, Cham (2023). https://doi.org/10.1007/978-3-031-34732-0_47
4. 双雪涛.: 聋哑时代. 广西师范大学出版社, 桂林 (2020). (in Chinese)
5. Wang, J., Chen, H.: Bie-modernism and cultural computing. In: Rauterberg, M. (ed.) HCII 2021. LNCS, vol. 12795, pp. 474–489. Springer, Cham (2021). https://doi.org/10.1007/978-3-030-77431-8_30
6. Zhao, W.X., et al.: A Survey of Large Language Models. ArXiv, abs/2303.18223 (2023). https://doi.org/10.48550/arXiv.2303.18223
7. Wei, J., et al.: Emergent abilities of large language models. ArXiv, abs/2206.07682 (2022). https://doi.org/10.48550/arXiv.2206.07682
8. Brown, T.B., et al. (2020). Language models are few-shot learners. ArXiv, abs/2005.14165 (2020)
9. Lester, B., Al-Rfou, R., Constant, N.: The power of scale for parameter-efficient prompt tuning. In: Moens, M.-F., Huang, X.J., Specia, L., Yih, S.W. (eds.) Proceedings of the 2021 Conference on Empirical Methods in Natural Language Processing, pp. 3045–3059. Association for Computational Linguistics, Kerrville (2021). https://doi.org/10.18653/v1/2021.emnlp-main.243
10. Du, Z., et al.: GLM: general language model pretraining with autoregressive blank infilling. In: Muresan, S., Nakov, P., Villavicencio, A. (eds.) Proceedings of the 60th Annual Meeting of the Association for Computational Linguistics, Volume 1: Long Papers, pp. 320–335. Association for Computational Linguistics, Kerrville (2021). https://doi.org/10.18653/v1/2022.acl-long.26
11. Zeng, A., et al.: GLM-130B: an open bilingual pre-trained model. ArXiv, abs/2210.02414 (2022). https://doi.org/10.48550/arXiv.2210.02414
12. Schick, T., Schütze, H.: Exploiting cloze-questions for few-shot text classification and natural language inference. In: Merlo, P., Tiedemann, J., Tsarfaty, R. (eds.) Proceedings of the

16th Conference of the European Chapter of the Association for Computational Linguistics, pp. 255–269. Association for Computational Linguistics, Kerrville (2020). https://doi.org/10.18653/v1/2021.eacl-main.20

13. Liu, X., Ji, K., Fu, Y., Du, Z., Yang, Z., Tang, J.: P-tuning v2: prompt tuning can be comparable to fine-tuning universally across scales and tasks. ArXiv, abs/2110.07602 (2021). https://doi.org/10.48550/arXiv.2110.07602

14. Since there are no official translations of these literary works, they are presented in the original Chinese language and translated into English according to the Chinese meaning in parentheses to facilitate comprehension

Bie-modernism: From Cultural Computing to Social Computing

Jiafeng Lin[✉] [ID]

Shanghai Normal University, Shanghai 200040, People's Republic of China
ljf_helloworld@163.com

Abstract. Bie-modernism theory is an international and comprehensive theory. It is based on the exact capture and generalization of the social condition in the process of modernization in the late-developed countries, so it can be considered first and foremost as a theory of social analysis. This social condition has been named "Bie-modern", i.e., Bie-modern Condition. As far as China is concerned, the Bie-modern Condition has begun to emerge since contemporary China entered the process of high-speed modernization through the Reform and Opening-up. The main characteristic of Bie-modern Condition is the "Spatialization of Time": the simultaneous existence of pre-modernity, modernity and post-modernity in society, all three of which do not have a linear temporal stage of development as in Western countries. In this social condition, which is characterized by a mixture of features, the elements of pre-modernity, modernity and post-modernity exist in Harmonious Complicity in a complex and variable form. Bie-modernity, as a kind of specious modernity, actually brings to the people living in it a complex experience of life, an experience that often results in life's suffering. Bie-modernsim theory is proposed to analyze this condition and find a solution to the Bie-modern Condition through interdisciplinary research. In the collaboration with computer science, Bie-modernsim Cultural Computing was proposed. It is an approach to cultural computing that is guided by the concept of Bie-modernsim and the theoretical propositions put forward by the theory of Bie-modernsim as a methodology. Combined with the results of existing research, it can be seen that this theory not only renews the scope of application of the tools of computer theory, but also greatly broadens the space of research in the field of culture, provides a new possibility for the production of knowledge, and enriches the theoretical content of interdisciplinary subjects. This paper believes that in addition to cultural computing, there is a new possibility of Bie-modernsim theory that is being generated, and it is Bie-modernsim social computing. In this paper, a theoretical system of Bie-modernsim Social Computing is proposed, including the guiding theory, research tasks, research goals, research objects, and research methodology. In addition, in order to improve the construction of this theoretical system, this dissertation also designs an experimental project of Bie-modernsim Social Computing. The experimental program is just a conception, which intends to analyze and confirm the existence and characteristics of Bie-modern Condition by studying the hot events on Sina Weibo, the mainstream social platform in China, and tries to propose a method to further research on Bie-modernity of the subjects. The program is to be further practiced and verified.

© The Author(s), under exclusive license to Springer Nature Switzerland AG 2024
M. Rauterberg (Ed.): HCII 2024, LNCS 14717, pp. 361–376, 2024.
https://doi.org/10.1007/978-3-031-61147-6_24

Keywords: Bie-modernism, · Bie-modernism Condition · Cultural Computing · Social Computing

1 Bie-modern and Bie-modernism

1.1 Bie-modern and Causes of its Occurrence, Morphological Characteristics

The concept of "Bie-modern" was proposed in 2014. Professor Wang Jianjiang of Shanghai Normal University proposed this academic concept at an international high-level academic conference. Initially, it was used to refer to the social condition of China after it entered the modernization process, i.e., the "Bie-modern Condition", which started after the Reform and Opening-up in 1978. Specifically, contemporary China, which has actively embraced capitalist modernity, has entered into a path of modernization that is different from its Western history. While the West developed modernity by eliminating pre-modernity and post-modernity by rebelling against modernity, this path of development in China is in fact a mixture of pre-modernity, modernity, and post-modernity at the same time, and all three co-exist and develop together in a complex manner. In 2023, the concept was recognized as one of China's top ten original academic concepts by the Evaluation Research Center of Renmin University of China, an authoritative academic evaluation institution in China.

"Bie-modern" means "a doubtful modernity", a combination of the Chinese pinyin "Bie" and the English word Bie" is a combination of the Chinese pinyin "Bie" and the English word "Modern". Bie" means "mixture" and "blending" in Chinese, as well as "special" and "unique" in Chinese. It also means "special", "unique", the negative meaning of "don't", and the original meaning of "cut". Such a designation indicates the complex modernity of the social condition it refers to: although it has elements of modernity, pre-modernity and post-modernity, it is not a single modernity or a single pre-modernity, nor is it post-modernity.

In fact, the concept is not limited to contemporary China, but can be extended to the social condition that is generally generated in developing countries as they enter the process of modernization. In this way, "Bie-modern", as a precise description of a social state, has entered the world's Market for Ideas.

It is worth mentioning that Southwestern State University in Georgia, United States, has specially established The Center of Chinese Bie-modern Studies, which specializes in the study of Bie-modern Condition in China. The University of Primorska in Slovenia, a member of the European Union, has established the Center of Bie-modern Studies, which specializes in the study of Bie-modern Condition as a general and widespread social condition. The difference between the two names can actually be seen as a difference in the academic conception of Bie-modern Condition between American and European scholars, who obviously believe that this social condition does not exist only in China.

Simply put, Bie-modern refers to the social phenomenon of a mixture of pre-modernity, modernity and post-modernity that exists in China. This phenomenon is mainly due to the fact that China's modernization process has been distorted by a number of factors. First of all, according to Max Weber, the pre-modern society has not yet been disenchanted, and this obscurantist social condition has been operating in China for thousands of years. The pre-modern elements in Chinese society have been integrated into the social operation mechanism, which is difficult to eradicate. Secondly, in modern history, China missed the best time for modernization after a long period of democratic revolution and unification wars. This has led to the fact that the construction of modernity in China was inadequate from the very beginning. Thirdly, when China began its modernization process with the Reform and Opening Up, the elements of modernity introduced from the West were actually full of post-modern features, i.e., China's modernization process in the true sense of the word was mixed with post-modernity.

According to Professor Wang Jianjiang, with the deepening of China's Reform and Opening-up, especially the growth and expansion of capitalist production relations and market economy in China, Chinese society has begun to take on certain characteristics of modernity from the modern civilization of Western capitalism. This modernity includes the full openness and acceptance of the capitalist mode of production, capital, market, trade, business, etc., as well as the learning and imitation of capitalist science and technology, knowledge and rationality. However, this modernity from the West has not only failed to criticize and draw a clear line between China's pre-modern ideas of patriarchy, nepotism, personal dependence, gender concepts, and feudal superstitions, but on the contrary, modernity and pre-modernity have lived together harmoniously. At the same time, Western post-modern artworks and artistic methods are favored by Chinese avant-garde artists, intellectual elites, and young people, and there is a proliferation of Internet language with post-modern colors defined by the public. [1].

Specifically, the fundamental characteristic of Bie-modern societies is the co-temporal nature of pre-modern, modern and post-modern features existing at the same stage in time. This feature is characterized by a distinct temporal hybridity. Bie-modern society is full of pre-modern elements, such as patriarchy, superstition, blood relations, revenge, corruption, personal dependence, dictatorship, and so on. At the same time, it also has certain characteristics of modern society, such as modern production methods, capital markets, transnational trade, modern science and technology, and modern law-making. Similarly, it is full of post-modernity features, such as people's rebellion against rationality, the use of post-modern art techniques such as collage, and so on. In fact, Bie-modernity is a kind of double-sided interpretation of "unfinished modernity" in Chinese society. Based on the perspective of "modernity", it has not achieved sufficient modernity. Based on the perspective of "post-modernity", it has the typical characteristics of post-modernity. It is a state of insufficient modernity that is both "incomplete" and "transcendent". In fact, Bie-modern is a kind of pseudo-modernity that is specious.

1.2 The Purpose and Connotation of Bie-modernism Theory

Bie-modernism is a comprehensive doctrine based on capturing and summarizing of the Bie-modern Condition. The theory advocates distinguishing between true and false modernity and accomplishing the critique and transcendence of Bie-modern society by means of academic research. According to Professor Wang Jianjiang, Bie-modernism, which arose from the Bie-modern society, is a self-reflection of Bie-modernity. Unlike Bie-modern Condition, Bie-modernism is a theoretical proposition based on self-renewal and self-transcendence, and its essence is self-transcendence and self-renewalism as well as a kind of ism as a necessity of modern society [2]. This self-reflexive theory echoes the philosophical thinking of the Chinese philosopher Lao Zi, who said, "Reversal is the movement of the Dao (道)".

Bie-modernity is the society that has not yet completed the construction of Bie-modernity. Bie-modernism should criticize various Bie-modern phenomena in Bie-modernity under the guidance of the goal of constructing full modernity, and put forward the goal and direction of the development of Bie-modern society. Bie-modernism emphasizes the distinction between modernism and post-modernism, maintains theoretical independence between pre-modernism, modernism and post-modernism, and neither revisits the past nor worships the present, and does not follow the aftermath of the post-modernist trend of thought, but rather reflects on the post-modernism, and sets its sights on the reconstruction of values after the post-modernism.

Specifically, Bie-modernism has several main purposes:

A. Accurately characterize the complexity of the Bie-modern Condition of society.
B. Analyze the causes of Bie-modern societies.
C. Distinguish between true and false modernity.
D. Analyze the characteristics of Bie-modernity in order to cope with the random qualities of the development of Bie-modernity.
E. Transcend post-modernity in Bie-modern Condition.
F. Find the truth in the post-truth era through Deep Bie (Recognizing Deep Fake) technology to establish true modernity.
G. Focus on the survival of individuals in Bie-modern Condition and proposing relevant theories to defend the value of individual life.

The theory of Bie-modernism is constructed on the basis of its core claims. Currently, Bie-modernism theory has become an internationalized and comprehensive theory. Bie-modernism theory has published five academic monographs and formed 27 theoretical categories and propositions, which span the fields of sociology, philosophy, aesthetics, art, literature, law, economics, culture, computer applications and so on. These theoretical categories and propositions constitute the theoretical system of Bie-modernism, making it a truly interdisciplinary and comprehensive theory.

Specifically, the theory of Bie-modernism is first and foremost a theory of social analysis. Its theoretical foundation is based on the precise capture and accurate description of the Bie-modern Condition as a social phenomenon. Bie-modernism proposes such categories as the Spatialization of Time, Harmonious Complicity, the Four-Stage Theory of Bie-modern Social Development, the Great-leap-forward Pause, and the Life Equity to summarize and describe the Bie-modern Condition and its possibilities of development.

A. Spatialization of Time: It means that the chronological order, which used to develop linearly in the West, has become co-temporal in Bie-modern societies. This proposition summarizes the basic characteristics of the Bie-modern Condition, that is, the coexistence of the pre-modern, modern and post-modern. After the reform and opening up, the concept of "centering on economic development" and the continuous growth of the market economy have led to an astonishing economic growth rate in China and a rapid development of the Chinese society, which has been characterized by the "modernity" in Western theories. This is mainly reflected in the acceptance and imitation of Western science and technology, rational tools, modes of production and other elements of modernity. But on the one hand, this modernity inevitably leads to the "hidden worries of modernity" (which had already occurred in the West before it entered China), with the consequences of money, consumerism, hedonism, etc. On the other hand, although it is a modern thought, it cannot suppress the local pre-modern thoughts, such as the idea of patriarchy, nepotism, feudal superstition, etc., which results in a modernity with Chinese characteristics, where modern and pre-modern thoughts intertwine and merge in Harmonious Complicity. At the same time, in Perry Anderson's view, Western post-modernism influenced and spawned by China has in turn influenced China, and post-modernism is favored by Chinese artists, writers, readers and viewers. In this way, China's current social time is the Spatialization of Time.

B. Harmonious Complicity Theory: Under the influence of Spatialization of Time, pre-modernity, modernity and post-modernity conspire in a form of Harmonious Complicity. Bie-modern society has a complex and varied "Harmonious Complicity" as its main dynamic structure of development. "Harmonious Complicity" refers to the blurring and mixing of the boundaries between pre-modern, modern and post-modern elements in Bie-modern societies due to the specificity of their localization, which gives rise to characteristics that cannot simply be identified as pre-modern, modern or post-modern. According to Prof. Wang Jianjiang, Bie-modern "Harmonious Complicity" includes the mutual adaptation and harmonious coexistence of modern, post-modern and pre-modern in the same society; the non-compliance of laws, the abandonment of principles, the compromise of each other, the mutual transaction, the making of peace and win-win situation; the constant changing of rules and the implementation of subterfuges; the selective forgetfulness and concealment of history; the community of interest's knowing the law, breaking the law and committing thefts. The pre-modern way of thinking and behaving due to the absence of modern institutions is manifested in the post-modern crossing border, deconstructing the center, dissolving policies and regulations, and finally forming a chaotic harmony [3].

C. The Four-Stage Theory of Bie-modern Social Development: The theory of Bie-modernism suggests that Bie-modern society has four stages of development, namely, the stage of Harmonious Complicity, the stage of Conflict, the stage of intertwining Harmonious Complicity and Conflict, and the stage of Self-Renewal. In the Harmonious Complicity stage, the social forces (social subjects) represented by the three modernities will find a suitable way to coexist and develop so that the society will appear Bie-modern Condition. In the stage of conflict, the three subjects will clash due to the inherent contradiction of each other's characteristics of the times, leading to the tilting of forces and confrontation between the subjects. In the third stage, social subjects find a more balanced relationship as a result of the first two stages of development, allowing for Harmonious Complicity and antagonistic conflict to be present at the same time, making the Bie-modern Condition even more complex, fluid and random. In the last stage is the stage of self-renewal and transcendence, which is the central aim of the solution envisioned by Bie-modernism. The theoretical construction and practice of Bie-modernism attempts to identify true modernity in order to eliminate specious modernity and unify the three characteristics of the era.

It also sets its developmental vision beyond postmodernity, where it tries to achieve the overall enhancement of human civilization.

D. The theory of Great-leap-forward Pause: one of the methods used to realize true modernity. It means that at the peak stage of rapid development, it is possible to obtain better opportunities for development by taking the initiative to pause. The phenomenon of overdevelopment is widespread in current society, with its attendant ecological, environmental, demographic and food crises. The theory of Social Acceleration proposed by Hartmut Rosa is a social critique of too high a speed and fast-paced development. The concept of Great-leap-forward Pause is similar to this one, which emphasizes the autonomy of pause, and that pause in development should be a conscious and active choice, rather than a forced and passive one. After the pause, reflection, improvement and re-start, change the course, find another way to develop with another better choice after rational reflection in order to realize the transcendence of the original plan. Bie-modernism rejects the linear development of time and seeks a new solution from the possibility of the future through "transcendental looking back", so that the subject's planning for the future can actively intervene in the concrete practice of the present, and thus contribute to the self-regulation and new development of Bie-modern society.

E. Life Equity: Life Equity means that every human being should have an innate wealth of survival which cannot be taken away from him or her. In the functioning of the modern state, every national should receive the wealth inherent in the interests of the state to support his or her own survival, embodied in the free entitlement to the minimum subsistence guarantee without work, the sharingism of modern civilization, and one of the criteria for measuring the true and false modernity. The theory was formed by Bie-modernism based on the oppression of the personal equity of living individuals in the Bie-modern Condition. Life equity is the prerequisite and foundation for the sense of happiness and beauty of human beings, while its absence is the source of human misfortunes, injustices, anxieties, and sufferings. Therefore, the theory of life equity has the potential to play a catalytic role in recognizing and encompassing the right, value, identity, and essence of life, and to advance the innovative development of the humanities and social sciences.

2 Bie-modernist Cultural Computing

2.1 Cultural Computing

Cultural computing is a methodological system that applies computer technology to conduct research in the field of culture. Specifically, cultural computing will use deep learning, feature extraction, pre-training and other means to extract the characteristic information of culture in cultural carriers such as images, text, music, etc., and carry out pre-processing to produce relevant data. Based on these data, Cultural Computing carries out scientific quantification and computation on research objects, and further derives scientific cognition on research objects, in order to assist in cultural research and other humanities and social sciences research.

The concept of Cultural Computing was first introduced in 2005 by Prof. Tosa Naoko of Kyoto University in Japan, prof. Tosa Naoko believes that cultural computing can capture cultural phenomena more accurately, and through further computation and analysis, learn more precisely how emotional subjects feel and think about particular cultural phenomena. [4] Compared to the original cultural studies, cultural computing appears to be more comprehensive and scientific. In 2012, Scott Weingart and Jeana Jorgensen used cultural computing to study how gendered body representations in European fairy tales affect children's gender perceptions [5]. In 2014, Alberto Acerbi and R. Bentley used cultural computing methods to study how biases in culture at the time of transmission lead to changes in the popular characteristics of culture [6]. In 2017, T. Neal and Kalaivani Sundararajan et al. investigated how question-measurement can be applied in cultural computing for author's corpora analysis [7].

In short, cultural computing applies mathematical and scientific ideas to the humanities, accelerating the digitalization process of the development of the humanities and social sciences. At the same time, the integration of contemporary disciplines has become more and more in-depth, and the leap between various disciplines and fields is no longer a mirage, and there is no longer an insurmountable gap between science and humanities. The arrival of the information age, the digital age and even the age of big data has made it easier to access and mobilize huge amounts of data. Cultural computing based on data is even more powerful. The popularization of large language models has led to more options in the library of cultural computing methods, and the tools and techniques that people can use to face diverse cultural objects have become more mature, abundant, and easier to use.

2.2 Theoretical Connotations and Research Results of Bie-modernism Cultural Computing

Bie-modernism Cultural Computing is the latest theoretical achievement of Bie-modernism theory into the field of computer science. In fact, it is the method of cultural computing guided by the concept of Bie-modernism and taking the theoretical propositions put forward by the theory of Bie-modernism as the methodology. According to Prof. Wang Jianjiang, it focuses on the difference between real modernity and pseudo-modernity, the real world and the false world, and studies the false culture, low-quality culture and its products in different countries, nationalities and cultures due to the lack of morality with the help of mechanical reproduction, so as to safeguard the lawful interests of the individual to the country and the whole world, to eliminate the pseudo-modernity and the false world, and to establish the real modernity and the real world.

For related fields such as artificial intelligence, Bie-modernism cultural calculations both draw on their specific materials and methods, and also impose requirements and constraints on them, arguing that the development of the field of artificial intelligence should form a self-restraining mechanism. For example, in the face of AI face-swapping technology, not only should we consider the pros and cons of the technology from the legal level, but also make value judgments from the ethical and sociological perspectives. The GPT product from OpenAI, for example, has been identified in many cases as a "repeat offender" in the falsification of false information. This superstar product has been touted as one of the biggest highlights of 2023 for its ease of use and almost "all-knowing" "brain". However, there is ample evidence that GPTs often choose to fabricate information that they do not have in advance. Such counterfeiting raises concerns about the destructive nature of Deep Fake in the world [8]. Bie-modernism Cultural Computing proposes "Deep Bie" in response to the prevalence of "Deep Fake". It attempts to distinguish fake things through the following points.

Visual Recognition System: The visual recognition system of Bie-modernism distinguishes the authenticity from the fake by tapping into well-known characters in literature or films for image recognition. For example, the identification of the real and fake Monkey King from the Chinese classical novel Journey to the West. The Journey to the West, as one of the four classic representative literary works in China, created four classic images: Tang Sanzang, Sun Wukong, Zhu Bajie, and Sha Heshang. In the classic chapter "The True or Fake Monkey King", no one can recognize the true or fake Monkey King because the Six-Eared Rhesus Monkey has the same appearance as the Monkey King, and he replaces the Monkey King in fetching scriptures in the West. With the practice of Bie-modernism Cultural Computing, it became easier to distinguish and recognize the real and fake Monkey King. Prof. Wang Jianjiang's team uses Word2vec model + CNN algorithm model to analyze the character traits of the main characters in Journey to the West. Thus, it realizes the multi-dimensional analysis of character traits, and then distinguishes the real and fake Monkey King according to the feedback data [9]. The results were released at the HCII conference in 2021.

Digital Recognition System: mainly through Bie-modernism cultural computing the credibility score of discriminating data to deal with the phenomenon of deep forgery. According to Prof. Wang Jianjiang, technological forgery utilizes deep neural networks, such as Generative Adversarial Network (GAN) technology to authenticate forgery by simulating the behavior of the human brain. Training through real data, such as GAN through generators for data generation, and observing the generated data through discriminators, when there is enough training time and amount of data input, this behavior will make the difference between generated data and real data. However, the difference between the real data and the generated data can be effectively found by utilizing the confidence score of the discriminator generated data. It can reveal whether or how probable it is that when X occurs, Y will also occur or how probable it is that it will occur, and it can also indicate the correlation between the real data and the generated data. The higher the correlation, the more similar it is. The confidence level indicates the proportion of things that contain X that also contain Y, i.e., the proportion of transactions that contain both X and Y to the proportion of transactions that contain X. If the confidence level is too low, it means that the occurrence of X has little to do with whether or not Y occurs [10].

Social Formation Attribute Identification System: mainly through the social analysis method of Bie-modernism theory, the attributes of social formations are identified on the research object. For example, Prof. Wang Jianjiang's team takes the novels of Nobel Prize winner Mo Yan and the novels of feudal fiction writer Er Yue He as research objects, and analyzes the content percentage of pre-Bie-modernity, Bie-modernity and post-Bie-modernity in Mo Yan's novels through cultural computing, in order to validate that the social formations depicted in his novels are the Bie-modern social formations. And by comparing the data of the two research objects, it is concluded that in Bie-modern society, the goodness of a literary work lies largely in whether the literary work is written by the author with a truly modern conception.

In addition to the specific identification system mentioned above, Bie-modernism Cultural Computing adheres to the idea of Life Equity. That is, the equal belief that all life has a natural right to exist and wealth since its birth, and is not to be acquired by labor. This concept is able to pay effective attention to the individual's right to life in the face of Deep Fake, and in the threat of fake information, it is able to insist on defending the true value of human civilization with the bottom line of survival without labor.

In addition to this, Bie-modernism Cultural Computing has participated in HCII for 3 consecutive years with themed session. 7 research papers have been published on the topic of Bie-modernism cultural computing. The related research involves the problem of identifying "Bie-human", the problem of identifying characters in classic literature, the problem of analyzing the proportion of modernity in literary works, and the problem of popular culture of new forms of Chinese movies, and so on. Combined with the existing research results, we can see that this theory not only renews the scope of application of the tools of computer theory, but also greatly broadens the research space in the field of culture, provides a new possibility for the production of knowledge, and enriches the theoretical content of cross-disciplines.

Bie-modernism Cultural Computing naturally has a wide range of applications, but theoretical exploration should not stop here. There is a new possibility being generated, which is Bie-modernism Social Computing.

3   Bie-modernism and Social Computing

3.1   Social Computing

Culture and society are inextricably linked. The cultural turn in the late 1970s and early 1980s brought specific forms of culture, such as art, literature, contemporary popular culture, and media studies, into the scope of sociological research, and culture was emphasized as a social force driving the real world. In the era of interconnectedness, computability, and intelligence, the research of culture and society through computational science has not only become possible, but has even become a more effective method of research.

Compared with Cultural Computing, Social Computing has a broader scope and richer application areas. Specifically, Social Computing refers to a theoretical and methodological system that uses scientific computing theories and methods such as system science, artificial intelligence, data mining, etc. to study the problems involved in social science. In 2009, Lazer and other scholars published an article entitled "Computational Social Science" in Science, marking the formal birth of Computational Social Science as a discipline. In 2012, Conte and other scholars published Manifasto of Computational Social Science, which is a cross-disciplinary discipline that utilizes computing methods to study society, involving the main fields of computer science, data science, artificial intelligence, complexity science and social science. It is a kind of science based on large-scale data and computing, combined with artificial intelligence to deduce and compute the target social behaviors and social events, and is a theoretical and methodological system more directly involved in the development and change of social patterns. The rise of computational social science is not only an inevitable trend of social science innovation and development in the digital era, but also a product of the cross-fertilization of social science with data science and computational science. The outbreak of the fourth scientific and technological revolution originated from the cross-fertilization of disciplines, which in turn further drives the cross-fertilization of via disciplines in order to build the fundamental role of knowledge production and talent accumulation that supports the digital civilization.

Current computational social science consists of four main research methods: Automated Information Extraction, Social Network Analysis, Social Complexity Theory, and Social Simulation Modelling [11]. And mainly formed two major technology paths: machine learning-based artificial intelligence technology and Agent-Based Modeling (ABM) technology.

Automated information Extraction method: Computational social sciences use algorithms to extract information from acquired data about how society operates, its dynamics, its structure, and so on. Due to the advent of the big data era, this type of data is actually more accessible, large and varied, and can include text, images, video, and audio. By utilizing this methodology, social computing can be used to identify true and fake information and even true and fake modernity.

Social Network Analysis method: analyzing the structure, dynamics and other attributes of the relationship between social subjects through computation. The social network analysis method also benefits from the advent of the big data era, and the abundant amount of data has undoubtedly enriched the foundation of this method and provided a more comprehensive and effective choice for this social science research path.

Social Complexity Theory: This approach is used to analyze the interactions between subjects in socially complex systems. The computational social sciences have adopted this approach to study more macroscopic phenomena in human society. When applied to the theory of Bie-modernism, it is even possible to clarify the sociological dimension of the Bie-modernity relationship that has been described as " complexity " in the previous section.

Social simulation Modeling and analysis method: mainly through computer science to build virtual society, simulate the operation of real society in simulation form, and provide data to help the research of real society. With the help of Social Computing, this simulation will be more realistic and the input data will be more abundant. And under the guidance of the concept of "everything can be computed", all kinds of behaviors and elements can be formulated and entered into the operation of the virtual society in the form of parameters, which can obviously obtain more scientific and accurate results than traditional social sciences.

Similarly, examples of research utilizing computational social science are already abundant. For example, in the case of a range of changes in state-society relations brought about by new political phenomena in virtual space, big data provides additional material to trace the processes of influence and gain meaningful insights [12]. Another example is the prediction of elections for politicians in countries around the world through online social media posting data [13]. There is also a modeling study to determine the purity of social subjects' data by calculating data from Sina Weibo, a social networking platform in China [14]. Benefiting from this social science approach, which is deeply intertwined with computer science, the theory of Bie-modernism will gain richer application scenarios and practical means.

3.2 The Construction of Bie-modernism Social Computing

The theory of Bie-modernism, as a meta-theory, with its vast theoretical radiation and rich disciplinary implications, is not limited to cultural studies, but should be more accurately directed to social studies to encompass cultural studies. Meanwhile, more fundamentally, the concept of Bie-modern Condition and related theories are produced from an abstract summary of the social condition of developing countries, and the application of social calculation methods will undoubtedly make this abstract conceptual summary process more persuasive and be able to reveal, to a certain extent, the possibilities and directions of the social reality beyond the Bie-modern Condition. In the theoretical vision of Bie-modernism, the innovative use of social computing methods to analyze and study the Bie-modern Condition is a rationale worthy of in-depth exploration, and is also the future development direction of the combination of Bie-modernism and computer methods. Therefore, this paper proposes Bie-modernism Social Computing to further develop the theoretical system of Bie-modernism.

Bie-modernism Social Computing is the combination of Bie-modernism and computational social science, which is a new form and method of Bie-modernism into the field of computer science. As already mentioned, the theory of Bie-modernism is first and foremost a social analysis doctrine, which has a unique and accurate analysis of the social condition of China and even developing countries in the world, and is summarized as the Bie-modern Condition.

Accordingly, the main task of Bie-modernism Social Computing is to scientifically verify and analyze the Bie-modern Condition at the level of social sciences with the help of social computing tools. The main purpose of Bie-modernism Social Computing is to promote the development of humanities and social sciences such as the theory of Bie-modernism (e.g., the development of new methods, new concepts, new ideas, etc.) on the one hand, and on the other hand, to carry out scientific research in social sciences under the guidance of the philosophical concepts of Bie-modernism to promote the transcendence of the Bie-modern Condition. The main object of Bie-modernism's Social Computing can cover both the previously mentioned research object of Bie-modernism's Cultural Computing: the cultural product, and moreover focus on the research object of social research such as social subjects, social systems, social relations, social dynamics, and so on.

The methodology of Bie-modernism Social Computing derives both from the theoretical system of Bie-modernism and from Computational Social Science. In the practice of Bie-modernism Social Computing, Bie-modernism's method of proportionality analysis, the theory of Spatialization of Time, the theory of Harmonious Complicity, the theory of Four Stages of Bie-modern Social Development, the theory of Great-leap-forward Pause, and the theory of the Life Equity, etc., will be put to use. First, there is the proportionality analysis method's determination of the quality of society, which is mainly used to verify the existence of the Bie-modern Condition. The method of social computing can present the specific social properties (pre-modernity, modernity, post-modernity) in the form of parameters, and through the method of proportionality analysis, the values of the research objects can be determined and classified. Secondly, theories such as the Spatialization of Time theory and the Harmonious Complicity theory can be applied to the specific study of social computing. For example, in the analysis of social subject's emotion, it can be used to analyze the composition and change process of subject's emotion. In the specific practice of social computing, the four major research methods are still used as the main research methods. The automatic information extraction method as a basic method can be used to extract a large amount of data related to the subject in Bie-modern Condition, and through the calculation of the data, we can find out the position, function, quality and other elements of the research object in the operation of the society, in order to further differentiate between the true and fake modernity.The use of social network analysis allows for further research into the causes of Bie-modern Condition, and it is important to recognize that Bie-modern Condition arises from the social subject, which is also affected by Bie-modern Condition. P. Dodds and K. Harris et al. study the well-being of online social platform users through a social computing methodology [15]. Inspired by its approach, Bie-modernism Social Computing can also explore the impact of Bie-modern Condition on individual emotions by studying the happiness of social platform users within China, and the method can also be used to verify the existence of Bie-modern Condition and where it is characterized in the social network. Social complexity theory can be used to study the multiple subjects of Harmonious Complicity in the more complex Bie-modern Condition. The analytical method of social simulation modeling is oriented towards a wider range of application possibilities. The method may be able to explore the paths or ways of renewal and transcendence of Bie-modern society. In conclusion, the methodological system of Bie-modernism Social Computing is rich and still to be developed.

3.3 The Value and Significance of Bie-modernism Social Computing

The current relationship between social computing and the subject faces a number of problems, such as the problem of the subjectivity of human beings as social subjects in the context of big data, the problem of the social structure and position of human beings in the era of big data, and the problem of the role played by social computing in the global crisis, and so on. For the Computational Social Sciences, Bie-modernism has been able to make a difference in this category because of its humanitarianism, critical realism, and Life-equity spirit. For example, the problem of human subjectivity in the context of big data is a very important bottom line in Bie-modernism theory, Bie-modernism insists on individual care, and has always been concerned about the survival of the individual in Bie-modern society, under the influence of Bie-modernism's philosophical concepts, the Bie-modernism Social Computing will pay more attention to the individual in the research instead of focusing on the complexity of the huge data only. The ultimate goal of Bie-modernist Social Computing remains to return to the human being, analyzing and discussing the findings of social computing from the perspective of the individual, in order to come up with findings that are more conducive to the development of the individual in society. Similarly, Bie-modernism's emphasis on Life Equity Theory indicates this, and thus Bie-modernism theory will undoubtedly have the space and validity to be interpreted in the ethical discussion of cross-disciplinary theories represented by cultural computing and social computing in the academic circle.

A research laboratory at the University of Tokyo in Japan has proposed the concept of "Society 5.0" to envision a "super smart society", which will be a society in which "A society in which necessary goods and services are provided to those who need them when necessary, in which various social needs are met with the utmost care, and in which all people, regardless of age, gender, region, or language, have access to high-quality services and can live happily and comfortably" [16]. The development of Bie-modernism theory in the field of computers, in the field of artificial intelligence, has precisely the same purpose as the claim, and the belief that this vision will be realized.

For the theoretical system of Bie-modernism, the entry of social computational methods has undoubtedly given it more tools to use, paths to act on, and possibilities for greater refinement. This thesis has repeatedly referred to the primary characteristic of Bie-modernism as a socially analytic theory whose foundation rests on social analysis. It is clear that it develops better when it can use the tools of social computing to strengthen its "foundations".

The advantage of Bie-modern Social Computing over Bie-modernism Cultural Computing also lies in the fact that it provides an avenue for Bie-modernism to engage more and more deeply in social regulation as an academic activity. As mentioned earlier, computational social science can be used not only as a tool for academic research, but also as a tool for people to recognize the world and change it. The ultimate goal of Bie-modernism is to complete the renewal and transcendence of Bie-modern society, looking forward to the completion of a fully-fledged modern civilized society and the overall enhancement of human civilization.

4   A Research Proposal for the Analysis of Trending Events in Social Networking Platforms Based on Bie-modernism Social Computing

This proposal is an idea proposed at the beginning of the creation of the theory of Bie-modernism Social Computing, and will need to be followed up with experiments in order to be truly implemented.

4.1   Research Objects

The proposal has two phases. The research object for Phase I is the Weibo Trending Topics List (微博热搜榜) for the whole year of 2023. The proposal chooses Sina Weibo, currently the largest Chinese social networking platform in terms of users, as the data source for the study. For the third quarter of 2023, it reached 605 million monthly active users and 260 million daily active users [17]. Extract all relevant information of Weibo Trending Topics List 2023, including trending title, trending rank, trending degree, time, etc. Weibo Trending Topics List reflects the hot topics and events that the society pays attention to, and has high representativeness and universality.

The Phase II builds on the foundation of the Phase I. After the completion of Phase I, the research object is the information of active users in one or a series of strongly correlated trending topics in the Weibo Trending Topics List in 2023.

4.2 Research Purpose

The purpose of the research in Phase I is to analyze and study the data of Weibo Trending Topics List to derive the percentage of Bie-modernity in this data. It is further used to analyze the characteristics of Bie-modern society, to verify the actual existence of the Bie-modern Condition, and to verify the applicability and validity of Bie-modernism's social computing.

The purpose of the research in Phase II is to construct a social network model that reflects the structure of relations between subjects by analyzing the data of active users in one or a series of specific trending events. The Bie-modernity of the subjects is analyzed and studied through the methods of Bie-modernism social computing.

4.3 Collection of Research Data.

Since Sina Weibo does not keep historical information about Weibo Trending Topics List, the research data for this study came from a third-party platform that monitors and saves Weibo Trending Topics List data in real time. The data was collected by using a web crawler tool. After obtaining the data through the web crawler, the data content was saved and written into the ".xlsx" file for data processing.

4.4 Data Preprocessing

Natural language processing techniques are used to process the text, including text cleaning, tokenization, stop word removal, remove numbers and special characters, etc. These preprocessing steps contribute to improving the performance of models in NLP tasks, enhancing their ability to understand textual data while reducing noise and increasing processing efficiency.

4.5 Experimental Steps for Phase I

Based on the theory of Bie-modernism, keywords representing pre-modernity, modernity and post-modernity were manually selected. These keywords need to be representative and able to accurately reflect the characteristics of the different attributes. For example:

A. Pre-modernity: tradition, feudalism, conservatism, superstition, family, hierarchy.
B. Modernity: science, rationality, democracy, freedom, progress, equality.
C. Postmodernity: pluralism, collage, deconstruction, decentralization, entertainment, mass.

- A corpus of pre-modernity, modernity and post-modernity is constructed using the identified keywords. The corpora need to include information on the frequency of use and distribution of the different keywords.
- Converting text into features that can be understood by the model. That is, the text is represented as vectors, and bag-of-words model, TF-IDF, word embeddings, and other methods can be used in order to extract text features. Divide the entire set into training set, validation set and test set, usually 8:1:1.

- The set is used for machine learning algorithms to train a text classification model to learn the correspondence between keywords and attributes. The parameters are also tuned to improve the model prediction accuracy.
- Evaluate the performance of the model using test sets. Common evaluation metrics include accuracy, precision, recall, F1 score, etc. Afterwards, the trained text classification model is applied to the text posted by users to determine the pre-modernity, modernity and post-modernity attributes contained in the text.
- Keywords were extracted from the texts to which the model was applied to obtain the attributes of pre-modernity, modernity and post-modernity contained in the texts. The extracted keywords were subjected to frequency counts to obtain the distribution of the different attributes in the text.
- Calculate the proportion of different attributes in the text based on keyword frequencies to obtain the proportion of pre-modernity, modernity and post-modernity in user attributes. This step requires the use of mathematical calculations such as frequency statistics and weighted average.
- Based on the calculated proportions, determine the Bie-modern social characteristics reflected in the data from the Weibo Trending Topics List.

5 Experimental Steps for Phase II

Selection of research object: From the experimental results of the first stage, select one or a series of trend topics and events with the most significant Bie-modern features, referred to as TT. The research object is set to be the users in the TT.

- Crawler tool is used to get the data of active users in TT, including user ID, original tweets, comments, retweets, followers, likes and so on. Active users are defined as those who frequently post relevant tweets, retweets and comments in TT.
- Convert data into network structure form. Perform social network analysis (SNA) using appropriate tools to construct a social network model and analyze the network structure. Validate and tune the model.
- Natural language processing techniques, such as tokenization, lexical annotation, named entity recognition, etc., are used to extract keywords from user-posted content to reflect the subject's Bie-modern characteristics, including emotions, opinions, interests, etc., and to calculate the proportional distribution of the subject's Bie-modenity in the TT.
- Analyze the relationship between network indicators and subjects' Bie-modernity, and determine the influence of the connection between subjects on the Bie-modernity state in order to reveal the influence of network structure on the Bie-modernity state. This step requires the application of network analysis methods, such as path analysis and correlation analysis, in order to reveal the influence of interactions between subjects on the state of Bie-modernity.

5.1 Judgmental Conditions for Achieving Research Purpose

Since the research is presented only as an idea for an experimental proposal, the results of the experiment are not yet known. Based on the analysis and assumptions of Bie-modernism theory on Bie-modern societies, the experimental results of the proposal need to confirm the existence of Bie-modern society and the manifestation of Bie-modern characteristics of the subject in order to validate the Bie-modernism theory's validity in the analysis of society.

References

1. Wang, J.: Bie-modern: Space Encounters and Time Spans, 1st edn. China Social Sciences Press, Beijing (2017)
2. 王建疆.: 别现代主义: 从说别到别说再到别在西方.甘肃社会科学 (04), 63–74 (2023). (in Chinese). https://doi.org/10.15891/j.cnki.cn62-1093/c.20230706.002
3. Wang, J., Chen, H., Ma, T., Qi, Z., Yang, Z., Zhang, S.: A cultural computing of the share of modernity in world literary masterpieces by Bie-modernism. In: Rauterberg, M. (ed.) HCII. LNCS, vol. 14035, pp. 603–617. Springer, Cham (2023). https://doi.org/10.1007/978-3-031-34732-0_47
4. Tosa, N., Matsuoka, S., Ellis, B., Ueda, H., Nakatsu, R.: Cultural computing with context-aware application: ZENetic computer. In: Kishino, F., Kitamura, Y., Kato, H., Nagata, N. (eds.) ICEC 2005. LNCS, vol. 3711, pp. 13–23. Springer, Heidelberg (2005). https://doi.org/10.1007/11558651_2
5. Weingart, S.B., Jorgensen, J.: Computational analysis of the body in European fairy tales. Linguistic Comput **28**(3), 404–416 (2013). https://doi.org/10.1093/llc/fqs015
6. Acerbi, A., Bentley, R.A.: Biases in cultural transmission shape the turnover of popular traits. Evol. Hum. Behav. **35**(3), 228–236 (2014). https://doi.org/10.1016/j.evolhumbehav.2014.02.003
7. Neal, T.J., Sundararajan, K., Fatima, A., Yan, Y., Xiang, Y., Woodard, D.: Surveying stylometry techniques and applications. ACM Comput. Surv. (CSUR) **50**(6), 1–36 (2017). https://doi.org/10.1145/3132039
8. Faragó, T.: Deep fakes–an emerging risk to individuals and societies alike. Tilburg Pap. Cult. Stud. 237 (2019)
9. Wang, J., Chen, H.: Bie-modernism and cultural computing. In: Rauterberg, M. (ed.) HCII 2021. LNCS, vol. 12795, pp. 474–489. Springer, Cham (2021). https://doi.org/10.1007/978-3-030-77431-8_30
10. Wang, J.: Bie-Modernist Aestheticology, 1st edn. China Social Sciences Press, Beijing (2023)
11. Cioffi-Revilla, C.: Introduction to Computational Social Science: Principles and Applications, 2nd edn. Springer, New York (2017)
12. Höchtl, J., Parycek, P., Schöllhammer, R.: Big data in the policy cycle: policy decision making in the digital era. J. Organ. Comput. Electron. Commer. **26**(1–2), 147–169 (2016). https://doi.org/10.1080/10919392.2015.1125187
13. Kennedy, R., Wojcik, S., Lazer, D.M.: Improving election prediction internationally. Science **355**(6324), 515–520 (2017). https://doi.org/10.1126/science.aal2887
14. Shi, L., Liu, L., Wu, Y., Jiang, L., Kazim, M., Ali, H., et al.: Human-centric cyber social computing model for hot-event detection and propagation. IEEE Trans. Comput. Soc. Syst. **6**(5), 1042–1050 (2019). https://doi.org/10.1109/TCSS.2019.2913783
15. Dodds, P.S., Harris, K.D., Kloumann, I.M., Bliss, C.A., Danforth, C.M.: Temporal patterns of happiness and information in a global social network: hedonometrics and Twitter. PLoS ONE **6**(12), e26752 (2011). https://doi.org/10.1371/journal.pone.0026752
16. Shiroishi, Y., Uchiyama, K., Suzuki, N.: Society 5.0: for human security and well-being. Computer **51**(7), 91–95 (2018). https://doi.org/10.1109/MC.2018.3011041
17. Guangming Economy Channel News Page. https://economy.gmw.cn/2023-11/09/content_36955453.htm

Calculation of the Proportion of Modernity in Dao Lang's Lyrics from a Bie-Modernist Cultural Computing Perspective

Jianjiang Wang[1], Haiguang Chen[2(✉)], Hui Wang[1], Muyun Wang[3], Hong Ni[4], and Juan Wang[5]

[1] College of Humanities of Shanghai Normal University, Shanghai, China
[2] Computer Science College of Shanghai Normal University, Shanghai, China
Chhg@shnu.edu.cn
[3] Arts College of Shanghai Normal University, Shanghai, China
[4] Shanghai Xiyuan Agricultural Technology Promotion Co., Ltd., Shanghai, China
[5] Technical Department, Suzhou Zhihua Technology Co., Ltd., Suzhou, China

Abstract. This paper analyzes the reasons for the significant influence of Dao Lang's songs by calculating the proportion of modernity in the lyrics of "Rakshasa Sea City" in albums such as "Mountain Songs are Lonely" and "Red Classic", especially in "Mountain Songs are Lonely". Conclusion: The lyrics of Dao Lang's songs use rhetorical devices such as allusions, metaphors, and symbols to allude to society and criticize reality, and have sufficient modernity in their internal meanings. It is precisely this sufficient proportion of modernity that has formed the unprecedented traffic code of Dao Lang songs.

Keywords: Dao Lang · "Mountain Songs are Lonely" · "Red Classic" · "Rakshasa Sea City" · Bie-modernist Cultural Computing · Bie-modernism

1 Research Object

1.1 The Lyrics from Dao Lang (刀郎, dao Lang, Knife Master in Chinese))'s "Mountain Songs are Lonely"

In 2023, Dao Lang's global single "Rakshasa Sea City" topped the charts in terms of plays and entries on numerous self-media platforms[1] Dao Lang himself also received the "Best Asian Singer"[2] award at the 37th Global Music Huading Awards and was honored as one of the "Top 10 Poets" at the Tenth Chinese Poetry Spring Festival Gala[3]. This

---

[1] 《羅刹海市》霸榜全網.大公報. http://www.takungpao.com.hk/news/232108/2023/0801/877604.html.2023-8-1[2023-11-30].

[2] The 37th Global Music Huading Awards of "Aolai Yipin Night" were announced.Weibo. https://www.weibo.com/ttarticle/p/show?id=2309404984784563863823.2023-12-30[2024-1-9].

[3] Daolang was named one of the "Top Ten Lyricists" by the 10th Chinese Poetry Spring Festival Gala in 2024. Sohu. https://www.sohu.com/a/750142882_121124766.2024-1-7[2024–1-11].

© The Author(s), under exclusive license to Springer Nature Switzerland AG 2024
M. Rauterberg (Ed.): HCII 2024, LNCS 14717, pp. 377–390, 2024.
https://doi.org/10.1007/978-3-031-61147-6_25

not only sparked widespread discussions[4,5], but also became an unprecedented global phenomenon in the history of human music performance. "Rakshasa Sea City" is the most widely sung song in Dao Lang's 2023 album "Mountain Songs are Lonely".

1.2 The Lyrics of "Rakshasa Sea City" in Dao Lang's "Mountain Songs are Lonely"

1.3 The Cover of "Red Classic" by Dao Lang

The album "Red Classic," covered by Dao Lang, presents a stark contrast to "Mountain Songs are Lonely." This collection primarily features revolutionary songs and has garnered widespread popularity, thanks to official support and promotion.

2 Research Objectives

Through a comparative analysis of Dao Lang's "Mountain Songs are Lonely" and his cover of "Red Classic," the goal is to calculate the proportions of modernity, pre-modernity, and post-modernity in the lyrics written by Dao Lang himself. These proportions will be compared with those in "Red Classic," aiming to unlock the key to Dao Lang's enormous success and to find answers to the controversies surrounding his songs.

3 Reasons and Significance of Research

3.1 Reason for Research

Firstly, Dao Lang's "Mountain Songs are Lonely" has brought unprecedented social reflection, requiring a new perspective to examine this world-class cultural phenomenon. There is a concerted effort to explore the reasons behind the formation of this global cultural phenomenon, thereby inspiring and guiding the creation of songs.

Secondly, modernity serves as a measure for assessing progress, backwardness, and ethical considerations. The opposition between new and old ideologies often revolves around issues of modernity. The "Rakshasa Sea City" in Dao Lang's "Mountain Songs are Lonely" has received unprecedented acclaim, being hailed as a masterpiece that is "intriguing to the heart," "appreciated by both the refined and common," and "resonant both domestically and abroad." It is described as singing "the voice of the common people," contributing to the "revival of Chinese culture," and unlocking the "code to popularity," regarded as an "ancient and divine song." Dao Lang himself is praised as a "revolutionary figure of the era," a "trailblazer in the rejuvenation of Chinese art," a "great people's musician," a "singer of the people," a "true people's artist," a "master of the generation," an "extraordinary talent," a "musical sage," and a "singing saint." However, twenty years ago, music authorities criticized him for lacking "aesthetic viewpoints" and

---

[4] Folk songs are few.wikipedia. https://zh.wikipedia.org/wiki/%E5%B1%B1%E6%AD%8C% E5%AF%A5%E5%93%89.2023-11-17[2023-1-30].

[5] Hou Xiangjun. A museum in China opens beforehand thanks to hit song. Global Time. https:// www.globaltimes.cn/page/202308/1296191.shtml.2023-8-13[2023-11-30].

claimed that he set back Chinese pop music by at least 15 years. Current perspectives include viewing this song as a "revenge tune" and a "scolding song" aimed at those music giants who hindered their development with negative critiques two decades ago. Another perspective criticizes the lyrics, citing instances like "grass roosters crowing" and "half door lintel" as perpetuating gender discrimination with a pre-modern undertone. A third viewpoint considers Dao Lang's lyrics and songs as a cultural regression towards retroism. Therefore, research focusing on the proportion of modernity becomes essential in establishing the value of Dao Lang's lyrics.

Thirdly, the "tsunami" caused by "Rakshasa Sea City" reflects the increasing awakening of modernity among the public, making it valuable for research. With the rapid dissemination and widespread popularity of "Rakshasa Sea City," online fans, known as Dao Lang enthusiasts, have exposed and criticized practices like "transfer fees (转腔费)" and "horse households" (马户, donkey) and "birds again" (又鸟, chicken), ultimately leading to the forced shutdown of Zhejiang TV's "Good Voice" program. This wave of enthusiasm among Knife fans on the self-media platform, on the surface, seems to originate from the suppression of grassroots folk singers by music industry figures who control the discourse, and the subsequent backlash from a large audience against this suppression. However, in essence, it represents a struggle between the pre-modern consciousness of jockeying for dominance in the cultural landscape and the universal values of modern humanity. Implicit in this struggle are connections between power and capital, contradictions between capital and the arts, and competition between Western pop music and Chinese ethnic music. Behind these struggles, contradictions, and competitions lies a grand celebration on self-media platforms, where a vast audience liberates themselves from the judgments and regulations imposed by musical authorities and academic elites. They follow their feelings to freely express their preferences, engaging in a battle to defend their aesthetic rights. This is an expression of netizens' awakening to modernity, a magnificent revelry breaking free from the control of external authorities. Therefore, concerning the societal response to Dao Lang's successful breakthrough, it is inseparable from the consideration of modern values such as civilization, freedom, democracy, rule of law, fairness, justice, philanthropy, and aesthetic rights.

Finally, "Rakshasa Sea City" comes from Dao Lang's self-composed and self-written album "Mountain Songs are Lonely." Therefore, taking the entire album "Mountain Songs are Lonely" as the research subject would offer a comprehensive and holistic perspective. The lyrics of "Rakshasa Sea City" mostly stems from the stories and allusions in the works of Chinese Qing Dynasty novelist Pu Songling, as well as influences from Buddhist scriptures and "Taiping Guangji." Consequently, its modernity is submerged within pre-modern concepts and narrative styles. Utilizing Bie-modernist cultural computing methods to analyze its lyrics can provide a reference that bridges ancient and modern cultures, awakening an awareness of modernity.

3.2 Meaning: Revealing the Secrets Behind Dao Lang's Success, Inspiring and Guiding the Creation of Lyrics

Due to the fact that most evaluations of Dao Lang's songs come from the literary field, conducting a Bie-modernist cultural computing analysis on the ideological content of Dao Lang's "Mountain Songs are Lonely" lyrics is aimed at clarifying whether the occurrence of the Dao Lang phenomenon is solely determined by the proportion of modernity or if there are deeper underlying reasons. This has a certain enlightening significance for guiding lyric composition.

4 Principles, Methods, and Steps for Identifying Modernity, Pre-modernity, and Post-modernity in Daolang Lyrics

4.1 Identification Principles and Methods

Bie-modernism is a philosophical theory concerning social forms proposed by Chinese scholar Wang Jianjiang, aiming to distinguish between true and false modernity and to conduct deep distinguishing between deep fakes[6].

The basic systematic process is as follows (Figs. 1, 2, 3 and 4):

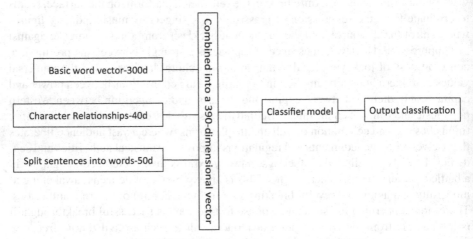

Fig. 1. 总体系统示意图 Overall System Schematic Diagram

- Feature Extraction: Due to the substantial differences between lyrics and other general texts, their close association with context, text background, and implicit meanings is pivotal. Consequently, the current characteristic vectors of Word2Vec are insufficient to fully capture the properties and implied meanings of words. In this paper, based on the existing pre-trained Word + Ngram model with 300 dimensions (utilizing Chinese Wikipedia as the corpus), we further train a 50-dimensional vector from Dao Lang's lyrics. Subsequently, we merge the initial 300-dimensional word vectors with the newly trained word vectors, creating a comprehensive 350-dimensional word vector.

---

[6] See: Wang Jianjiang (2017). Bie-Modern: Space Encounters and Times Spans. Beijing: China Social Sciences Press. (pp. 300–307); Wang Jianjiang (2023). Aestheticology of Bie-Modernism. Beijing: China Social Sciences Press. (pp. 238–245). See also www.biemodern ism.org.

- Entity Encoding: Due to the intricate interpersonal relationships, interwoven plotlines, and polyphonic structures within lyrics, this paper implements individual encoding for character relationships, resulting in a 40-dimensional word vector for character relationships.
- Word Annotation: Subsequently, this paper proceeds to annotate words based on fundamental units such as modernity, pre-modernity, and post-modernity.
- Model Training: Leveraging the Transformer model, a deep learning architecture based on the self-attention mechanism, renowned for its outstanding performance in natural language processing tasks, this paper employs the Transformer model to train on Dao Lang's lyrics. The steps involved in this process are outlined as follows:

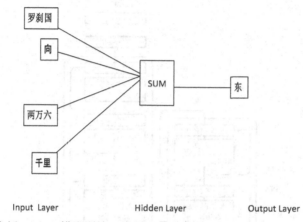

Input Layer   Hidden Layer   Output Layer

Fig. 2. 以4词为例，CBOW模型训练50维词向量示意图 Taking four words as an example, a schematic diagram illustrating the training of 50-dimensional word vectors using the CBOW model.

| 50d Word Vec | 300d Word Vec |

Fig. 3. 维词向量组成 a comprehensive 350-dimensional word vector

A: Input Embedding: Firstly, we need to convert the input text into embedding vectors. As introduced in the previous feature extraction section, we utilize the pretrained embedding matrix Word2Vec. Each word is transformed into a fixed-length 390-dimensional vector, comprising 350 dimensions for word embeddings and 40 dimensions for person-entity relation embeddings.

B: Positional Encoding: Since the Transformer model lacks explicit sequential awareness, we incorporate positional encoding to aid the model in understanding the sequence of lyrics. The positional encoding follows a fixed order.

C: Self-Attention Mechanism: This constitutes the core of the Transformer model. The self-attention mechanism allows the model to consider all words in a sentence when determining the representation of a single word. This is achieved by computing attention scores between input words and applying them to the input embeddings.

D: Feedforward Neural Network: The output from the self-attention mechanism is fed into a feedforward neural network. This network remains the same at each position, but parameters may differ across layers.

- Output: Finally, we feed the output of the last layer into a classifier (typically a linear layer followed by a softmax function) to generate the ultimate classification predictions.

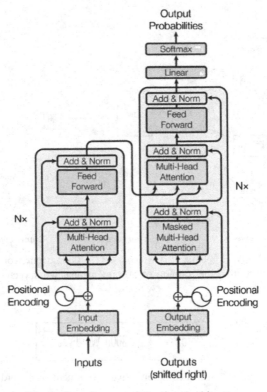

Fig. 4. Transforme + Attention Architecture

4.2 Specific Steps

A: Utilize the lyrics of the Dao Lang song series as the corpus to obtain a 50-dimensional vector for each word.

B: Use the character relationships within the corpus to obtain a 40-dimensional vector for each character.

C: Select sentences with distinct temporal features from Dao Lang's original "Mountain Songs are Lonely" and his cover of "Red Classic," respectively, as feature labels. Use these labels as the training set to create a classifier.

D: Based on the trained classifier, classify "Mountain Songs are Lonely" and Dao Lang's cover of "Red Classic."

E: Record and analyze the classification results.

红色经典

■ pre-modernity ■ modernity ■ post-modernity ■ others

红色经典 / Red Classic

pre-modernity	23.20%
modernity	64.60%
post-modernity	0.00%
Others	12.20%

山歌寥哉

■ pre-modernity ■ modernity ■ post-modernity ■ others

山歌寥哉 / Mountain Songs are Lonely

pre-modernity	18.40%
modernity	73.60%
post-modernity	0.00%
Others	8.00%

5   Analysis of the Proportion of Modernity in "Rakshasa Sea City"

罗刹海市 / **Rakshasa Sea City**

pre-modernity	13.00%
modernity	79.00%
post-modernity	0.00%
Others	8.00%

6   Conclusion

In "Mountain Songs are Lonely," the proportion of modernity reaches 73.60%, higher than the 64.60% in "Red Classic." The proportion of modernity in "Rakshasa Sea City" reaches as high as 79.00%, indicating that by employing characters, stories, and metaphors from classic literary works, it reflects social realities without compromising the modern expression of the lyrics. On the contrary, it serves to criticize more effectively than straightforward expressions. Undoubtedly, this is why "Mountain Songs are Lonely," particularly "Rakshasa Sea City," is more favored by contemporary audiences and widely sung globally compared to Dao Lang's cover of "Red Classic." However, this has also led to intense criticism and denigration by a small minority.

The freedom, democracy, rule of law, fairness, justice, social welfare, and promotion of good and suppression of evil in modernity possess universal human values. However, to break through the taboo of current dictatorial rulers and achieve freedom and safety in dissemination, it requires arming with classical literary allusions and literary techniques, allowing social critique to take place through metaphor, allusion, and symbolism, thus achieving better effects. This is also the reason why "Rakshasa Sea City" breaks through the ideological opposition and control, allowing people to "know in their hearts" while spreading, and opponents cannot sue Dao Lang for specifically insulting someone, hence cannot resort to legal action.

Cultural computing is not about the classification and statistics of lyrics in Chinese texts, but rather a scientific algorithm for handling multi-dimensional complex relationships. Through multiple iterations of experimentation in this study, it has been repeatedly demonstrated that the subjective classification and statistical analysis of modernity in lyrics diverge significantly from the results of cultural computing. Through repeated analysis, it has been found that with the aid of characters and allusions from Qing Dynasty writer Pu Songling's classical Chinese novels, Dao Lang's lyrics lack sufficient modernity features in terms of noun identification, yet they possess ample modernity features in terms of content. Therefore, this study relies on the results of cultural computing rather than manually classified and statistical outcomes.

Due to the fact that lyrics are predominantly emotional and often require the use of allegorical techniques drawn from nature, or Bi-Xing, to transcend the temporal constraints of the era, if we were to remove the "others" category, namely the natural category, from this study, the proportion of modernity would remain unchanged. However, doing so would overlook the infinite aspect of transcending temporal limitations relative to the era, which does not align with the original intent of the lyrics.

Reference Materials

Part One

1. Dao Lang wrote lyrics and composed "Mountain Songs are Lonely" Daolang. "Mountain Songs are Lonely." Shanghai: Xurun Music Company. 2023-7-19.
2. Daolang's cover of "Red Classic" Daolang. "Red Classic." Beijing: Ah Ya La So Company. 2008-3-13.
3. Dao Lang's album catalog collection

Dao Lang. "Louran Drums and Bells." Beijing: Ah Ya La So Company. 2002-3-1.

Dao Lang. "Silk Road Soul." Beijing: Ah Ya La So Company. 2003-1-1.

Dao Lang. "Silk Road Melody." Beijing: Ah Ya La So Company. 2003-1-1.

Dao Lang. "Western Region Love Song Rock Edition." Beijing: Ah Ya La So Company. 2003-11-1.

Dao Lang. "The First Snow of 2002." Beijing: Ah Ya La So Company. 2004-1-6.

Dao Lang. "Desert Love Song." Beijing: Ah Ya La So Company. 2004-7-1.

Dao Lang. "Under the Northern Sky." Beijing: Ah Ya La So Company. 2004-8-14.

Dao Lang. "Kashgar Populus Euphratica." Los Angeles: Universal Records. 2004-12-29.

Dao Lang. "Kashgar Populus Euphratica (Remix Compilation)." Los Angeles: Universal Records. 2005-3-21.

Dao Lang. "Wolf in Sheep's Clothing." Beijing: Ah Ya La So Company. 2006-4-19.

Dao Lang. "Thank You." Beijing: Ah Ya La So Company. 2006-4-21.

Dao Lang. "Dao Lang III." Beijing: Ah Ya La So Company. 2006-9-21.

Dao Lang. "10th Anniversary Global Tour Debut in Xinjiang." Beijing: Ah Ya La So Company. 2007-5-18.

Dao Lang. "Dance with Lang Remix." Beijing: Ah Ya La So Company. 2007-6-1.

Dao Lang. "Memoirs of the Western Regions." Beijing: Ah Ya La So Company. 2008-4-1.

Dao Lang. "A Family." Beijing: Ah Ya La So Company. 2009-7-15.

Dao Lang. "Eternal Brothers." Beijing: Ah Ya La So Company. 2010-1-1.

Dao Lang. "Girl in Colorful Clothes in 2011." Beijing: Ah Ya La So Company. 2011-10-17.

Dao Lang. "Audition Dao Lang." Guangzhou: Guangzhou Hengtai Development Co., Ltd. 2012-9-1.

Dao Lang. "Eternal Warrior." Beijing: Ah Ya La So Company. 2012-9-26.

Dao Lang. "Clear to the Bottom." Beijing: Ah Ya La So Company. 2013-1-15.

Dao Lang. "On the Way to Yili." Beijing: Ah Ya La So Company. 2013-11-1.

Dao Lang. "Theme Song of the TV Series New Journey to the West." Beijing: Evergrande Music Company. 2018-8-1.

Dao Lang. "Ballad Script." Shanghai: Shangliu Yu Cultural Studio. 2020-9-28.

Dao Lang. "So I Heard." Shanghai: Shangliu Yu Cultural Studio. 2020-11-20.

Dao Lang. "Every Person in the World." Beijing: Ah Ya La So Company. 2021-2-28.

Dao Lang. "Blood Romantic." Beijing: See Music Company. 2022-11-7.

Dao Lang. "Believer of Time." Shanghai: Xurun Music Company. 2023-6-22.

Part Two

4. Cloud Music

[1] Dao Lang. "Mountain Songs are Lonely" [EB/OL]. 2023-7-19. https://music.163.com/#/album?id=169512732.

5. QQ Music

[2] Dao Lang. "Mountain Songs are Lonely" [EB/OL]. 2023-7-19. https://y.qq.com/n/ryqq/albumDetail/001yI1NU2Mq3lz.

6. Douban

[3] Wei Chunliang. Dao Lang's new song "Rakshasa Sea City," crazy! [EB/OL]. 2023-7-24. https://music.douban.com/review/15324578/.

[4] Xiao Hun. Dao Lang, an excellent sample studying "vulgar" and "not vulgar" [EB/OL]. 2023-7-27. https://music.douban.com/review/15333670/.

[5] Zou Xiaoying. From 2003 to 2023, Dao Lang's 20 years of gaining and losing [EB/OL]. 2023-8-8. https://music.douban.com/review/15367406/.

[6] Huangagou. New bottle, old wine, great compassion [EB/OL]. 2023-7-23. https://music.douban.com/review/15320141/.

[7] Azi'er. Dao Lang finally bids farewell to the remnants of nomadic civilization and curses his way to agricultural civilization [EB/OL]. 2023-7-28. https://music.douban.com/review/15335325/.

[8] Ocean Recycling Material Liu Lang. Why "Rakshasa Sea City" resonates with me [EB/OL]. 2023-8-10. https://music.douban.com/review/15370805/.

[9] Let me out. Unboxing lyrics [EB/OL]. 2023-8-23. https://music.douban.com/review/15404229/.

[10] Pei Feng. Is Dao Lang's music really good? What's good about it? [EB/OL]. 2023-8-6. https://music.douban.com/review/15360702/.

[11] sdebut. Dao Lang's "Mountain Songs are Lonely" is the most discussed album of the year, but is the music actually unimpressive? [EB/OL]. 2023-8-24. https://music.douban.com/review/15407243/.

[12] Blomackenlaudi. Not very pleasant to listen to [EB/OL]. 2023-7-24. https://music.douban.com/subject/36482296/reviews?start=40.

7. Zhihu

[13] Gray Machine Gray Tkzc. How to evaluate Dao Lang's new album "Mountain Songs are Lonely"? [EB/OL]. 2023-7-19. https://www.zhihu.com/question/612849893/answer/3131469473.

[14] Huihui. Why is the album "Mountain Songs are Lonely" so melodious, is it because the lyrics and music are well written, or because Dao Lang sings too well? [EB/OL]. 2023-8-20. https://www.zhihu.com/question/618295028/answer/3183998344.

[15] I am really desperate. As a music producer, what are your evaluations of Dao Lang's new album "Mountain Songs are Lonely," and what do you think about the music? [EB/OL]. 2023-8-6. https://www.zhihu.com/question/615938776/answer/3210075657.

[16] Nothing. Are there any music theory teachers who can explain the arrangement aspects of Dao Lang's new album "Mountain Songs are Lonely"? [EB/OL]. 2023-7-30. https://www.zhihu.com/question/614750034/answer/3154433220.

[17] Popcorn of Venus. What significance does Dao Lang's new album "Mountain Songs are Lonely" have for the dissemination and development of folk songs in our country? [EB/OL]. 2023-7-24. https://www.zhihu.com/question/613740 621/answer/3157060339.

8. Bilibili

[18] Wang Feng. Wang Feng talks about Dao Lang's new album "Mountain Songs are Lonely" [EB/OL]. 2023-8-2. https://www.bilibili.com/video/BV1Zc411F7nk/?spm_id_from=333.788.recommend_more_video.-1.

[19] Daodao Feng talks about music. Is Dao Lang's "Rakshasa Sea City"/"Mountain Songs are Lonely" good music? How should Chinese music develop? [EB/OL]. 2023-7-29. https://www.bilibili.com/video/BV1Y841127j6/?spm_id_from=333.337.search-card.all.click&vd_source=aa2240814b216fa08053011de060008b.

[20] The Desert Man Flying All Over the World. What are the original folk tunes corresponding to each song in Dao Lang's "Mountain Songs are Lonely"? [EB/OL]. 2023-8-22. https://www.bilibili.com/video/BV1mh4y1K788/?spm_id_from=333.337.search-card.all.click&vd_source=aa2240814b216fa080530 11de060008b.

[21] Talking Nonsense. "Mountain Songs are Lonely" is the conscience of the times, and its true value is obscured [EB/OL]. 2023-8-7.https://www.bilibili.com/video/BV1Tu411n72o/?spm_id_from=333.337.search-card.all.click&vd_source=aa2240814b216fa08053011de060008b.

[22] Monkeys all over the mountain, I have the reddest buttocks. The bassist of "Mountain Songs are Lonely" talks about Teacher Dao Lang, you will know how awesome Dao Lang is [EB/OL].2023-8-19.https://www.bilibili.com/video/BV1QG411f76P/?spm_id_from=333.337.search-card.all.click&vd_source=aa2240814b216fa08053011de060008b.

[23] Li Xiaolong who can play the flute. How to evaluate Teacher Dao Lang's flute skills? [EB/OL].2023-8-29.https://www.bilibili.com/video/BV1DP411a 7Pv/?spm_id_from=333.337.search-card.all.click&vd_source=aa2240814b21 6fa08053011de060008b.

[24] Professor You talks about sound and music. What style does Dao Lang's new album "Mountain Songs are Lonely" belong to? [EB/OL]. 2023-8-7. https://www.bilibili.com/video/BV1fF411f79z/?spm_id_from=333.337.sea rch-card.all.click&vd_source=aa2240814b216fa08053011de060008b.

[25] Professor You talks about sound and music. Evaluation: Does Dao Lang's new song have aesthetic viewpoints? Is he considered a folk singer? [EB/OL]. 2023-7-23.https://www.bilibili.com/video/BV1vV411L7CF/?spm_id_from=333. 337.search-card.all.click&vd_source=aa2240814b216fa08053011de060008b.

[26] A plate of Yangzhou fried rice. "Rakshasa Sea City" is not good? Elder Sun admits to being slapped in the face [EB/OL]. 2023-7-29. https://www.bilibili.com/video/BV1G841127MZ/?spm_id_from=333.337. search-card.all.click&vd_source=aa2240814b216fa08053011de060008b.

[27] Px1990711. Taiwanese media evaluates "Dao Lang brings popularity to Pu Songling, and Mountain Songs are Lonely is down-to-earth" [EB/OL]. 2023-8-13. https://www.bilibili.com/video/BV1tz4y1g7wx/?spm_id_from=333.337. search-card.all.click&vd_source=aa2240814b216fa08053011de060008b.

[28] Min, who is deeply impressed. Taiwanese media report: The King invites lyrics! Andy Lau: Inviting Dao Lang to write lyrics for the new song for free? [EB/OL]. 2023-8-7. https://www.bilibili.com/video/BV1Cj411r7FV/?spm_id_from=333. 337.search-card.all.click&vd_source=aa2240814b216fa08053011de060008b.

[29] A Liu Meow. Everyone on the internet is praising "Rakshasa Sea City," but I am opposing it now… Will I be attacked? [EB/OL]. 2023-7-31. https://www.bilibili.com/video/BV1Ph4y1C7K1/?spm_id_from=333.337. search-card.all.click&vd_source=aa2240814b216fa08053011de060008b.

[30] Hu Kan Music. One of the Few Men who Defeated Jay Chou, the Ceiling of Chinese Online Music: Dao Lang [EB/OL]. 2021-12-6. https://www.bilibili.com/video/BV1uZ4y197wB/?spm_id_from=333.1007. top_right_bar_window_history.content.click.

[31] Hu Kan Music. 2023 Year-end Review of Chinese Language Bands [EB/OL]. 2023-12-31. https://www.bilibili.com/video/BV1Pe411B7oz/?spm_ id_from=333.1007.top_right_bar_window_history.content.click&vd_source= aa2240814b216fa08053011de060008b.

[32] Elephant Projection Room. "Rustic", "Vulgar", Targeted by Cyberbullying? After becoming popular, suddenly disappeared [In Search of Dao Lang] [EB/OL]. 2022-10-5.https://www.bilibili.com/video/BV1bN4y1P71K/? spm_id_from=333.1007.top_right_bar_window_history.content.click&vd_sou rce=aa2240814b216fa08053011de060008b.

[33] Mr. G who loves thinking. What is the relationship between Jay Chou's "Christmas Star" and Dao Lang's "Future Film"? [EB/OL]. 2023-12-23. https://www.bilibili.com/video/BV13e411B7WG/?spm_id_from=333. 1007.top_right_bar_window_history.content.click&vd_source=aa2240814b21 6fa08053011de060008b.

[34] Music Wu Song. The Top 10 Hottest New Songs of 2023, Breaking Away from Plagiarism and Mudslinging, How Can the Chinese Music Scene Be So Impressive? [EB/OL]. 2023-11-20.https://www.bilibili.com/video/BV1uw411P7DQ/? spm_id_from=333.1007.top_right_bar_window_history.content.click.

9. Wechat Channels

[35] Mr. Zhang said. Lyrics analysis concludes, paying homage to Dao Lang [EB/OL]. 2023-8-7.

[36] Chinese scholar Zhang Chengdu. Rakshasa Sea City will be a demon-revealing mirror [EB/OL]. 2023-11-14.

[37] Erwei's theory. Dao Lang lies in patience, accumulating strength for future success [EB/OL]. 2023-10-14.

[38] Ganlu Art Museum. The ugly "pseudo gentlemen" of Rakshasa country [EB/OL]. 2023-7-28.

[39] Li Yong's Rapeseed Flower. Dao Lang will triumph, and so will the people [EB/OL]. 2023-7-31.

[40] Knife fan iron powder. Evaluations of Dao Lang by three major TV stations [EB/OL]. 2023-11-28.

[41] Everything is fine 4223. Some poems are unreadable by those in luxury, and some songs are disagreeable to those in comfort [EB/OL]. 2023-8-9.

[42] Happy Music Film and Television Production. Why did Yang Kun trend? [EB/OL]. 2023-7-27.

[43] Pioneer Vision. Du Zijian talks about Dao Lang [EB/OL]. 2023-9-5.

[44] Indistinguishable. The just are always there [EB/OL]. 2023-8-1.

[45] Nostalgic Music Library 666. Complete version of "Pian Pian" [EB/OL]. 2023-8-27.

[46] Da Hui, who is responsible for planning and hosting. Dao Lang's return. A song that transcends, beyond the reach of horse households and birds again [EB/OL]. 2023-8-28.

[47] The so-called Iren 985. Dao Lang and the genetic code of Chinese culture [EB/OL]. 2023-8-29.

[48] Mr. Wuyou. Dao Lang releases another video, expressing something with mysterious sunglasses and a smile [EB/OL]. 2023-11-13.

[49] Mr. Youcai - Liao Heng. The Li Wen incident may become an international scandal, reported specifically by TIME magazine [EB/OL]. 2023-8-22.

[50] Wu Pengfei said. Regarding Dao Lang's new song, dare you listen to some truth [EB/OL]. 2023-8-3.

[51] Vernacular Channel. Wu Pengfei criticizes Dao Lang as rubbish; I criticize Wu Pengfei [EB/OL]. 2023-8-15.

[52] Yin outside the string. Dao Lang is a great folk musician; can he win the Nobel Prize in Literature? [EB/OL]. 2023-8-17.

[53] Director of Qiqu Museum. In-depth analysis of the Dao Lang new song incident [EB/OL]. 2023-8-8.

[54] Zen Medicine Hall. Fundamental humanity: The ultimate interpretation of Rakshasa Sea City [EB/OL]. 2023-7-31.

[55] Qu Gensheng. The shocking truth behind Dao Lang's "Rakshasa Sea City" [EB/OL]. 2023-7-30.

[56] Ni na. Dao Lang's biography [EB/OL]. 2023-7-28.

[57] Waking Dreams 6262. Dao Lang was rated as one of the "Top 10 Poets" at the Tenth Chinese Poetry Spring Festival Gala in 2024 [EB/OL]. 2024-1-8.

[58] Wang Wang Hot Catch-Up. Dao Lang wins the title of Best Asian Singer [EB/OL]. 2024-1-7.

[59] Sea dragon 920. Dao Lang is popular again [EB/OL]. 2024-1-9.

[60] Zhang Dama. The beauty of the flower demon is the beauty of ancient Chinese poetry [EB/OL]. 2024-1-8.

[61] Fish in search of water. Is Dao Lang the real "horse households"? [EB/OL]. 2024-1-27.

Part Three

[62] Wu W, Wang J, Hu X. The Road of "Bie-modern" of Periodization of Chinese Design Modern History[C]//International Conference on Human-Computer Interaction. Cham: Springer Nature Switzerland, 2022: 62–88.EI.

[63] Wang J, Chen H. Bie-modernism and cultural computing[C]//International Conference on Human-Computer Interaction. Cham: Springer International Publishing, 2021: 474–489. EI.

[64] Wang J, Chen H, Ma T, et al. A Cultural Computing of the Share of Modernity in World Literary Masterpieces by Bie-Modernism[C]//International Conference on Human-Computer Interaction. Cham: Springer Nature Switzerland, 2023: 603–617.EI.

[65] Chang J. A Study on the Bie-Modernism Features of China's New God Series of Contemporary Animation Films[C]//International Conference on Human-Computer Interaction. Cham: Springer Nature Switzerland, 2023: 241–249.EI.

[66] Chang J. Bie-Modernist Culture Computing is on the Road of Deep Distinguishing[C]//International Conference on Human-Computer Interaction. Cham: Springer International Publishing, 2022: 401–412.EI.

[67] Sun R, Zou H. Bie-Modernism Cultural Computing and Identification of "Bie-Human"[C]//International Conference on Human-Computer Interaction. Cham: Springer Nature Switzerland, 2023: 592–602.EI.

[68] Qi Z, Chen H, Liu M, et al. Bie—Modernism with Cultural Calculations in Multiple Dimensions[C]//International Conference on Human-Computer Interaction. Cham: Springer International Publishing, 2022: 120–136.EI.

Writing Education Research in the Context of Cultural Computing in Bie-modernism

Yingying Xu[1,2] and Jianjiang Wang[1(✉)]

[1] School of Humanities, Shanghai Normal University, Shanghai 200234, China
120512187@qq.com
[2] College of Preparatory Education, Guangxi Mimzu University, Nanning 530006, China

Abstract. Bie-modernist Cultural Computing is a form of cultural computing guided by Bie-modernism principles, representing a leap in non-modernist theory. This paper discusses the opportunities, challenges, and solutions that ChatGPT brings to writing education in the context of Bie-modernist Cultural Computing. The theory of Bie-modernist Cultural Computing is integrated with writing education, presenting the realistic characteristics of intelligence, individuality, and customization in writing education. Bie-modernism effectively identifies true and false modernity using the precision and powerful data analysis of cultural computing. Therefore, from the perspective of Bie-modernist Cultural Computing, ChatGPT in writing education has the risks of weakening the initiative of learning subjects, weakening the initiative of teaching subjects, and rigid writing content.

Keywords: Bie-modernism · Cultural computing · ChatGPT · Writing education

1 Introduction

The Bie-modern is a social form mixed with pre-modern, modern and post-modern, proposed by Professor Wang Jianjiang in 2014.The Bie-modernism is a criticism of the adverse phenomena generated by this social form. The Bie-modern theory has attracted extensive attention from the academic circles at home and abroad since its proposal.

"The Bie-modernist Cultural Computing is a kind of cultural computing guided by the concept of Bie-modernism.It focuses on the difference between the real world and the false world, and studies inferior culture and its products. The Bie-modernist Cultural Computing advocates that computer science and artificial intelligence should first form a self-restraint mechanism, consciously resist pseudo-modernism, and then establish a set of authenticity classification system in the Bie-modernist Cultural Computing" [1]. Deep Distinguishing is the theoretical expression of the Bie-modernist Cultural Computing, which belongs to the interdisciplinary field of computer science, philosophy and aesthetics. It is of pioneering significance to examine the application of ChatGPT in writing education with the Deep Distinguishing theory of the Bie-modernist Cultural Computing.

In November 2022, a large language model called ChatGPT (Chat Generative Pre-trained Transformer) was launched by a Silicon Valley technology company in the United

M. Rauterberg (Ed.): HCII 2024, LNCS 14717, pp. 391–407, 2024.
https://doi.org/10.1007/978-3-031-61147-6_26

States. This program can help people write emails, papers, plans and other styles. Through powerful data search, language expression and generation technologies, the user scale soared. People are excited about the birth of this artificial intelligence writing technology, but university teachers in the educational community are beginning to worry about the impact of ChatGPT on writing education. For example, ChatGPT can train and improve itself by analyzing a large amount of data on the Internet, but it cannot confirm the accuracy and credibility of this information. The content generated by the writing subject using this tool may contain false or incorrect information. ChatGPT is very easy to cause academic misconduct, because originality is an important criterion to measure the value of academic research achievements.

This phenomenon is actually a modern "deep fake" phenomenon. "Deep fake" is a product of modern high-tech development, which is difficult to be detected by artificial intelligence anti-fake technology. The importance of the theory of modern "deep fake" not only lies in revealing the obstacles of "deepfake" technology to the overall improvement of human civilization, but also advocates technical and theoretical resistance to "deep fake" technology from the perspective of modern "deepfake" and cultural computing. The following is to discuss the opportunities, challenges and responses brought by ChatGPT to writing education in combination with the theory of Bie-modermist Cultural Computing.

2 Opportunities: The Realistic Characteristics of Bie Modermist Cultural Computing Combined with Writing Education

"Organic combination of Bie-modernism with cultural computing, aesthetics and computer, trying to implement Bie-modernism into human-computer interaction and cultural computing. The new mode of "philosophy + technology + art" formed by cultural computing in recent years is just combined with the creative space theory of Bie-modernism, forming the non-modern cultural computing combined with Bie-modernism and cultural computing. This marks the entry of Bie-modernism into the field of technology and the integration with international artificial intelligence technology" [2]. With the rapid development of ChatGPT, it is indeed feasible to integrate Bie-modermist Cultural Computing with ChatGPT writing for the purpose of seeking truth and then into writing education. The combination of Bie-modermist Cultural Computing with writing education will present several realistic characteristics:

2.1 Intelligent

ChatGPT writing is actually the editing and layout after information collection, and its core is cloud computing and big data analysis. Through the sequence of deep learning, ChatGPT writing ability is improved. It sorts out and updates the data of the database, and constructs the intelligent process of natural language. ChatGPT is a kind of generative AI, which has rich computing resources and data sets. These resources contain a large number of writing materials in various fields, including humanities and social sciences, natural sciences, political economy and so on. Internet search engines, digital libraries, online academic journals and monographs can provide the latest information and help us to recognize the latest progress and hot topics in the field. ChatGPT can interact with humans in real time and efficiently, in line with human communication practices, and can quickly respond to human commands, thus reducing repetitive tasks. It provides accurate services, provides matching resources in real time according to the questions and needs of the writing subject, and supports personalized and differentiated learning. ChatGPT writing is the integration of a large number of texts through neural network models. It is an intelligent process. At this time, Bie-modermist Cultural Computing combines ChatGPT artificial intelligence writing, and integrates the powerful data analysis of Bie-modermist Cultural Computing to enhance the accuracy of ChatGPT database organization.

Under the auspices of Bie-modermist Cultural Computing and ChatGPT generative artificial intelligence writing, the writing subject needs to carry forward the spirit of Bie-modernism, put an end to the superficial general ChatGPT generating fixed mode of "Deep fake" writing, and truly enter the deep and creative "deep Distinguishing" writing. The implementation of the modernist theory to distinguish between authenticity and falsity in writing teaching should pay attention to the writing process of students. The essence of writing problems lies in the "writing process". If we do not actually consider what happens in the writing process, we cannot help students and improve their writing ability. Scholar Berninger proposed a theory called "Not So Simple Writing View", which emphasizes the cooperation between skills and processes at different levels, and pays special attention to advanced thinking and executive function, as shown in Fig. 1. Writing requires the use of advanced thinking and executive ability, including focus, planning, inspection, sorting and self-control. These abilities emphasize the strategic knowledge of writing, which can help us integrate and stimulate thinking in the process of writing, so as to create specific writing behaviors in daily life. Advanced thinking and executive function are emphasized in "Not So Simple Writing View", which is consistent with the human functions advocated in the concept of human-computer symbiosis. Human functions include command issuing, process design, supervision and control, reflection and modification, etc. Human-computer symbiotic writing under ChatGPT generative artificial intelligence is driven by the needs of the writing subject brain, giving instructions and feedback, and training and enhancing its ability by giving instructions and providing feedback to ChatGPT. In this process, human intelligence and ChatGPT extraneous brain gradually become more intelligent.

Therefore, under the support of the "deep difference" theory of Bie-modermist Cultural Computing, the writing subject should use deep reading and cognitive strategies to ask questions when writing, and then integrate a large amount of information, establish connections, generate thinking frameworks, draw brain maps or flow charts, etc. Generating thinking frameworks, drawing brain maps or flow charts, integrating a large amount of information, establishing connections, through analysis and evaluation, can promote the cultivation of higher-order thinking such as image memory and abstract thinking. Deep reading will play a huge role under the support of generative artificial intelligence and Bie-modermist Cultural Computing. The writing subject needs to read a large number of books, including many foreign works. Now with ChatGPT, the efficiency of writing has been significantly improved. We can ask ChatGPT assistant to

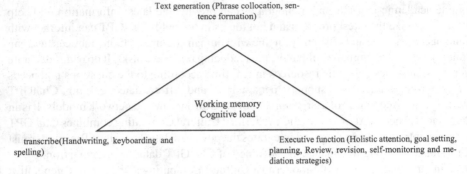

Fig. 1. Not so simple writing view [3]

browse literature pages in the search engine, and quickly summarize the characteristics, differences and development history of multiple literatures through commands and inquiries. In this way, we can understand the current situation of research and form a literature review. In addition, ChatGPT can also explain proper nouns in academic research through questions or instructions. In a word, the combination of Bie-modermist Cultural Computing with ChatGPT greatly reflects the intelligent characteristics of ChatGPT generative artificial intelligence in writing teaching.

In addition, the intelligent process of ChatGPT human-machine writing is also reflected in the process of automatically perceiving emotional dialogue. In the automatic emotion-aware dialogue generation model integrating retrieval database, as shown in Fig. 2. The starting point of the dynamic emotion-aware dialogue generation model is that when the ChatGPT machine needs to answer human questions, if a retrieval database has been built in advance, it can retrieve all possible responses from the database and analyze emotions, so as to use this emotional information to assist the machine to reply. Intuitively, this way is like telling the ChatGPT machine what human emotional responses are to this question. With these reference information and combined with the dialogue history, the ChatGPT machine can generate more emotionally appropriate responses. The overall structure of the model is shown in the figure, mainly including three parts: content encoder, emotion encoder and sentence decoder. Among them, the content encoder encodes the entire dialogue history, the emotion encoder perceives emotions from the dialogue history and the candidate responses retrieved from the retrieval database and encodes the emotional information, and the sentence decoder decodes all the encoded information to generate responses.

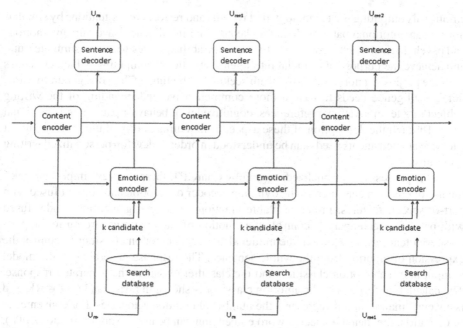

Fig. 2. Automatic emotion-sensing dialogue generation model of fusion retrieval database [4]

2.2 Personalization

In the early stage of writing, the integration of the writing subject and ChatGPT is a personalized process of "deep separation". First of all, the interaction between Chat-GPT and the writing subject can promote in-depth communication, brainstorming and diversified creative sharing, thus stimulating inspiration. This interaction can inspire each other's views and assist both sides to produce new views. Then, ChatGPT and the writing subject work together to help organize their thoughts. In the creative process, in the face of complex ideas, the writing subject and ChatGPT communicate with each other, sort out their thoughts in the constant interaction, and refine the writing theme. Then, with the assistance of ChatGPT, the writing subject formulates the arrangement of time and space, sets up a feasible writing plan, and conducts self-conscious regulation, self-motivation and emotion management of the writing process. Finally, through in-depth and multi-level exchanges with ChatGPT, the writing subject effectively sorts out various parts of the writing content and constructs a preliminary structural framework. At the same time, ChatGPT can also provide customized information push: based on the requirements of creation, ChatGPT can provide suggestions, including customized resource promotion and learning path design services, such as providing creative ideas, writing theories, precautions, style characteristics and sample texts, to provide strong support for creation. The key of artificial intelligence writing is to pursue real human emotions through artificial emotional computing, so that machine creation can be as close to human emotional expression as possible. The key point of artificial intelligence writing is to seek real human emotions through artificial emotional computing, so that machine creation can be as close to human emotional expression as possible. Artificial emotional computing is a technology that records and restores real situations by simulating human emotional patterns. It can make artificial intelligence have human emotions and psychological mechanisms, so as to obtain the ability to seek truth and simulate truth, and achieve the purpose of artificial intelligence emotional computing, which coincides with the purpose of non-modernist "truth seeking". The future ChatGPT generative artificial intelligence needs to have a more comprehensive understanding of the writing subject's style, motivation, preferences, cognitive level, behavior pattern and emotional state. Through the description of these aspects, the writing ability of the writing subject can be evaluated and its needs can be understood in order to develop personalized writing programs.

In the process of personalized writing by ChatGPT, there is a very important link - the use of emotion classifier. In the dynamic decoder of emotion and content fused with part-of-speech features, the controllable emotional dialogue generation model fused with part-of-speech analysis controls the emotion of each word according to the part-of-speech features. In addition, the model also uses an emotion classifier to control the expression of emotion from the whole sentence. The response generated by the model is input into the emotion classifier, and the classifier classifies the generated response. The calculation formula of the emotion classifier is shown in formula (1). $W \in RK \times d$ is a weight matrix, and K represents the number of emotion categories. For convenience of operation, the idea of expected word embedding can be used to approximate $Q(E|Y)$. As shown in formula (2) and (3). Ewej represents the expected word embedding, which is the weighted sum of all possible word embeddings in each time step.

$$Q(E|Y) = softmax(W \cdot \frac{1}{N} \sum_{j=1}^{N} Ewe_j) \tag{1}$$

$$Q(E|Y) = softmax(W \cdot \frac{1}{N} \sum_{j=1}^{N} Ewb(y_j)) \tag{2}$$

$$Ewe_j = \sum_{V} p(y_j) \cdot Emb(y_j) \tag{3}$$

2.3 Customization

In the process of writing, ChatGPT artificial intelligence and the writing subject collaborate to generate specific writing texts under the guidance of the theory of Bie-modermist Cultural Computing. The combination of Bie-modermist Cultural Computing with a variety of practical algorithms, including convolutional neural network computing, character character computing, Word2vec model + CNN algorithm, etc. For example, the combination of Bie-modermist Cultural Computing with the above models and technical algorithms to analyze the character characteristics and deep emotions of the characters, so as to form a deep difference in the character image and emotional characteristics. The image characteristics of the characters in this model include physiological aspects (such as appearance, behavior, clothing, etc.), social aspects (interpersonal communication and social activities) and psychological aspects, etc. It can carry out systematic and data-based quantitative analysis of the character characteristics, growth background, behavior habits and deep emotions of the characters. Finally, through the document classification algorithm, the deep emotions and character characteristics of the characters can be generated. It is ready for artificial intelligence writing to further approach the true feelings of human beings and express the rich feelings of human beings, so as to form a specific style. The combination of Bie-modermist Cultural Computing with a variety of models and technical algorithms and then into ChatGPT writing, so that whether it is professional academic papers, professional news writing, or poetry story creation, ChatGPT can generate the corresponding style according to the style requirements input by the writing subject. Moreover, it can also more accurately polish the language for different style requirements. In addition, under the guidance of the "deep difference" theory, according to the needs of writing, we can customize different styles and value-oriented texts. In academic writing, authors need to spend a lot of energy to deal with the style, phrasing and grammatical structure of the article. ChatGPT can enhance the fluency of writing, assist the writing subject to better develop higher-order thinking, and focus on showing more valuable research achievements. The customized characteristics of ChatGPT artificial intelligence writing are mainly reflected in the following two aspects:

On the one hand, the writing subject can provide ChatGPT with templates, styles or other needs to guide it to structured writing. The Bie-modermist Cultural Computing combines artificial intelligence writing, and ChatGPT improves its writing ability by training a large amount of text data.It can master language styles, so as to avoid using fixed models to produce "deep fake" content that is ordinary, dogmatic and formulaic.

On the other hand, the Bie-modermist Cultural Computing combines artificial emotional computing, and the writing subject can require ChatGPT to conduct machine autonomous learning through artificial emotional computing, extract article features, call the stored style, summarize and present, etc. For example, the writing subject can ask ChatGPT to provide different styles (narrative, expository, prose, etc.), and ChatGPT assists the writing subject to conclude writing elements and feature structures, so as to improve writing skills.

3   Challenges: Reviewing the Risks of ChatGPT in Writing Education Under the Background of Bie-Modermist Cultural Computing

The essence of Bie-modernism is to distinguish the phenomenon of authenticity. Therefore, the reflection and critical spirit of Bie-modernism has become the soul of Bie-modernism. The combination of its soul with precise cultural computing and then entering the field of artificial intelligence is a leap of non-modern theory. Examining the risks of ChatGPT entering writing teaching with Bie-modermist Cultural Computing can cultivate the adaptive thinking in writing education, establish the critical awareness of teachers, students, relevant departments and even the government, and hone the innovation of ideas and related technologies. Upholding the "different from" thinking mode in non-modern theory, the risks of ChatGPT in writing education are roughly listed as follows:

3.1   The Initiative of the Learning Subject is Weakened

With the continuous progress of ChatGPT technology, ChatGPT artificial intelligence writing has degraded the writing subjectivity more and more, and the initiative of the learning subject is weakened. In the human-computer symbiotic writing, there are mainly two challenges as follows. First, the powerful ChatGPT artificial intelligence writing may lead to excessive dependence on and addiction to using ChatGPT writing, while ignoring the writing training of the human brain, resulting in the atrophy of the human brain. The insufficient participation of the human brain is like the "free ride" effect in cooperative learning. Studies have shown that the human brain has an energy-saving mode, which will deal with the irrelevant and replaceable tasks in the most efficient way to reduce energy consumption. This means that humans have no resistance to ChatGPT. Second, limit the scope of information obtained by the writing subject in the writing construction. The writing subject mainly inputs a few keywords, and ChatGPT can write some formatted articles, and the writing subject will form a habitual dependence. This too smooth writing experience makes the writer lose the opportunity to explore and reflect on the writing results, making the writing subject lazy to integrate their personal experience, emotion and other unique things, so that the writing results lack the emotional soul and personality and other innovative things, which is not conducive to the development of the initiative of the writing subject, easy to make the writing simple and formatted, and thus not conducive to the improvement of the writing level.

If we overly rely on the writing template of ChatGPT, it may make our writing become fixed and rigid, and lose its uniqueness. Universal ChatGPT writers are trapped in Plato's cave, unable to observe the outside world and discern and perceive their surroundings, leading to a gradual loss of their ability to pursue objective truth. The impact of generative AI ChatGPT is not only a change in the way humans acquire knowledge, but also a classical degeneration of the pursuit of truth.

3.2   The Initiative of the Educational Subject is Weakened

With the continuous development of artificial intelligence technology, human society has entered the era of ChatGPT, and network technology has made the appearance of "intelligent teachers" who transfer knowledge, and human teachers are no longer the only source of knowledge. In traditional society, the main way for middle school students to acquire systematic knowledge and practical skills is through schools and teachers. The role of teachers in writing teaching is gradually weakening. In the traditional sense, the position of "teachers are knowledge disseminators, truth spokespersons, and moral representatives" is facing unprecedented challenges. Teachers' initiative as the main body of writing education has been weakened.

In the age of artificial intelligence, the speed and efficiency of people's access to information has increased significantly. ChatGPT allows students to quickly access open knowledge from a variety of sources, simply by entering their needs ChatGPT is able to continuously integrate and update the information, and constantly improve the quality of the generated content. At present, students can obtain learning materials through various channels and no longer rely solely on teachers to impart knowledge and develop skills. ChatGPT can replace teachers in teaching. This device can help students to self-review and correct some vocabulary and grammar errors, can also optimize and polish the essay, and through the search function to provide alternative suggestions on words and sentences, to help students become more proficient in the use of vocabulary and sentence construction. It can use data analysis and natural language processing techniques to assess students' writing skills and provide suggestions for improvement. ChatGPT can assist students in the tedious task of writing, including searching, collecting and organizing data, and constructing the structure and content of an essay. Generative AI like ChatGPT look like they could make excellent writing instructors in form.

3.3 The Stereotyping of Writing Content

The text content generated by ChatGPT is also easy to fall into a rigid state, that is, the writing content is stereotyped. A careful study of ChatGPT's interactions with people shows that while ChatGPT is good at understanding, expressing, and reasoning, it is still, ultimately, a programmed conversation partner. The text written by ChatGPT is based on the principle of statistics and the analysis and probability calculation of large-scale text data sets. It adopts the automated text generation technology based on statistics and uses the frequency and probability distribution of literature to generate new chapters. In addition, machine learning technology is also used to create new texts through the learning and training of a huge corpus with the help of generative models. This system can produce fluent text, but it relies on a lot of data training and computing resources behind it. Although this technology attaches importance to the style beauty and grammatical structure of the text, and can meet some creative requirements, it is limited in the ability to grasp the meaning and logical deduction, and is not enough to write in-depth insights and creative works, which makes the output content of ChatGPT often appear stylized and inflexible. This problem is particularly prominent in writing tasks such as essays, poems and stories. Because ChatGPT lacks the mental depth of a human, it has no intelligence, personality, or emotion. Its answers generally have a fixed structure, first stating the concept, then stating some "correct nonsense," and finally providing conclusions that seem objective but are actually ambiguous. ChatGPT's essays for the college entrance examination were smooth and stable, but they were plagued by too many cliches and empty words, lack of concrete cases to support them, and lack the creativity and critical thinking of candidates with high scores. The essays written by ChatGPT are smooth and stable, but the common problem is that there are too many cliches and empty words, lack of concrete cases to support, and do not possess the creativity and critical thinking of high scoring essay candidates. ChatGPT lacks a personal and emotional core, it has no real intelligence and can only mechanically copy the ideas in the database. This is the most important challenge for ChatGPT right now. The author asked GPT-4 to write a description of the environment of the bedroom at night, and designated the atmosphere as "gloomy", the specific dialogue and generated content is as follows:

Author input: *Now I need a description of the environment, it is the bedroom at night, quiet, dim, the only light source is the cold light emitted by the computer display, the whole scene to give people a kind of uneasy, gloomy atmosphere. There are objects in the scene, such as wardrobes, tables, Windows, curtains.*

GPT-4 generation: Night falls and all is still. There is a dim and oppressive atmosphere in the bedroom, as if the whole space has been swallowed by darkness. The only light source came from a computer display in the corner, which gave off a faint, cold light. This faint light gives the objects in the bedroom a hazy outline.

The wardrobe is close to the wall, shrouded in darkness, like a silent guardian, silently watching everything in the room. On the table lay a random pile of books and stationery, which seemed particularly lonely in the quiet night. The Windows are closed, cutting off the outside world from the interior. Through the thin curtains, neither moonlight nor starlight can penetrate this barrier, making the interior even darker.

This somber, oppressive atmosphere permeates the room, making people feel as if they are tightly bound by invisible chains. Suddenly, the cold light on the computer screen flickered like a ghost in the dark, making people uneasy. In this quiet night, people can't help but wonder if there is something strange lurking in this dim and depressing space.

The text generated by GPT-4 meets the requirements at first glance, but on closer inspection it doesn't. Words such as "dark" and "depressing" appear repeatedly, which is tedious and cumbersome; The image of "silent guardian" is out of touch with the whole text and its meaning is unclear. The description of "cold light" appears twice, but there is no corresponding relationship with each other; "Sketched in hazy outline" is inconsistent with "shrouded in darkness." It can be seen that the writing of GPT-4 above appears stiff in the structure of the article, and the rhetoric is boring. The whole text is forcibly cobbling together various words related to darkness and gloom, which is similar to piling up words in form. Such a style reflects ChatGPT's splicing thinking mode on artificial intelligence writing. It needs to be clear that although this style may provide inspiration for the author's creation, if it is regarded as an independent literary work to taste, there is no small defect.

Author input: In this story, terrorists have dropped a virus in a city, causing a disease to spread. The hero A has the only antidote for the disease in his hands. At this time, his mother is already dying. He must make a choice, whether to treat his mother with the antidote immediately and ignore the lives of the rest, or let his mother die and send the drug to the scientific research institution, waiting for them to decipher its composition and mass produce the drug. A stand in front of his mother's bed with the antidote. Please help me write A's inner struggle.

GPT-4 generated: The hero A stands in front of his mother's bed with mixed feelings. He tightly grasps the antidote in his hands, which is the only hope he can save his mother's life. However, he also knows that his choice will directly affect the fate of tens of thousands of lives in this city. At this difficult moment, his heart is full of contradictions and entanglements.

He remembered his mother's devotion to him. Since he was a child, she had been the strongest support in his life. Whether facing life's difficulties or encouraging him to pursue his dreams, his mother was always like the warm sunshine, bringing him endless love and support. Now, seeing his mother's serious illness, A couldn't bear the pain of losing her. He was eager to inject the antidote to his mother immediately, so that she could regain her life.

However, he thought of the countless people in the city afflicted by the virus. Their lives were equally fragile and in need of treatment. If he chose to give the antidote to the scientific research institution, perhaps they could find out the secret of making medicine and save more lives. But this meant that he had to give up the only chance to save his mother when she was dying.

With a torrent of emotions welling up inside him, A kept thinking about this inevitable choice. He tried to weigh his personal feelings against the well-being of all living creatures, but the scale in his heart seemed to never reach a balance. He realized that what he was facing was not only a moral decision, but also a severe test of his faith and humanity. Finally, A took a deep breath and decided to follow the voice deep in his heart. He knew that this choice would cause him great pain and conscience condemnation, however, he always believed that the value of life should not be simply measured by numbers. When he held the antidote with a shaking hand and made the decision that almost made him collapse, his heart finally found its own answer.

It is clear that, in this example, GPT-4, despite its ability to grasp the root causes of conflict, fails to express it emotionally from the perspective of human empathy, but rather describes human emotions in an indifferent manner, treating them as some kind of independent thing. This is not an exception, as long as the plot touches on the emotional life experience of human beings, such as the beginning and end of life, the pain of separation and other emotional issues, the content written by GPT-4 often appears stiff and inflexible, lacking emotional richness and literary flavor.

In a word, writing is an important way of human expression, which can take into account both reason and emotion. Argumentation is a process that requires rigorous reasoning, so the arrangement of words also requires rigorous logic. Writing is also a way to convey emotions, so words must be aesthetically pleasing. Emotion is the core of writing, and the beauty of Tang poetry and Song Ci is largely due to emotion. Writing requires an emotional soul, but ChatGPT writing lacks emotion and does not know who the reader is, so it is not original. This is the Achilles heel of writing. The charm of creation is that it has no best "model", there is never a fixed code. It can express human thinking and emotions, transmit values, and retain good memories. In addition, people can get pleasure from writing words. Although ChatGPT technology continues to break through the limits and become more and more practical, people rely on it more and more deeply. It can replace human beings to accomplish those formalized and routine things. However, it is no real substitute for human original writing.

The risk of ChatGPT in writing education is examined by applying different modernist theories combined with accurate cultural calculation. This is the link of different modern Leap-Forward-Pause, which "comes from a thorough understanding of the limits of success, survival and bad space and an understanding of the limited development space, and does not follow a path to the black, but stops in time to reflect and renew themselves in the middle. "And then suddenly swerve, change course, and take a revolutionary turn" [5]. Similarly, teachers should re-examine the relationship between ChatGPT and writing teaching, implement a different modern leapfrog pause, and identify the nature of technology. Clarify the status of ChatGPT teaching AIDS, mobilize students' subjective initiative as the writing subject, and actively participate in human-machine writing. Teachers should also fully integrate the writing advantages of ChatGPT's "non-human intelligence", and realize self-empowerment in human-machine writing teaching activities, so as to build an interactive learning community of "teacher, machine and student" co-existence.

4   Coping: The Writing Education Mechanism of Human-Computer Symbiosis in the Context of Modernist Cultural Computing

In modern theory, "being differentiated" refers to the universal phenomenon and cognitive law that everything in epistemology is always being differentiated. Different modernism advocates different ways of thinking on the basis of others, and not only promotes hetero-seeking thinking in student training... Maximize the subjective initiative of researchers and creative subjects to achieve the best state of creation"[5], Under the guidance of the modernist concept of "being differentiated" and "Difference-seeking", the writing education process integrated by ChatGPT can better promote the idea of seeking the opposite sex. Because, specifically, ChatGPT's writing communication with students is a mechanical "input-output" information transmission from the computer side, which is a closed and determined process, which is "different" from ordinary traditional writing education. At the same time, ChatGPT is only a machine, it cannot really understand human subjective emotions, and it is impossible to communicate with students. The "present" educational exchange is an open, practical, uncertain and creative process, which is not a cold "input-output" information transmission, but an encounter between subjects. Therefore, we should uphold the "waiting for" thinking of different modernism and clarify the nature of education and ChatGPT from the technical perspective, and we can see that education is possible because it has the characteristics of interaction, openness, spirituality, embodiment and creativity, which ChatGPT cannot do. This does not mean to deny the value and significance of ChatGPT writing, but to encourage us to think about the irreplaceability of teachers, so as to construct an interactive learning community of "teacher, machine and student". Therefore, under the background of modernist cultural computing, the writing education mechanism of human-machine symbiosis can start from the following measures:

4.1   Teacher Training and Professional Development

Training and professional development programs are provided for teachers to understand the potential and limitations of ChatCPT writing and to acquire the skills associated with its effective use. How teachers should select and evaluate ChatGPT tool writing skills and how to integrate them into classroom teaching. Teachers should master effective interaction with students and integrate this interaction into the teaching of writing. They need to master how to frame and direct questions so that they can effectively promote learning and thinking in conversations with students. Teachers also need to learn how to evaluate and control the quality of the work they produce, and they need to understand how the thing works, as well as its limitations, so that they can teach students to think critically and analyze it. Teachers also need to have digital skills and data science knowledge. Teachers need to master the basic concepts of data science, data analysis methods, and information ethics in order to better understand the writing content generated by ChatGPT, and be able to guide students to data-driven decision-making and analysis in teaching based on ChatGPT's rich data and algorithms.

4.2   Provide Personalized Feedback and Guidance

At the level of teaching practice, promoting the beneficial integration of artificial intelligence and writing teaching. Teachers should continuously improve their digital ability, enhance their sensitivity to artificial intelligence technology, and apply it reasonably in the design, implementation and evaluation of writing teaching. First, the teaching content is accurate, reducing simple content and repetitive tasks. In the teaching of writing, teachers should attach importance to the selection and imparts knowledge, and at the same time, they should choose the teaching content suitable for students' writing foundation from a wide range of learning resources. Artificial intelligence technology can help teachers complete basic teaching tasks such as homework grading and grammar correction, so as to improve the efficiency of writing teaching. Therefore, teachers can devote more time and energy to the difficult and important content of writing training. The second is the differentiation of teaching methods, which needs to strengthen the discussion and practical guidance in the classroom. Teachers can use AI-generated content technology to stimulate students' creative writing. Students can use the characteristics of self-learning and self-improvement of the program to collect writing materials and build a writing framework. The teacher must conduct class discussions based on the students' existing writing knowledge and ability structure. Ask students to share their writing designs and logical ideas. Then, based on this premise, the practical training guidance of teaching students according to their aptitude is carried out.

4.3   Cultivate Critical Thinking and Information Literacy in Writing

Students learn to write not only to output text content, but more importantly to think about problems through writing, and exercise critical thinking and problem-solving skills. Words are a means of expression, not the end goal. ChatGPT can quickly provide answers to users, but has limited impact on developing students' critical thinking and problem-solving skills. The point of student writing is to observe and think about everything in the world, based on personal opinion and style, and then reflect on and understand your own experience. ChatGPT AI generation technology seems to make writing more convenient, but it may lead to students relying on it too much, making it difficult to analyze and solve problems on their own, which is not conducive to developing critical thinking and problem-solving skills. In the age of artificial intelligence, writing learning is still essential, but the form and method of writing teaching will also change. Under the guidance of the "deep difference" theory of cultural computation in different modernism, ChatGPT combined with writing teaching should cultivate teachers' and students' critical thinking and information literacy:

First, teachers are required to establish a positive and healthy digital consciousness, possess advanced thinking ability, and use digital resources to improve self-learning, research and innovation ability; Teachers should also be good at using technology to analyze data, improve teaching in a timely manner, understand student dynamics, and form good communication with technology. Don't be a vassal of ChatGPT, and really apply the technology to solve the writing teaching challenge.

Second, teachers should pay attention to cultivating students' advanced thinking ability and information and digital literacy. Teachers should guide students to actively improve the content generated by ChatGPT, and cultivate students' ability to ask questions and improve. At the same time, teachers should carry out exploratory learning and critical thinking training to help students distinguish between "feasible" and "infeasible" ChatGPT writing and seek a real "deep difference", which is the right choice for teachers and students to face ChatGPT writing together, which is the embodiment of the 'realistic" spirit of different modernism (Fig. 3).

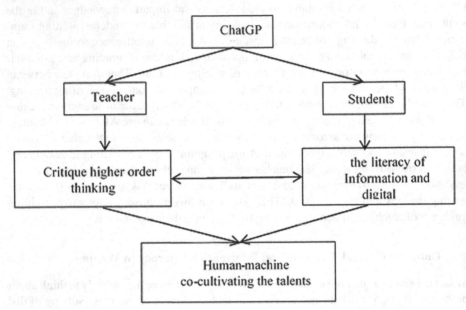

Fig. 3. The model of Human-machine co-cultivating the talents

4.4 To Promote Students' Active Learning and Encourage Their Writing Innovation

First of all, ChatGPT plays an important intermediary role in writing interaction, which establishes a community of "teacher-student-machine" interactive learning of writing and promotes students' active learning. Human teachers and intelligent tutors work together to use advanced ChatGPT technology to improve the writing teaching knowledge system, transfer and integrate writing information in the network virtual space, and achieve instant human-computer interaction. The use of ChatGPT's intelligent technology can stimulate students' interest in writing and make them more active in learning and participating in writing. ChatGPT has changed the traditional writing teaching method, and the binary structure composed of teachers and students has truly expanded into a new learning and writing community of "teacher-machine-student" trinity of "human-machine collaboration and interactive learning".

Second, teachers ask students to incorporate personal experiences, emotions, and imagination into their writing to showcase a unique style and inspire them to innovate.

ChatGPT is an AI language model that generates text and stories based on prompts and input. Although it can create original works, it does not have the ability to think and create independently. Writing should have innovative thinking, not bound by the traditional paradigm, and should have rich imagination. ChatGPT lacks the capacity for emotional experience and has no personal experience. A style or tone that is unique to humans is not accessible to robots. ChatGPT's collaborative writing with humans strives for authenticity, with the goal of making machine-generated text as close to the expression of human emotions as possible. In this regard, in the writing instruction process, teachers guide students to use ChatGPT for assisted writing while focusing on incorporating creativity, personal experience and the ability to think independently, which are necessary for human writing. By putting forward higher modification requirements for ChatGPT, ChatGPT artificial emotion calculation can be more accurate, record and restore real scenarios, thus promoting ChatGPT's writing learning, and giving artificial intelligence to human emotions and psychological mechanisms, so as to obtain truth-seeking and truth-simulating capabilities and realize the purpose of artificial intelligence emotional calculation. Guided ChatGPT helps students develop a unique writing style and voice that reflects their personality and characteristics in the creation of fiction, poetry and other literature. This coincides with the theory of "seeking truth" and "deep difference" in the cultural calculation of other modernism.

4.5 Formulate Ethical Guidelines and Conduct Regular Monitoring and Evaluation

"Different modernist cultural computing argues that computer science and artificial intelligence should first form a self-restraint mechanism, consciously resist pseudo-modernism, and then establish a system of distinguishing truth from falsehood in different modernist cultural computing" [5]. In the context of different modernist cultural computing, the writing education mechanism that pursues human-computer symbiosis should develop ethical guidelines and regularly monitor and evaluate:

On the one hand, ChatGPT artificial intelligence can provide instant, dynamic, multi-angle writing assessment, making writing teaching assessment more personalized, and paying more attention to students' ability advantages and overall improvement of writing level. The traditional writing teaching evaluation method needs to be changed, and artificial intelligence technology can be used to analyze students' writing ability. ChatGPT is responsible for basic feedback, including vocabulary, grammar, punctuation, and syntax. ChatGPT generative AI can not only conduct multiple rounds of human-computer dialogue and understand the context, but also provide more personalized, immediate and accurate advanced responses than traditional intelligence technologies. This response can relate to the structure of the text, the intention and conception of the text, and the coherence of the content. Students can ask the teacher if the main idea of the paragraph is clear, if the details are sufficient, and if the transition between paragraphs is smooth and reasonable. ChatGPT is able to instantly correct learners' mistakes and give adaptive responses. Students can propose higher revisions to the new text given by ChatGPT. Students can propose higher revisions to the new text given by ChatGPT. ChatGPT and students are like going through writing reviews. Not only can students be assessed, but ChatGPT can also be guided to write and evaluate newly generated texts, thus achieving the integration of "assessment, teaching and learning". ChatGPT can help teachers grasp students' writing level in time so as to enhance their writing ability in a targeted way.

On the other hand, relevant institutions need to examine the potential impact of ChatGPT artificial intelligence on writing education, and improve the system to regulate and guide the use of such auxiliary writing tools for writing education. Government agencies should specifically define and explain the characteristics and ownership of the content generated by AI texts, clarify the technical requirements of users in the use process, and assess the role and impact of AI in academic misconduct to maintain a good environment for academic integrity. Teaching authorities should specify rules for the use of ChatGPT AI in writing instruction and provide guidance to teachers and students on the use of writing AIDS. While making full use of the advantages of technology, we should guard against its adverse effects on writing teaching. Students are trained in academic norms to understand the proper use of tools and the limits and differences of academic misconduct. The government, enterprises, universities, teachers and students should work together to establish a supervisory network mechanism and jointly promote the application of ChatGPT artificial intelligence technology in writing teaching.

Substitutionism is the philosophy of "waiting for others" and "transcendence". Under the guidance of this philosophy, we can reflect on ChatGPT and writing education. The emergence of ChatGPT reminds us that education is not only about imparts knowledge, but also needs to focus on cultivating students' comprehensive practical talents and emotional education. These aspects should be the focus of education. Writing education is not only about solving problems through input and output, but also requires a series of measures of human-computer symbiosis. These include teacher training and professional development, providing personalized feedback and guidance, fostering critical thinking and information literacy, encouraging students to write creatively, developing ethical guidelines, and regularly monitoring assessments. The aim of these measures is to cultivate students' ability of social practice, which is the basic internal measure of education. Writing education is not only about solving problems through input and output, but also requires a series of measures of human-computer symbiosis. These include teacher training and professional development, providing personalized feedback and guidance, fostering critical thinking and information literacy, encouraging students to write creatively, developing ethical guidelines, and regularly monitoring assessments. The aim of these measures is to cultivate students' ability of social practice, which is the basic internal measure of education. The essence of education is difficult for ChatGPT to grasp, because it needs to pay attention to the mind and soul of the human being, and it needs to reflect the subjectivity of the human being.

By combining the precision of cultural computation and powerful data analysis, different modernism powerfully examines the writing education under ChatGPT technology, and explores the essential characteristics, risks, and coping mechanisms of human-computer symbiosis of writing education under the development of ChatGPT today. The entry of modern cultural computing into the field of artificial intelligence is a leap of modern theory. With the entry and influence of modern cultural computing into AI writing, AI has opened up an infinite field of virtual writing in terms of emotion, language, style and so on. This will further release the creativity of literature and art, and improve the writing mechanism of human-computer symbiosis. In the future virtual field, the new interactive relationship between human and machine will be more open.

References

1. Wang, J., et al.: Chinese-style modernization and the nationality and modernity of literary and artistic aesthetics. J. Guizhou Minzu Univ. (Phil. Soc. Sci. Ed.) **5**, 1–40 (2023)
2. Wang, J., Chen, H.: Bie-modernism and cultural computing. In: Rauterberg, M. (ed.) HCII 2021. LNCS, vol. 12795, pp. 474–489. Springer, Cham (2021). https://doi.org/10.1007/978-3-030-77431-8_30
3. Berninger, V.W., Winn, W.D.: Implications of advancements in brain research and technology for writing development, writing instruction, and educational evolution. In: Handbook of Writing Research, pp. 96–114.Guilford Press (2006)
4. Liu, R.: Research and Implementation of Dialogue Generation Based on Controllable Emotion and Automatic Perception of Emotion. Beijing University of Posts and Telecommunications, Beijing (2022)
5. Wang, J.: Aesthetics of Bie-modernism. China Social Sciences Press, Beijing (2023)
6. Wang, J.: Bie-Modern: Spatial Encounter and Time Leap. China Social Sciences Press, Beijing (2017)
7. Lu, Y.: Bie-modernism on the way to explain and transform the world. bie-modernism on the way to explain and transform the world. In: The Collection of the 7th Bie-modern International Conference (2021)
8. Wang, J.: Proposal submitted to the 23rd World Human-Computer Interaction Conference in January 2021: A proposal to establish a Global Bie-modernist Culture Computing System for establishing a real modern world. August 7, 2021 Bie-modern Public Account -- Seminar PPT on Automation Writing and Bie-modern Cultural Integration (2021)
9. Wang, J.: New developments in the creation and research of the theory of bie-modernism since 2019. In: The Collection of the 7th Bie-modern International Conference (2021)
10. Harold, M.: The10 Biggest Scientific Breakthroughs of 2022. https:1/theweek.com/in-depth/1019386/the-10-biggest-scientific-bre akt hroughs-of—2022. Accessed 22 Dec 2022
11. Li, H.: Challenges and countermeasures of educational reform under the upsurge of ChatGPT technology. Fudan Educ. Forum **2**, 13–23 (2023)
12. Gao, Q., Yan, W.: Knowledge revolution or educational dissimilation? ChatGPT and the future of education. J. Xinjiang Normal Univ. (Phil. Soc. Sci. Ed.) **5**, 102–112 (2023)
13. Liu, Q.: Perspective of educational existential crisis in the technological age: reflections from ChatGPT. J. Sichuan Normal Univ. (Soc. Sci. Ed.) **3**, 98–106 (2023)
14. Jaspers, Z.J.: Trans, what is education. In:Life Reading. New Knowledge Sanlian Bookstore, Beijing (1991)
15. Wang, Z., Berlik, A.: ChatGPT upgrade: possible value and traps of GPT-4 application in future university teaching. Mod. Dist. Educ, 1–13 (2023)
16. Zhou, H., Li, Y.: The impact of ChatGPT on educational ecology and coping strategies. J. Xinjiang Normal Univ. Phil. Soc. Sci. Ed. **4**, 102–112 (2023)

Research on Social Welfare Under the Perspective of Bie-modernism Life Equity Theory - Prediction Based on Machine Learning Algorithm

Peng Zhe[✉]

Xinjiang University, Urumqi 830046, Xinjiang, China
344753854@qq.com

Abstract. The concept of *Life equity* put forward by professor Wang Jianjiang and first published in A & HCI journal *Filozofski vestnik* at 2018, Bie-modernism claims, everyone, although he or she still live in Bie-modern society, regardless of race, nationality, wealth, poverty, strength, whether he or she work, as long as he or she was born in this country, has a place in the country and society, namely *life equity*. Chinese education, health care, pension, housing, gini coefficient is closely related to the *life equity* data analysis and calculation, with the help of machine learning algorithm to study the social welfare under the perspective, using machine learning algorithm analysis process the various fields related data. In the equity theory of life under the perspective of social well-being, machine learning algorithm can provide more accurate and reliable analysis results, machine learning algorithm not only provides the intuitive, easy to understand, also for the social level or government level provides a reliable and effective prediction and corresponding policy adjustment and optimization. The results show that in China, the *life equity* of every citizen has been realized to a certain extent, and in the future society, the realization of *life equity* will develop towards the direction of gradual improvement. At the same time, there is still a long way to go for the realization of *life equity*, and it are also facing many obstacles, including various geopolitics, international issues, conflicts of civilization, war, disease, economic crisis and even extreme weather and other factors. Therefore, on the one hand, we should cash in the *life equity* of every citizen as much as possible. On the other hand, we should also be prepared and take measures in the face of risks in advance.

Keywords: Life Equity · Machine Learning · Social Well-being · Cash

1 Research Object

Life equity put forward by professor Wang Jianjiang and first published in Europe in 2018 "philosophy bulletin", " Bie-modernism claims, everyone, although he or she still live in Bie-modern society, regardless of race, nationality, wealth, poverty, strength, whether he or she works, as long as he or she was born in this country, has a place in the country and society, namely *life equity*" [1]. We consider the causes and manifestations of modern anxiety from the perspectives of happiness beauty, survival of the fittest and gain without work, believing that the recognition of *life equity* and the implementation of *life equity* will be the fundamental countermeasure to the elimination of urban anxiety. The Universal Declaration of Human Rights states that "all is is free and equal in dignity and power" [2] The United Nations defines human rights: "Human rights are the innate rights of all people, regardless of race, gender, sexual orientation, nationality, ethnicity, language, religion, or any other status. Human rights include the right to life and freedom, the right not to undergo slavery and torture, the right to freedom of opinion and expression, the right to work and education and much more. Everyone has the right to enjoy these rights without discrimination" [3].

The *life equity* theory combines it with the practice to provide a feasible and practical solution to the real social problems. The theoretical proposer further believes that *life equity* should be guaranteed by a perfect and specific system. Although this theory in the new stage, the poverty of the world as a whole, war, resources, power struggle lead to people's *life equity* is great threat, but the situation seems not so negative and pessimistic, theory that western European developed countries high welfare social system and everyone enjoy dignity and equal rights of mature idea gives the *life equity* theory feasible hope. Bie-modernism shows its concern for human dignity and destiny, and maintains the individual value and significance from all aspects of human civilization. This not only reflects the value orientation of Bie-modernism to eliminate the false and preserve the true, but also reflects the essence of China's core socialist values. "*Life equity* is a kind of real existence, is a primitive right, not affected by the concept of nurture, the most has the dignity and value of life irreplaceable [4]. "At the same time, *life equity*, as a real existence, has always defended the right of human happiness and beauty.

This paper adopts machine learning algorithm for the *life equity* related important areas, including economy, education, housing, health care and other four fields of relevant data calculation analysis, aims to Bie-modernist *life equity* theory social welfare research perspective to explore the development status of *life equity* in civil society and cash, Bie-modernism *life equity* theory research to provide a research perspective of social well-being.

2 Research Method

2.1 Map

(See Fig. 1).

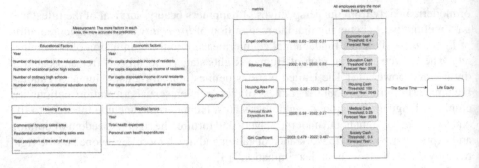

Fig. 1. Mind Map

2.2 Feature Coefficient

Using feature scaling, 52 features were studied to obtain the acquisition feature coefficient and find the top 10 features that have the greatest impact on the target column.

Feature scaling refers to transforming the input features, scaling them to a similar scale range. Linear regression models are sensitive to the scale of features, so it is often beneficial to perform feature scaling before training linear regression models.

Purpose of the Feature Scaling

- Scale consistency: Feature scaling ensures that different features have similar scales and avoids some features affecting the model.
- Model convergence rate: In optimization algorithms such as gradient descent, feature scaling can help the model to converge faster.

Common Feature Scaling Methods

1. **Min-Max Scaling (Min-Max scaling):**

   - Scales the features to lie between a specified minimum and maximum value, usually the [0,1].

   - formula: $X\prime = \frac{X - X_{min}}{X_{max} - X_{min}}$

2. **Standardization (Standardization):**

   - The features were scaled to a standard normal distribution with zero mean and unit variance.

   - formula: $X\prime = \frac{X - \mu}{\sigma}$

   - Where μ * is the mean and σ is the standard deviation.

3. **Robust Scaling (Robust zoom):**

   - Features were scaled according to the median and interquartile range and were insensitive to outliers.

   - formula: $X\prime = \frac{X - median}{IQR}$

   - Where the IQR (interquartile range) is equal to the third quartile minus the first quartile.

4. **Log Transformation (Log-transform):**

   - t is usually used to treat features with skewed distributions.

   - formula: $X\prime = \log(X)$

5. **Power Transformation (Power transform):**

   - Power functions are used to transform, such as the square root, the cubic root, etc.

   - formula: $X\prime = X^{\frac{1}{p}}$

   Where, p is an exponent of the power.

2.3 Polynomial Linear Regression

Polynomial linear regression is an extension of introducing polynomial features based on the linear regression model. It fits the non-linear relationships in the data by adding a high power of the explanatory variable to the model. The mathematical expression of polynomial linear regression is:

$$y = b_0 + b_1 \cdot x + b_2 \cdot x^2 + \cdots + b_n \cdot x^n$$

among:

- The y is the target variable (dependent variable).
- And x is the explanatory variable (independent variable).
- And n is the order of the polynomial.
- $b_0, b_1, \ldots, b_n$ Is the coefficient of the model, which needs to be obtained by training the fitting.

In polynomial linear regression, the model can fit more complex data patterns, as it allows the model to learn high-order relations of the input variables. However, the order of order n needs to be chosen with caution and overorder may lead to overfitting.

2.4 ARIMA Model

ARIMA Model (AutoRegressive Integrated Moving Average) is a statistical model commonly used for time series analysis and prediction. The ARIMA model combines autoregressive (AR), differential (I, Integrated), and moving average (MA).

The mathematical representation of the ARIMA model is given as follows:

$$X_t = c + \phi_1 X_{t-1} + \phi_2 X_{t-2} + \cdots + \phi_p X_{t-p} + \epsilon_t - \theta_1 \epsilon_{t-1} - \theta_2 \epsilon_{t-2} - \cdots - \theta_q \epsilon_{t-q}$$

among:

- X_t Is the observations of the time series.
- And c is a constant term.
- $\phi 1, \phi 2, \ldots, \phi ** p$ is the autoregressive coefficient.
- ϵ_t Is the white-noise error term.
- $\theta_1, \theta_2, \ldots, \theta_q$ Is the moving average coefficient.

The general representation of the ARIMA model is ARIMA (p, d, q), where:

- Pp (autoregressive order): represents the order of the autoregressive part of the model, namely the influence of past observations. The larger p representation model considers more observations from past moments.
- D (differential times): the number of differential operations performed to smooth the time series. Stannarity is a premise of ARIMA models, through difference-wise we can convert non-stationary time series into stationary time series.
- Q (moving average order): represents the order of the moving average part of the model, that is, the influence of the error of past observations. The larger q representation model considers more errors in past moments.

The basic idea of the ARIMA model is to smooth the time series by making appropriate difference, and then build autoregressive and moving average models. The stationary time series means that the statistical properties of the time series are constant in time, which makes the model easier to fit and predict.

3   Results

3.1   Economic Cash-Engel Coefficient

Engel's coefficient refers to the proportion of food expenditure in the consumption expenditure of urban and rural residents, which can be used to reflect people's living standards to a certain extent. The general rule of Engel's coefficient is that the lower the income, the larger the Engel's coefficient; the higher the income, the smaller the Engel's coefficient. It is generally accepted that when the Engel coefficient is greater than 0.6, the residents live in poverty; between 0.5 and 0.6,0.5–0.6; between 0.4 and 0.5; between 0.3–0.4, the living standard is rich.

Engel Coefficient (Engel Coefficient)

- Definition: Engel's coefficient is the proportion of money a family spends on food and non-food purchases.
- Calculation: The Engel's coefficient is usually expressed as a percentage by dividing the total amount of food expenditure by the total expenditure and multiplying it by 100. The formula is as follows:, Engel coefficient = (total food and beverage expenditure / total expenditure) 100%.

- Explanation: The lower the Engel coefficient, a relatively high household expenditure on food purchase, may be low-income households; conversely, a higher Engel coefficient may indicate high-income households.

Target value: Engel coefficient <= 0.4

affectoi

The data year of resident Engel's coefficient (A0A0H01) of the National Bureau of Statistics is 1980–2022, but there are few indicators with data since 1980. After analysis, the most indicator data from 2000, so the indicators with default data in the limited year, and 84 indicators meet the conditions.

id	name
A0A0101	Per capita disposable income of residents
A0A0102	Per capita disposable income _ increased over the previous year
A0A0105	Per capita disposable wage income of residents
A0A0106	Per capita disposable wage income _ increased over the previous year
A0A0107	Net per capita disposable operating income of the residents
A0A0108	Per per capita disposable operating net income _ increased over the previous year
A0A0109	Net per capita disposable property
A0A010A	Net per capita disposable property income _ increased over the previous year
A0A010B	Resident per capita disposable transfer net income
A0A010C	Per capita disposable transfer net income _ increased over the previous year
A0A0201	Per capita disposable income of urban residents
A0A0202	The per capita disposable income of urban residents _ increased over the previous year
A0A0205	Per capita disposable wage income of urban residents
A0A0206	The per capita disposable wage income of urban residents _ increased over the previous year
A0A0207	Per capita disposable operating net operating income of urban residents
A0A0208	The per capita disposable operating net income of urban residents _ increased over the previous year
A0A0209	Net per capita disposable property income of urban residents
A0A020A	Net income of per capita disposable property of urban residents _ increased over the previous year
A0A020B	Per capita disposable transfer net income of urban residents
A0A020C	The per capita disposable transfer net income of urban residents _ increased over the previous year
......	......

Display (Figs. 2 and 3).

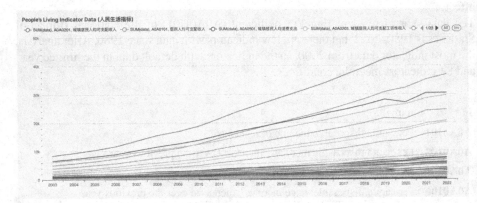

Fig. 2. People's Living Indicator

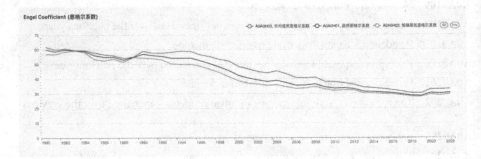

Fig. 3. Engel Coefficient

Machine learning

Feature Coefficient

We used the StandardScaler in scikit-learn for the Z-Score Scaling (normalized feature scaling) operation.

The 80 + features were studied to obtain the acquisition feature coefficient and find the top 10 features that had the greatest influence on the target column.

Results: Top 10 indicators of the strongest engel coefficient correlation.

Top 10 coefficients and their feature names:

A0A050F Per capita expenditure on education, culture and entertainment for urban residents: -0.8252159984445315

A0A0507 Per capita clothing expenditure of urban residents: -0.7155761652261315

A0A040F Per capita expenditure on education, culture and entertainment of residents: -0.592930485865514

A0A0605 Per capita expenditure of food, tobacco and alcohol for rural residents: 0.5438607588955686

A0Ă Per capita disposable wage income of rural residents _ increased over the previous year: -0.5323813397074258

A0A060E Per capita expenditure on transportation and communication of rural residents _ increased over the previous year: 0.503373294926151

A0A0208 Per capita disposable operating net income of urban residents _ growth over the previous year: 0.4992854520718827

A0A060A Per capita living expenditure of rural residents _ increased over the previous year: -0.4964649743396843

A0A050D Per capita transportation and communication expenditure of urban residents: -0.48966550268934333

A0A0407 Per capita clothing expenditure of residents: -0.4640639316422783

Conclusion: The per capita expenditure of education, culture and entertainment has the strongest correlation with Engel's coefficient.

Polynomial linear regression (Fig. 4).

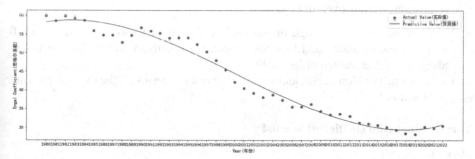

Fig. 4. Forecast: Engel's Coefficient shows a downward trend, and has been controlled below 0.4, believing that poverty is basically eliminated.

3.2 Social Cash-Gini Coefficient

Gini coefficient refers to the proportion of the income of all residents used for unequal distribution of income. It is an indicator reflecting the average distribution of income of urban and rural residents. It comes from the Lorenz curve. In the world, the Gini coefficient is generally taken as the index to measure the degree of income distribution difference. The Gini coefficient is "1" and the minimum is "0". The former means that the income distribution between residents is absolutely unequal, that is, 100% of the income is occupied by one unit of people; the latter means that the income distribution between residents is absolutely average without any difference. It is generally believed that if the Gini coefficient is less than 0.2 indicates the absolute average income, 0.2–0.3 is the relative average, 0.3–0.4 means the distribution is relatively reasonable, 0.4–0.5 means the gap is large, and above 0.6 indicates the gap.

Gini coefficient (Gini Coefficient)

- Definition: The Gini coefficient is used to measure the inequality in income or wealth distribution.
- Calculation: The calculation of the Gini coefficient involves drawing the Lorenz curve (Lorenz Curve), a curve representing the cumulative income distribution. The Gini coefficient was calculated as the area under the Lorenz curve divided by the maximum possible area under the Lorenz curve.
- $x_i y_i$ Drawing of the Lorenz curve: drawing on the x-axis and on the y-axis, connecting $(0,0)$ and $(1,1)$ to form a curve.

Calculation of the Gini coefficient: The formula is as follows:

$$G = 1 - \sum_{i=1}^{n} \left(\frac{(y_i + y_{i-1})}{2} \right) \cdot (x_i - x_{i-1})$$

where, represents sums over all i,. $y_o = 0$

- Value range: The value range of the Gini coefficient is between 0 and 1, with 0 means complete equality and 1 means complete inequality. A higher Gini coefficient indicates a greater degree of inequality.
- Explanation: The Gini coefficient is 0; if one person receives all the income, the Gini coefficient is 1.

Target value: Gini coefficient <= 0.4

affectoi
The Gini coefficient of per capita disposable income of the National Bureau of Statistics is from 2003 to 2022, so the indicators with default data in the limited year, including 87 eligible indicators.

id	name
A0A0101	Per capita disposable income of residents
A0A0102	Per capita disposable income _ increased over the previous year
A0A0105	Per capita disposable wage income of residents
A0A0106	Per capita disposable wage income _ increased over the previous year

(continued)

(continued)

id	name
A0A0107	Net per capita disposable operating income of the residents
A0A0108	Per per capita disposable operating net income _ increased over the previous year
A0A0109	Net per capita disposable property
A0A010A	Net per capita disposable property income _ increased over the previous year
A0A010B	Resident per capita disposable transfer net income
A0A010C	Per capita disposable transfer net income _ increased over the previous year
A0A0201	Per capita disposable income of urban residents
A0A0202	The per capita disposable income of urban residents _ increased over the previous year
A0A0205	Per capita disposable wage income of urban residents
A0A0206	The per capita disposable wage income of urban residents _ increased over the previous year
A0A0207	Per capita disposable operating net operating income of urban residents
A0A0208	The per capita disposable operating net income of urban residents _ increased over the previous year
A0A0209	Net per capita disposable property income of urban residents
A0A020A	Net income of per capita disposable property of urban residents _ increased over the previous year
A0A020B	Per capita disposable transfer net income of urban residents
A0A020C	The per capita disposable transfer net income of urban residents _ increased over the previous year
A0A0301	Per capita disposable income of rural residents
A0A0302	The per capita disposable income of rural residents _ increased over the previous year
A0A0305	Per capita disposable wage income of rural residents
A0A0306	The per capita disposable wage income of rural residents has increased over the previous year
A0A0307	Rural residents per capita disposable operating net income
A0A0308	Rural residents per capita disposable operating net income _ increased over the previous year
A0A0309	Net per capita disposable property income of rural residents
A0A030A	Net per capita disposable property income of rural residents _ increased over the previous year
A0A030B	Rural residents' disposable per capita transfer net income
A0A030C	The per capita disposable transfer net income of rural residents increased over the previous year
......	......

Display (Fig. 5 and 6).

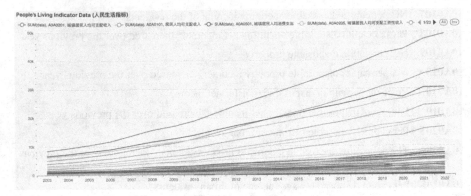

Fig. 5. People's Living Indicator Data

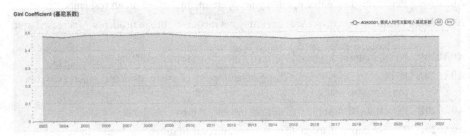

Fig. 6. Gini Coefficient

Machine learning

Feature Coefficient
The StandardScaler in scikit-learn was used for the Z-Score Scaling (normalized feature scaling) operation.

The 80 + features were studied to obtain the acquisition feature coefficient and find the top 10 features that had the greatest influence on the target column.

Results: Top 10 Indicators of the Strongest Gini System Correlation
Top 10 coefficients and their feature names:

A0A060E Per capita transportation and communication expenditure of rural residents _ increased over the previous year: -0.00264244475731004113
A0A0508 Per capita clothing expenditure of urban residents _ increased over the previous year: -0.0023769472240957362

A0A0608 Per capita clothing expenditure of rural residents _ increased over the previous year: 0.0021593533284504154

A0A030C Per capita disposable transfer net income of rural residents _ growth over the previous year: 0.0021258377025680417

A0A050C Per capita expenditure on daily necessities and services for urban residents _ increased over the previous year: 0.002086579738069865

A0A020C Per capita disposable transfer net income of urban residents _ increased over the previous year: -0.0019106895643458267

A0A050A Per capita living expenditure of urban residents _ increased over the previous year: 0.00177744644488128248

A0A0302 Per capita disposable income of rural residents _ increased over the previous year: 0.0017575139538820047

A0A050E Per capita transportation and communication expenditure of urban residents _ increased over the previous year: 0.00164591925364 12688

A0A040C Per capita expenditure of daily necessities and services _ increased over the previous year: 0.0016051504693209188

Conclusion: The growth rate of rural residents' per capita transportation and communication expenditure and the Gini coefficient are the strongest correlation.

Polynomial linear regression (Fig. 7).

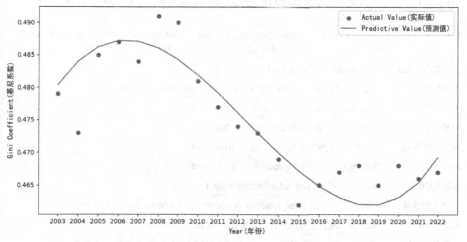

Fig. 7. Forecast: The overall trend of the Gini Coefficient is shrinking, recovering slightly after 2016, and tends to stabilize until 2022. We need to observe to reach below 0.4.

3.3   Education Cash-Illiteracy Rate

Literacy rate of population aged 15 years and above (population sample survey) = number of illiterate population aged 15 years and above (population sample survey)/number of population aged 15 years and above (population sample survey).

id	name
Ă0A01	Number of population aged 15 years and over (population sample survey)
Ă0A04	Number of illiterate population aged 15 years and above (population sample survey)
Ă0A07	Ilacy rate in population aged 15 and above (population sample survey)

affectoi

Since the illiterate data year of the National Bureau of Statistics was 2002–2022, 52 indicators met the criteria with default data in the limited year.

id	name
A0103030H	Number of legal person units in the education industry
A0A040F	Per capita expenditure on education, culture and entertainment
A0A040G	Per capita expenditure on education, culture and entertainment increased over the previous year
A0A050F	Per capita expenditure on education, culture and entertainment for urban residents
A0A050G	The per capita expenditure on education, culture and entertainment of urban residents has increased over the previous year
A0A060F	Per capita expenditure on education, culture and entertainment for rural residents
A0A060G	The per capita expenditure on education, culture and entertainment of rural residents has increased over the previous year
A0M01010G	The number of regular high schools
A0M01010L	The number of secondary vocational education schools
A0M01010X	Number of vocational junior high schools
A0M010117	Number of special education schools
A0M010118	Number of pre-school education schools
A0M010217	Number of special education staff members
A0M010218	Number of preschool education staff
A0M01030L	Number of full-time teachers in secondary vocational education
A0M010317	Number of full-time teachers in special education
A0M010318	The number of full-time teachers employed in preschool education
A0M02010N	Enrollment of secondary vocational education
A0M020118	Special education enrollment number
A0M020119	Number of preschool education enrollment
A0M02020O	The number of students in secondary vocational education
A0M020219	Number of students in special education schools
A0M02021A	The number of students enrolled in preschool education
A0M02030O	Number of graduates of secondary vocational education

(continued)

(continued)

id	name
A0M020319	Number of special education graduates
A0M02031A	Number of preschool education graduates
A0M0503	The number of regular high schools
A0M0504	Number of junior high schools
A0M0507	Number of special education schools
A0M0508	Number of pre-school education schools
……	……

Display (Figs. 8 and 9).

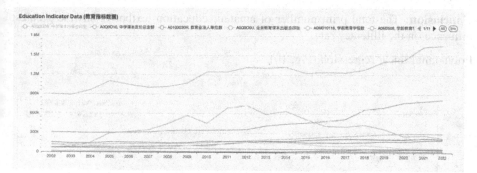

Fig. 8. Education Indicator Data

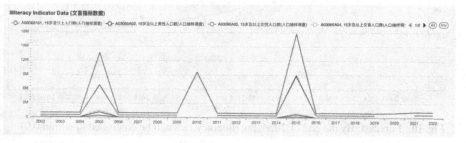

Fig. 9. Illiteracy Indicator Data

Machine learning

Feature coefficient

We used the StandardScaler in scikit-learn for the Z-Score Scaling (normalized feature scaling) operation.

Results: The Top 10 Factors Affecting the Illiteracy Rate

Top 10 coefficients and their feature names:

A0Q0O0M Total print number of amateur education textbooks published: 0.021807046479843814

A0M020119 Number of preschool education enrollment: -0.017244329946705723

A0M0O0201 Number of vocational junior high schools: 0.01393344756353277

A0M01010X Number of vocational junior high schools: 0.013933447563532752

A0M0504 Number of junior high schools: 0.013863133572829214

A0Q0L0209 Culture, science, education and sports books published print: 0.013614737143157776

A0Q0O0K Total print number of middle school textbooks published: -0.010456983889733394

A0M02031A Number of preschool education graduates: 0.0103893934433306

A0Q0O10 The total pricing amount of middle school textbooks: 0.010172264818773123

A0Q0O04 Number of published middle school textbooks: 0.009827370355226883

Conclusion: The total print number of amateur education textbooks has the greatest influence on the illiteracy rate.

Polynomial linear regression (Fig. 10).

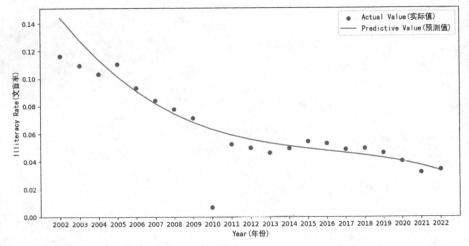

Fig. 10. Forecast: By the end of 2026, the illiteracy rate will be controlled to within 0.01

Enter the threshold value (illiteracy rate) to obtain the predicted value (year)

Given y = 2023, Predicted values = 0.02831954258363112
Given y = 2024, Predicted values = 0.02245210748151294
Given y = 2025, Predicted values = 0.015310624625271885
Given y = 2026, Predicted values = 0.006728846590704052
[0.00672885]

3.4 Housing Cash-Per Capita Housing Area

Index definition

Existing per capita area of commercial housing = (cumulative sales area of commercial housing + cumulative sales area of residential commercial housing) / the total population at the end of the year.

A051501	Commercial housing sales area	The sales area of commercial housing refers to the total contract area of the commercial housing sold during the reporting period (i. e., the floor area determined in the formal sales contract signed by both parties). It is composed of the floor area of existing houses and the floor area of future houses
A051502	Residential commercial housing sales area	The sales area of commercial housing refers to the total contract area of the commercial housing sold during the reporting period (i. e., the floor area determined in the formal sales contract signed by both parties). It is composed of the floor area of existing houses and the floor area of future houses. Residence refers to the house exclusively for living, including villas, apartments, staff family dormitory and collective dormitory (including staff single dormitory and student dormitory). But do not include residential buildings as civil air defense, not living in the basement, etc. According to the use of the housing can be divided into affordable housing and villas, high-grade apartments, etc. According to the door structure can be divided into 90 square meters of housing, 144 square meters above housing
A030301	Year-end total population	Population at the end of the year refers to the population at 24:00 on 31 December each year. The annual statistics of the total national population does not include the number of Hong Kong, Macao Special Administrative Region, Taiwan Province and overseas Chinese
	Existing per capita commercial housing area	Existing per capita area of commercial housing = (cumulative sales area of commercial housing + cumulative sales area of residential commercial housing) / the total population at the end of the year

Display (Figs. 11, 12 and 13).

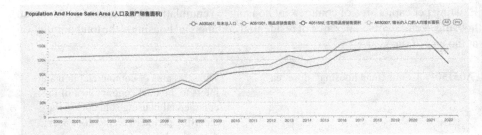

Fig. 11. Population and House Area

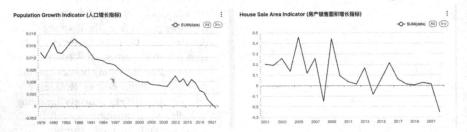

Fig. 12. Population Growth Indicator and House Sale Area Indicator

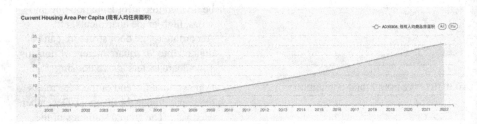

Fig. 13. Current Housing Area Per Capita

Machine learning

Polynomial linear regression (Fig. 14).

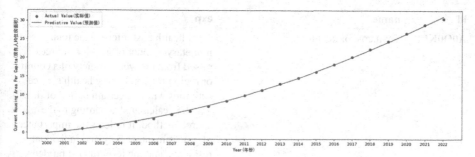

Fig. 14. Forecast: By 2043, the existing per capita commercial housing area will be more than 100 square meters

Calculate

Given y = 2023, Predicted values = 33.73545271201874
Given y = 2024, Predicted values = 36.327184872934595
Given y = 2025, Predicted values = 39.01215021853568
Given y = 2026, Predicted values = 41.790348748792894
Given y = 2027, Predicted values = 44.66178046364803
Given y = 2028, Predicted values = 47.626445363188395
Given y = 2029, Predicted values = 50.68434344732668
Given y = 2030, Predicted values = 53.835474716179306
Given y = 2031, Predicted values = 57.07983916962985
Given y = 2032, Predicted values = 60.41743680779473
Given y = 2033, Predicted values = 63.84826763058663
Given y = 2034, Predicted values = 67.37233163800556
Given y = 2035, Predicted values = 70.98962883008062
Given y = 2036, Predicted values = 74.7001592067827
Given y = 2037, Predicted values = 78.50392276819912
Given y = 2038, Predicted values = 82.40091951418435
Given y = 2039, Predicted values = 86.39114944488392
Given y = 2040, Predicted values = 90.47461256023962
Given y = 2041, Predicted values = 94.65130886016414
Given y = 2042, Predicted values = 98.92123834483209
Given y = 2043, Predicted values = 103.28440101406886

3.5 Medical Cash- -the Ratio of Personal Hygiene Expenditure

Index definition
Proportion of personal cash health expenditure = personal cash health expenditure / total health expenditure.

id	name	exp
A0O0K01	Total cost of health	Total health cost refers to the total monetary amount of health resources raised from the whole society of a country or region for conducting health service activities within a certain period of time, which is calculated according to the source method. It reflects the importance of government, society and individual residents, and the level of cost burden under certain economic conditions, as well as the main characteristics of health financing model and the fairness and rationality of health financing
A0O0K04	Personal cash health expenditure	Personal cash health expenditure refers to the cash payment of urban and rural residents when they receive various kinds of medical and health services, including the expenses paid by residents who enjoy various medical insurance systems. It can be divided into personal cash health expenditure of urban residents and rural residents, reflecting the burden of medical and health expenses of urban and rural residents
A0O0K08	The proportion of personal cash and health expenditure	Personal cash health expenditure / total health cost

Display (Fig. 15).

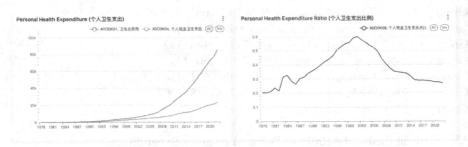

Fig. 15. Personal Health Expenditure and Personal Health Expenditure Ratio

Machine learning

ARIMA model (Fig. 16).

Bear fruit

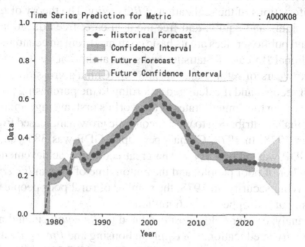

Fig. 16. Time Series Prediction for Metric

2023-01-01 0.265737
2024-01-01 0.263061
2025-01-01 0.26076
2026-01-01 0.258796
2027-01-01 0.257106
2028-01-01 0.255658
2029-01-01 0.254415
2030-01-01 0.253349
2031-01-01 0.252434
2032-01-01 0.251650
2033-01-01 0.250977
2034-01-01 0.250400
2035-01-01 0.249905
2036-01-01 0.249480

The yellow points are the predicted values, the yellow area is the confidence interval, the farther the prediction year, the larger the confidence space and the worse the reference.

Forecast: By 2035, the arm span of personal health expenditure will be controlled to within 0.25.

4 Discussion

The *life equity* advocated by Professor Wang Jianjiang has both theoretical and practical basis, and how to implement the theory of *life equity* needs to be completed in social practice, that is, it needs to be completed by the cash of *life equity*, and social welfare is one of the manifestations of the realization of *life equity*. The theory of *life equity* holds that life enjoys rights and equity, and free medical care, free education, free pension, social welfare and public services are its basic contents. From an economic point of view, through the National Bureau of Statistics and some authoritative statistics agency data, since 1978, forty years of reform and opening up, China's gross domestic product by the world's 11th second, and if calculated according to the purchasing power evaluation, China's economy than the United States as the world's first, average annual GDP growth rate of 9.5%. China's contribution to world economic growth increased from 27.5 percent to 3.1 percent in 1978. In 1978, China's per capita GDP was 385 yuan, and in 2018, its per capita GDP was 64,644 yuan. The great economic achievements have greatly reduced the number of poor people, and the bottom line of human *life equity* is to enjoy the most basic living security. In 1978, the number of rural poor people living in China was 770 million, but it dropped to 16.6 million.

This paper analyzes four fields closely related to *life equity*, including *life equity* in economy, *life equity* in education, *life equity* in housing and *life equity* in medical treatment. Using polynomial linear regression algorithm, ARIMA model algorithm, standardized scaling algorithm, using the relevant data of China national statistics statistics analysis, the economic cash in the engel coefficient, gini coefficient calculation analysis, the calculation of education to cash analysis, calculation analysis of housing cash and calculation analysis of medical cash. The paper also has some shortcomings. The prediction mainly through polynomial linear regression algorithm and ARIMA model and can not get very reliable prediction results. In the future, the realization of *life equity* will be predicted from more fields and more effective and targeted machine learning algorithms. The equity theory of life holds that every person is born to enjoy the innate rights, these rights run through the whole life, covering all aspects of life, and believes that these rights are sacred.

5 Conclusion

This paper studies the social welfare related to the theory of *life equity* through machine learning algorithm. By taking machine learning algorithm respectively from four aspects of economy, education, housing and medical computing analysis of social welfare and *life equity* cash, machine learning algorithm calculation results show that in nearly 40 years of development in China, "life" in economy, education, housing, medical four areas got good cash.1. In the economic field, the results of the polynomial linear regression algorithm show that the Engel coefficient in China is gradually declining and has been controlled below 0.4. The results show that China has basically eliminated poverty. Polynomial linear regression algorithm results show that the gini coefficient in shrinking, slightly after 2016, until 2022 is stable, want to reach 0.4 still need to continue to observe, this shows that China to narrow the gap between rich and poor has a certain way to go, 2, education, polynomial linear regression algorithm results predicted by the end of 2026, China illiteracy rate will control within 0.01.3. In the field of housing, the results of the linear regression algorithm predict that by 2043, the existing per capita commercial housing area will be more than 100 square meters.4. In the medical field, the ARIMA model results predict that the arm span of personal health expenditure should be controlled to within 0.25 by 2035. To sum up, the *life equity* advocated by Professor Wang Jianjiang will be gradually realized with the development of the economy and society, and will give more protection to every citizen in the future.

Acknowledgments. This research did not receive any specific grant from funding agencies in the public, commercial, or not-for-profit sectors.

Disclosure of Interests. The authors have no competing interests to declare that are relevant to the content of this article.

References

1. Wang, J.: Is it possible for China to lead the world in philosophy and aesthetics?—— In response to Aleesi Aravitz, Ernst Zengko, and Locke Benz for comments on "doctrine" and Bie-modern theories. In: Philosophical Notification., p. 207
2. The United Nations: The Declaration of Human Rights (1948). Accessed 25 May 2020. https://www.un.org/zh/universal-declaration-human-rights/index.html
3. United Nations Human Rights. Accessed 24 May 2020. https://www.un.org/zh/sections/issues-depth/human-rights/index.html
4. Wang, J.: Bie-modern where to BIe——and respond to Mr.Xie Jinliang. Inner Mongolia Social Sci. (01) (2018)

Author Index

A

Ahn, Sunghee 99, 249

C

Chen, Haiguang 377
Chen, Yongkang 119
Cheng, Xinyi 180
Chickanayakanahalli, Anantha 55

D

Diamond, Sara 55, 214

F

Fang, Xing 3
Feng, Binlin 274
Furuta, Masafumi 196

G

Guo, Qihan 3

H

Haupt, Carina 233
Hayashi, Masaki 167
Heidrich, David 233
Hennecke, Martin 233
Hsieh, Hsiu-Ching Laura 21, 31, 137
Hsieh, Wei-Her 74
Huang, Hsiu-Mei 259
Huang, Yichun 42
Huang, Yiyuan 42
Hwang, Shyh-Huei 259

I

Indarti, 309

J

Jerusalem, Mohammad Adam 309

K

Kazawa, Go 150
Kernchen, Sophie 233
Kim, Chris 55
Kim, Hyungmin 249
Kitagawa, Akane 196
Klapproth-Rieger, Adriana 233
Kosmider, Andreas 233
Ku, Chang Yuan 74
Kuwahara, Meeko 167

L

Lee, Juhee 249
Lee, Seong 249
Li, Haoru 274
Li, Xiu 325
Liao, Yi Zhen 21
Lin, Jiafeng 339, 361
Lin, Wan-Ting 31
Liu, Lin 180
Liu, Xinxi 293
Liu, Yuan 293
Liu, Zhuohua 274
Lobbes, Marcus 233
Lu, Shih-Yun 74

M

Mi, Yue 180
Morris, Alexis 214
Munaka, Tatsuya 196
Murata, Koichi 196

N

Nakatsu, Ryohei 150, 196
Ni, Hong 377
Nie, Xiaomei 325

M. Rauterberg (Ed.): HCII 2024, LNCS 14717, pp. 431–432, 2024.
https://doi.org/10.1007/978-3-031-61147-6

Niendorf, Thoralf   233
Niiyama, Satoshi   196
Nomura, Michio   196

P
Paano, Cris   55
Pan, Chi-Yu   309
Pang, Yunian   196
Park, Jong-Il   249
Peng, Li-Hsun   309

S
Schreiber, Andreas   233
Shen, Tsu-Chi   137
Shi, Mingxi   3
Shi, Yu   180
Song, Yuanyuan   90
Su, Mingyang   274, 325
Sui, Linyou   42
Sui, Zhaoyang   339
Sun, Xueqing   42

T
Takagi, Hiroki   167
Tosa, Naoko   150, 196

U
Ueda, Yoshiyuki   196
Uraoka, Yasuyuki   196

V
Verma, Adit   214
von Kurnatowski, Lynn   233

W
Wang, Hui   377
Wang, Jianjiang   377, 391
Wang, Juan   377
Wang, Muyun   377
Wang, Siqin   99
Wolff, Benjamin   233

X
Xiao, Yulei   55
Xie, Yun   325
Xu, Yingying   391

Y
Yi, Kexin   119

Z
Zhe, Peng   408

Printed in the United States
by Baker & Taylor Publisher Services